FIRST IMPRESSIONS

The Tauber Institute Series for the Study of European Jewry

The Tauber Institute Series is dedicated to publishing compelling and innovative approaches to the study of modern European Jewish history, thought, culture, and society. The series features scholarly works related to the Enlightenment, modern Judaism and the struggle for emancipation, the rise of nationalism and the spread of antisemitism, the Holocaust and its aftermath, as well as the contemporary Jewish experience. The series is published under the auspices of the Tauber Institute for the Study of European Jewry—established by a gift to Brandeis University from Dr. Laszlo N. Tauber—and is supported, in part, by the Tauber Foundation and the Valya and Robert Shapiro Endowment.

For the complete list of books that are available in this series, please see https:// brandeisuniversitypress.com/series/tauber

JOSEPH A. SKLOOT
First Impressions: Sefer Ḥasidim and Early Modern Hebrew Printing

*MARAT GRINBERG
The Soviet Jewish Bookshelf: Jewish Culture and Identity Between the Lines

ARTHUR GREEN
Defender of the Faithful: The Life and Thought of Rabbi Levi Yitshak of Berdychiv

GILAD SHARVIT
Dynamic Repetition: History and Messianism in Modern Jewish Thought

YOSEF HAYIM YERUSHALMI in Conversation with SYLVIE ANNE GOLDBERG
Transmitting Jewish History

CHARLES DELLHEIM
Belonging and Betrayal: How Jews Made the Art World Modern

CEDRIC COHEN-SKALLI
Don Isaac Abravanel: An Intellectual Biography

CHAERAN Y. FREEZE
A Jewish Woman of Distinction: The Life and Diaries of Zinaida Poliakova

CHAVA TURNIANSKY
Glikl: Memoirs 1691–1719

DAN RABINOWITZ
The Lost Library: The Legacy of Vilna's Strashun Library in the Aftermath of the Holocaust

JEHUDA REINHARZ and YAACOV SHAVIT
The Road to September 1939: Polish Jews, Zionists, and the Yishuv on the Eve of World War II

*A Sarnat Library Book

First Impressions

Sefer Ḥasidim and Early Modern Hebrew Printing

JOSEPH A. SKLOOT

Brandeis University Press

WALTHAM, MASSACHUSETTS

Brandeis University Press

Manufactured in the United States of America
Typeset in Arno Pro by Robert Slimbach

LIBRARY OF CONGRESS CATALOGING-IN-PUBLISHING DATA
Names: Skloot, Joseph A., 1983– author.
Title: First impressions : Sefer ḥasidim and early modern
Hebrew printing / Joseph A. Skloot.
Description: Waltham : Brandeis University Press, [2023] | Series: The Tauber Institute series for the study of European Jewry | Includes bibliographical references and index. | Summary: "In 1538, a partnership of Jewish silk makers in the city of Bologna published a book entitled Sefer Ḥasidim, a compendium of rituals, stories, and religious instruction that primarily originated in medieval Franco-Germany. This book tells the story of how these men came to produce such a book" — Provided by publisher.
Identifiers: LCCN 2022050290 | ISBN 9781684581498 (paperback) | ISBN 9781684581504 (cloth) | ISBN 9781684581511 (ebook)
Subjects: LCSH: Judah ben Samuel, approximately 1150–1217. Sefer ḥasidim—Criticism, Textual. | Judah ben Samuel, approximately 1150–1217. Sefer ḥasidim—First editions. | Froben, Ambrosius, 1537–1602. | Printing, Hebrew—Italy—Bologna. | Printing, Hebrew—Switzerland—Basel. | Hebrew imprints—Italy—Bologna. | Hebrew imprints—Switzerland—Basel.
Classification: LCC BJ1287.J83 S55 2023 |
DDC 686.2/1924—dc23/eng/20221228
LC record available at https://lccn.loc.gov/2022050290

5 4 3 2 1

Contents

List of Illustrations

Acknowledgments

ACKNOWLEDGMENTS are the most human of paratexts (documents that surround the core of a book, a term that we will discuss at length in the introduction). Through them, we can discern the people and places that lurk in the background of a book, uncover clues to the circumstances of its creation, the networks of ideas and patronage and capital that made it come to be. Acknowledgments are a modern innovation, an outgrowth of the much older tradition of the dedication, which is perhaps as old as writing itself.* In appending either acknowledgments or dedications to a book, a writer implicitly confirms a truth that has often, since the early modern period, rarely been stated explicitly, one at the center of this monograph: Writing is a collaborative act.

There is no such thing as a solitary author. (Premodern and early modern Hebrew writers made this point clear with elaborate pious dedications: Only God creates out of nothing. Human beings merely channel the creativity of the Author of All.) I make this plain at the outset of this monograph not to deny my own responsibility for the statements and arguments herein. They are, of course, my own. Rather, I hope to signal to readers that this book could not have become what it is without the piercing insights, dogged questioning, and unceasing encouragement, not to mention material support, of numerous individuals and institutions.

This monograph began as a mere inkling of an idea in my doctoral advisor Elisheva Carlebach's seminar room over a decade ago. In the interim, Professor Carlebach has been a steadfast guide and interlocutor, and has read too many drafts of this book to count. David Ellenson, my rabbi and mentor, read it in its many iterations and shepherded it to publication. Several colleagues, esteemed scholars all, read and commented on the manuscript,

*Helen Smith, "Acknowledgements and Dedications," in *Book Parts*, eds. Dennis Duncan and Adam Smyth (Oxford: Oxford University Press, 2019), 93.

or portions of it; they include A. J. Berkovitz, Yoram Bitton, Gordon Dale, Tamara Cohn Eskenazi, Kristi Garroway, Anthony Grafton, Lisa Grant, Alyssa Gray, Jennifer Grayson, Susannah Heschel, Lawrence Hoffman, Jason Kalman, Jan Katzew, Sharon Koren, Olga Litvak, Dalia Marx, Richard Sarason, Nancy Weiner, Jacob Wright, and Adina Yoffie. It was enriched by conversations with my uncle, Michael Bamberger, with my godmother, Marie-Thérèse Daniëls-Dirven, and with Bernard Cooperman, Barbara Friedman, Michael Marmur, Amy Perlin, Judith Plaskow, Haim Rechnitzer, Andrew Rehfeld, Claudia Rosenzweig, Adam Shear, Ellen Umansky, and Wendy Zierler. Some of the scholars above participated in HUC-JIR's faculty works-in-progress seminar where sections of this monograph were presented. I am also grateful to rabbinical students George Altschuler, Noah Lawrence, Eliza Scheffler, and Samuel Weiss, who participated in my seminar on the history of the Jewish book at HUC-JIR in the autumn of 2021.

Through the peer-review process at Brandeis University Press, I received invaluable comments and suggestions from two anonymous readers. I am grateful for their candor, meticulousness, and appreciation of the book and its arguments. I am also grateful for the guidance of the press's editorial director, Sylvia Fuks Fried, and the commitment of the editors of the Tauber Institute Series for the Study of European Jewry, Jehuda Reinharz, ChaeRan Y. Freeze, Sylvia Fuks Fried, and Eugene R. Sheppard.

The research and writing of this book was made possible with financial assistance from HUC-JIR's provost, Andrea Weiss, and HUC-JIR's Samek Fund, under the direction of Lawrence Hoffman, as well as Bonnie and Daniel Tisch, through the remarkable fellowship program they created at HUC-JIR. I am also grateful to the many generous donors who established the Rabbi Aaron D. Panken Professorships at HUC-JIR, of which I am an inaugural recipient, and to my teacher, Rabbi Panken, of blessed memory, and to his wife, Lisa Messinger.

Throughout the preparation of this book, I received research support from the Klau Libraries at HUC-JIR in New York and Cincinnati, and the Columbia University Library. All of the images reproduced here were generously provided by the Klau Library. Over several years, I have been the beneficiary of generous assistance from library professionals, including Yoram Bitton, HUC-JIR's director of libraries, Abigail Bacon, Emily Cramton, Jordan Finkin, Eli Lieberman, Jason Schapera, Tina Weiss, and Chana Wolfson, as well as Michelle Margolis at Columbia.

Books are bound up in lives. This one was researched, written, and edited in offices, libraries, airports, dining rooms, and coffee shops around the world, from Morningside Heights to Maplewood, from Venice to Jerusalem. My parents, Suzanne and Edward Skloot, and my in-laws, Patsy and Donald Glazer, watched this project grow with pride and appreciation. My children, Maya and Solomon, were born and have grown into themselves alongside this book. Through it, they have come to see how the past can be brought to life through stories and how books—physical, inky, smelly, beautiful books—are embedded in our family's life and in Jewish culture.

And finally, *aḥronah aḥronah ḥavivah*, my wife Erin. When we married, she did not realize that she would have to share her life with sixteenth-century Hebrew printers. Erin, who is the consummate thinking partner and life partner, has always seen rays of light amid darkness and has never lost faith in this project or in me.

Pesaḥ 5782
April 2022

Notes on the Text

BECAUSE THE PAGINATION of the early modern editions of *Sefer Ḥasidim* cited herein is inconsistent, I have chosen to identify passages using their numeration, which is more reliable. For ease of comprehension as well, block quotations are broken into thematic sections denoted by the letters (a), (b), and so on.

Translations of biblical verses generally follow the Jewish Publication Society (JPS, 1917) translation, which, while sometimes stilted, accords well with the biblical syntax, unless noted otherwise in a footnote.

Transliterations from Hebrew follow the simplified scheme of the *Encyclopedia Judaica,* 2nd edition, except where a particular spelling at variance with this scheme has entered common English usage.

For simplicity's sake, I identify all individuals who possess the title "Rabbi" with the abbreviation "R." Similarly, I abbreviate *ben,* meaning "son of," in Hebrew patronymics, as "b."

Dates of birth and death are provided for figures mentioned more than once in the text, with the caveat that in premodern times, such dates are often inexact or unavailable.

FIRST IMPRESSIONS

Introduction

> There is no text apart from the physical support that offers it for a reading (or hearing), hence there is no comprehension of any written piece that does not at least in part depend upon the forms in which it reaches its reader.
>
> Roger Chartier, *The Order of Books* (1994)

• • • • •

During the twelfth and thirteenth centuries, a remarkable diversity of Hebrew texts emerged in the Rhineland and Northern France (Ashkenaz), circulating under the name *Sefer Ḥasidim* (*The Book of the Pious*) and variations thereof. These texts describe a world of temptation, sin, and penance; ghosts, demons, and werewolves; rabbis, monks, and crusading armies; moneylenders, scribes, and witches. They are rooted in the culture of the High Middle Ages and have been seen as a prime historical witness to the period and to a group of religious innovators known as *Ḥasidei Ashkenaz* (the Rhineland pietists). Alongside these realia, they contain a mix of normative, homiletical, and exegetical material: guidance about prayer, commerce, and family relations, as well as testimony to the unique Jewish customs of the region. Nonetheless, these texts, preserved today in nearly twenty medieval manuscripts, possess no overarching line of argument, organizational structure, or ideological posture. Some advocate novel positions—such as the radical immanence of God, the efficaciousness of extreme corporeal penances, or the superiority of practical wisdom over Talmudic dialectics. Others are entirely conventional Jewish religious literature—paeans to repentance, study, and fear of God.[1]

In the sixteenth century, however, these texts underwent a material and conceptual transformation. They became a book, a single treatise with a stable text, attributed to R. Judah he-Ḥasid of Regensburg (Judah the Pious, 1150–1217), a canonical work of religious and moral edification keyed to the concerns of early modernity.[2] (By "early modern" and "early modernity," I refer to the period roughly from 1492 to 1789, with special emphasis on the sixteenth and seventeenth centuries and the cultural movements known as the Renaissance and Reformation.[3]) This transformation occurred through the medium of printing, carried out by Hebrew printers in the cities of Bologna and Basel. The subject of this monograph is that transformation and those printers. It argues that Hebrew printing was not a passive mode of communication, but rather an active means of literary, artistic, and material production, involving several interrelated processes: textual assembly and editing; authorial attribution; the fashioning of reference tools, as well as front and back matter; and censorship. Through them, the book known as *Sefer Ḥasidim* came to have a decisive influence on the religious culture of early modern and modern Ashkenazic Jewry, shaping the community's religious practice and self-understanding.[4] Hebrew printing, thus, did much more than transmit and perpetuate older manuscript traditions; it created new versions of Hebrew texts, versions that remain definitive today.

The field of the history of the early modern printed book has developed prodigiously in the years since Lucien Febvre and Henri-Jean Martin's *L'apparition du livre* (1958) and Elizabeth L. Eisenstein's *The Printing Press as an Agent of Change* (1979).[5] The spread of printing technology and printed books across Europe and beyond is now widely acknowledged to have had transformative implications, though the specific nature of those implications remains much debated.[6] Historians of the Jews have generally agreed that the printing of Hebrew books—a process that began in the mid-fifteenth century—was a signal event for Jewish culture. David Ruderman has, for example, described the effects of printing on Jewish culture as a "knowledge explosion," arguing that it led to the emergence of "a shared cultural experience between disparate Jewish communities" and the diminution of "the exclusivity and hegemony of the rabbis."[7] But what printing did to Hebrew texts themselves has not been extensively explored.

This monograph takes up that challenge, pinpointing what early modern printing and printers did to Hebrew texts systematically and precisely through a close reading of the first two printed editions of *Sefer Ḥasidim* (1538 and 1580), in light of their manuscript antecedents. Chapters 2 and 3 of this monograph analyze the first edition of 1538 and how, through it, *Sefer Ḥasidim* became a book with a stable text and a known author. Chapters 4, 5, and 6 analyze how that first edition was adapted and transformed by a new generation of printers in 1580. While it is an investigation into the construction of these printed books, this monograph is not a work of bibliography; no attempt is made to chronicle the totality of *Sefer Ḥasidim* editions, and there are many. Eschewing encyclopedic comprehensiveness in favor of granular analysis, this monograph does not consider, for example, the third edition of *Sefer Ḥasidim* printed in Krakow in 1581, as it represents a secondary if not tertiary stage of the book's development. By the time of that edition's appearance, *Sefer Ḥasidim* had already found a wide readership and, unlike the second edition, its printers merely reproduced the text of the first edition with few modifications.

This monograph also eschews questions of reception—how *Sefer Ḥasidim* was read and understood by subsequent generations of readers. It does so in order to home in on "the vast labour of adaptation" and creation undertaken by early modern Hebrew printers.[8] While an investigation into the creation of the first printed editions of *Sefer Ḥasidim* may be a foundation for future work on *Sefer Ḥasidim*'s reception, this monograph is not merely the preliminary stage of a reception history. The printing of *Sefer Ḥasidim* for the first time merits a monograph in its own right because of what it can teach about how printers fashioned the cultural legacy of the Middle Ages in the early modern period.

In its methodology, this monograph takes its cue from microhistory. Microhistory has been described as the "intensive historical investigation of a relatively well defined smaller object," often a person, a family, a village, or an event.[9] Through these investigations, microhistorians demonstrate how the quotidian can illuminate, clarify, and/or challenge regnant understandings of large-scale political, social, religious, and cultural phenomena—investigations into the realm of what has been called the "exceptional normal."[10] Carlo Ginzburg, one of microhistory's pioneers, has written that, by diving deep into a discrete body of sources, "it is possible to trace, as in a microcosm, the characteristics of an entire social stratum in a specific historical period."[11] Rather than perceive history as the working out of historical forces (of a Hegelian or Marxist or evolutionary variety, for example), microhistorians highlight the power of individuals and groups to shape their fates through conscious choice and resistance, that is, their agency.

Microhistory is particularly useful for the study of printing because, like

Christianity, capital, and democracy, printing has sometimes been depicted as an autonomous, revolutionary, world-historical force. Yet, printing was a creative process undertaken by people, living in specific contexts, who made decisions about how, and in what circumstances, to deploy a new technology.[12] In exploring the lives and work of specific printers, their contexts and choices, this monograph, in the tradition of microhistory, emphasizes that printing was a realm of human agency and contingency. In particular, by comparing the first two printed editions of *Sefer Ḥasidim*, this monograph shows how printers actively transformed a corpus of manuscripts into a printed book, and how the identity of that book was contested from the moment it rolled off the presses.

Sixteenth-Century Printing and *Sefer Ḥasidim*

The sixteenth century looms large in the history of Hebrew books because only then, nearly thirty years after the appearance of the first printed Hebrew book, did the Hebrew press come into its own.[13] While only about 140 Hebrew titles were printed prior to the year 1500, primarily Bibles and halakhic (legal) works, that number increased nearly twenty times during the following century, and those titles displayed a dizzying thematic range and technical complexity.[14] Most appeared on the Italian peninsula, and the presses of Venice, especially Daniel Bomberg's press, achieved prominence because of the quality of their editions.[15] Toward the middle of the sixteenth century, however, Hebrew presses in other cities outside Italy—including Prague, Krakow, Salonica, Constantinople, and, importantly for this monograph, Basel—emerged and began to compete, satisfying the ever-increasing demand for Hebrew books among both Jews and Christians.

From the quantitative analyses of Shifra Baruchson-Arbib and Anat Gueta, we know that, during the sixteenth century, the most printed and purchased Jewish books were liturgical (prayer books), scriptural (Bibles and associated commentaries), and legal (halakhic codes). Such books helped direct the daily practice of the faithful.[16] Books in other genres (such as the Talmud, philosophy, or mysticism) were printed, read, and achieved notoriety—perhaps none more so than Bomberg's Babylonian Talmud (1519–1523). The print runs of sixteenth-century Hebrew titles were comparable to those in other languages: between 500 and 1,000 copies.[17]

Bomberg's Rabbinic Bible (1517) was printed in 1,000 copies, for example. Of course, because initial outlays for raw materials (paper, type, and ink) and labor were significant, economies of scale necessitated printers produce the maximum quantities the market could bear: The Conti Press of Cremona printed 3,000 copies of its first edition of the esoteric work *Sefer ha-Zohar* (known as "the Zohar," 1558), but it printed other titles in more modest runs of 650 copies.[18] (It perhaps goes without saying that print runs dwarfed the maximum number of manuscripts a scribe might copy in a lifetime.[19]) In general, quartos and octavos, in which eight and sixteen pages, respectively, were printed per sheet of paper and then folded into a booklet (a "quire" of four or eight leaves, respectively) to be bound with others, could be printed more quickly and in greater quantity than folios (four pages per quire) and sold more cheaply. A specialized laborer in the mid-sixteenth century might spend a day's earnings on an octavo and nearly four days' wages on a folio.[20] On the other hand, a middling Italian rabbi might spend one-sixth of his yearly wages on an octavo, and a folio would simply be too dear. Distinguished rabbis with wealthy patrons, on the other hand, could afford larger and more expensive books.[21]

Sefer Ḥasidim was printed for the first time in Bologna in 1538 by a group of silk manufacturers who called themselves "the partners" (*ha-shutafim*). Ambrosius Froben (1537–1602), scion of a famed Basel printing dynasty, printed a second edition, based on the first, in 1580. While there is no direct evidence testifying to the size of either edition's print run, we can assume that both presses produced between 500 and 1,000 copies, as was customary at the time.[22] Both appeared in an octavo format, affordable for a wide array of readers. These were not, like Bomberg's folio-size Bibles and Talmuds, specialty items for European Jewry's scholarly elite. They were intended, rather, to be read by a growing readership of rabbis and students in Italy and central Europe, and, in the case of Froben's edition, by Christian students of Hebrew as well.

Why *Sefer Ḥasidim*?

The printing of *Sefer Ḥasidim* is an ideal "exceptional normal" subject for a microhistorical study of sixteenth-century Hebrew printing. It is "normal" in that its manuscript and printing history shares much with other ancient and medieval works assembled by early modern printers, including the Zohar and the Palestinian Talmud.[23] Yet, it is "exceptional" in that its social world, literary qualities, and manuscript history have generated prodigious scholarship and sophisticated analytical tools—the foundation upon which this monograph stands. It is especially indebted to the pioneering work of Peter Schäfer and his team at the Princeton University *Sefer Ḥasidim* Project (PUSHP). The PUSHP has cataloged and analyzed twenty medieval *Sefer Ḥasidim* manuscripts, transcribing them digitally and developing search and comparison applications.[24] Because the manuscripts, as well as the printed editions, are divided into discrete passages of generally no more than 1,000 words and often far fewer, they may be easily compared one to the next using the PUSHP's database. In fact, *Sefer Ḥasidim* is one of the few early modern printed texts to have its related manuscripts so thoroughly analyzed and digitized. The longest of these manuscripts, the Parma manuscript, was discovered in the late nineteenth century and contains nearly 2,000 passages.[25] The shortest manuscripts are a mere few passages. The Bologna first printed edition and the Basel second edition are about half the length of the Parma manuscript, containing just under 1,200 passages each. The investigations at the heart of this monograph compare these two editions and their manuscripts, on both the microscopic level (their words, sentences, and paragraphs) and the macroscopic level (their collective structure and organization), throwing light on the ways in which printers adapted and transformed preexisting medieval materials.

Peter Schäfer and Ivan Marcus, separately, have described the *Sefer Ḥasidim* manuscripts as representative of much medieval Ashkenazic Jewish literature: marked by frequent and drastic variation and lacking an original version or *Urtext*.[26] In his recent book, *Sefer Hasidim and the Ashkenazic Book in Medieval Europe* (2018), Marcus has called *Sefer Ḥasidim*, in its medieval instantiations, an "open book," meaning that it was composed of textual blocks without linear coherence, circulating in various collections and sequences.[27] He compares the *Sefer Ḥasidim* manuscripts to the children's toy Lego, whose users create "modular and disjunctively constructed" structures from blocks that may be arranged and rearranged time and again.[28] The passages that comprise the *Sefer Ḥasidim* manuscripts are akin to those Lego blocks, and the manuscripts show evidence of frequent rearrangement and adjustment. This modular form was, Marcus asserts, common to most medieval Ashkenazic texts, in contrast to those originating in Muslim lands.[29]

This monograph pushes this line of argument further, asserting that, prior to its being printed, *Sefer Ḥasidim* was not a book at all, if "book" means a relatively stable text attributed to a specific author or authors.[30] Rather, in the medieval period, the title *Sefer Ḥasidim* was a catchall used to describe various concatenations of texts from Ashkenaz. Only when early modern printers came into possession of at least two versions of that text, edited and adapted them into a single volume, emblazoned the cover page with the title *Sefer Ḥasidim* or *Sefer ha-Ḥasidim* (with the definite article), and ascribed that volume to R. Judah he-Ḥasid, was it possible to speak about the existence of a book by that name. Continuing Marcus's Lego analogy, printing *Sefer Ḥasidim* glued its textual blocks together such that it acquired a cohesive form and a modicum of fixity; after that, there was less room for play.[31] Less room, but not no room. Indeed, the fact that we possess other manuscript versions of *Sefer Ḥasidim* that postdate the first printed edition indicates that other forms of *Sefer Ḥasidim* continued to circulate after 1538—in some cases, for generations.[32] At the same time, it may also be argued that printing did for Ashkenazic literary culture and *Sefer Ḥasidim* what the Muslim conquest did for Sephardic literary culture, that is, prioritize the single-author treatise by superimposing this literary model on formerly "open" medieval Hebrew texts.

As much as the medieval *Sefer Ḥasidim* manuscripts are characteristic of medieval Ashkenazic literary culture, the first and second printed editions of *Sefer Ḥasidim* may be read as witnesses to the social and cultural history of early modern Bologna and Basel, as well as early modern Jewish culture more generally. The partners' Hebrew press in Bologna was a short-lived start-up, located in the heart of the Papal States, a territory with a venerable Jewish community. The Basel second edition, on the other hand, was printed by one of Europe's foremost Christian printing houses, in a Protestant city where Jews had been prohibited from residing for two centuries. Both editions appeared during the tumultuous years following the rise of Protestantism, as European policy regarding Jews turned more severe, and as Jews and Christians explored new sources of religious authority, from *sola scriptura* to *Kabbalah* to the *Hebraica veritas*. One example of this context's direct impact on the form and content of both printed editions of *Sefer Ḥasidim* foreshadows the following chapters: The Papacy's changing attitudes toward Jews and Jewish books over the course of the sixteenth century led the printers of these editions to censor them in surprisingly different ways. Terms deemed acceptable by the printers of the first edition, which appeared just prior to the Council of Trent, were rejected by the printers of the second edition and replaced with alternatives, as Catholic press censorship intensified. In this way, *Sefer Ḥasidim,* in its first two editions, which were the basis of all successors until the late nineteenth century, was an early modern book, whose component parts originated in the Middle Ages but were reformulated, reconceptualized, and repackaged during the early modern period, reflecting the concerns of that time.

Prior to the appearance of the Bologna *editio princeps, Sefer Ḥasidim* was neither widely known nor cited.[33] Its relative obscurity before printing contrasts with its reputation in subsequent generations. The Bologna and Basel editions were the basis of the more than fifty successive editions, most produced in the Polish-Lithuanian Commonwealth and Russia, through the end of the nineteenth century, when the Parma manuscript was printed for the first time.[34] Thus, through the Bologna and Basel editions, *Sefer Ḥasidim* came to be known among early modern and modern Ashkenazic Jews. As Edward Fram has written, the printing of *Sefer Ḥasidim* "allowed the ideas and values of *Ḥasidei Ashkenaz* to return and influence Polish Jewish culture long after the German pietist movement itself had disappeared" and "Polish rabbis turned to the book as a source for instruction on how to improve their own level of religiosity."[35] In other words, unlike well-known and well-studied sixteenth-century Hebrew printed titles such as the Bomberg Bibles and Talmud editions, which achieved canonical status long before they were printed, *Sefer Ḥasidim* was launched out of obscurity and became a staple of the Ashkenazic religious library because of printing and its printers.

Book History and the History of the Hebrew Book

This monograph is one of a small but growing number of studies arguing that printing played an essential role in fashioning early modern culture. In focusing on Hebrew printers, their practices and contexts, it follows in the footsteps of Alexandra Gillespie and Craig Kallendorf, who have identified far more than duplication in the practices of early modern printers of editions of medieval and ancient works. Gillespie has shown how the printers of Geoffrey Chaucer and John Lydgate grouped texts together within the same volume or the same series, attributed a collection of texts to one author or the other, and composed introductions and commentaries to excite readers' interest and favor particular interpretations. "The press made it possible to make something new out of old books and old stories," Gillespie has written, through "coherent pre-packaging."[36] Kallendorf, writing about early modern editions of Virgil, moreover, has argued that printing served as an "*agent* of transformation," an arena in which received texts were refashioned through diverse (and contested) practices of commentary, translation, attribution, and censorship.[37] These processes of literary and material creation are emblematic of the larger interconnectedness of high and low knowledge in the early modern period, as emphasized by Pamela Smith.[38] The history of the printed editions of *Sefer Ḥasidim*—just as that of editions of Chaucer and Virgil—highlights how the print shop was a place where technical skill, business acumen, religious devotion, and philological scholarship intersected to produce desirable material goods.

This monograph also explores how the material form of the printed book and the social form of the print shop shaped religious knowledge in the early modern period. In the history of science, Simon Schaffer and Steven Shapin have discerned the ways social structures—such as the Royal Society—lent credence to new scientific paradigms, even inventing the concept of the Scientific Revolution as we know it.[39] Similarly, Adrian Johns has argued that the social context of the print shop shaped the production of scientific knowledge during the same period: A book's meaning, authority, and value, Johns argued, were closely associated with "the identities, representations, and practices of the people" who printed it.[40] Johns has encouraged book historians to consider the range of editorial and promotional strategies employed by printers, as well as the social networks they engaged to win authority for their books.

This monograph details the ways in which the printers of the first two *Sefer Ḥasidim* editions, along the lines of Johns's findings, sought to cultivate the support of existing institutions by employing a number of editorial and promotional strategies: pursuing official licenses and institutional support; bestowing upon their books a recognizable title; ascribing authorship to a venerated medieval saint; editing and adapting medieval manuscripts for comprehensibility and clarity; portraying their works variously as works of moral edification or rabbinic lore; producing reference tools to help readers navigate them; censoring texts to remove polemical references to Christians and Christianity and thereby avoid condemnation; and glossing to clarify difficult terms and concepts. All of these strategies show how, in Johns's words, the "identities, representations, and practices" of *Sefer Ḥasidim*'s printers shaped the editions they produced.[41]

One of the distinctive contributions of early modern Hebrew printers was the composition of "paratexts"—subsidiary documents, from title pages to colophons (concluding statements), from headings to pagination—that, in the literary theorist Gérard Genette's words, "surround" a text "and extend it, precisely in order to present it . . . to ensure the text's presence in the world, its 'reception' and consumption in the form . . . of a book."[42] The printers of *Sefer Ḥasidim* invested creativity and capital in their paratexts, especially their title pages (*sh'arim*), introductions (*hakdamot*), tables of contents (*mafteḥot* or *simanim*), and glosses (*haggahot*), and this monograph pays special attention to these documents. As Genette explained when coining the term, paratexts constitute "a privileged place of a pragmatics and a strategy, of an influence on the public, an influence that . . . is at the service of a better reception of the text and a more pertinent reading of it."[43] They are thus an attempt to situate a book in a given context and to shape and color readers' understandings and appreciation of it. And while Genette emphasized that paratexts are an expression of an author's intentions (they "ensure for the text a destiny consistent with the author's purpose"), recent studies have highlighted the role of printers in fashioning paratexts and their concomitant pragmatics and contextualization.[44] Indeed, the paratexts that accompanied printed editions of premodern works are best understood as an expression of printers' intentions, that is, their desire to promote their preferred reading or readings of a text at the expense of other possible interpretations.

Paratexts began to proliferate in books during the sixteenth century, having been fairly scarce prior to 1500.[45] Sixteenth-century printers and editors padded their publications with a dizzying variety: introductions, imprimaturs, glossaries, dedications, commentaries, finding aids, charts, and illustrations. As Anthony Grafton has emphasized, sixteenth-century editors "enjoyed displaying their ability to create new aids for readers," and they touted the usefulness of these materials on title pages.[46] Title pages, in particular, were especially important for identifying a book in crowded shops, where books were sold unbound, enticing potential readers to make a purchase.[47] Paratexts thus served a promotional function, distinguishing titles from one another and creating a venue for the printer to appeal directly to potential readers and testify to his work's authority and superiority.

Because of this promotional role, early modern paratexts were replete with commonplaces and clichés, such as "this edition should supersede all others" or "despite its errors, give this book the benefit of the doubt." Yet, they also offered data about a printed book's formation, often (though not always) identifying key participants, their social circle and cultural profile, and the sources of their capital. An "impressum," for example, was a statement, often on a title page, identifying who printed a book and where. A "chronogram" was a phrase, often a biblical quotation, found on the title page, that alluded to the content of a work and whose numerical value was equivalent to the date of a book's printing. Interpreting paratexts like these in the first and second printed editions of *Sefer Ḥasidim* is the focus of chapters 3 and 5 of this monograph.

Importantly, these paratexts ascribe *Sefer Ḥasidim* to R. Judah he-Ḥasid. The printers of the first edition of *Sefer Ḥasidim*, in particular, used paratexts to craft a presentation of R. Judah he-Ḥasid as a saint whose magnum opus, their book, contained wisdom directly relevant to the concerns of sixteenth-century spiritual seekers. The significance of this kind of authorial ascription was highlighted by theorist Michel Foucault in his well-known 1969 lecture, "What Is an Author?" There, Foucault linked recognizably modern notions of authorship to the development of modern doctrines of private property and social discipline. An author, in the modern sense, was an autonomous creator and owner of textual goods that could be sold, pirated, and made to stand in for their creator. Foucault's implication was that texts became perpetually linked to those to whom they were ascribed, and those people "became subject to punishment . . . to the extent that [their] discourses could be transgressive."[48] The emergence of modern notions of authorship has been explored with greater precision by a succession of historians. Most important for this study is the work of Lisa Jardine, who has shown how the Renaissance theologian and humanist Desiderius Erasmus of Rotterdam (1466–1536), together with his Basel printer Johann Froben (c. 1460–1527), used printed textual and paratextual devices to craft his self-presentation and a "multidimensional cultural persona" meant to win authority and credibility for Erasmus's revolutionary ideas and written works.[49]

Beyond authorial attribution, the printers of *Sefer Ḥasidim* also innovated through the production of reference tools. The tables of contents these printers fashioned are emblematic of the proliferation of reference tools and reference works during the sixteenth and seventeenth centuries, as Ann Blair has shown. While such tools occasionally appeared in manuscripts, during the sixteenth and seventeenth centuries, authors and printers developed ever more sophisticated aids for readers.[50] Adam Shear has pointed out that the history of such tools in Hebrew and Jewish books has yet to be thoroughly explored by historians.[51] With a close, comparative analysis of the tables of contents in the first two printed editions of *Sefer Ḥasidim*, this monograph takes up that challenge.

Another editorial process that the printers of *Sefer Ḥasidim* undertook was censorship. In preparing the text of *Sefer Ḥasidim* for print, they removed references to Christians and Christianity. In so doing, they sought to ensure their editions a wide distribution, and thus impact, in the Christian world and to avoid the Roman Church's condemnation. Annabel Patterson has described censorship as a pervasive feature of early modern culture and a "highly sophisticated system of oblique communication, of unwritten rules whereby writers could communicate with readers or audiences… without producing a direct confrontation."[52] Censorship, therefore, forced authors to encode ideas that could not be stated explicitly, generating the possibility of new interpretations—leading to what Patterson has called the "hermeneutics of censorship."[53] Recently, Hannah Marcus has similarly shown how novel and controversial ideas were permitted to circulate in early modern medical textbooks after a process of expurgation—the deletion of problematic words or phrases after publication. Expurgation functioned to preserve and propagate knowledge in tumultuous times on the grounds of "scientific utility."[54] Censorship, Patterson and Marcus demonstrate, could thus be constructive, as well as destructive.

Amnon Raz-Krakotzkin has applied this insight to early modern Hebrew texts, arguing that the process of censorship was contiguous with other editorial processes (such as proofreading), and that print-shop workers (both Jewish and Christian) undertook these tasks simultaneously. According to Raz-Krakotzkin, the printing of early modern Hebrew books was marked by a creative interplay of Jewish and Christian artisans, in which Jewish texts were rewritten to soften polemical elements and to make them fit within the limits of discourse defined by the Church.[55] This application of the "hermeneutics of censorship" to Hebrew texts is apposite to the case of *Sefer Ḥasidim*, for censorship in both editions generated new meanings within the text while helping to ensure it a wide readership.

The case of censorship also, crucially, illustrates the interconnectedness of the history of Hebrew and non-Hebrew books. As a result of the Counter-Reformation, the sixteenth century was a period of increased surveillance and censorship; Christian sovereigns were as much concerned about the spread of heterodoxy and subversion in printed Hebrew books as they were about this phenomenon in books in other languages. The same printers and print shops produced both Hebrew and non-Hebrew works: At the beginning of the sixteenth century, Aldus Manutius (1449–1515), the famed Venetian printer of classical Greek and Latin, printed in Hebrew as well.[56] Later on, as will be discussed at length in chapter 4, Ambrosius Froben printed both Hebrew and humanist Latin titles. Printers of Hebrew books engaged in the same editing and packaging processes employed in the production of non-Hebrew titles. Above all, printed Hebrew and non-Hebrew books attracted many of the same readers, particularly those in the burgeoning community of Christian Hebraists—Christian scholars who studied Hebrew and Jewish texts in order to further Christianity's mission and deepen their faith.[57] By the same token, Jewish scholars, such as Azariah de' Rossi and R. Isaac Lampronti, among many others, avidly read the works and employed the ideas of Renaissance humanists in their historical, scientific, and legal treatises.[58] There were, in other words, no rigid disciplinary, religious, or linguistic boundaries that differentiated the printing of Hebrew books from the printing of books in other languages during the early modern period, though such boundaries may exist today. Indeed, while book history has been an especially fertile field in recent decades, book historians have largely invested their energies in exploring the printing of titles for Christian and humanist readers in classical and European languages, as well as cheap-print and popular culture.[59] Thus, while this monograph seeks to apply the insights of book history to the history of the Hebrew book, it also seeks to integrate Hebrew books into the history of the book more broadly. Indeed, the history of the early modern book cannot be told adequately without sufficient consideration of Hebrew books and their role in the early modern print shop.

A Book about Books

This monograph is rooted in a close reading of the texts and paratexts contained in the first two printed editions of *Sefer Ḥasidim*, situating them within their local and institutional contexts.

Chapter 1 offers an overview of the content of *Sefer Ḥasidim* and the "prehistory" of these printed editions, exploring the diversity of *Sefer Ḥasidim*'s medieval manuscript witnesses and the work's origins in medieval Europe. It describes how *Sefer Ḥasidim* in its medieval context was not a single coherent treatise but, rather, a catchall term for a variety of texts that emerged in medieval Ashkenaz. These texts were not attributed to R. Judah he-Ḥasid, and the concept of authorial attribution as it is understood in modern literature is not applicable to medieval "open books" like *Sefer Ḥasidim*.

Chapters 2 and 3 focus on the Bologna *editio princeps*. Chapter 2 examines the historical background of this edition and its creators, their social position within Bolognese Jewry, and the legal and institutional frameworks that regulated the production of Hebrew books in Bologna. It argues that "the partners" drew on capital and expertise acquired in the burgeoning sixteenth-century Bolognese silk trade to open and operate their print shop. *Sefer Ḥasidim*, as well as the other books they printed, represented an attempt to serve an increasingly ethnically diverse Italian Jewish community following the migration of Iberian Jews to Italy, and to offer religious guidance at a time of doubt and anxiety.

Chapter 3 offers a close reading of the partners' edition of *Sefer Ḥasidim*, its paratexts and text, in comparison to extant medieval *Sefer Ḥasidim* manuscripts. It highlights how the partners assembled their edition from preexisting sources, ascribed a title and authorship to it, prefaced it with a lengthy table of contents, and censored it. This edition became the standard edition of *Sefer Ḥasidim*, the basis of all future editions of the work until the late nineteenth century.

Chapters 4, 5, and 6 turn to the second printed edition of *Sefer Ḥasidim* and its Basel printer, Ambrosius Froben. Chapter 4 argues that Froben's edition of *Sefer Ḥasidim* was an outgrowth of his edition of the Babylonian Talmud (1578–1580). It was also an attempt to profit by supplying books to emergent communities of readers in the late sixteenth century, including Jewish students (*talmidim*) in the Polish-Lithuanian commonwealth and

Christian Hebraists. Chapter 5 is an analysis of the paratexts in Froben's *Sefer Ḥasidim* edition: its title page, two introductions, and table of contents. The chapter argues that, in these documents, Froben and his editors presented *Sefer Ḥasidim* as a canonical work of *aggadah* (lore), part of the larger sixteenth-century rediscovery of this ancient genre.

Chapter 6 explores the relationship of Froben's edition to the partners' edition and the various ways in which Froben's edition differed from its predecessor and model. This chapter illuminates how Froben's editors censored the text more aggressively than the partners had, removed phrases in languages other than Hebrew, and introduced punctuation and explanatory glosses into the text. These emendations created the impression that *Sefer Ḥasidim* was much older than it was and thus buttressed the assertions offered in the accompanying paratexts. They were also reflective of the increased surveillance of both Jews and Hebrew books in the period of the Counter-Reformation.

An epilogue concludes the monograph, reflecting on the relationship of manuscript to printed-book production and the distinctive achievements of *Sefer Ḥasidim*'s printers.

THE TRANSFORMATION of *Sefer Ḥasidim* into a book during the sixteenth century is thus not merely the story of *Sefer Ḥasidim*. It is the story of printers who actively made their medieval cultural inheritance into something new, fit for their time and place. It is the story of Jews and Christians engaged in negotiations over the deployment of new technologies for the communication of contested religious wisdom. It is the story of a changing Jewish community, its expanding geographic and cultural horizons, and its relationship to Christian neighbors and rulers. It is an early modern story set within the larger movements of the Renaissance and Reformation. It is the story of the creation of a Hebrew book and all the worlds that book contained.

CHAPTER 1

Sefer Ḥasidim in the Middle Ages

A wise man commanded his son to avoid taking too much pleasure in the world and to avoid allowing thirty days to pass without a fast. When he died, they took him from his grave and flogged him. They grieved very much on account of this.* The man came to one of them in a dream and said to him, "This happened because I would see books erased and in tatters and I did not repair them and retire them."

Sefer Ḥasidim (Bologna, 1538), §97

. . . . .

IN THE MANUSCRIPTS and printed editions of *Sefer Ḥasidim*, books assume an outsize role and an almost totemic status. In the epigraph, the wise man's failure to accord them proper respect made him subject to grievous postmortem punishment. Other passages deal with the relative sanctity of different types of books, the placement of books in one's home and synagogue, the reuse of book covers, and Jews' possession of Christians' books.[1] These passages are concerned as much with books' material form—their pages, ink, and bindings—as with their content. (They were, of course, in their original medieval context, manuscript scrolls and codices, not printed works.)

These *Sefer Ḥasidim* passages manifest a particular type of bibliophilia common to religious Jews to this day. The assumptions undergirding them, however, assumptions about what a book is, differ from those of our own era. The eighteenth-century philosopher Immanuel Kant, in *The Metaphysics of Morals*, offered what may be taken as a paradigmatic modern definition of a book:

*The pronouns in this passage are ambiguous.

> A book is a writing (it does not matter, here, whether it is written in hand or set in type, whether it has few or many pages), which represents a discourse [*Rede*] that someone delivers to the public by visible linguistic signs. One who *speaks* to the public in his own name is called the *author* (*autor*).[2] One who, through a writing, discourses publicly in another's (the author's) name is a *publisher*. When a publisher does this with the author's permission, he is the legitimate publisher; but if he does it without the author's permission, he is an illegitimate publisher, that is, an *unauthorized publisher*. The sum of all the reproductions of the original writing (the copies) is an *edition*.[3]

For Kant, a book was speech ("discourse," *Rede*) communicated to a "public" through intelligible "linguistic signs" instantiated as a "corporeal artifact."[4] A book possessed stability; it could be "reproduced" and transmitted to readers over and over again. It was also perpetually linked to its creator, its "author," who retained authority over how and when it might be communicated. The author delegated the work of communication to a "publisher," giving him a "mandate" to reproduce the discourse and to profit from it.[5]

Two elements of Kant's definition of a book are of import for this study and continue to define our understanding of books today: first, textual stability and replicability, and, second, authorial attribution. In medieval Ashkenaz, however, these two were not givens. The medieval manuscripts of *Sefer Ḥasidim*, like medieval open books in general, possess no uniform or consistent text. The epigraph, for example, is found in two distinct versions across six manuscripts and the Bologna *editio princeps*, with numerous more minute variations among them.[6] Further, the medieval *Sefer Ḥasidim* manuscripts, again like other medieval open books, make no claims about their authorship or the sources of many of the traditions they contain. The authorities quoted throughout, as in the passage here, are often anonymous. Thus, lacking a consistent text or an author, we might say that *Sefer Ḥasidim* in the medieval period was not a book at all—at least not from a modern, Kantian perspective. What was it? This chapter endeavors to answer that question.

Sefer Ḥasidim or *Sifrei Ḥasidim*?

Sefer Ḥasidim's preprint history was marked by instability; many heterogeneous *Sifrei Ḥasidim* (plural of *Sefer Ḥasidim*, "books of the pious") circulated under similar titles during the medieval period. The scribes who created these manuscripts were anthologists, gathering from diverse sources, some known to us today and some not, some entitled *Sefer Ḥasidim* and some not, often adding their own distinctive contributions. Indeed, in a world of open books, the distinctions between "writer" and "scribe" are slippery, because creative writing involved quotation, and copying involved creative rewriting. Yet, for over a century, much *Sefer Ḥasidim* scholarship has revolved around attempts to uncover a definitive *Sefer Ḥasidim Urtext*. These investigations began with the publication of the Parma manuscript by Jehuda Wistinetski in 1891.[7] In 1903, the Russian *maskil* and philologist Abraham Epstein opined that the Bologna printed edition included "many additions from different times" and thus was not a reliable witness "to the book's [meaning, *Sefer Ḥasidim*'s] principal content." On the other hand, Epstein stated, the Parma manuscript "was edited in ancient times, and lacks the many additions" of the Bologna text and, therefore, was the superior exemplar.[8] Jacob Freimann, the German rabbi and encyclopedist who supplied a scholarly introduction and appendix to the second edition of the Parma manuscript (1924), noted that, while groupings of passages on the same topic (such as the laws of prayer or the Sabbath) were found in multiple locations across the Parma manuscript, passages on the same topic were grouped together in the Bologna edition. Freimann concluded: "The Parma edition was edited in ancient times, closer to the time of the creation of the book [again, meaning *Sefer Ḥasidim*] . . . and the editor of the Bologna edition came afterwards at a later time and composed the book so that there was one section for every topic on its own."[9]

Such historical-critical investigations have continued into the present century. Scholars continue to depict the longer Parma manuscript as closer to a purported *Sefer Ḥasidim Urtext* than the Bologna printed edition.[10] Given the weight of this consensus, Peter Schäfer and Ivan Marcus's claims about the "openness" of *Sefer Ḥasidim* and the absence of a *Sefer Ḥasidim Urtext* represent a dramatic historiographic revision.[11]

The number and diversity of the extant *Sefer Ḥasidim* manuscripts is the clearest evidence in support of this revision. Marcus has cataloged thirty-seven *Sefer Ḥasidim* manuscripts, almost two-thirds of which date from the medieval period. The remainder date to the period after the appearance of the Bologna edition. It is clear that at least some of these later manuscripts were copied by readers of printed editions. As a result, the manuscripts that predate the Bologna printed edition may be considered the most reliable witnesses to *Sefer Ḥasidim*'s preprint history.[12] These medieval manuscripts are conspicuously heterogeneous in their content, structure, and titling.

Six medieval *Sefer Ḥasidim* manuscripts lack titles. Some are missing initial pages and/or colophons, and thus it is impossible to know the names under which they circulated. The remainder, however, are variously titled: Four are called by the familiar appellation *Sefer Ḥasidim* (or, relatedly, *Sefer ha-Ḥasidim,* including the definite article *hey*).[13] These are alike in that they are composed of the first 152 passages of the Bologna edition or a portion thereof.[14] A fifth manuscript containing the same cluster of 152 passages is entitled *Sefer ha-Ḥasidut* (*The Book of Piety*).[15] Haym Soloveitchik has argued, on the basis of their language and theology, that most of these 152 passages were a separate and distinct work from *Sefer Ḥasidim*. This separate work, which he dubbed "SH I," emerged not from the milieu of the *Ḥasidei Ashkenaz* but, rather, from medieval France, among followers of the philosopher Moses Maimonides (1138–1204). Marcus similarly has suggested that SH I—which he calls *Sefer ha-Ḥasidut*—circulated on its own and as a unit within *Sefer Ḥasidim* during the medieval period.[16] Thus, though SH I/*Sefer ha-Ḥasidut* was known to some of its readers as *Sefer Ḥasidim,* according to Soloveitchik and Marcus, it was both quantitatively and qualitatively different from other works called *Sefer Ḥasidim*.

A further ten of the medieval *Sefer Ḥasidim* manuscripts are entitled *Likkutim mi-Sefer Ḥasidim* (*Gleanings from Sefer Ḥasidim*) or similar descriptors, such as *Katuv be-Sefer Ḥasidim* (*Written in Sefer Ḥasidim*) and *Nimẓa be-Sefer Ḥasidim* (*Found in Sefer Ḥasidim*).[17] The prominence of these terms among the manuscripts indicates that their scribes rarely perceived themselves as writing out a full, definitive *Sefer Ḥasidim*—if such a work existed at all. Rather, they saw themselves as recording bits and pieces of a larger work by that name.[18]

Tellingly, one of the longer medieval manuscripts, and perhaps the oldest extant today, the Cambridge University Library's Ms. Add. 379, concludes with the colophon: "Completed is the work of *Sefer ha-Ḥasidim* which was gathered [or gleaned, *nilkat,* related to *likkut*] like 'berries in the top of the uppermost bough' [Isaiah 17:6] or 'choice grapes' [picked] 'from among the wild sort' [Isaiah 5:4]."[19] With these biblically inflected phrases, the scribe indicated that he did not copy a preexisting exemplar whole cloth but, instead, collected the best material (the "gleanings") from various sources, anthologizing them in a single document. In other words, through anthological activity, the scribe perceived himself as creating a book he called *Sefer ha-Ḥasidim.*

The Bologna printed edition itself may be characterized as a compilation of three self-contained works, each marked with a heading or title.[20] The first passage of the book begins with the enlarged words, in square type: "This book is called *Sefer Ḥasidim*"—the standard beginning of the so-called SH I/*Sefer ha-Ḥasidut.*[21] Several pages later, prior to §162, there is another enlarged heading in square type: "*Sefer ha-Ḥasidim.*"[22] Later, toward the end of the text, prior to §1,136, there is the pious formula with which many Hebrew books close: "The end, blessed is the Merciful and our help," followed by the statement, in enlarged square type: "This [i.e., the following] was copied from another *Sefer Ḥasidim* [*Sefer Ḥasidim aḥer*]."[23] These three headings testify to the existence of various works circulating under the same or similar titles. (Chapter 3 will consider when and how these three works were joined to one another.) Similar groupings of passages marked by the same headings are present in the medieval manuscripts.

Within the text of the Bologna printed edition and the manuscripts, moreover, there are numerous extracts from well-known medieval sources. The bibliographer and *Sefer Ḥasidim* commentator Hayim Yosef David Azulai (1724–1806) noticed that SH 1/*Sefer ha-Ḥasidut* contained lengthy excerpts from Moses Maimonides's legal code, the *Mishneh Torah.*[24] While most are not identified as originating outside *Sefer Ḥasidim,* one passage (numbered §20 and comprising an excerpt from Maimonides's *Laws of Repentance,* chapters 1 and 2) is preceded in both the manuscripts and the Bologna edition by the heading "Laws of Repentance."[25] There are also lengthy extracts from R. Nissim b. Jacob b. Nissim ibn Shahin's (990–1062) *Megillat setarim,* R. Isaac Alfasi's (1013–1103) commentary on the Babylonian Talmud, and R. Sa'adia Gaon's (882–942) *Emunot ve-de'ot.*[26] Each is either preceded or followed by a heading acknowledging its origins in another work by a named author. There is also the text of a responsum (a halakhic query sent to a rabbinic court and their reply) from the "elders of Regensburg," dealing with the question of whether synagogue honors may be purchased by transgressors, set off with its own heading.[27] Marcus, following Abraham

Epstein, identified §§153–162 as *Sefer ha-yir'ah* (*The Book of God-Fearing*), a work attributed to R. Judah he-Ḥasid's father, R. Samuel b. Kalonymus he-Ḥasid, based on its own distinctive content.[28]

While a detailed exposition of the structures of the medieval *Sefer Ḥasidim* manuscripts is beyond the scope of this chapter, the Parma manuscript, though the longest, is characteristic. It, too, is a compilation. It begins with the title *Sefer Ḥasidim* but proceeds directly to the text of the work Marcus has called *Sefer ha-yir'ah*. Passage 14 begins with the centered heading "*Sefer Ḥasidim* 2 [*bet*]." Passage 27 begins with another enlarged heading, "This is *Sefer Ḥasidim*," and, shortly thereafter, there is a series of extensive quotations from medieval works, including the *She'iltot* of Ahai Gaon (eighth century) and Sa'adia Gaon's *Emunot ve-de'ot*, each preceded with its own heading. Passage 545 is derived from Shabbtai ben Abraham Donnolo's (tenth century) commentary on the mystical work *Sefer Yeẓirah*. Passage 721 is preceded by the heading, "This I found in another book [*sefer aḥer*]." Passage 1,592 is the responsum of the court of Regensburg, mentioned previously. Passage 1,792 is introduced by the heading "*Sefer Ḥasidim* on the Proverbs of Solomon." And these are just some of the divisions within the manuscript.

The presence of differing headings, distinctive subsections and extracts, and varied organizational structures within the various *Sefer Ḥasidim* witnesses we possess today lends credence to the view that *Sefer Ḥasidim* was never a single, definitive work in the medieval period. Only when the partners of Bologna printed their edition in 1538—the edition that served as the basis of every other edition for centuries thereafter—did *Sefer Ḥasidim* acquire a single standard text.

Who Wrote *Sefer Ḥasidim*?

Just as manuscript culture led to textual instability, it also fostered authorial instability. Scholars of literature and the history of the book have noted that, in medieval Europe, readers did not necessarily link a text's meaning and value to the identity of a named individual. Its authority reflected its dependence on other works previously deemed canonical. The term *auctor* (author)—"one whose words possess authority"—was bestowed on writers whose works had acquired the halo of canonicity, whose words were quoted and anthologized by others over generations. This led to a cultural conservatism; literary creativity was considered a reflection of a work's kinship with an acknowledged body of texts.[29] Writing was a collaborative or iterative act, one generation adapting and reworking the previous generation's efforts.[30] Such norms of literary creativity did not prioritize attributing texts to specific individuals.

The medieval manuscripts that circulated under titles like *Sefer Ḥasidim* were anthologies of passages composed by many hands—some named individuals such as Maimonides, and many anonymous. The scribes who wrote these manuscripts did not attribute them to a specific named individual.[31] Their lack of attribution corresponds to advice given in one *Sefer Ḥasidim* passage (§367 in the Bologna edition): Writers should be like the "sages of old" who "would not write their books in their own names and did not allow others to put their names on their books . . . They would not write in their books, 'I so-and-so son of so-and-so wrote and composed this book,' so that they would not benefit in this world and damage their reward in the world to come."[32]

Yet, despite these realities, and despite newfound recognition of *Sefer Ḥasidim*'s "openness," scholars continue to write as if R. Judah he-Ḥasid were its author. Even Marcus has asserted, "It is likely that R. Judah *he-hasid* [*sic*] was the author of most of these single paragraphs and also of the sequences of topics [in *Sefer Ḥasidim*] . . ."[33] In fact, the only medieval source attributing a book known as *Sefer Ḥasidim* to Judah is a manuscript of Judah's commentary on the Pentateuch transcribed by his son, R. Moses Zaltman. There, at the beginning of the section on Genesis 12:1–17:27, Moses explains that he witnessed his father "write two pages [*dapim*] of *Sefer Ḥasidim*" shortly after receiving a premonition about his (Judah's) impending demise.[34] Yet, there is much to suggest that this is not a full-fledged statement of attribution. First, the medieval manuscripts associated with the title *Sefer Ḥasidim* are longer than two pages. Second, as David Shyovitz has noted: "The fact that Judah composed two pages of *Sefer Ḥasidim* does not preclude anyone else from having contributed to the same endeavor."[35] Third, Moses's testimony is a brief aside in an obscure manuscript, uncited and uncorroborated in the works of Judah's contemporaries or successors. We do, in fact, possess several medieval sources that quote Judah's teachings by name, parallels of which may be found in *Sefer Ḥasidim* witnesses, but they do not cite a book known as *Sefer Ḥasidim* as their source.[36] We also possess a smaller number of medieval sources that cite a work entitled *Sefer Ḥasidim*, but, as one would expect, they do not attribute that work to Judah.[37] Above all, we do not have manuscripts entitled *Sefer Ḥasidim* in which Judah is identified as the author of the text. Neither do we have medieval works (other than the manuscript quoted here) that attribute a work entitled *Sefer Ḥasidim* to Judah.

Moses's testimony and that of other medieval authorities thus suggests, at most, that Judah may have composed some of the passages anthologized in a work entitled *Sefer Ḥasidim*, but Judah was not considered "the author" of any definitive *Sefer Ḥasidim* by his colleagues or successors. To paraphrase Kant (in translation), he was not the creator of a stable "discourse" known as *Sefer Ḥasidim* and did not "mandate" its replication and communication. Medieval writers were participants in a collective and iterative enterprise that often resulted not in single definitive editions but, rather, a diversity of editions. In the early modern period, however, the act of printing, as we will see in the coming chapters, had a constricting effect, reducing the sphere of authorship from a plurality to the person of a single, named individual. And so it was in the case of *Sefer Ḥasidim*: As a result of the efforts of the printers of the Bologna *editio princeps*, Judah became known as *Sefer Ḥasidim*'s author.

What Is *Sefer Ḥasidim*?

The textual and authorial instability of the medieval *Sefer Ḥasidim* witnesses is mirrored by their lack of thematic or ideological coherence—qualities carried forth into the Bologna printed edition and its successors. Until recently, as was the case with the question of authorial attribution, much scholarship has portrayed *Sefer Ḥasidim* as a single, unified treatise (or fragments of a single long-lost *Urtext*). Scholars have sought to uncover, as Yizhak F. Baer did in a seminal study, the "socioreligious orientation of *Sefer Ḥasidim*," and, in doing so, have played down contradictions.[38] What follows is an attempt at undoing this consensus.

If anything unites the various *Sefer Ḥasidim* witnesses, it is a recurring protagonist: the anonymous *ḥasid* (male pietist, plural *ḥasidim*). Yet, what the *ḥasid*'s pietism entails is difficult to pin down. The very first passage of the Bologna printed edition describes *ḥasidim* as "God-fearers and ones who dwell on His name," who saw themselves as subject to a second set of religious guidelines parallel to the standard commandments revealed at Sinai.[39] Haym Soloveitchik has argued that this was a major theological innovation with social ramifications.[40] It was not enough, for example, for a *ḥasid* to offer the thrice-daily prayers; he had to do so with exceptional concentration and in a state of physical purity. If he felt he could not attain the requisite focus in his local synagogue, or that his fellow worshippers were not sufficiently virtuous, he might pray on his own at home.[41]

Elitism and esotericism of this sort are not manifested consistently in the various *Sefer Ḥasidim* witnesses. Another passage, by contrast, lauds the piety of an uneducated shepherd who, not knowing the words of the Hebrew prayers, praised God in simple and spontaneous terms, saying: "For while I take wages from all others, if you hired me to look after beasts, I would take nothing from you, for I love You."[42] The passage's unqualified admiration for the shepherd's virtuous intentions and spiritual authenticity conflicts with passages like those quoted previously that laud the pursuit of esoteric knowledge and uncompromising ritual observance. It appears that the various *Sefer Ḥasidim* witnesses do not advocate a single theology or religious path.

Many *Sefer Ḥasidim* passages depict the *ḥasid* and his society as marked by a constant temptation to sin. Separation and vigilance were necessary to overcome it:

> Anyone who wants to enter into the depth of piety [*ḥasidut*], the depth of the Creator's palaces, the depth of His majesty, the only way for him to do so is if he is a sage, wise and possessing a willing soul without anger, forsaking worldly things, casual conversation among people, the pleasure of children, and conversation with his wife except during sexual relations.[43]

Some *ḥasidim* reinforced this separation by adopting nonnormative religious practices, such as donning a fringed garment (*ẓiẓit* or *tallit*) and phylacteries (*tefillin*), which, while common among Jews today, according to Elisheva Baumgarten, were not widespread in medieval Ashkenaz.[44] *Ḥasidim* sometimes encountered hostility for these practices. In the face of opposition, one *Sefer Ḥasidim* passage counsels *ḥasidim* to see themselves as knights (*parashim*) in armor, who "descend into the depths of battle and sacrifice themselves for their glory."[45] Yet, other passages emphasize the *ḥasid*'s humility and his refusal to do anything that might set himself apart from his fellows: "One should distance oneself from a situation where one might accrue eminence or honor."[46] Again, on questions relating to religious behavior and worldview, the passages in the *Sefer Ḥasidim* witnesses do not present a united front.

Other passages express contradictory opinions of Talmudic dialectics, the development of which reached new heights in High Medieval Ashkenaz. One expounds upon the teaching in Ecclesiastes 4:6: "Better is a handful of quietness, than both the hands full of labor."[47] It is better, the passage explains, for "a man to know the practical application of the laws ['a handful of quietness'] than to know how to pose difficult questions, to reconcile contradictions, and to plunder the Talmud for sources ['hands full of labor']."[48] These verbs (to question—*lehakshot*; to reconcile—*letareẓ*; to plunder—*lahafokh*) referred to the hallmarks of the new school of Talmudic dialectics established in medieval Ashkenaz known as Tosafism.

Yet, Ephraim Kanarfogel has shown that there was no rigid division between proponents and opponents of Talmudic dialectics in medieval Ashkenaz and *Sefer Ḥasidim*. He highlights passages in the *Sefer Ḥasidim* witnesses that encourage a traveler far from home to buy books "unavailable in his city, such as commentaries, *tosafot*, and homilies . . . since it is a commandment to buy books." With its reference to *tosafot*, the passage makes explicit positive mention of the literature of Tosafism.[49] Kanarfogel similarly points out that in the responsum cited previously, the court of Regensburg applied an "amalgamation of halakhic and pietistic principles," invoking precedents of the Tosafists.[50] Kanarfogel's investigations reinforce the conclusion that the various *Sefer Ḥasidim* witnesses cannot be typecast as either hostile to Tosafistic analysis or entirely favorable to it. At best, they represent a hybrid approach.

Among the best-known and most controversial passages associated with the *Sefer Ḥasidim* witnesses are those prescribing rituals that bruise the body for the purpose of purifying the soul. One passage states succinctly: "With every pain one accepts God's will."[51] Another describes a *ḥasid* who "in summer lay on the ground among fleas and in wintertime put his feet in a pail of water until they became frozen in ice."[52] While passages like these seek to negate and brutalize the human body, others, recently considered by David Shyovitz, underscore the wondrousness of the body and advise close attention to its care and inner workings. One, for example, recalls a liturgy a *ḥasid* offered in praise of "each and every one of his limbs."[53] Another suggests that one's internal organs are obligated to offer blessings to God during worship.[54] Some uphold submission to martyrdom as the greatest expression of faith.[55] Others, by contrast, offer guidance on how to preserve oneself and avoid martyrdom during times of persecution.[56]

The analogy of the *ḥasid* to a knight is one of the many evocative references in the texts of *Sefer Ḥasidim* to the realia of medieval European life. Again, the attitudes these passages display to the dominant culture are not uniform. On the one hand, a notable passage mentions non-Jewish courtly literature, called "romances," and prohibits the *ḥasid* from reusing parchment upon which such literature was written as bindings for Hebrew books.[57] A *ḥasid* should not teach priests Jewish songs and should avoid setting Jewish prayers to Christian melodies.[58] Some passages describe Jews' commerce with Christians and the challenge of doing business without unintentionally affirming or impugning Christianity and its symbols—a problem for Jews in Christian Europe writ large, not just *ḥasidim*.[59] While some passages seek to impose distance between Jews and Christians, others testify to a common culture, especially with regard to magic and the supernatural. One describes "women, called *striya, mares,* and werewolves, who were created at dusk and who are able to perform an action and change their appearance."[60] Another describes a metamorphosing, demonic dragon.[61] And still another, discussed in chapter 6, recounts that, at various times, including the seventh day of the Festival of Sukkot (known as *Hoshana Rabba*), "souls come out of their graves" and "go out and pray" on behalf of the living.[62]

The prominence of the supernatural in the *Sefer Ḥasidim* witnesses has attracted the attention of scholars since the early modern period, as we will see later. Yet, no matter the fantastical and unique aspects of some passages, these details should not lead one to conclude that the *Sefer Ḥasidim* witnesses represent a novum in Jewish theology or metaphysics. As both Soloveitchik and David Shyovitz have pointed out, there is much that is entirely conventional in the *Sefer Ḥasidim* witnesses.[63] As noted earlier, for example, there are extensive quotations from the works of the medieval philosophers, including, among others, Moses Maimonides and Sa'adia Gaon, as well as frequent quotations from the Talmud and other rabbinic sources. Many of the supernatural elements cited in the passage find their *locus classicus* in the Babylonian Talmud. Passages very often recapitulate and adumbrate traditional material. The ghosts who rise from their graves in prayer do so only to teach the living an entirely conventional rabbinic lesson, that prayer, fasting, and charity can save one from death (cf. Proverbs 10:2).

Conclusion

Evocative passages advocating nontraditional theologies, unsophisticated spirituality, and self-abnegation, alongside stories of knights, holy men, and ghosts, make clear why *Sefer Ḥasidim*, in its various witnesses, has attracted the attention of historians of medieval Jewry for more than a century. They have often used passages like those cited here to draw conclusions about the ways medieval Ashkenazic Jews related to their non-Jewish neighbors. Marcus, for example, proposed the concept of "inward acculturation" to describe the ways in which the Jews of medieval Ashkenaz integrated into northern European society while maintaining difference.[64] Baumgarten has proposed that Jews engaged in a dialectic of "appropriation" and "differentiation."[65] These important conversations, however, have tended to reify the perception of *Sefer Ḥasidim* as a single work with a single author and a single "socioreligious orientation." In reality, the sources at our disposal give the impression of heterogeneity; there were multiple works entitled *Sefer Ḥasidim*, multiple works written by multiple hands, containing a multiplicity of concepts and views.

With due appreciation for the generations of scholars who have illuminated the richness of medieval Jewish culture by studying the various *Sefer Ḥasidim* witnesses, this monograph now turns to its primary subject: how and why *Sefer Ḥasidim* became a book (in the Kantian sense of a stable, replicable discourse with an author), who was responsible for that transformation, and what it can teach us about the history of printing and Hebrew books generally.

CHAPTER 2

The Partners of Bologna

They received the secret of the correct prayers, and the rest of the secrets, rabbi from his rabbi, until Aaron . . . who . . . had to wander from place to place, until he came to the land of Lombardy, to a city named Lucca. . . . [Rabbi Moses b. Kalonymus] was the first to leave Lombardy, he and his sons . . . and the rest of the important people there. King Charles brought them with him from the land of Lombardy, and settled them in Mainz.

R. Eleazar of Worms (c. 1220),
quoted in Joseph Delmedigo,
Sefer meẓaref leḥokhma (1629)

• • • • •

THE JEWS OF MEDIEVAL ASHKENAZ proudly traced their ancestry to northern Italy, from where, they believed, Charlemagne providentially had carried them forth to the budding cities of the Rhineland.[1] The pioneers who made the trek across the Alps included the venerable Kalonymus family, from which R. Judah he-Ḥasid descended. From Judah, R. Eleazar of Worms received "the secret of the correct prayers." R. Eleazer then promulgated those secrets in a thirteenth-century manuscript, a quotation from which was printed in the sixteenth-century chronicle cited previously.[2]

Persecution led the Jews of the Rhineland to cross the Alps once again in the late fourteenth and fifteenth centuries and establish new settlements in northern Italy.[3] The fact that several of the extant medieval *Sefer Ḥasidim* manuscripts were copied in late-medieval Italy suggests that the Ashkenazic migrants may have carried the traditions associated with the name *Sefer Ḥasidim* southward. It is thus fitting that *Sefer Ḥasidim* became a book in the city of Bologna, just over a day's walk from the Rhenish Jews' ancestral home, Lucca, the foremost producer of silk in medieval Europe. Lucca ceded that position to Bologna after some of its craftsman decamped to *La Grassa* ("the fat one," Bologna's moniker) during the fourteenth century. Jews were active in Bologna's silk trade, and three Bolognese Jewish silk makers, who called themselves "the partners" (*ha-shutafim*), printed the *editio princeps* of *Sefer Ḥasidim* in 1538. It is perhaps surprising, then, that at least one of the partners was not Ashkenazic but rather Sephardic, and that their *Sefer Ḥasidim* edition was made possible with the financial and textual contributions of the Castilian sage R. Abraham b. Moses ha-Cohen. With its content rooted in medieval Ashkenazic culture, and Sephardic Jews among its creators and promoters, the *editio princeps* of *Sefer Ḥasidim* was thus a symbol of a new multiethnic Jewish community and culture that was coming into existence in early modern Italy. That first edition testifies to the role of printers and printing in creating that culture and to the central preoccupations of that community: in particular, improving religious devotion in light of the temptations of Aristotelian philosophy.

Jewish Life and Printing *nella Grassa*

There is evidence of Jews in Bologna from at least the fourteenth century, though they may have resided there long before.[4] In 1416, the city was the site of the first synod of Italian Jewish leaders.[5] Throughout the medieval period, control of the city alternated among Italy's noble families. From 1506, however, it found itself squarely in papal hands. By then, its Jewish population totaled around 1,000 individuals; out of a total population of 60,000, it was one of the larger, though not the largest, Jewish communities on the Italian Peninsula.[6]

Bologna's Jewish population grew during the sixteenth century as a result of an influx of refugees from the Iberian Peninsula following the expulsion of the Jews of Spain in 1492. Perhaps 9,000 Spanish Jews landed on the Italian Peninsula after 1492, with some settling only temporarily and others permanently.[7] The numbers of newcomers increased further in 1527 with the arrival of loan-bankers from Florence.[8] That year, Florence's ruling family, the Medici, lost control of the city in the War of the League of Cognac. Florence's new imperial rulers did not renew the residence and banking privileges of the city's Jews, forcing them to flee to neighboring towns—especially those under (friendlier) papal control, such as Bologna. According to Bernard Cooperman, these bankers transformed Bologna into "the financial capital of Jewish Italy," operating more than seventeen loan-banks.[9]

The arrival in Bologna of these groups of Jewish migrants, Iberian and Florentine, led to conflict: Iberian refugees sought to impose their practices and halakhic traditions on the preexisting community, while the Florentine bankers sought to displace the city's older commercial elite.[10] This fractiousness, however, did not impede Bologna from becoming a vibrant center of Jewish learning and religious culture. By 1554, according to a papal census, there were at least eleven synagogues in the city.[11] Torah scholars and students praised Bologna for the dynamism and sophistication of its scholarship. In a letter to his father from 1540, for instance, Elhanan da Rieti, the son of the Sienese banker R. Ishmael da Rieti, asked if an associate of his father who was visiting Bologna could "gather the spirit of wisdom by the handful there, Bologna, and novellae of the *yeshivah* [rabbinical academy, plural *yeshivot*], and bring it back to me safely."[12] During the 1540s, two confraternities (*ḥavurot*) were established for Jews who wished to commit themselves to pious strictures and perform charitable acts.[13] The city was also home to one of Europe's oldest and most prestigious universities, where Jews were known to sit in on classes, especially at its medical school.

The university spurred demand for printed books, and, as early as 1471, a press was operating in the city.[14] That press was established by three men—Francesco dal Pozzo, Baldassarre Azzoguidi, and Annibale Malpigli—who shared in funding, editing, and printing editions of classical and medieval texts.[15] Financial partnerships of this nature, in which several individuals pooled capital to underwrite the printing of books, were especially common during the first centuries of printing. Printers required enough capital to make significant initial investments in raw materials (paper, type) and labor, and then they had to be content with profits realized many months or years later, when books were sold at market.[16] Bologna's first Hebrew press was also established by a partnership of three men: Meister Joseph, Neriyah Hayyim Mordecai, and Hezekiah of Ventura produced the city's first Hebrew books in 1477. Like the university press, its founding was likely tied to student demand for its books—in this case, from the city's *yeshivah* students. Its total output totaled three editions of the book of Psalms with R. David Kimḥi's commentary.[17] Given the constant Christian proselytizing during this period, it is not surprising that they chose to print a work known for its anti-Christian polemics.[18] In 1482, the itinerant R. Abraham b. Hayyim dei Tintori ("Abraham of the Dyers") of Pesaro printed an edition of the Pentateuch with vowels, cantillation, and commentaries in the city—another practical choice given the centrality of scriptural recitation in Jewish worship.[19] After Abraham's Bible, from 1482 until 1537, no Hebrew books were printed in Bologna. Then, in 1536, another triumvirate, "the partners," laid the groundwork for a new Hebrew printing enterprise in Bologna.[20]

The Partners and Their Press

What we know of the partners' press comes primarily from the paratexts, especially the introductions and colophons, of the books they printed and from papal *condotte* (singular *condotta*, "license") recorded in the Vatican Apostolic Archives. In the introduction to the last of their publications, a massive two-volume liturgy for weekdays and festivals (Hebrew, *maḥzor*), the book's editor, R. Yoḥanan b. Joseph Treves, wrote the following encomium:

> For this reason, the nobles of the people [Numbers 21:18] opened their eyes and arose, and drew their shields. It is not for nothing that they spent their money, they acted, copied texts, and waxed mighty in power [Job 27:1], in their craft, the sacred labor, at their presses. The learned, holy people of [the Lord's] jubilation [Leviticus 19:24], whose names were set down as "the partners of Bologna," that faithful town [Isaiah 1:21]. Behold these three of stately stride [Proverbs 30:29] in integrity and faith: Rabbi Menaḥem, may he live and be well, son of Rabbi Abraham of Modena, of blessed memory; Rabbi Yeḥiel of Verona son of Rabbi Solomon, of blessed memory; and, Rabbi Don Aryeh, may he live and be well, son of Rabbi Solomon Ḥayyim of Monselice, of blessed memory. The Lord touched their hearts to enlarge Torah [Leviticus 14:32]. They sought a wise artisan [Isaiah 40:20], Rabbi Raphael Talmi son of Rabbi Emanuel, of blessed memory, of Forli, to oversee the work and to do it, and they printed many books.[21]

The partners were thus: R. Menaḥem b. R. Abraham of Modena, R. Yehiel of Verona b. R. Solomon, and R. Don Aryeh b. R. Solomon Hayyim of Monselice.[22] On the title pages of their other volumes, these men also called themselves "the partners—makers of silk crafts" (*ha-shutafim . . . osim malekhet ha-meshi*), recalling their association with the trade that powered Bologna's prosperity in the sixteenth century.[23] Assisted by R. Raphael Talmi b. R. Emanuel of Forli, whom Treves compared, by way of allusion, to the biblical craftsman Bezalel b. Uri (Exodus 31:3), the partners printed nine titles over four years, from 1537 to 1540.

In his encomium, Treves characterized the partners as entrepreneur-scholars, investing both capital and religious knowledge in the titles they produced. On the financial side, Treves, as was common in Hebrew introductions, deployed Scripture to note the investment the partners made in their books: They "spent their money and fulfilled the words of the prophet Job [21:7]: 'they copied [books] and acted with courage' in the sacred work of printing." As for their scholarly credentials, when listing their names, Treves preceded them with suggestive honorifics: All three had acquired a kind of rabbinical ordination synonymous with expertise in Talmudic learning that granted them license to render halakhic decisions.[24] Given this learning, it is thus likely that the partners were engaged in the editorial work of producing books as well. This was not unusual in the sixteenth century, when printers performed multiple roles, from financier to editor, from bookseller to anthologizer.[25] It was even more the case among Hebrew printers—perhaps most famously, Bomberg—who were known to be intimately involved in the preparation of their editions.[26] The partners were not, then, merely entrepreneurial laypeople seeking to profit from a new commodity. They were scholars well versed in the Jewish textual tradition who exploited that knowledge *and* the new technology of printing to produce books for the Jews of Bologna and beyond. To do so, however, they required a *condotta* from the Pope.

The *condotta* was a legal instrument through which the papacy bestowed privileges and imposed obligations on those under its sovereignty. Jewish settlements in premodern Christian Europe were notoriously precarious. Jews possessed no rights, only privileges—privileges of settlement, of self-government, of commerce—granted by their sovereigns and perpetually subject to renewal, modification, and retraction.[27] Jews solicited *condotte* from the Pope in order to establish settlements and business activities in the papal domains in exchange for fees, taxes, and tributes. The *condotte* preserved in the Vatican archives frequently mention the Jews of Bologna, both as individuals and as a corporate body, and their efforts to secure privileges great and small, as well as the revenues they provided to the Holy See. In particular, they testify to how the Jews of sixteenth-century Bologna struggled to negotiate their financial burdens and ward off impoverishment.[28]

They engaged the levers of power seeking to ensure their own security, but the possibility of expulsion always lurked in the background.

Hebrew printing, like any other Jewish trade, required a *condotta*. Such licenses, as in the partners' case, often conferred on their holders a limited monopoly and/or a copyright. Outside of Bologna, we know of Bomberg's efforts to secure permission from the Venetian Senate for his press, as well as to prevent others from reprinting his books or entering the field of Hebrew printing at all. Bomberg and the Senate engaged in regular negotiations over the fees for his license, monopoly, and copyright, but he, ultimately, was a Christian residing in a city ruled by a Christian merchant elite. He could (and ultimately did) leave with his wealth and return to his native land if the Senate's terms were too onerous.[29] The partners, by contrast, were Jews—a perpetually maligned, subject minority under the auspices of the princes of the Church, living under the near-constant threat of impoverishment and expulsion. The balance of power was entirely different.

To win a printing *condotta*, in the autumn of 1536, if not earlier, the partners solicited the support of influential members of the curia and family of Pope Paul III (Alessandro Farnese, 1534–1549). We know of their lobbying efforts through the testimony of Aleandro Girolamo (1480–1542), the archbishop of Brindisi and a scholar of Hebrew, whose guidance the Holy See sought in determining whether to permit a Hebrew press in Bologna.[30] According to Girolamo, the partners first petitioned Nicholas of Aragon, the dean of the Roman Rota (the Church's highest appellate court) and the papal *referendarius*, the senior Vatican official in charge of receiving petitions. This was the standard tactic, but it is notable that Nicholas's father Ferdinand was the Pope's physician and a formerly Jewish convert to Christianity.[31]

Upon receipt of the petition, Paolo Capizucchi, Bishop of Nicastro, papal vicar, and an auditor (member) of the Rota, advised against "granting quick permission" to the request and suggested seeking Girolamo's opinion. Girolamo, too, was disinclined to approve the partners' request because "the Hebrew teaching contains, after the arrival of the Lord, ignorances that violate our Holy Scriptures."[32] He recommended that the petition be referred to the papal governor in Bologna. However, Girolamo and Paolo's efforts were short-circuited by the partners, who sought assistance from another member of the Pope's inner circle: Pier Luigi Farnese (1503–1547), Duke of Castro and Captain-General of the Church, as well as the Pope's illegitimate eldest son.

Girolamo wrote derisively of the partners' attempts to bypass the standard policy-making avenues and involve Pier Luigi: "There is no doubt that the Jews, if the usual ways to the Pope are not possible, tried to influence his son with courteous [*facilis*] petitions." While he and Cardinal Tommaso Badia, Master of the Sacred Palace (the Pope's senior policy advisor), were visiting the home of Cardinal Nicholas Schòmberg, Bishop of Capua, Girolamo witnessed Pier Luigi's pressuring of Badia to write an opinion in favor of the partners' request. Apparently, Badia declined to intervene, but, Girolamo suggested, through Pier Luigi's efforts, the partners succeeded in acquiring a *condotta*.[33]

Pier Luigi's intervention was likely rooted in self-interest and the interests of the Church: A swashbuckling mercenary who earned fame fighting for the Holy Roman Emperor Charles V and against his father in the Sack of Rome in 1527, Pier Luigi was an expert in mustering Jewish wealth for his own purposes.[34] In 1538, he arranged for his father to grant the annual revenue from the Jews of Cesena to an associate.[35] He and his father would profit, indirectly of course, through the success of the partners' enterprise. Pier Luigi's wife, Gerolama, was raised in Pitigliano in Tuscany, which had a large and prosperous Jewish population from the fifteenth century. She was a supporter of Ignatius Loyola's missionary activities and intervened in papal proceedings to force a Jewish woman whose husband had been baptized to relinquish their son.[36] Perhaps she believed a Hebrew press under the auspices of the Church could further the Church's mission to the Jews. Regardless of motivation, Pier Luigi's intervention led Pope Paul III to grant the partners their *condotta* in December 1536.

The text of that *condotta* permitted one "Emanueli Habraham" (the aforementioned R. Menaḥem b. R. Abraham of Modena) "and his Jewish associates" to

> print or have printed ... the Jewish Books of the Old Testament with ancient commentaries, and official books which are read in the synagogue, in which nothing blasphemes against Jesus Christ our Lord and Savior, as well as blessings for mealtimes, written in Hebrew letters.[37]

Three months later, Pope Paul III headed off any interference from local Bolognese authorities by reaffirming this license and commending it to Gregory Magalotto, Bishop of Chiusi and Governor of Bologna. Finally, in October 1537, the partners once more received the affirmation of the Holy

See with a grant of a ten-year copyright from Cardinal Antonio Pucci, the head of the Supreme Tribunal of the Apostolic Penitentiary.[38]

Under this legal framework, the partners printed nine titles, including a newly composed philosophical treatise by R. Obadiah b. Jacob Sforno (1475–1550); a translation of the daily liturgy into Judeo-Italian; and, of course, *Sefer Ḥasidim*. They never did print a Bible or the mealtime blessings. The *condotta*'s February 1537 reconfirmation further permitted them to print a Hebrew grammar.[39] That book also never came to be.[40]

From Silkworms to Bookworms

While no explicit evidence testifies to why the partners chose to enter the printing business when they did, certainly the growth of Bologna's Jewish population and its *yeshivot* during the first half of the sixteenth century brought new sources of wealth and learning, including R. Abraham b. Moses ha-Cohen, Bologna's leading rabbi in the early 1500s. The partners also began printing books just when Bomberg's press appears to have floundered. Beginning in the early 1530s, its output began a precipitous decline. In 1536, its government-granted monopoly lapsed.[41] By 1538, Bomberg had headed home to his native Antwerp. Perhaps the partners were aware of these events and believed Bomberg's weakened position created an opening for competition.[42]

The growth and prosperity of the silk trade in Bologna by mid-century no doubt also stimulated the partners' printing enterprise.[43] It is likely that the partners employed capital they generated in the silk trade to underwrite the substantial starting costs of their printing venture. While the prominence of Bologna's Jewish loan-bankers has been widely recognized, Jews' involvement in the city's silk trade has received little scholarly attention.[44] In fact, the partners were participants in what Carlo Poni has termed a "proto-industrial revolution" in Bologna.[45] There were essential similarities, moreover, between early modern silk and book production.

According to the economic historian Stephen R. Epstein, competing claims of sovereignty, war, and plague during the thirteenth and fourteenth centuries led to "increased artisan mobility [which] accelerated cross-fertilisation between industrial sectors and economic regions."[46] By the middle of the fourteenth century, silk workers from Lucca (at the time,

Europe's foremost producer) brought their craft knowledge to Bologna and established the world's first water-powered silk mill.[47] This was one of three jealously guarded innovations—along with mechanical winding machines and the use of bobbins for spinning thread—that became characteristic of the "*alla Bolognese*" method of silk production.[48] The *alla Bolognese* system transformed a laborious home-based craft into an urban factory-based trade, led to at least a hundredfold increase in productivity, and fashioned thinner and stronger threads, especially the desirable *orsoglio* (organzine) thread.[49] Bologna benefited from a topography and hydrology that permitted the creation of a network of underground capillaries and aboveground canals, allowing mills to be hidden inside buildings and preventing their valuable technologies and techniques from being observed by outsiders.[50] As a result of these innovations and advantages, estimates of the percentage of the city's population involved in silk production during the sixteenth century range from forty to sixty percent.[51]

Aside from the partners' own testimony, papal *condotte* bear witness to Jews' involvement in Bologna's silk trade during the first decades of the sixteenth century. These particular *condotte* permitted Jews to trade in textiles, especially *strazzaria* (rags and other secondhand cloth, including silk), alongside the more common profession of moneylending.[52] In one case, on December 22, 1529, Pope Clement VII granted "Salomon, son of David of Monselice" a "license to trade in secondhand cloth (*strazzaria*), silk and the like, in Bologna."[53] Three years earlier, the papal chamberlain, Francis Armellinus Medici, had granted Salomon a license to "trade in old clothes and other merchandise and to enjoy the rights of the Jewish bankers."[54] This Salomon may have been none other than the father of one of the partners, R. Don Aryeh b. R. Solomon Hayyim of Monselice. Moreover, because the *alla Bolognese* method brought the various steps of silk textile production, from spinning to weaving, under one roof, Bolognese silk was generally sold as a finished and semifinished product. It is thus likely that Solomon and his son Don Aryeh may have been involved in silk manufacture, not merely reselling finished goods. Indeed, it is known that the city's powerful silk-makers guild (*l'Arte della Seta*) enrolled Sephardic exiles.[55] On the basis of the Spanish honorific "Don" before his name in Treves's *maḥzor* introduction, we can conclude that Aryeh's father and perhaps Aryeh himself were Spanish exiles.

The transfer of capital and knowledge from silk to printing in Bologna may be another example of Epstein's theory of early modern "cross-fertilization" among artisans and across geographies. Later in the century, Poni identified an example of this phenomenon in reverse. In 1570, Giovan Battista Guidoboni received a patent from Bologna's Senate to replace the wooden bobbins then used in silk winding with metal ones, improving the bobbins' durability and the homogeneity of resulting threads. Guidoboni, Poni notes, was born into a family of printers from Lucca and may have devised the notion of replacing the irregularly shaped wooden bobbins with uniformly cast metal ones by reflecting on "the substitution of wooden with lead or tin typeface."[56]

There were important structural similarities between Bolognese silk manufacture and Hebrew book printing as well. Prior to the advent of the *alla Bolognese* method, silk production was a multistep process comprising winding (twice), spinning, dyeing, and weaving, each carried out in its own locale, especially in artisans' homes. Poni has noted that mechanization led to the concentration of these steps "under the same roof," leading to reductions in "manpower employed, improved product quality control, shortened production times, [and] decreased capital immobilization and production costs."[57] This process was overseen by entrepreneurs who invested significant starting capital in building and maintaining machinery. Skilled and semiskilled female laborers, who had previously spun and woven thread at home under a piecework system, were replaced with skilled male weavers and a much smaller number of unskilled children who tended to spinning machines.[58]

Hebrew printing was, similarly, a mechanical multistep process carried out under a single roof. Printing occurred in urban shops established by entrepreneurs with enough starting capital to procure the use of a press, type, paper, and skilled labor.[59] Determining which titles to print involved risk, and printers weighed the significant costs of raw materials against the size of a potential readership and thus future revenue. Patience was imperative, as these investments were not realized until months, if not years, later, when books made it to market.[60] To print a text, an exemplar was prepared and edited, and the type composited and then often edited again. All these processes were undertaken by skilled craftsmen, like R. Raphael Talmi b. R. Emanuel of Forli. As Anthony Grafton has written, such artisans worked at the "inky crossroads where publishing and scholarship intersected."[61]

The Partners' Publications

With capital earned in the silk trade and a *condotta* from the Pope, the partners began to print Hebrew books in Bologna for the third time in the city's history. Their nine titles, most first editions, can be seen as a uniquely early modern Jewish library, drawing on the cultural patrimony of, and intended to appeal to, scholars and students of diverse Jewish backgrounds.

EARLY MODERN BOUNDARY CROSSING

David Ruderman has identified "mingled identities" as one of the hallmarks of a distinctive early modern Jewish culture.[62] The Italian Peninsula, at the crossroads of Europe's trade networks and the producer of most of its printed books, was the crucible where this new culture first emerged.[63] Printed titles, such as the halakhic code *Shulḥan Arukh* (Venice, 1565), blurred and blended the traditions of Sephardim and Ashkenazim, leading to the emergence of "a unified culture fusing Sephardic law with Ashkenazic custom."[64] We can think of the partners' publications as engaged in a similar process.

Taken together, the partners' list represents the collective traditions of Ashkenazic, Sephardic, and Italian Jewry. Several titles emerged from the Italian milieu, including Sforno's philosophical treatise *Or amim* (*Light of Nations*, 1537); a *siddur* (weekday and Sabbath liturgy, 1537) according to the Italian synagogue rite; a translation of the liturgy into Judeo-Italian, entitled *Tefilot Latini* (1538), only the second vernacular translation of the *siddur* ever printed; the *Piskei halakhot* (*Halakhic Decisions*, 1538) of the Italian halakhist R. Menaḥem Recanati (c. 1250–1310); and the aforementioned *maḥzor* (*Maḥzor k'fi minhag kehillat kodesh Roma*, 1540), with R. Yoḥanan Treves's commentary.[65] The *maḥzor,* which also included a commentary by Sforno on tractate *Avot* of the Mishnah, subsequently became the definitive text of the liturgy used by Italian Jews.[66]

Three titles had roots in Iberia or the Iberian diaspora: a philosophical treatise entitled *Torah or* (*Light of Torah*, 1538), by the scion of an illustrious Portuguese rabbinic family, R. Joseph b. David ibn Yaḥya (1494–1539); a commentary on the Five Scrolls (*Perush hamesh megilot*, 1538), also by Joseph; and the responsa (1539) of the Catalonian halakhist R. Solomon b. Abraham Adret (also known by the acronym RaSHbA, 1235–1310).[67]

One title, *Sefer Ḥasidim*, had a distinctly Ashkenazic pedigree.

But despite their association with the long-standing Jewish ethnic groups, the partners' titles are also notable in the way in which they represented a "mingling" of traditions and thus had the potential to generate crossover appeal. Recanati's *Piskei halakhot*, for example, while associated with a venerable Italian halakhist, was in fact an anthology of legal rulings by leading authorities of medieval Germany, Austria, Provence, and Catalonia.[68] It was a medieval attempt by an Italian scholar to integrate the halakhic traditions of Ashkenaz and Sepharad, repackaged by the partners for an early modern readership.[69]

The partners' Hebrew *siddur* of 1537 principally followed the Italian synagogue rite, but it also integrated Ashkenazic traditions. Its title page proclaimed that it was "ordered according to the custom of the holy community of Rome, but we have added according to our ability."[70] The most visible example of this adding was the inclusion of *seder ma'arakhah* (or, as the partners called it, *seder ma'arekhet Eliyahu*), a daily commemoration of ancient Temple sacrifices attributed to the medieval French mystic and poet R. Eliyahu b. Menaḥem of Le Mans.[71] In this way, the partners popularized a medieval Ashkenazic custom by welding it to established Italian tradition.

Perhaps surprisingly, the partners' *Sefer Ḥasidim* edition similarly represented an integration of Ashkenazic and Sephardic traditions. While the manuscripts on which it was based no doubt originated in Ashkenaz, and its religious guidance was embedded within medieval Ashkenazic culture, as we noted in chapter 1, the text of the partners' edition was a patchwork, including extracts from sources far beyond the Ashkenazic ken, such as Sa'adia Gaon's *Emunot ve-de'ot* and Maimonides's *Mishneh Torah*. While these extracts are found in older manuscripts of *Sefer Ḥasidim*—and thus we can assume that the partners were not responsible for introducing them into their text—the partners' edition should not be characterized as a squarely Ashkenazic work. It was, rather, composed of elements of diverse origins, much like the Jewish community of sixteenth-century Bologna.

The ethnic and cultural heterogeneity of the partners' titles was also manifested in the roster of the partners' collaborators, among them R. Abraham b. Moses ha-Cohen, as well as two of early modern Italian Jewry's most celebrated scholars, the aforementioned R. Obadiah b. Jacob Sforno and Azariah de' Rossi (1511–1578).

Born in Cuenca, Castille, Abraham was among Bologna's newly arrived Spanish exiles in the first decade of the century.[72] In 1519, he received a papal *condotta* to enjoy the privileges granted to the city's bankers, including permission to lend money at interest and to abstain from wearing the Jewish badge.[73] The *condotta* noted that Abraham had developed "great intimacy and conversation [*magnam familiaritatem et conversationem*]" with Christian scholars, who consulted his library of Hebrew and Latin books. In order to promote such exchanges, the Holy See granted Abraham permission to travel throughout the papal domains without paying tariffs on books.[74]

Despite being a newcomer to Bologna, Abraham became one of the city's leading rabbis, the head of its *yeshivah*, and the author of a series of halakhic opinions meant to preserve local custom and ward off outsiders' interference.[75] In a lengthy retort to an illustrious Ashkenazic colleague, R. Abraham Mintz (1440–1530) of Padua, in 1518, Abraham proudly asserted his priestly and Castilian heritage and the primacy of the Spanish halakhic tradition. "My ancestors and family were known all throughout Sepharad," he wrote, "they were the holy 'priests of Cuenca'... who martyred themselves publicly, were respected for their knowledge of Torah, [and were] people of substance and lovers of peace and its pursuit."[76] Yet, Cooperman has shown how Abraham was also a deft reader and interpreter of Ashkenazic *halakhah*.[77] His knowledge, and likely his library, encompassed sources from across the Jewish world.

It is possible that Abraham fled Castille with his library in tow. In 1498, Ercole I d'Este permitted a Castilian merchant by the name of Abraham Cohen to settle and do business in the city of Ferrara.[78] According to Attilio Milano, this Cohen was related to R. Moses b. Yekutiel ha-Cohen, a banker and textile merchant who is thought to have commissioned the celebrated Rothschild Miscellany, a late-fifteenth-century illuminated codex containing biblical, kabbalistic, and philosophical works.[79] Maria Giuseppina Muzzarelli has suggested, further, that this Moses was Abraham's father, and that the works found in the Rothschild Miscellany were the nucleus of Abraham's library.[80]

The paratexts in the partners' books, especially *Sefer Ḥasidim*, testify to Abraham's involvement in the partners' printing enterprise. Abraham wrote the introduction that preceded the text of *Sefer Ḥasidim* and the colophon that concluded it, along with a lengthy (fifty-page!) table of contents.[81] In the colophon, Abraham recounted that he was the owner of a manuscript included in the partners' edition. In his day, *Sefer Ḥasidim* was exceedingly rare, as it was "not found in this region as far as Jerusalem [Micah 1:9]... only one [copy] was hidden with me. Because of its abundant importance and the value of its ideas, in order to bring profit to the masses, I brought it out, and it came to the hand of the dear printers to print it."[82] Abraham's statement, "I brought it out, and it came [*hoẓetihu uva*]," implies that he also provided financial support for the publication, and perhaps played the role of *meivi l'veit ha-defus* (transmitter to the print shop), an ambiguous position that combined those of initiator, sponsor, and supervisor.[83] According to Shifra Baruchson-Arbib, Hebrew printers regularly drew on funding "combinations"—their own personal wealth, outside investors, and subscription revenue—to stabilize their operations during the time lag between the beginning of a project and the sale of completed volumes.[84]

None of the medieval *Sefer Ḥasidim* manuscripts we possess is sufficiently similar to the partners' edition to lead us to the conclusion that it served as their exemplar—that is, the basis for their edition. As a result, we do not know where Abraham's manuscript of this venerable Ashkenazic work originated. It is certainly possible that Abraham procured it in Italy after his arrival. We noted in chapter 1 that several of the extant *Sefer Ḥasidim* manuscripts were written in Italian script and likely originated in Italy. On the other hand, like other items in his library, it is possible that Abraham brought his *Sefer Ḥasidim* manuscript to Italy from Spain. The traditions of R. Judah he-Ḥasid were known in Iberia as early as the fifteenth century. R. Jacob b. Asher (1270–1340), the halakhic codifier who migrated to Castile from the Rhineland in 1303, cited traditions ascribed to Judah in his influential code, the *Arba'ah turim*.[85] Further, at least two of the extant *Sefer Ḥasidim* manuscripts, both dated to the fifteenth century, were copied in a Sephardic semicursive script, suggesting that they originated in Spain or among Sephardim.[86]

In his introduction to the partners' *Sefer Ḥasidim* edition, Abraham wrote that the book's appeal was contingent on his table of contents:

> For the sake of understanding the value of this book and its fruits, like a set table prepared before all who seek the Lord and His fear, I, the insignificant, the poorest among the greats who signed [their names] at the conclusion of this book, determined to open a doorway and a gate with a table of contents.[87]

Abraham thus deployed the standard hyperbole of sixteenth-century paratexts—references to the works' accessibility (it was like a "set table") and to his own poverty and insignificance—to eulogize his efforts in composing this finding aid. It is notable that both the partners' editions of Recanati's *Piskei halakhot* and Adret's responsa included tables of contents and that the one in the Adret volume is, like the table in *Sefer Ḥasidim*, especially lengthy. Isaiah Sonne suggested that Abraham composed both of these tables—one in a work of Italian, and the other in a work of Spanish, origin—in addition to the one in *Sefer Ḥasidim*. Further, Sonne noted that Abraham, as a Jew of Spanish extraction, would likely have been interested in disseminating the responsa of an illustrious medieval Spanish halakhist in Italy.[88] Thus, in his work with the partners, as in his communal leadership, Abraham played the role of cultural mediator, facilitating the dissemination and mingling of Sephardic, Ashkenazic, and Italian traditions.

ALONGSIDE ABRAHAM, R. Obadiah Sforno, the lion of early modern Italian Jewish culture, was also involved in the partners' printing venture. His role, however, is not as well documented.[89] Sforno was a physician and teacher who kept company with Christian scholars and is known today primarily for his Bible commentaries.[90] Around 1527, fleeing the Sack of Rome, Sforno moved to Bologna, where he practiced medicine, wrote, taught, and served on rabbinical courts alongside Abraham.[91] It is possible that the partners established their press initially with the intention of producing a Hebrew grammar with Latin translation by Sforno, though the work was never printed.[92]

Sforno's name is found in two of the partners' titles: He was the author of *Or amim* (*Light of Nations*, 1537), a synthesis of Jewish tradition and Aristotelian rationalism, and a commentary on tractate *Avot* of the Mishnah printed within the partners' *maḥzor*. We will have occasion to discuss *Or amim* in greater detail, but here it is worth noting that Sforno also published a Latin version of this treatise, known by the abbreviated title *Lumen Gentium*, at the Bologna press of Anselmo Giacarelli in 1538.[93]

AZARIAH DE' ROSSI was another giant of sixteenth-century Italian Jewish culture involved in the partners' press, though at an early stage of his career. De' Rossi was the author of *Me'or einayim* (*Light of the Eyes*, 1573–1575), one of the first Hebrew works of historiography.[94] Born in Mantua, he spent much of his life in and around Ferrara, along with stints in Bologna. From his own testimony, we know that he attended lectures in geometry at the University of Bologna, and that he was in the city in 1569 when Pope Pius V expelled its Jews.[95] De' Rossi's first printed work was a laudatory poem for the partners' edition of R. Joseph b. David ibn Yaḥya's *Torah or*, which they published the same year as *Sefer Ḥasidim*.[96] As a literary artifact, this poem, which the partners set strategically before the colophon, is the standard promotional fare of early modern paratexts. De' Rossi advises those seeking the "path where enlightenment dwells" to "look within me—*Torah or*" and purchase the book. He also, in typical Hebrew poetic fashion, inscribed the letters of his name into the first word of each stanza.[97]

Throughout his life, it seems, de' Rossi had a sideline composing laudatory poems, like the one in *Torah or*, for printed books—akin to today's blurbs.[98] When the poem appeared in *Torah or*, de' Rossi would have been in his mid-twenties. Joanna Weinberg has uncovered the testimony of a physician whom de' Rossi consulted at the age of thirty-five (during the mid-1540s). De' Rossi told the physician, who recorded de' Rossi's words in his medical casebook, that he had previously worked as a censor of Hebrew books.[99] Weinberg has suggested that de' Rossi was likely "working on behalf of the Jewish community" to ensure that newly printed Jewish books did not cause controversy among their Christian neighbors.[100] Given the timing of this conversation, and the limited number of Hebrew presses operating at the time, it is possible that de' Rossi worked in Bologna at the partners' press censoring manuscripts prior to publication.[101] Censorship was indeed a pervasive feature of the partners' *Sefer Ḥasidim* edition, one that we will discuss in detail in chapter 3.

Thus, another triumvirate, one of scholars—Abraham, Sforno, and de' Rossi—joined the partners in printing Hebrew books in Bologna. Rooted in both Spain and Italy, they helped fashion a library of books that blended these cultures with that of northern Europe.

HEBREW HIGH CULTURE

The partners marketed their books, including *Sefer Ḥasidim*, to readers like themselves and their learned colleagues, Jewish scholars and intellectuals on the Italian Peninsula. Many addressed these readers' central preoccupation: the compatibility of Jewish theology and non-Jewish philosophy (which, in this period, was synonymous with Aristotelianism). As Robert Bonfil has shown, the question of the legitimacy of philosophic study animated rabbinic circles in Italy, especially in Bologna, during the early sixteenth century.[102] The partners offered a range of responses to this question, seeking to attract a wide readership and engage all sides.

The partners' edition of R. Solomon b. Abraham Adret's responsa contained both a condemnation and an endorsement of philosophy, or *ḥokhmot ḥiẓoniyot*. In 1305, along with the other leading rabbis of Barcelona, Adret imposed a ban (*ḥerem*) on those under the age of twenty-five who dared to explore this field.[103] He believed that philosophy had lured young Jews, unschooled in *halakhah*, away from faith into heresy. While editions of Adret's responsa had been printed previously, none included Adret's ban, as the partners' edition did. Further, following the ban, the partners appended R. Jedaiah b. Abraham Bedersi's response to Adret, his *Ketav ha-hitnaẓelut* (*Apologia*). In *Ketav ha-hitnaẓelut*, Bedersi, a Spanish scholar and poet, defended philosophy as a legitimate way of understanding the universe and, therefore, one compatible with Judaism.[104]

R. Joseph b. David ibn Yaḥya, in his *Torah or*, took a harder line against philosophy. Joseph—whose family history and life story, recounted in his introduction to *Torah or*, were marked by persecution and predation—perceived his existence as a testament to his progenitors' faith, and his own.[105] This faith, manifested in a life of devotion to the commandments, was the essence of Judaism and the reason for Jews' exalted place above all other nations. Joseph attacked Maimonides, whom, he said, "assents to the words of philosophy [*filosofia*] that the soul is the first perfection [*sh'leimut rishon*], namely the intellect realized through intelligible concepts [*muskalot*], and that immortality can only be achieved through philosophical speculation [*iyun*] and mathematics [*midot*]." Were this the case, Joseph suggested, the entire corpus of God-given ritual would serve no purpose. Only the very few, capable of engaging in such sophisticated investigations, would achieve salvation; the rest of the Jewish people, present and past, would be damned to oblivion.[106] This was untenable because Joseph, following rabbinic tradition, stressed that "All of Israel has a share in the World to Come," and that "share" was a consequence of their having received the commandments from God at Mount Sinai.[107] What followed, then, in *Torah or*, was an extensive defense of the commandments and the Jewish people's chosen status.[108]

In contrast to Joseph's rejection of philosophy, Sforno, in his *Or amim*, charted a more moderate course.[109] He regretted that, in his day, some Jews felt that the "principles of our Torah could not be rendered indubitable" through rational proofs (*moftim sikhli'im*). This led some to advocate blind faith and others to doubt.[110] But this dichotomistic thinking, he argued, was misplaced. In fact, Sforno argued, Aristotelian philosophy and Judaism were not incompatible, for the most part. Some Aristotelian principles, which had been accepted by Maimonides, such as the eternity of the universe, were incompatible with Judaism. But they were also incorrect, as Sforno endeavored to show.[111] Much else in Aristotle's philosophy was in harmony with Judaism. In fact, when interpreted allegorically, the Torah elucidated the same principles as philosophy—a point of view associated with Ibn Rushd (1126–1198, known as "Averroes" in the West), the twelfth-century Islamic defender of Aristotle. For this reason, Sforno has been called "the last Averroist" among Jewish philosophers.[112]

Another early modern approach to the question of the legitimacy of philosophy was offered by advocates of Kabbalah. Two centuries after Adret's ban, some kabbalists took Adret's line of argument even further: The principles of philosophy were antithetical to Jewish faith. Kabbalah, however, was an indigenous Jewish form of wisdom that led its students to greater truths than could ever be uncovered through philosophy.[113] Over the course of the sixteenth century, Kabbalah study became increasingly popular among the Jews of Bologna, and of Italy more generally.[114] Ariel Toaff has suggested that the partners catered to readers' interest in Kabbalah by printing kabbalistic texts, singling out *Sefer Ḥasidim* and R. Menaḥem Recanati's *Piskei halakhot*.[115] Yet, the reality of the partners' efforts was more complex.

In fact, the partners did not print any of the classic works of medieval Kabbalah, such as the Bible commentaries of Naḥmanides or the *Sefer ha-bahir*.[116] The most explicit reference to Kabbalah in their publications is found on the title page of Recanati's *Piskei halakhot*, where the work is called *Piskei halakhot me-ha-mekubbal Rebbeinu Menaḥem . . .* (*Legal Decisions of the Kabbalist Rabbi Menaḥem*). Indeed, Recanati was a well-known, late-thirteenth to early-fourteenth-century Italian kabbalist, one of the first to make extensive use of the literature of the Zohar in his writings.[117] However, Recanati's legal decisions are remarkably free of references to kabbalistic texts or ideas.[118] The fact that the partners identified Recanati prominently as a kabbalist on their title page suggests that they sought to benefit from the rising prominence of Kabbalah in Italy and to attract readers to their publication by emphasizing the author's kabbalistic pedigree—despite the fact that the text itself contained little Kabbalah. This kind of legerdemain was a common feature of early modern title pages.[119]

On the other hand, in his commentary in the partners' *maḥzor,* entitled *Kimḥa d'avishuna* (*Flour Milled from Roasted Grain*), R. Yoḥanan b. Joseph Treves included kabbalistic traditions and extracts from texts associated with the Zohar in order to interpret the meaning of Jewish rituals.[120] He did so, as was common in sixteenth-century paratexts, while professing that he intended to elucidate only the "straightforward meaning" (*peshat*)—not its *sodot,* or mystical secrets.[121] On the one hand, Treves sated demand for esoterica among his readers while seeking to avoid offending those scholars who wished for this literature to remain the prerogative of the elite. On the other hand, he asserted that the kabbalistic interpretations of the prayers in his commentary were synonymous with their "straightforward meaning." In essence, he claimed that, far from being novel, kabbalistic interpretations of Jewish practices and texts were entirely in keeping with venerable Jewish tradition.

RELIGIOUS EDIFICATION

Toaff's claim that the partners' edition of *Sefer Ḥasidim* was meant to appeal to readers interested in Kabbalah is dubious.[122] It is unlikely that Italian Jewish readers would have equated the ideas and practices found in the partners' edition of *Sefer Ḥasidim* with Kabbalah at all. It contains little that could be characterized as kabbalistic. With few discourses on "secrets" (*sodot*) or theosophy and its focus on piety, penance, and faith, the partners' edition reads more like a Hebrew guidebook for moral and spiritual instruction, and that was exactly how R. Abraham b. Moses ha-Cohen characterized it in his introduction. "In every generation," Abraham wrote, God appointed pious people (*ḥasidim*) to "bestow merit upon and purify and sanctify the masses, to teach them and instruct them in the way and manner whereby one praises and acclaims God's name." Such people set the moral and religious standards of their communities and demonstrated proper comportment. In this characterization, *Sefer Ḥasidim* was thus not a work of esotericism; rather, it was manifestly exoteric, full of practical ethical and spiritual teachings, "pearls of wisdom and the important values."[123] This characterization of *Sefer Ḥasidim* does not much differ from how the text of the book in the partners' edition describes itself. Its first passage reads: "Thus, *Sefer Ḥasidim* was written for the sake of those who fear the Lord, and those returning to their Creator with a perfect heart, that they may know and understand what is incumbent upon them to do and what they must avoid."[124] Such an exhortation to piety was one way of counteracting the spiritual challenge posed by philosophical study.

The partners characterized other titles in similar terms, seeking to fill the same educational niche. In his *maḥzor* commentary, Treves described his work as a devotional guide. It would help worshippers achieve the proper concentration and avoid mistakes in prayer by helping them comprehend the meaning of the obscure words of the prayer book. He urged his readers to think of prayer as an act as sacred as the public reading of Scripture, or perhaps even more so. A person could fulfill the commandment of reading from the Torah even if he made an error, if he had the proper focus or intention (*kavvanah*), Treves explained. But prayer was different; in order for a person to fulfill the commandment of daily prayer, a worshipper had to both have the proper focus and make no mistakes—and, to do this, he had to comprehend the meaning of the words he was uttering.[125] This was especially difficult because, despite the fact that prayer was a fact of daily life for Jewish men, the liturgy (especially the festival services) was a patchwork of abstruse texts. Moreover, the printing process had introduced numerous "corruptions" (*shibushim*) and "variants" (*ḥilufim*). Uneducated worshippers often read the prayers without "understanding" (*havanah*) and did not notice these errors. They thus failed to fulfill their religious obligation. Thus, the purpose of the *maḥzor* and his commentary, Treves explained, was to correct this state of affairs by producing as accurate a text as possible and by explaining its meaning clearly. With these tools, Treves believed his coreligionists would finally be able to fulfill their religious obligations and improve their spiritual condition.[126]

A similar educational vision may be discerned in the partners' vernacular prayer book, *Tefillot Latini*. According to the title page, the initiative for its publication came from potential readers, "kind and gentle women" who "forced and persuaded" the partners to print a translation of the prayers. (Of course, touting the fervid requests of potential readers was another commonplace of early modern paratexts.)[127] In doing so, the partners hoped their prayer book would have a positive spiritual effect: female readers "would come to know the Almighty." This title should also be seen as part of a broader trend in women's religious engagement and education among Italian Jews during the early modern period. Scholars have noted that Italian Jewish women participated in religious activities often reserved for men, including leading the obligatory daily prayers aloud (in the synagogue's women's section), wearing phylacteries, and ritually slaughtering animals. There are also notable examples of female scholars of rabbinic texts and of women's serving as Hebrew teachers.[128] *Tefillot Latini* was the male printers' response to women who wished to cultivate a deeper involvement with the synagogue rituals and to improve popular comprehension of the liturgy. Of course, there were also many Italian Jewish men whose command of Hebrew and Aramaic was such that the liturgy was inaccessible—"men who are like women," in the phrasing of early modern Jewish paratexts—and *Tefillot Latini* served their needs, too.[129]

Alongside these efforts at liturgical education, Italian Jewish leaders (lay and rabbinic) sought to improve Jewish knowledge and piety in their communities by establishing the position of the "communally-appointed rabbi," who oversaw teaching, especially the teaching of children and young adults, and regular synagogue preaching. Bonfil has noted that this institution was likely modeled on the position of *marbiẓ Torah* (communal teacher and preacher) in Spain and was brought to Italian soil by Spanish exiles.[130] R. David ibn Yaḥya, the father of R. Joseph b. David ibn Yaḥya, for example, was the community-appointed rabbi in Naples. He recorded that much of his day was spent in teaching the community's youth basic Jewish texts (an activity, he noted acerbically, for which he felt he was not adequately compensated).[131] Further, David Ruderman has called the sixteenth and seventeenth centuries the "age of the sermon," as evinced by the new prestige accorded to preachers, the practice of printing and disseminating sermons after they were delivered, and the development of a literature of handbooks for aspiring preachers.[132] Preaching and printing thus went hand in hand during the sixteenth century as modes of popular religious edification.

Conclusion

The partners' Hebrew print shop and the books they produced, especially *Sefer Ḥasidim*, represent the dynamics of Jewish life in Bologna, and Italy more generally, in the early sixteenth century. By this time, as a result of immigration and the *alla Bolognese* method of silk manufacture, the city had become exceedingly prosperous. Jews, especially those who worked in silk, were the engines and beneficiaries of this prosperity. Recently arrived Sephardim integrated into the city's commercial and Jewish institutions, such that they were members of the silk guild and served as its most prominent rabbis. New opportunities were possible, not least in the establishment of a Hebrew press and the printing of new and formerly obscure Hebrew texts.

The printing of *Sefer Ḥasidim* by the partners in 1538 was emblematic of Italian Jewry's cultural creativity, which was manifested in Bologna's thriving *yeshivot*; its integration of Jewish traditions and customs from the Italian, Ashkenazic, and Sephardic worlds; and its efforts to improve popular religious devotion. Abraham highlighted the latter rationale in his introduction and his table of contents. *Sefer Ḥasidim* was neither esoteric nor kabbalistic; it was, rather, a work of moral and spiritual edification designed for regular consultation.

The richness of Jewish cultural life, both material and spiritual, in Bologna, however, would not survive the Counter-Reformation. For reasons unknown, Hebrew books ceased being printed in Bologna in 1540, following the publication of the partners' *maḥzor*. In 1553, Pope Julius III ordered the public burning of the Talmud and other Hebrew books in the city. Three years later, its Jews were confined to a ghetto. A decade later, they were expelled. Indeed, Pope Paul III, who granted the partners their *condotta*, began to turn the tide against the Jews of Bologna and the Papal States with increasingly exorbitant taxation during the 1530s. Bologna's Sephardim, like Aryeh and Abraham, who had found stability in La Grassa, were once again cast out to search for a new home.

CHAPTER 3

The Partners' *Sefer Ḥasidim*

PARATEXTS AND TEXT

A man should not store an unused notebook inside a book for safekeeping. He should not store a notebook that contains Written Torah inside a book that contains Oral Torah. He should not store a notebook that contains Oral Torah inside a book that contains Written Torah. A man should not write his accounts in a book. He should not write, "I am testing the ink," or "I am testing the pen," since it is forbidden to add to the book.

Sefer Ḥasidim (Bologna, 1538), §921

• • • • •

REFLECTING A TIME when paper, parchment, ink, and quills were scarce and expensive, several *Sefer Ḥasidim* passages evince concern for the care and reuse of these writing materials.[1] In particular, they prohibit writers from combining different genres of texts within the same volume—Written Torah (Scripture) with Oral Torah (rabbinic texts), Scripture with the ephemera of everyday life—despite the pressures they faced to do so. The operative principle governing these passages is *kedushah* (sanctity), and different sorts of texts possessed differing amounts of it. To write mundane words within a book, a *sefer*, even to write something as necessary and as innocuous as "I am testing the ink," was a violation of the book's sanctity.

The passage assumes, moreover, that books (*sefarim*) possess the highest level of sanctity. A notebook (*kuntres*)—used for a student's notes, a merchant's accounts, or simply recording the details of everyday life—possesses a lower level of sanctity, even if it contained quotations from canonical works.[2] Indeed, speakers of Yiddish and Jewish English, a distinctive mode of communication common among Jews today, retain this elevated definition of the word *sefer*, associating it only with canonical books and scrolls, while, in modern Hebrew, it can refer to any bound volume.[3] Forceful prescriptions like the ones in this passage also suggest that, in medieval Ashkenaz, some Jews were not scrupulous in their writing practices. They did, in fact, intermingle texts of differing sanctity within the same volume and store them together. They "added" (*hosif*) to works that should not have been added to.[4] Another passage thus condemns copyists who "add words or subtract words or intend to allude to their own names" within their manuscripts.[5] Intermingling, reuse, and adaptation were, of course, part and parcel of manuscript culture, and they were practices that continued in early modern print shops

The partners' *editio princeps* of *Sefer Ḥasidim* is marked by that intermingling, reuse, and adaptation. This creative labor is evident when the partners' edition is compared to its manuscript antecedents. The partners' *Sefer Ḥasidim* differs from those manuscripts in four principal ways: It features novel paratexts, including an introduction, a colophon, and a lengthy table of contents; it possesses an authorial attribution; it contains a new, composite *Sefer Ḥasidim* text assembled from preexisting sources; and it is marked by censorship. Because of these labors, *Sefer Ḥasidim* became a book, in the Kantian sense, with a stable text and an author, a book unlike any manuscript that had existed previously. It became the definitive *Sefer Ḥasidim,* reprinted over and over again for the better part of four centuries. And though it was entitled "*Sefer*" *Ḥasidim,* it was not a *sefer* in the canonical sense implied in the previous passage and according to contemporary Jewish English usage. The latter transformation occurred with the printing of the second edition and will be discussed in chapters 5 and 6.

This chapter sheds light on the partners' creative labors in fashioning *Sefer Ḥasidim* into a book by comparing their edition to its manuscript antecedents. It begins with an overview of their edition and its component parts. Subsequent sections explore how those parts are illustrative of the partners' creativity. The primary assumption undergirding this comparative project is that textual or paratextual features present in the partners' edition and not found in extant medieval manuscripts were introduced by the partners. Because none of the manuscripts is sufficiently similar in either structure or content to the partners' edition, it is clear that none of the manuscripts served as the partners' exemplar(s). Absent an exemplar, we cannot be certain whether a particular feature present in the partners' edition, but absent in the manuscripts, was uniquely present in an exemplar to which we no longer have access. But because the number of *Sefer Ḥasidim* manuscripts available today is considerable, we may assume that the extant manuscripts collectively represent the totality of what the title *Sefer Ḥasidim* entailed in the medieval period. As a result, we may further assume that the partners' exemplar(s) was not substantially different from the aggregate text of the medieval manuscript witnesses that have come down to us.

The Anatomy of a Hebrew Book

Holding the partners' *Sefer Ḥasidim* edition, one is struck by its diminutive size.[6] It is an octavo, a small format pioneered by Aldus Manutius in the early sixteenth century, inexpensive and ideal for transport. Aldus earned fame for his pocket-size editions of classical works in a novel italic typeface intended not for the wealthy elite but for a broader range of readers and for his departure from manuscript precedents, their unwieldy folios and challenging scripts.[7]

At the start of the partners' *Sefer Ḥasidim* was a title page (figure 1), a ubiquitous paratext in printed books but not in manuscripts.[8] Over the course of the sixteenth century, title pages became more and more elaborate, including illustrations and promotional verbiage, yet early in the century they tended to be brief. The title page of the partners' *Sefer Ḥasidim* edition included only the words "*Sefer ha-Ḥasidim,*" centered, in large, square Hebrew type, and the impressum, "Printed here, Bologna, by the partners, may they succeed and live, in fear of God" below it, in smaller type. That impressum also identified that the partners, in Foucauldian terms, were legally and morally responsible for the book's content. (It did not make mention of an author, because in the early sixteenth century title pages generally lacked authorial attributions. Such detail appeared in an introduction.[9]) Aesthetically, the title page shares much with the title pages of other early-sixteenth-century printed Hebrew books, such as the title pages of Daniel Bomberg's first Talmud edition, which included only the names of the tractates contained in the volume and an impressum (figure 2).[10]

The title page was followed by R. Abraham b. Moses ha-Cohen's one-page introduction, his lengthy table of contents, the text of *Sefer Ḥasidim* itself, and a brief colophon also written by Abraham. The simplicity of the title page is emblematic of the visual layout of each of these sections, and of the volume as a whole. When compared to the highly ornamented printed Hebrew books of the later sixteenth century, such as the second printed edition of *Sefer Ḥasidim*, the partners' edition is characterized by an aesthetic clarity, even elegance.

Abraham's introduction begins with an enlarged initial word—"may He be praised" (*yitbarakh*)—surrounded by a rectangular frame of vines (figure 3).[11] This frame reappears later in the book, surrounding the initial word of the *Sefer Ḥasidim* text: "this" (*zeh*, figure 4).[12] These frames are the only nontextual, decorative elements in the book, and they stand out—distinguishing the beginning of the front matter and the text, respectively. The majority of that text, aside from the initial words of each passage, as well as the introduction, table of contents, and colophon, is set in a Sephardic semicursive typeface, known today as "Rashi-script." This typeface was used by the partners' Bologna predecessor Abraham b. Hayyim dei Tintori in his Bible of 1482, to distinguish noncanonical commentaries (such as that of the eleventh-century exegete R. Solomon b. Isaac, known as RaSHI, of Troyes) from scriptural texts when they appeared on the same page.[13] The fact that the partners set their entire text of *Sefer Ḥasidim* in this typeface indicates their judgment about the canonicity of the work. Again, no matter how important the book was, it was not canonical.[14]

Despite the compact size of the book and its type, the pages of the partners' *Sefer Ḥasidim* edition are highly legible. From their signatures (Hebrew and Arabic numerals at the bottom of every eight pages designed to assist in the assembly of the book's quires), as well as Abraham's comment in his introduction that he was "the poor and insignificant one among the thousands signed at the end of this book," it is evident that the partners first printed the text itself and then added the front matter (title page, introduction, table of contents) after the fact, as was common. The *Sefer Ḥasidim* text is set in a single, fully justified column, with the initial word of each passage in square type, so that it is visually distinguished from what precedes and follows it. The number of each passage, in Hebrew alphabetical characters, is listed near the left margin on the preceding line, leaving space between it and the final words of the preceding passage. Pages of the *Sefer Ḥasidim* text, though not the table of contents, are numerated with Hebrew characters. There are also catchwords at the end of every quire, in both the table of contents and the *Sefer Ḥasidim* text, to aid in the proper ordering and assembly of the book's quires. Page numeration, catchwords, and passage numeration were all common features of manuscript codices that the partners presumably carried over into their edition.

In contrast to their *Sefer Ḥasidim* text, the partners printed Abraham's table of contents in two columns of semicursive type. This table will be discussed in greater detail, but here it is worth noting that printing led to the proliferation of finding aids like it in Hebrew and non-Hebrew books. Its length and detail, moreover, differentiate it from the more rudimentary finding aids in medieval manuscripts.

Finally, at the very end of the book, directly below the last *Sefer Ḥasidim* passage, the partners printed Abraham's colophon. Colophons were common paratexts in manuscripts and, though often brief, were the venue where a writer would speak directly to readers, note the date of a text's completion, and offer praises to God.[15] Abraham's colophon is no different in these respects. As we discussed in chapter 2, Abraham also used his colophon to describe his involvement in the production of the partners' *Sefer Ḥasidim* edition as that of an initiator and sponsor. Yet, the fact that the colophon was written by Abraham in the first person—and not the partners themselves—is indicative. In providing his manuscript and funds to the partners, he clearly perceived himself, and the partners similarly perceived him, as sharing responsibility for the work.

Introducing *Sefer Ḥasidim* and Its Author

Neither the writers of the various medieval *Sefer Ḥasidim* manuscripts nor those of the medieval works that cited the title *Sefer Ḥasidim* attributed them to R. Judah he-Ḥasid. This was in keeping with medieval notions of literary creativity and was emblematic of the practice of anonymity advocated by some *Sefer Ḥasidim* passages: Be like the "sages of old" who "would not write their books in their own names and did not allow others to put their names on their books."[16] It thus comes as a surprise that, in his introduction, Abraham wrote these words:

> [God] established for us righteous and upright people who will defend their generations...grace them with the spirit of knowledge and fear of the Lord, author books to augment their already considerable sanctity and

> their purity... just as the mighty, holy, our rabbi, Judah he-Ḥasid did, who is the greatest of the pious ones. He weighed, investigated, and established this wondrous book, which put its name on the earth [Psalms 46:9]: *Sefer ha-Ḥasidim*.[17]

Judah, as Abraham conceived of him, "authored" (*ḥiber*) books that called the Jewish people to righteousness. The Hebrew verb Abraham employed referred, in the Bible, to the joining together of objects.[18] Yet, especially in the early modern period, it took on connotations of composition and authorship in a Kantian and Foucauldian sense.[19] For Abraham, Judah was *Sefer Ḥasidim*'s "author" (*meḥaber*, the nominal form of the Hebrew root *ḥet-bet-resh*), and thus the discourse contained in the partners' edition was Judah's, meaning, the result of his creative process of composition, his "weighing, investigating, and establishing."[20] That process could certainly involve the joining together of preexisting materials, but the work of gathering those sources did not efface the personage of the gatherer, as it had for medieval writers, but, rather, elevated it. Abraham asserted that *Sefer Ḥasidim*, the book printed by the partners, was linked to Judah because it was the product of his quill.

Scholars of literature and the history of the book have noted that authorship underwent a conceptual transition during the early modern period: What was once a conservative and collective enterprise came to be centered around, as Elizabeth Eisenstein wrote, "possessive individualism." The "fixity" of the printed text, Eisenstein asserted, led to its association with a named individual responsible for it.[21] Adrian Johns, by contrast, has shown that early modern readers evinced skepticism toward printed texts, perceiving printing as more vulnerable to error, deception, heresy, and piracy. Lisa Jardine has shown that the Renaissance Catholic theologian and humanist Desiderius Erasmus, together with his printers, used printed textual and paratextual devices to craft a "self-presentation" and "multidimensional cultural persona" meant to win authority and credibility.[22] Printers, thus, whether because of the stability or instability of the printed text, elevated the personage of the author and the practice of authorial attribution in the sixteenth century. While the partners' name appeared on the title page, they had, according to Abraham, reproduced Judah's discourse for public consumption. In Kantian terms, they were the "publishers" and Judah was the "author." That discourse was worthy of reproduction, moreover, because

Judah was a person of authority who played a time-honored, prophetic role: that of moral exemplar and rebuker. Judah, Abraham wrote in his introduction, "purified and sanctified the masses, to teach them and instruct them in the way and manner whereby one praises and acclaims His Name" through *Sefer Ḥasidim*.

While hardly as complex a marketing strategy as Erasmus's (in collaboration with his printer, Johann Froben), Abraham's hagiographic introduction created a "cultural persona" for Judah, endowing the partners' *Sefer Ḥasidim* edition with prophetic authority. In an environment where textual errors, distortions, and corruptions were ubiquitous, as Treves noted in his introduction to the partners' *maḥzor*, hagiographies like Abraham's instilled credibility and legitimacy.[23] They nudged readers to give printed books, as Abraham wrote in his colophon, "the benefit of the doubt":

> I came to tell the person who searches in it [this book] that if he were to find somewhere distorted or unclear language, or he sees an apparent error in it, may he give it the benefit of the doubt [Mishnah, *Avot* 1:6]. May he decide in favor of the multifarious benefits of the pearls of its words, important principles, manners, and teachings more valuable than gold [Psalms 19:11] . . . tolerating [the infelicities of] everyday speech in the mouth of the typesetter, for he merely used the customary phraseology in correcting the language of this book.

While it was a commonplace in early modern paratexts to beg forgiveness for errors, Abraham's colophon reveals the manifest fear of printers that errors would scare off readers and render their investments worthless. In Abraham's view, the partners' *Sefer Ḥasidim* likely contained such errors, as well as linguistic oddities that would taint the work's credibility (*lashon niftal ve-lo ẓah*). Such errors were neither his nor Judah's fault; they were the result of the carelessness of the typesetter (*ha-mesader*)—perhaps R. Raphael Talmi b. R. Emanuel of Forli. Printed at the end of the book, this blame game was an exercise in justification after the fact. At the front of the book, though written and printed chronologically after the colophon, Abraham's introduction set the scene, seeking, by building up the persona of R. Judah he-Ḥasid, to generate sufficient confidence in the book's text that readers might be willing to overlook any infelicities they would subsequently find there.

"A set table prepared before all who seek the Lord": Abraham's Table of Contents

In 1518, a dispute over the relationship of rabbinic courts to each other and the power of wealthy individuals to affect their decisions roiled the Jewish communities of northern Italy. Known as the "Finzi-Norsa controversy," it involved Immanuel b. Noah Raphael da Norsa (1457–1523/4) of Ferrara and Abraham Raphael b. Jacob da Finzi of Bologna. Norsa, one of the wealthiest Jews in Italy at the time, operated a bank in Ferrara with Finzi's help. In addition to being business partners, the two men were related by marriage. Yet, they had a falling-out over Finzi's attempts to sell his stake in the Ferrara bank. The men sued each other in rabbinic courts in both Bologna and Ferrara and sought support from rabbis elsewhere on the peninsula.

Among the documents that testify to this controversy is a letter written by R. Abraham Mintz of Padua, a supporter of Norsa, in which he proudly declared that his legal opinions were "not supported by… the canes of weaklings [Mishnah Shabbat 5:6], [namely] on the decisions of the rabbis of tables of contents, those seekers in notes and searchers of references."[24] Mintz was accusing his adversaries, prominently among them R. Abraham b. Moses ha-Cohen, of taking shortcuts in their research, of drawing conclusions from the study of reference tools found in newly printed volumes of rabbinic texts: "tables of contents" (or "indices," literally, "keys," *maftehot*), "notes" (*simanim*), and "references" (*ẓiyyunim*).[25] Mintz's accusation recalls a criticism that sixteenth- and seventeenth-century Christian scholars leveled at one another, that their works relied overmuch on quotations from reference books, with which, in the words of one seventeenth-century French Jesuit, "minds feeble in invention or weak in knowledge can supplement their indigence."[26]

Christian scholars had occasion to rely on such reference works, because, as Ann Blair has shown, the sixteenth and seventeenth centuries were a period of prodigious development in this field of literature: The number, topical diversity, and sheer size of reference works increased, while authors and printers developed ever-more-sophisticated finding aids to help readers access the vast quantities of information books contained. The table of contents—a lengthy document summarizing each of *Sefer Ḥasidim*'s 1,178 passages, composed by R. Abraham b. Moses ha-Cohen—is emblematic of the many cultural tendencies reflected in the early modern humanist and Christian reference works and finding aids analyzed by Blair.

Blair has portrayed the growth in number and diversity of early modern reference works and their accompanying finding aids as a reflection of an early modern "stockpiling mentality," that is, a need to collect and categorize knowledge and render it intelligible, accessible, and immune to loss. This "info-lust" was a consequence of both the trauma of the loss of Europe's classical heritage during the Middle Ages and the popularization of knowledge in diverse fields through print.[27] While finding aids, such as lists of headings and indices, were known in the Middle Ages, these tools became indispensable for navigating the early modern period's expansive and unwieldy reference titles.[28] They also encouraged readers to dip in and out of books in search of specific data, a practice Blair calls "consultation reading," rather than reading from cover to cover.[29]

Similarly, Peter Stallybrass has demonstrated how consultation reading, or what he calls "nonlinear reading," could serve political or religious agendas.[30] Newly created indices and concordances in sixteenth-century Bibles directed Protestant readers to biblical verses that affirmed specific theological positions, such as those that seemed to contradict Catholic dogma. These verses would likely have been obscured or ignored if readers had not been alerted to them through accompanying finding tools.[31]

Abraham's table of contents exhibits many of the hallmarks of these reference works and finding aids. Moreover, its specifically early modern features come to light when it is compared to the only extant medieval table of contents to *Sefer Ḥasidim*, which is found in the Cambridge University Library Add. 379.2 manuscript.[32] This manuscript was copied in thirteenth- or fourteenth-century Ashkenaz and includes a version of *Sefer Ḥasidim* in 579 passages, of which the first 400 mirror the partners' edition closely in both arrangement and content.[33] The table of contents, copied by the same hand as the text, is found after the scribe's colophon.

The two tables of contents, one in manuscript and one in print, are similar in that both are arranged according to the sequence and numeration of the passages of the accompanying *Sefer Ḥasidim* text, meaning that there is one entry in the table of contents for each passage, and each entry is preceded by a passage number. Similarities end there, however.

Above all, the Cambridge manuscript's table of contents is briefer than

Abraham's: It encompasses eight pages, while Abraham's spans over fifty. The brevity of the entries in the Cambridge manuscript appears to have been influenced by spatial and visual considerations. The manuscript's pages are ruled in two columns of thirty-six to forty lines, with considerable empty space left for both the right and the left margins, as well as a gutter between the columns. In general, each entry fills no more than a single line of text (though, occasionally, an entry flows into the marginal space or gutter). For this reason, entries are generally no more than ten words in length, and very often far fewer.

Following Blair's taxonomy of finding aids, the Cambridge manuscript table of contents may be categorized as an "*elenchus*" or "*series titulorum*," a list of chapter headings following the order they appear in a text. Entries often recapitulate the first words or heading of a passage. For instance, the first words of §319 (§317 in the partners' edition) are: "There are things that a man may steal which are more grievous than [typical] theft." These words reappear without modification as the entry for the passage in the table of contents. The entry for §37 is the first three words of the passage, "Fear of the Lord is pure [*yir'at Adonai tehorah*]," including its slightly enlarged, centered heading, "Fear."[34]

Frequently, the spatial constraints of the Cambridge manuscript's table of contents mean that entries offer precious little information about the content of associated passages. The entry for §87 (§88 in the partners' edition), for instance, reads simply, "The sage said," but it fails to offer any more detail about the passage's content (avoid mockery and nastiness). The entry for §102 reads, "It is forbidden to murder a louse" (the first words of the passage) but fails to explain that this prohibition applies only when the louse in question is found on one's dinner table, or to state that the passage in fact includes a number of other prohibitions relating to good manners.[35]

Given its laconic style, the Cambridge manuscript's table of contents would have been most useful either to readers who knew the accompanying text of *Sefer Ḥasidim* well and wanted to locate familiar passages or to copyists who wished to check their manuscripts against an abbreviated list of passages. By contrast, Abraham's table of contents is more like readers' notes, with each entry summarizing the corresponding passage, often in multiple sentences.

Early modern humanists cultivated the practice of note-taking. Notetaking manuals counseled readers to engage in a multistep process, first marking up a text itself, then copying choice passages into a separate notebook in the order they originally appeared (either abridged or as is), and then indexing those passages according to relevant keywords.[36] Abraham's table of contents recalls the second step in this process: the excerpting and abridging of passages in the order they appear in the text. Yet, absent the third step (indexing and cross-referencing), it has little utility as a finding aid. One searching for a particular passage or material on a specific theme would have to slog through the entire table of contents in order to find what one desired. Abraham's table of contents thus did not transform *Sefer Ḥasidim* into a "navigable book" appropriate for "consultation reading."

Early modern authors and printers also, according to Blair, "invested considerable creative and financial resources" in producing new finding aids, such as tables of contents, indices, marginal notes, and the like, in order to attract the interest of readers.[37] As we noted in chapter 2, Abraham, similarly, saw his table of contents as a selling point:

> For the sake of understanding the value of this book and its fruits, like a set table prepared before all who seek the Lord and His fear, I, the insignificant, the poorest among the greats who signed [their names] at the conclusion of this book, determined to open a doorway and a gate with a table of contents. To this awesome book, all who fear the Lord and contemplate His name will come, and they will find easily all the pleasures of the King [Genesis 49:20], King of the universe, which are in it.[38]

Abraham here explained that his table of contents (literally, "keys," *mafteḥot*) was meant to be more than an aid for consultation reading: It rendered the discursive text of *Sefer Ḥasidim* accessible. In a play on words common to early modern Hebrew paratexts, Abraham exploited the various meanings of the Hebrew word "key," which, as in English, can refer both to a legend or reference and to an object used to open locks. Abraham's table of contents ("keys") unlocked the religious meaning of *Sefer Ḥasidim*, placing it before his readers like a "set table" (*shulḥan arukh*).[39] This religious meaning, a close reading of Abraham's table indicates, was synonymous with the homiletic content of each passage, its capacity for moral and spiritual inspiration, and its function as a practical guide for pious living.

Abraham's homiletic approach to abridging and adapting the content of *Sefer Ḥasidim* is evident when one compares the entries in his table to their associated passages. One passage, §72, is divided into four thematic subsections:

> (a) "Banish care from your mind, and pluck sorrow out of your flesh" [Ecclesiastes 11:10]. This is a good virtue and more excellent than all the other virtues.
>
> (b) When you hear a man or a woman speak about you or against you a thing which is not proper, put your fingers in your ears. For thus the sages said: "For what reason do a man's fingers resemble pegs? For if a man hears something that is not proper, he should place his finger in his ear, or you should force your earlobe into it, and you should not hear anything" [Babylonian Talmud, *Ketubot* 5b].
>
> (c) Even more so, if you hear a different woman or a man speaking about your friend, or a woman speaking about her friend, one should not reply at all, for what is it to him but trouble? Rather, block up your ears and don't hear them abusing each other. And this is good for you!
>
> (d) Control your spirit and restrain yourself, and place in your mouth an obstacle so as not to abuse your relative. Even if he speaks against your father or your mother something that is not proper, do not reply improperly; rather, set his teeth on edge and say to him, "You do not speak the truth." Do not answer him anything more, neither much nor little.[40]

This passage appears in nearly identical form in the Cambridge manuscript, except that there it lacks all of section (a). For this reason, the corresponding entry in the manuscript's table of contents is not the quotation from Ecclesiastes ("Banish care from your mind") but, rather, a brief description of the passage's content. This contrasts with Abraham's lengthy summary. Table 1 presents a side-by-side comparison of the two entries:

Abraham's Table of Contents	Cambridge Manuscript Table of Contents
When a man hears that they say improper words about him, he does not get upset and does not reply. Rather, he puts the fingers of his hands into his ears. If he hears something about his father or his mother, he should not respond, only say, "You don't speak the truth," and he should not add [anything more].	A decree [concerning] one who hears something bad.

TABLE 1

In his entry, Abraham focuses on the two homiletical messages in the passage: (1) Shut your ears to slander, even going so far as to literally stuff your ears, and (2) when someone insults your parent, respond as minimally as possible.[41] This summary hews closely to the language of the passage, though Abraham changes the original second-person imperative to a neutral third-person summary. Abraham leaves out section (c), perhaps because he considers it an extension of the preceding section (b). He neither references the passage's narrative content—that, according to the Talmud, fingers resemble pegs—nor does he cite the biblical verse with which the passage begins. The lack of the verse is somewhat unusual, given that Abraham cites biblical verses frequently in other entries. One explanation for this absence may be that Abraham thought it related to the theme of the passage—slander—only when read in the context of the passage itself. On its face, its connection to the theme was not explicit enough to merit mention in the table.

Abraham's entries frequently bypassed tales, case studies, and moral exempla (known as *aggadot,* singular *aggadah*) in favor of practical ethical guidelines. While the entry in the Cambridge manuscript's table of contents for §174 reads, simply, "Two human beings," Abraham's entry for the same passage summarizes a specific, practical lesson:

> More sin is accounted to the person who adorns himself in such a way as to show himself pleasingly to women—who comes into transgression through them—than the person who does not adorn [himself].

In the text of §174, this lesson is explicated by two exempla (*ma'asim*).[42] The first features a comparison of two adulterers, one who "adorned [*mekashet*] himself" to provoke the attention of women and one who did not. The text asks rhetorically, "Which is preferred?" meaning, "Who committed a less grievous sin?" The text proposes that the man who adorned himself committed a more grievous sin, as epitomized by the second case: that of David and Solomon. David inappropriately provoked the attention of Bathsheba, while Solomon only "taught his evil inclination to desire" by maintaining a harem of one thousand wives.[43] Abraham left these narrative elements out of his summary in order to highlight the moral lesson the cases taught. Had Abraham mentioned the references to David and Solomon, he would have risked undercutting those moral messages by popularizing the licentious exploits of two of biblical Israel's heroes, one of them the progenitor of the future king-messiah.

The consequence of Abraham's emphasis on the homiletical aspects of *Sefer Ḥasidim* was that his table ignored many of the text's fantastical tales—including those of holy men, witches, demons, and ghosts—which no doubt would have been of interest to readers. Thus, for instance, Abraham's entry for §170 reads: "One should not steal a field, since there is no rest for the thief after having committed this act." While this is a summary of the passage's ethical lesson, Abraham gave short shrift to the two ghost stories in the passage: one about the redemptive power of almsgiving in memory of the dead and a second about the troubles a thief experienced after death because he failed to make restitution while alive. Abraham's summary made no reference to these stories, most likely because he considered them irrelevant to *Sefer Ḥasidim*'s ethical teachings. Indeed, he only cited the moral lesson derived from the second story in general terms.

Given Stallybrass's research on the ways finding aids colored readers' receptions of texts, it is worth considering how Abraham's truncating or eliminating many of the narrative elements in *Sefer Ḥasidim* may have affected readers' understanding of the book—especially readers who read *only* his table of contents. Such readers had ready access to the practical, spiritual, and ethical lessons contained in *Sefer Ḥasidim*, that is, its homiletic content, but they would not have encountered one of the distinctive features of R. Judah he-Ḥasid's theology. Stories, especially those involving ghosts or magic, were, for Judah, "manifestations, or even revelations, of divine truth." They were more than fables that taught a moral or spiritual lesson; they were evidence of "God's essence and power revealed in the world."[44] While the text of *Sefer Ḥasidim* recorded examples of those revelations for posterity, Abraham's abridgments removed those elements and presented *Sefer Ḥasidim* as a conventional religious manual.

Assembling the Text

From Abraham's colophon, one might reasonably conclude that the partners simply reproduced a manuscript he provided to them from his impressive library. As Abraham wrote, *Sefer Ḥasidim* was "not found in this region as far as Jerusalem [Micah 1:9] . . . only one [copy] was hidden with me. . . . I brought it out, and it came to the hand of the dear printers to print it."[45] Yet, just as medieval scribes intermingled texts, anthologizing works of differing origins in the same manuscript—an activity they called "gleaning" (*likut*)—the partners fashioned the text of *Sefer Ḥasidim* in their edition by combining at least two preexisting *Sefer Ḥasidim* manuscripts.

The bulk of that text, §§1–1,135, appears to have originated as one manuscript (A), to which the partners joined another, briefer manuscript encompassing §§1,136–1,178 (B). While the passages in B manifest many of the same themes as those in A—mortality, repentance, and the soul—they are not attested in any extant medieval *Sefer Ḥasidim* manuscript; in other words, they have no parallels.[46] The partners distinguished between these two sources by inserting between them the standard Aramaic formula used to conclude manuscripts and printed books in enlarged square type: "The end, blessed is the Merciful and our help." They then wrote, "This [i.e., the following] was copied from another *Sefer Ḥasidim* [*Sefer Ḥasidim aḥer*]" (figure 5). These statements are not used in any of the medieval *Sefer Ḥasidim* manuscripts to divide subsections.

Further, in his table of contents, Abraham wrote explicitly that A and B were distinct sources. Following his entry for §1,135, Abraham wrote, "The end, blessed is the Merciful and our help, concluding [*ligmor*] *Sefer ha-Ḥasidim*," and, on the next line, "This was copied from another *Sefer Ḥasidim*." Abraham's addition of the phrase "concluding *Sefer ha-Ḥasidim*" is telling. He perceived the preceding passages (A) as *Sefer ha-Ḥasidim* proper, just concluded; what followed, B, was "another" text, subsidiary to what preceded it. If Abraham perceived A as the true *Sefer Ḥasidim*, then it is also likely that source A was the manuscript he provided to the partners.

Interestingly, the fact that Abraham knew of the existence of at least two manuscripts, A and B, entitled *Sefer Ḥasidim*, suggests that his comment in the colophon, about his having the only copy of *Sefer Ḥasidim* in the region, was hyperbole. Indeed, at least four of the medieval *Sefer Ḥasidim* manuscripts extant today (cataloged by Marcus) were copied in Italy. These include Ms. Vatican Library, ebr. 285/20 (which actually includes two manuscripts); Ms. Zurich Zentralbibliothek, Heidenheim 51; Ms. Parma Biblioteca Palatina H 2486 (De Rossi 1420/5); and the manuscript previously known as the Jewish Theological Seminary Ms. Boesky 45, now in a private collection.[47] Thus, *Sefer Ḥasidim* manuscripts other than the ones printed by the partners were likely circulating in Italy during the sixteenth century, but it seems the partners had access only to the two they printed.

When printing sources A and B in their edition, the partners could have chosen to disguise the fact that A and B were separate documents. They could have refrained from printing the concluding formula and avoided mentioning that B was "another *Sefer Ḥasidim*." And, in fact, they did subtly elide the difference between these sources by employing continuous numeration; source B began with §1,136 and did not restart with §1. Yet the overall impression is that the partners saw value in preserving and acknowledging the difference between these sources.

Even if Abraham's introduction described Judah as the author of *Sefer Ḥasidim*, the partners' edition retained certain medieval qualities. It was a compilation of two texts joined together, a joining accomplished by printers. In this way, the partners also became *meḥaberim*, "authors," as well, in the biblical sense of the term—those who "join" preexisting materials together. Thus, it was fitting that their names appeared on the book's title page instead of that of Judah—who would be clearly listed there as the author in the second edition and subsequent editions—because the two sources at the heart of the book, though composed by Judah (according to Abraham), originated in two separate works. We can see, then, that in the early sixteenth century, modern notions of authorship and literary attribution began to emerge, while also retaining a certain medieval slipperiness, as literary creativity remained compilatory and anthological.

"Touched by the Censor"

Over the last century, scholars have generally agreed that the systematic censoring of Hebrew books began in the 1550s as a result of Christian sovereigns' increased concern for features of Jewish literature that, they perceived, contradicted or impugned Christianity. This was part and parcel of an expansion of surveillance during the period of the Counter-Reformation, as the Roman Church and states both Protestant and Catholic sought to control the spread of printed information.[48] Most accounts portray the burning of the Talmud in Italy in 1553 as a signal event, either as a symbol of a new kind of anti-Jewish hostility (according to Kenneth Stow) or as a catalyst for new, more subtle policies of social control (according to Amnon Raz-Krakotzkin).[49] Joseph Hacker has emphasized the importance of the 1550s as a period when Jewish authorities (including rabbis) also began to attempt the censorship of printed Hebrew books.[50]

This scholarly consensus about the importance of the 1550s in the history of Hebrew censorship has overshadowed the views of much earlier scholars, especially William Popper, who at the turn of the twentieth century described how, long before the 1550s, Jewish printers engaged in their own censorship efforts.[51] Popper even commented that Gershom Soncino's Talmudic tractates of the 1510s "anticipated the Church by thirty or forty years" in their elimination of seemingly anti-Christian passages.[52] More recently, Nurit Pasternak has shown that a unique trove of Florentine Hebrew manuscripts "bear the only physical evidence yet uncovered of Hebrew codices marked by censorship . . . prior to the Counter-Reformation and to the era of massive purges of Hebrew texts in its wake."[53] Popper's and Pasternak's works are important reminders that both Jews and Christians censored Hebrew books long before the 1550s, a point that the text of *Sefer Ḥasidim* in the partners' edition drives home.

Annabel Patterson has described censorship as a mode of communication that made possible "the equivocal and fragile relationship . . . between writers . . . and the holders of power, a relationship whose maintenance was crucial to all writers who aspired . . . to have influence, either on the shape of the national culture or more directly on the course of events."[54] While Patterson's analysis focuses on the literature of Elizabethan England, her conclusions may be applied to products of early modern Hebrew presses.[55] In order to carry out their work, the partners had to maintain a deferential relationship with the "holders of power"—in this case, the Holy See and its bureaucratic apparatus. To do this, as we noted in chapter 2, the partners lobbied influential individuals in the curia and committed themselves to producing only works that did "not contain any blasphemies against Jesus Christ."[56] With regard to *Sefer Ḥasidim*, this was no easy task, as its manuscript witnesses are replete with references to Christians and Christianity that Christian readers might have perceived as opprobrium. While their censorship was certainly more limited than that imposed by the Counter-Reformation Church a decade later, it is a vivid example of the adaptation and modification of received texts, on an almost microscopic level, by early-sixteenth-century printers in response to contemporary political concerns.[57] And, further, it contradicts the claim of Jacob

Freimann, who asserted that the partners' edition was "still untouched by the censor."[58]

Writing about the censorship of Jewish liturgical texts during the early modern period, Ruth Langer has discerned two approaches in the censors' work: One approach favored changes that would "merely remove the elements objectionable to Christians" but nevertheless did "not effectively change the inner-Jewish meaning of the text." A second approach was more aggressive, seeking "fundamentally to transform the intent of" the text.[59] Both approaches are evident in the partners' edition of *Sefer Ḥasidim*: Sometimes they replaced nicknames Christians found insulting with neutral descriptors, as when, for example, they substituted "priest" (*komer*) for "shaved-head" (*galaḥ*), the latter a derogatory reference to tonsured monks. On the other hand, sometimes their interventions transformed the meaning of passages by replacing direct references with ambiguous terms, introducing uncertainty about the subject under discussion. While it remained possible for a reader to interpret such a passage as it had once read, these more aggressive acts of censorship expanded interpretive possibilities. Semiotic ambiguity, moreover, gave the partners a measure of deniability if they were confronted with accusations of blasphemy. Following Patterson, for the partners, censorship was a form of "oblique communication"; while it functioned as insurance against Christian persecution, it also had the potential to sow confusion among readers, as it obscured the meanings of texts the partners hoped to popularize.[60]

Because passages in the partners' edition may be found in the medieval *Sefer Ḥasidim* manuscripts, it is possible to compare parallel passages and identify subtle differences between them.[61] These parallels are found in nearly all the available medieval *Sefer Ḥasidim* manuscripts. Here, I analyze three representative examples.

To begin, §188 is compared alongside a parallel version found in three manuscripts, with key phrases in bold (table 2). In this passage and its parallels, two variations are discernible: (1) In place of the phrase "converted from the law" (*hemir et ha-dat*) in the partners' edition, we find "apostatized" (*nishtammad*), and (2) in place of "among the foreigners" (*bein ha-nokhri'im*), a phrase repeated three times, we find "among the *goyim*" (*bein ha-goyim*). These two words—the verb *nishtammad* and the plural noun *goyim* (singular *goy*)—had profoundly negative significance for early modern Christians.

Partners' Edition	Manuscripts Parma, JTS Boesky 45, and Bodleian Oppenheimer Add. 34
(a) And one whose son has **converted from the law and gone among the foreigners** and followed their deeds: his mother and father would busy themselves to remove him [from among the gentiles] and to bring him into their houses and to entice him with money, so he would return [to Judaism]. (b) A sage said to them: "Stop and regret! For he will do more evil, for I heard that he wants to give bad counsel to induce and tempt his brothers and sisters to go **among the foreigners.**" (c) And further he says: "For when he was a Jew, he ate unfit flesh."[62] Better that they should leave him **among the foreigners** and he not cause others to transgress, and not cause them to eat forbidden foods. [Regarding one who is] bound to idols, it is better to leave him be [Hosea 4:17] than to bring him close and so that he might cause others to bind themselves to idols.	(a) And one whose son has **apostatized and gone among the *goyim*** and followed their deeds: his mother and father would busy themselves to remove him [from among the gentiles] and to bring him into their houses and to entice him with money, so he would return [to Judaism]. (b) A sage said to them: "Stop and regret! For he will do more evil, for I heard that he wants to give bad counsel to induce and tempt his brothers and sisters to go **among the *goyim*.**" (c) And further he says: "For when he was a Jew, he ate unfit flesh." Better that they should leave him **among the *goyim*** and he not cause others to transgress, and not cause them to eat forbidden foods. [Regarding one who is] bound to idols, it is better to leave him be [Hosea 4:17] than to bring him close and so that he might cause others to bind themselves to idols.

TABLE 2

Etymologically, the root of the verb *nishtammad* (*shin-mem-dalet*) denotes "destruction" and "cutting off."[63] There is some debate about the various meanings this root carried in rabbinic literature.[64] According to Langer, by the eleventh century, the nominal form, *meshummad*, became a pejorative term for Jews who had become Christians.[65] She asserts further that, by this time, most halakhic authorities understood a *meshummad* as a person who had "fully apostatized" from Judaism to Christianity.[66] Elisheva Carlebach has noted that the term's etymology implied "the absolute loss of that soul from the Jewish community," and its passive construction drove home the insult: "No Jew . . . would convert out of conviction."[67]

Needless to say, the term's negative connotations provoked, in Langer's words, "Christian sensitivity."[68] In 1596, Domenico Gerosolimitano, a Jew who converted to Christianity and made a career censoring Hebrew books for the Church, would write in his Hebrew censorship manual, *Sefer ha-zikuk*:[69]

> Every time the word *meshummad* is mentioned, when it does not recall something derisively, it should not be erased, and one should write in its place [the Hebrew acronym] *aleph-khaf-mem* [*akum,* meaning, "worshippers of the stars and constellations"].[70] However, if it is recalled derisively, it should be erased completely.[71]

The partners, by contrast, substituted the expression *hemir et ha-dat* ("converted from the law"), whose root (*mem-vav-resh*) denotes "exchange" or "change," for *nishtammad*. This expression was, as is clear in the translation, a more neutral turn of phrase, and Jewish readers had understood it as such since antiquity.[72]

Similarly, while in the Bible the noun *goy* was the generic term for "nation," the Israelite nation included, it took on profoundly negative meaning during the rabbinic period and beyond, coming to refer exclusively to non-Jews, both as individuals and as a group. According to Ishay Rosen-Zvi and Adi Ophir, this new sense of *goy* existed in two different guises:

> [F]irst the *Goy* is the one who does not stand before the law and . . . is a constitutive condition and external boundary of the halakhic discourse. Second, the *Goy* is an Other with whom the Jew is inevitably and commonly engaged. Commerce, communication and other various forms of mingling with them must be regulated, and, as such, the *Goy* is often degraded and presented as less than human.[73]

Interestingly, the partners replaced *goyim* with another word that, in both rabbinic and later literature, referred exclusively to non-Jews and possessed a negative connotation: "foreigners" (*nokhri'im,* singular *nokhri*). According to Rosen-Zvi and Ophir, *goy* and *nokhri* were "completely interchangeable in rabbinic literature."[74] Closer to our period, Domenico equated the terms when he wrote that the "names *goy, goyim, nokhri, nokhrit,* if understood as implying any disgrace, slander, and insult to that very *goy,* should be erased, and in their place [written] *akum.*"[75] Judging from their use of *nokhri,* however, the partners appear to have considered it less pejorative than its alternative. Perhaps this was because readers could still understand *nokhri* literally, as referring to anyone who was alien or foreign, and thus the term retained a certain ambiguity.

Another example of censorship in the partners' edition is §429, translated in table 3, dealing with the familiar themes of Christian books and clergy.[76] In comparing the partners' text of this passage to the three manu-

Partners' Edition	Manuscripts Parma, JTS Boesky 45, and Bodleian Oppenheimer Add. 34
(a) If there are **priests' books** that have a prayer to an idol in them, and they [the books] were erased, do not write on them [i.e., reuse them], even as a letter or register of a pledge. (b) And if a man has bindings of **their books**, do not bind them to Jewish books. (c) If there is a Bi ble that a **sectarian** wrote and did not inscribe it with his name or the name of an idol or the name of a holy thing, do not store it with Jewish books [i.e., books written by Jews], for "For the rod of the wicked shall not rest upon the lot of the righteous" [Psalms 125:3]. (d) If there is a **sectarian** who wants to make a hymn to an idol, or a **foreigner** wants to make [a hymn in honor of] a sin, and he says to a Jew, "Sing me a pleasant melody with which to praise your God," do not sing to him, so that [his transgression] will not occur on your account.	(a) If there are **shaved-heads' books** that have a prayer to an idol in them, and they [the books] were erased, do not write on them [i.e., reuse them], even as a letter or register of a pledge. (b) And if a man has bindings of **unfit books**, do not bind them to Jewish books. (c) If there is a Bible that a **shaved-head or priest** wrote and did not inscribe it with his name or the name of an idol or the name of a holy thing, do not store it with Jewish books [i.e., books written by Jews], for "For the rod of the wicked shall not rest upon the lot of the righteous" [Psalms 125:3]. (d) If there is a **shaved-head** who wants to make a hymn to an idol, or a ***goy*** wants to make [a hymn in honor of] a sin, and he says to a Jew, "Sing me a pleasant melody with which praise your God," do not sing to him, so that [his transgression] will not occur on your account.[77]

TABLE 3

script witnesses, we can discern that the partners made five substitutions: They substituted (1) "priests' books" (*sifrei komerim*) for "shaved-heads' books" (*sifrei galaḥim*); (2) "their books" (*sifreihem*) for "unfit books" (*sifrei pasulim*); (3) "sectarian" (*min*) for "shaved-head or priest" (*galaḥ o komer*) in the first instance, and (4) "sectarian" (*min*) for "shaved-head" in the second instance; and (5) "foreigner" (*nokhri*) for *goy*.

Once again, the partners substituted more neutral alternatives for terms that Christians perceived as disparaging. In section (a), they replaced the manuscripts' "shaved-head" (*galaḥ*) with "priest" (*komer*), a neutral title rather than a pejorative descriptor.[78] In section (b), they creatively employed the possessive pronominal suffix "their" (*-hem*) in place of the pejorative adjective "unfit" in the phrase "unfit books" (*sifrei pasulim*). This substitution was more aggressive than earlier examples because it substantially altered the meaning of the sentence: The original formulation included both a prohibition on the reuse of Christian book-bindings by Jews and a condemnation of those Christian books. The word *pasul* (unfit) had a strong pejorative connotation, as it was used in both the Bible and rabbinic literature for objects that were ritually impure.[79] In reformulating the sentence, the partners eliminated the condemnatory element while retaining the prohibition.

Finally, in sections (c) and (d), we encounter, once again, a more aggressive kind of censorship: The partners substituted the word *min* for two disparaging references to Catholic clergymen. The term *min* had a long and controversial history. While it could be translated literally as "kind" or "species," it was used in rabbinic literature to refer to schismatic groups, including atheists, baptized Jews, and Christians. According to Langer, in medieval Europe the term increasingly—but not exclusively—became synonymous with Christians, especially in R. Judah he-Ḥasid's circle. In his commentary on the Talmud, Rashi was even more specific: In some cases, he glossed *min* as semantically equivalent to *galaḥ*.[80] By the thirteenth century, Christian scholars were aware of this linkage and believed *min* was a word of opprobrium.[81] It is thus not surprising that, in his guide for censors, Domenico wrote that all instances of it should be erased.[82]

We can speculate that the partners substituted *min* for *galaḥ* in this passage in order to introduce some ambiguity. Despite its fraught history, *min* had a much broader semantic range than *galaḥ*. The manuscript versions of this passage prohibited certain kinds of exchanges with a very specific group of people: Catholic monks. However, by substituting *min* for *galaḥ*, the prohibition now encompassed exchanges with an undefined group that could have referred to many different kinds of people: heretics, baptized Jews, and Christian laymen and clergy. By choosing a word whose meaning was difficult to pin down, the partners encouraged readers to engage in what Patterson has called the "hermeneutics of censorship," asking them to work out for themselves to whom the prohibition applied.[83] Readers might very well continue to interpret the term as a reference to Christians, or more specifically Catholic monastics, but *min* afforded the partners some deniability because of the word's wider range of meaning.

Interestingly, in this and other passages, the partners did not change one controversial expression: *avodah zarah* (abbreviated with the Hebrew letters *ayin-zayin*), translated here as "idol" but also frequently translated as "idolatry." While in rabbinic literature this term referred to pagan practices and artifacts, by the Middle Ages it stood for Christianity too.[84] *Avodah zarah* thus possessed within itself an essential semiotic ambiguity, one that troubled Domenico enough to encourage Christian censors to replace the expression with the acronym *akum*.[85] Yet, it may be that the partners chose to leave the references to *avodah zarah* in the partners' text, again, because of its inherent ambiguity; readers could determine the focus of the passages for themselves. In an era preceding the formal, systematic censorship of Hebrew books by Christian sovereigns, when Jewish printers weeded out problematic words and phrases for themselves, the partners, we can speculate, hoped this ambiguity would protect them from the suspicion of the papacy.

The partners made even more dramatic changes to another passage, §427 (table 4).[86] Once again the partners substituted "foreigner" (*nokhri*) for *goy*, and, once again, the partners did not replace "idol" or "idolatry" (*avodah zarah*), even when it was linked to another controversial term, "festival" (*eid*). Early modern censors regularly erased or crossed out the latter term, and Domenico called it the "language of revilement" (*lashon ḥerpah*).[87] However, the partners evidently believed that it was not controversial, perhaps because, in the Talmud, it was frequently used to denote pagan festivals and therefore might not refer to Christian observances.[88]

At the same time, the partners made two substantive interventions in this passage that significantly changed its meaning. First, they removed a direct reference to Christianity in section (c), the Yiddish expression "*auf tin christianheit.*"[89] This explicit reference—easily comprehensible to anyone who could sound out the Hebrew characters—would no doubt have stoked controversy. In place of this expression, they substituted the more ambiguous locution, "by your faith." They thus replaced a direct reference to Christianity with a phrase that could be spoken to a person of any religion.

The partners adapted section (f) even more dramatically. It describes the case of a man who imagines disgracing an *avodah zarah* (translated here as "idol") by relieving himself upon it. In the manuscripts, the man's remarks employ biblical imagery encoding a scatological attack on Christianity:

> I will make a disgrace of an idol, I will urinate on it or defecate [on it] since **they [its adherents] would uncover themselves and do thusly to Pe'or.**

The man, speaking here about disgracing the idol, uses the term *Pe'or* as a reference to the Moabite god Ba'al-Pe'or, who, according to rabbinic tradition, favored these peculiar forms of worship.[90] According to Shai Alleson-

Gerberg, however, in this vignette, the medieval writer transposed the biblical pagan motif onto a reference to Jesus and Christianity: Pe'or came to signify Jesus or an icon of Jesus.[91] The man's actions, moreover, were part of a complex of Ashkenazic folk beliefs that associated Jesus with excrement.[92]

Medieval and early modern Christians knew of and were horrified by these associations. Likely for this reason, the partners removed this passage's allusion to Christianity by deleting the reference to Pe'or. Moreover, they changed the wording of the man's remark so that he might be understood as attacking idolatry directly, in the sense of the veneration of human images, and not Christian sancta. In the partners' reformulation, the idol (*avodah zarah*) becomes a mere statue, which represents, like the efflux from the man's body, mere flesh. The partners thus radically shifted the passage's polemical focus from powerful Christianity to harmless paganism.

Finally, it is interesting to note that, in this passage, two instances of the word *goy* remained, in sections (e) and (g). These examples demonstrate that the partners did not substitute *nokhri* for every instance of *goy*. The process of combing through texts and replacing or eliminating controversial material was tedious. As many scholars have pointed out, early modern censorship was hardly systematic or comprehensive. In Debora Shuger's words: "In practice, censorship tended to be a haphazard affair."[93] Or, in the context of the censorship of Hebrew books later in the century, as Gila Prebor has noted, censors' efforts very often failed to live up to their intentions.[94] This was certainly the case for the partners; even when they modified passages significantly, as in the passage quoted here, controversial words and phrases remained.

Censorship, embedding Christian sensitivities and interpretations within the text, became one of the features of *Sefer Ḥasidim* as a printed book. Amnon Raz-Krakotzkin has argued that, generally, censorship entered Hebrew books through the initiative of the Counter-Reformation Church.[95] From this study of the partners' edition of *Sefer Ḥasidim*, it is clear that this process began earlier, prior to the institutionalization of Hebrew press censorship in the aftermath of the burning of Hebrew books in the 1550s. The partners' textual interventions at times constrained and at times expanded the range of meanings readers could draw from that book. *Sefer Ḥasidim* passages record that, during the medieval period, some Ashkenazic Jews condemned writers who "added to" and modified preexisting sources. The

Partners' Edition	Manuscripts Parma, JTS Boesky 45, and Bodleian Oppenheimer Add. 34
(a) It is written, "Make no mention of the names of other gods; they shall not be heard on your lips" [Exodus 23:13], and this is joined to [the verse], "Three times a year you shall hold a festival for Me" [Exodus 23:14]. What does one deduce from them? To say to you that a Jew should not say to a **foreigner**, "I will make a loan to you until the day of some [non-Jewish] festival of idolatry or until the day of that holy thing." Rather say, "until so many weeks," as it is written, "Make no mention of the name of other gods," and [the verse uses the expression] "make no mention" [to mean] cause others to mention them. (b) You shall not swear to others by their names, and it is written, "You will call [Me] *Ishi*, And no more will you call Me *Ba'ali*. For I will remove the names of the *Ba'alim* from her mouth, And they shall nevermore be mentioned by name" [Hosea 2:18–19]. Even the name of their festival, which is called Michaelmas, a Jew should not mention. (c) Do not say to a **foreigner**, "By the faith that you have in your God" and do not say, "I swear to you **by your faith**." (d) And do not say to a convert the name of the idol, even to mock it: "Their names shall not be mentioned." And do not swear by his Judaism. (e) A man who wants to swear to a ***goy*** should not say, "I will swear by his god falsely"; even this is not done. (f) A man should not think, "I will make a disgrace of an idol, I will urinate on it or defecate [on it], **since they were flesh just like this**." (g) If the ***goy*** says, "Our God," or "May our Lord lengthen your [days]," or "bring you success," or "be with you," a Jew should not answer, "Amen," for his intention is for his god. But if he says, "Your God" or "May your Lord bring you success," then he may answer after him, "Amen."	(a) It is written, "Make no mention of the names of other gods; they shall not be heard on your lips" [Exodus 23:13], and this is joined to [the verse], "Three times a year you shall hold a festival for Me" [Exodus 23:14]. What does one deduce from them? To say to you that a Jew should not say to a ***goy***, "I will make a loan to you until the day of some [non-Jewish] festival of idolatry or until the day of that holy thing." Rather say, "until so many weeks," as it is written, "Make no mention of the name of other gods," and [the verse uses the expression] "make no mention" [to mean] cause others to mention them. (b) You shall not swear to others by their names, and it is written, "You will call [Me] *Ishi*, And no more will you call Me *Ba'ali*. For I will remove the names of the *Ba'alim* from her mouth, And they shall nevermore be mentioned by name" [Hosea 2:18–19]. Even the name of their festival, which is called Michaelmas, a Jew should not mention. (c) Do not say to a ***goy***, "By the faith that you have in your God" and do not say, "I swear to you **by your Christianity (*auf tin christianheit*)**." (d) And do not say to a convert the name of the idol, even to mock it: "Their names shall not be mentioned." And do not swear by his Judaism. (e) A man who wants to swear to a ***goy*** should not say, "I will swear by his god falsely"; even this is not done. (f) A man should not think, "I will make a disgrace of an idol, I will urinate on it or defecate [on it], **since they [its adherents] would uncover themselves and do thusly to Pe'or.** (g) If the ***goy*** says, "Our God," or "May our Lord lengthen your [days]," or "bring you success," or "be with you," a Jew should not answer, "Amen," for his intention is for his god. But if he says, "Your God" or "May your Lord bring you success," then he may answer after him, "Amen."

TABLE 4

heterogeneous corpus of *Sefer Ḥasidim* manuscripts extant today, marked by adaptation and modification themselves, indicates that adaptation and modification continued apace through the end of the medieval and into the early modern period. Censors in the early modern print shop continued to engage in those processes, shaping the meanings readers would draw from newly printed texts.

Conclusion

In the medieval period, *Sefer Ḥasidim* was marked by textual instability and authorial anonymity. In the sixteenth century, through the parallel processes of attributing, annotating, assembling, and emending, the partners and Abraham transformed *Sefer Ḥasidim* into a book with a stable, navigable, and (ideally) inoffensive text and a recognizable author. These innovations informed the range of meanings readers might draw from the book, "pre-packaging" the work, in Alexandra Gillespie's words, as a religious and moral manual.[96] Even as the printers of subsequent editions wrote openly about the inadequacy and unreliability of the partners' edition and their wish to replace it, the partners' edition served as the basis of every *Sefer Ḥasidim* edition nearly to the end of the nineteenth century. Through their efforts, the partners and their associates fashioned *Sefer Ḥasidim* into a classic of the Hebrew bookshelf.

CHAPTER 4

Ambrosius Froben of Basel

> Two *ḥasidim* had books that needed binding. There was a priest in the city who was more proficient at binding books than any of the Jews. One of the *ḥasidim* gave his books to a less proficient Jew, saying, "How can [the priest] toil over a book in which it is written, 'For the uncircumcised and the unclean shall never enter you again.' [Isaiah 52:1] ... Further, if the foreigner were to bind the books, he would render them contemptible..." His fellow said, "Of course it is forbidden for him to sew the panels of a Torah scroll with sinews, and it is forbidden for him to make anything else that would render the public reading of Scripture invalid, for instance writing [in the Torah scroll] or sewing it together with sinews, but regarding the binding of other kinds of books from which we study, with covers, it is not forbidden to give them [to a priest] to bind."
>
> *Sefer Ḥasidim* (Bologna, 1538), §280

• • • • •

THERE WAS A DIVERSITY of opinion in medieval Ashkenaz about what was at stake when non-Jews came into contact with Jewish sacred books.[1] The epigraph dramatizes that diversity, offering two views about whether, in a city where experts in manuscript maintenance were in short supply, it was permissible for non-Jews to bind Jewish books.[2] (In the medieval period, and in the centuries following the rise of printing, binding was a separate trade from manuscript or printed book production.) When raw materials and expertise were scarce, was it appropriate to turn to non-Jews for assistance in the manufacture and care of holy books? Earlier, we encountered a similar passage, instructing readers not to reuse books that had previously contained a Christian prayer, even if that prayer had been erased.[3]

These passages make clear that, in the medieval period, Jews and Christians found themselves in proximity to each other's sacred texts, even assisting in their production and care. In the early modern period, while Jews like the partners of Bologna and their itinerant predecessor Abraham dei Tintori pioneered Hebrew printing, by the mid-sixteenth century the production of Hebrew printed books was squarely in Christian hands.[4] The Counter-Reformation Church had prohibited Jews from owning or operating their own presses. In this, it was preceded by the Venetian Senate, which, in 1515 and at regular intervals thereafter, granted the Christian Daniel Bomberg a monopoly on Hebrew printing, and then, when that monopoly lapsed, prevented Jews from filling the vacuum.[5]

Northward from Venice, across the Brenner Pass, in the city of Basel, at the end of the sixteenth century, another Christian printer, Ambrosius Froben, immersed himself in the world of Hebrew books.[6] Froben printed eleven Hebrew titles in Basel between 1579 and 1581, though that number is misleading because his edition of the Babylonian Talmud and Mishnah comprised forty-four volumes. He then decamped to the nearby town of Freiburg-im-Breisgau, where he printed six to eight titles (the exact number is disputed) in Hebrew and Yiddish from 1583 to 1585. It was in Basel in 1580 that Froben printed a second edition of *Sefer Ḥasidim* based on the partners' first edition.

The next chapters take as their focus Froben's second edition of *Sefer Ḥasidim*, exploring how its particular social and cultural context shaped the volume that emerged from Froben's press. That context, needless to say, differed from that of early-sixteenth-century Bologna. While the latter was home to a venerable Jewish population, Froben's Basel had, since 1397, prohibited Jewish residents. Further, the years between the appearance of the partners' edition of *Sefer Ḥasidim* and Froben's witnessed dramatic events in the history of Hebrew books, from the condemnation and burning of the Talmud by the Church to the proliferation of printed Hebrew books for Christian readers. How Froben acquired the legal authority, knowledge, and assistance necessary to engage in the risky cross-confessional enterprise of Hebrew printing that ultimately produced, among other texts, his edition of *Sefer Ḥasidim* is the subject of this chapter. How the social and political contexts of the later sixteenth century were reified in his edition of *Sefer Ḥasidim* is the subject of the following two. Ultimately, the question that motivates these investigations is: How does a Hebrew book intended for both Jewish and Christian readers, printed by a Christian-owned print shop, differ from one printed exclusively by Jews?

In today's terms, the partners' Hebrew press might be characterized as a start-up: a group of entrepreneurs seeking to exploit the commercial potential of a new technology before the basic norms and institutions governing it are firmly established. Froben's press, on the other hand, might be called a legacy business: Froben was a third-generation printer who expanded into new markets, collaborated with expert Jewish artisans who learned their trade at other established shops, and was governed by institutionalized regulations.[7] Froben's press was thus emblematic of a broader professionalization and Christianization of Hebrew printing during the later decades of the sixteenth century.[8]

Basel and the Froben Family

Located on the Rhine, at the crossroads of France, the Holy Roman Empire, and the Italian Peninsula, early modern Basel, like Bologna, was a center of trade and scholarship. Its first press began producing books in 1468 (only a decade after Gutenberg's Bible appeared), and the city soon became known across Europe for its humanist and religious publications.[9] These specialties resulted from the close collaboration between scholars at the city's university (founded in 1460) and printers.[10] Catering to scholars' interest in Hebrew literature, especially the Bible, Basel's printers transformed the city into a center of Hebrew printing in the sixteenth century.[11] At the same time, it was a site of ongoing debate over the reform of Christianity. While the city officially broke with the Roman Church in 1529—a move led by professor, preacher, and book corrector Johannes Oecolampadius—the Basel city council and university attempted, in Stephen G. Burnett's words, "to maintain a less dogmatic preconfessional form of Protestantism from the early 1550s." As a consequence, Basel's presses continued to supply books to Catholic Italy long after the city sided with the Protestants.[12]

Ambrosius Froben's grandfather, the printer Johann Froben, is largely known today for his editions of humanistic and religious texts (including Luther's works) and for his close collaboration with Erasmus of Rotterdam, noted in chapter 3.[13] He also printed more than twenty titles containing varying amounts of Hebrew, many in collaboration with the Protestant Hebraist Sebastian Münster.[14] These works were intended for Christian readers. Upon Johann's death, his son Hieronymus and his son-in-law Nicolaus Episcopius took over their father's press and continued to print a similar list. They also attempted to expand their reach to Jewish readers by requesting permission from the Basel Council to print the Babylonian Talmud in 1561—just a few years after the Talmud (and other Hebrew books) was condemned, confiscated, and burned in Rome in 1553 and subsequently in other Catholic domains. The Basel Council, not wanting to provoke the Roman Church, denied their petition, and Hieronymus pushed no further. He continued to print books for Christians until his death in 1563.[15]

When Hieronymus's son Ambrosius assumed the leadership of the family business, he continued printing the humanistic and religious texts for which his father and grandfather had earned their reputations, among them Theodor Zwinger's *Theatrum vitae humanae* (1565) and Augustine's collected works in Latin translation (1569–1570). But, by the late 1570s, Ambrosius turned to printing in Hebrew and Yiddish. Why Ambrosius Froben made this shift from conventional humanist and Christian titles to Hebrew and Jewish ones is not clear. We can speculate that he resolved to accomplish what his father had failed to do: print the condemned Talmud. At the same time, he was likely influenced by changes in Catholic attitudes toward Jews and Hebrew literature during the later sixteenth century and, more generally, by the initiatives of the Counter-Reformation Church.

As the sixteenth century wore on, the Roman Church intensified its persecution of Jews through exorbitant taxation, ghettoization, and new efforts to stimulate mass conversion. For some church leaders, such as Cardinal Giampietro Carafa (subsequently Pope Paul IV), the Talmud was a fundamental impediment to Jewish conversion and had to be eliminated. For others, such as the humanists Petrus Galatinus and Andreas Masius, a proper understanding of the Talmud could help the Church achieve its goal; in Galatinus's words, "No book is more appropriate to convince the Jews than the Talmud."[16] These opposing viewpoints led to what Kenneth Stow has called a constant "fluctuation" in Church policy toward Hebrew books: from acts of violence, such as confiscations and burnings, to limited toleration, as articulated in Pope Julius III's bull *Cum sicut nuper* (1554), which permitted Jews to possess Hebrew books as long as they did not contain blasphemies.[17]

The promulgation of *Cum sicut nuper* has been called a landmark event, as it established the possibility that Hebrew books could exist legally within Catholic domains, and it enunciated the legal framework for Church-imposed censorship.[18] In 1561, at the behest of Pope Pius IV, Bishop Michele Ghislieri, the Roman inquisitor general and later Pope Pius V, proposed a policy of "expurgation"—deletion, after publication, of objectionable material in books deemed not wholly heretical—in his revision of the *Index librorum prohibitorum* (*Index of Prohibited Books*).[19] This principle was codified in the Tridentine Index of 1564, in which it became a primary Church strategy for controlling written heresy and blasphemy. As Amnon Raz-Krakotzkin has noted, the Tridentine Index was a formal representation of an "awareness of a need for a new kind of mechanism of control and new principles of surveillance" of printed literature.[20] The Index explicitly imposed (prepublication) censorship and expurgation on the Talmud (in addition to Protestant books), stipulating that Jews could publish it, "provided they [its volumes] are published without the name 'Talmud' and without offense and contumely against the Christian religion."[21] Thus, in contrast to his father's era, the time at which Froben took up the idea of printing the Talmud was one in which the Tridentine Index had enshrined the possibility of printing it anew, subject to the Church's oversight.

In the years that followed, Church policy vis-à-vis the Jews and Jewish books vacillated between the two poles of persecution and limited toleration. Gregory XIII's papacy (1572–1585) witnessed the emergence of a more aggressive conversionary policy.[22] As epitomized in his bull *Antiqua judaeorum improbitas* (1581), Gregory's strategy was to expose Jews to the truths of the Gospel by requiring their regular attendance at Christian sermons. The goal was to entice Jews to the baptismal font by demonstrating the kinship of Jewish and Christian exegesis and, conversely, by rooting out elements of Judaism that contradicted or dishonored Christianity. This policy led Church theologians to compose anthologies of rabbinic texts and commentaries upon them. These homiletical manuals, extant in manuscript in the Vatican archives, assisted preachers and Church theologians in demonstrating both the misconceptions of Jewish exegesis and the superiority of the Christian tradition.[23]

Gregory's interest in exploiting Christianity's theological "common ground" with Judaism to promote Jewish conversion may have been another impetus for Froben's decision to print a censored Talmud, as well as new editions of Hebrew texts. The titles—cleansed of their former blasphemies—would give Jews access to their sacred books without inculcating anti-Christian disdain, as the Church alleged that previous editions had.[24] Further, these editions would give Christian preachers and Hebraists new access to Jewish literature, freed of its calumnies against Christianity, so that it might become a Trojan Horse in the battle for Jewish converts. While Christians may have perceived Hebrew texts as anti-Christian, Jews may not have shared this view. Christian readers dwelled on passages they found scandalous, but many of those same passages were marginal for Jewish readers, who read their sacred literature for different reasons.

The Censored Talmud

"The sum of all the fairs of the whole world" (*omnium totius orbis emporiorum compendium*)—that was what the humanist printer Henri Estienne II called the Frankfurt book fair in 1574.[25] Twice yearly—in spring and autumn—booksellers, traders, and intellectuals of all kinds, along with paper makers, binders, and typesetters, would gather in the city on the Main to talk and trade in books, from manuscripts to printed volumes. By the sixteenth century, the Frankfurt fair was the world's most important gathering of bibliophiles and traders, as it remains today.[26]

It was at the fair in April 1578 that Froben contracted with a Jewish bookseller from Frankfurt named Simon zur Gemze (Günzburg) to print a new edition of the Babylonian Talmud. According to their contract, Simon provided a substantial investment, giving Froben one-third of an agreed-upon fee and committing to pay the remaining two-thirds over time, as he took delivery of a total of 1,100 printed volumes. The contract stipulated that Froben would produce an edition of the "entire Jewish Talmud" following Marco Antonio Giustiniani's Venice edition of 1547 "and its accompanying concordance, with no mistakes." The edition would adhere to the terms of the Tridentine Index; it would be printed "without the name 'Talmud' and without offense and contumely against the Christian religion." It would be subject to prepublication "correction" (*corrigirt*) by Inquisitor of Venice Marco Marini of Brescia (1542–1594), an Augustinian monk and Hebraist.[27]

Simon intended to sell the new Talmud to the Jews of the Polish-Lithuanian Commonwealth. By the late sixteenth century, the Commonwealth had become the site of the world's most demographically fertile, prosperous, and culturally dynamic Jewish community.[28] Because of the tolerance of the Polish nobility, Jews were permitted to settle widely and engage in diverse occupations, from tax farming to distilling. They were also afforded significant autonomy and developed their own governing institutions, forming associations at the local level (the *kahal*) and regional organizations, such as the Council of the Four Lands, a representative body of Jewish leaders.[29] Polish Jewry, with readers and disposable wealth aplenty, also became a significant market for Hebrew books.

Hebrew printing, moreover, began late in the Polish-Lithuanian Commonwealth. In 1534, the brothers Samuel, Asher, and Elyakim Helicz printed the medieval Ashkenazic guide to the dietary laws called *Sha'arey dura*. Following their conversion to Christianity, they continued to print Hebrew books, but Jewish readers found them suspect.[30] Other Hebrew presses were established in Krakow and Lublin in the 1570s, but throughout the sixteenth century Jews of the Commonwealth regularly purchased books from abroad, especially from Italy, the cradle of Hebrew printing—even if those books were printed by Christians.[31] (In the next chapter, we will explore how the title page of Froben's *Sefer Ḥasidim* showed the regard late sixteenth-century Jewish readers maintained for Hebrew books produced in Italy.) The transit of books from Italy to Poland was enabled by merchants who plied the roads from northern Italy to Krakow.[32] By partnering with Simon, Froben, who styled himself an Italian printer and employed Jews from Italy, hoped to profit by providing the growing Jewish population of Poland with another source of Hebrew books. Moreover, it is likely that Froben hoped his Talmud, censored by a leading Italian churchman, would become the favored edition for Polish Jews, who would not wish to offend their Catholic sovereigns.

In addition to producing books for Jews, Froben sought to attract the interest of Hebraists. While a few notable Christians undertook Jewish learning in the medieval period, the fifteenth and sixteenth centuries witnessed increasing numbers seeking the *Hebraica veritas*, the true meaning of Scripture in its original language.[33] On the one hand, Hebraism was an aspect of the larger Renaissance "revival of antiquity," in which Hebrew came to be seen as a classical language alongside Greek and Latin.[34] Humanists such as Giovanni Pico della Mirandola undertook explorations of Hebrew and Jewish texts as a facet of their larger pursuit of ancient truth. On the other hand, many churchmen sought knowledge of Hebrew and Jewish texts in order to deepen their faith and/or aid their mission to the Jews. For some Protestants in particular, Luther's principle of *sola scriptura* (Scripture as the sole source of religious authority) necessitated engaging the Bible in its original. Thus, Christian Hebraism has been described as, on the one hand, an attempt by Christians to appropriate Jewish religious literature for Christian missionary and Christological purposes, and, on the other, an effort "to forge some form of [Jewish-Christian] dialogue that bespeaks the potential (if not the reality) of mutual respect."[35] Regardless of motivation, Hebraists across Europe, but especially in Protestant cities such as Basel, were eager for copies of Hebrew texts in the original, including the Talmud, as well as learning aids such as grammars and lexicons. Froben's press endeavored to meet this demand.

Even prior to his contact with Simon, Froben was setting the stage for and making noise about printing a new Talmud edition. By 1577, according to the correspondence of Froben's print-shop employee Buonaventura Smet (also called Vulcanius, 1538–1614), Froben had already begun procuring the supplies necessary to begin the project, and Protestant leaders were debating its merits.[36] In the winter of 1578, prior to signing the Frankfurt contract, Froben, like his father had before him, petitioned the Basel Council for permission to go ahead. The council deliberated, requesting the endorsement of the University of Basel's theological faculty; by May, with the faculty's assent, the council approved Froben's request.[37] The first volume of the series—tractate *Eduyot* of the Mishnah—appeared in the summer of 1578, and subsequent Mishnah and Talmud tractates were produced into 1580. In October 1580, Simon dissolved his partnership with Froben, citing the poor quality of the volumes' printing, missing pages, and rampant damage due to improper packaging.[38] Simon was also displeased by the text's "radical expurgation." The book, he said, was "no longer that of the Talmud," and he feared his customers would not want to purchase it.[39]

Froben and Simon (and, following Simon's death in 1582, his heirs) waged a protracted, and ultimately unresolved, legal battle that lasted until 1590, with each side alleging that the other had failed to live up to the terms of their agreement. At one point, Simon went to Froben's home and repossessed Froben's furniture.[40] For his part, Froben continued to hold out hope that he might profit from the Talmud. In 1581, he petitioned Pope Gregory XIII for permission to sell the volumes in Italy and even traveled to Rome to win the

Pope's favor.[41] The Pope, however, on the advice of Cardinal Giulio Antonio Santoro, Prefect of the Congregation of the Inquisition and a critic of Hebrew books, condemned Froben's Talmud and accused Marini of failing to sufficiently censor the text and of delegating the hard work to others.[42] Jewish and Christian readers thus complained about the book's censorship; Jews felt it was too radically censored, and Christians sought even more changes. Even as Froben waged a battle on three fronts—with readers, with Simon, and with the Holy See—he turned his attention to producing other books for Jews, among them *Sefer Ḥasidim*.

Professionalization of the Hebrew Print Shop

In Bologna, the partners' Hebrew books were the result of a financial and creative partnership between the city's Jewish silk tradesmen and scholars. Yet, perhaps with the exception of R. Raphael Talmi, this group was composed of amateurs, newcomers to the print shop—a fact that makes the beauty of the resulting books even more surprising. By contrast, a team of seasoned professionals managed and operated Froben's press. Froben himself, of course, learned the trade at the feet of his father and grandfather. The work of printing was carried out by members of a new generation of Jewish printing experts, trained in Italy, who, beginning in the late sixteenth century, carried their skills to presses across Europe. These men formalized the interrelated tasks of assembling a text from preexisting manuscripts, censoring, composing paratexts, and correcting printed copy.[43] Among them were Cornelio Adelkind, Daniel Bomberg's right hand in Venice; Meir the Scribe at Venturin Ruffanello's press in Mantua; and Jacob b. Naftali ha-Cohen of Gazzuolo at R. Tobias Foa's press in Sabbionetta, and later in Mantua.[44] In the spring of 1578, Froben requested permission from the Basel Council to sidestep the city's official prohibition on the residence of Jews in order to recruit a Jewish printing professional. In his petition, Froben explained that the "special nature of the art" of printing Hebrew and the "inexperience" of Basel's existing printers necessitated the assistance of a Jew from abroad.[45] Shortly thereafter, he hired Israel Zifroni (or Zafroni).[46]

Prior to his involvement with Froben, Zifroni had worked for the Christian printer Vincenzo Conti at his Hebrew presses in Cremona and

Sabbionetta. Zifroni's name appears for the first time in Conti's publications of 1556. At Cremona, as at Basel, Zifroni signed his name "Israel Zifroni of Guastalla, residing at Gazzuolo," thus highlighting his ties to the towns of central and northern Italy. The mention of Gazzuolo has led some to conclude that he received his initial training from Jacob b. Naftali ha-Cohen of Gazzuolo.[47] A cache of letters sent to Zifroni while he was in Basel, excerpts of which the Christian Hebraist Johannes Buxtorf the Elder transcribed and published, indicates that Zifroni's peers and colleagues esteemed him for his Judaic knowledge.[48]

It is possible that, after the closure of Conti's press in Sabbionetta in 1567, Zifroni moved to Venice, where he worked for the printer Giovanni di Gara. (Zifroni worked for di Gara from the late 1580s through the first decade of the 1600s and perhaps developed a relationship with the celebrated Venetian at this earlier stage of his career.[49]) Then, by 1578, Zifroni was ensconced in Froben's shop in Basel; his name appears first in Froben's edition of tractate *Kiddushin* (1578).[50] In the books he produced with Froben, Zifroni is identified with terms that highlight the multifaceted work of early modern printing. In one reference, he is called "the man who oversees the work [*hukam al ha-malakhah*]," meaning that he oversaw the physical production of the books; this is a similar term to those with which R. Yohanan Treves described R. Raphael Talmi in his introduction to the partners' *maḥzor*.[51] Elsewhere, Zifroni is identified as a "corrector" (*megihah*), a "printer" (*meḥokek*), and even an "author" (*meḥaber*).[52]

Zifroni was assisted by a team of print-shop workers. Joseph Prijs estimated that, at minimum, ten skilled workers were needed to produce the entire set of Talmud tractates in two and a half years.[53] Some of them, likely the majority, were Christians. This is evident from the signatures at the bottom of the first page of every quire of *Sefer Ḥasidim*. In *Sefer Ḥasidim*, they included the word "Chasidim," in Latin characters—useful for differentiating quires in a print shop where multiple titles were being printed at the same time. Latin characters would have been unnecessary if the workers in charge of assembling finished books were Hebrew-reading Jews.

Further, in the colophon to the Talmudic anthology *Kavvanot ha-aggadot*, which Froben printed the same year as *Sefer Ḥasidim*, Zifroni highlighted the involvement of Christians in Froben's print shop and begged indulgence for errors that proliferated as a result:

> Do not judge a good book harshly, for one who understands the nature of the business of printing will know that this was not the will of the author; rather, it was on account of the craftsmen first and foremost, for they were not Jews, and the work was great [Mishnah, *Avot* 2:15], and when something is necessary you run and fall sometimes, and they also did so on the Jewish festivals.[54]

The errors in the book were the responsibility of non-Jewish, non-Hebrew-literate press workers who, presumably, under pressure to print as many books as they could as fast as they could and with little care for Jewish sensitivities, continued to set type and print even when there were no Jews to supervise their work.[55] Zifroni's comment also highlights an emerging late-sixteenth-century distinction between authors (*meḥab'rim*) and craftsmen (*omanim*). An author (in Kantian terms) "discoursed," that is, composed (*ḥiber*) a text, and craftsmen gave it material form, sometimes, as Zifroni tells us, at variance with the author's intention. Note, however, that in the case of *Kavvanot ha-aggadot*, Zifroni, who in this work called himself a "printer" (*meḥokek*), seems to have considered himself as occupying a liminal position between author and craftsman. To be a printer was to oversee the work of printing but not to work at the press, not to dirty one's hands with ink and type.

Even though Froben's petition to the Basel Council aimed at securing the residence of a single Jewish artisan, we know that Zifroni was assisted by other Jews, including one individual in particular: R. Jacob Luzzatto. Luzzatto was the compiler of the aforementioned *Kavvanot ha-aggadot* (also entitled *Kaftor va-feraḥ* and *Yash'resh Ya'akov*), and he edited and underwrote Froben's edition of R. Menaḥem b. Benjamin Recanati's *Ta'amei ha-mizṿoth* (1581).[56]

We know only bits and pieces of Luzzatto's background and biography. Prior to his arrival in Basel, Luzzatto corrected an edition of the kabbalistic homilies of the messianic pretender Solomon Molcho at the Krakow press of Isaac Prossitz.[57] In the colophon to *Kavvanot ha-aggadot*, Luzzatto called himself a "resident of Safed," the city in northern Palestine famous for kabbalistic ferment throughout the sixteenth century. The nineteenth-century Italian Jewish poet and antiquarian Samuel David Luzzatto (Shadal), who counted R. Jacob Luzzatto among his ancestors, asserted that Luzzatto was of German origin, and that he was a "true Kabbalist," one "all-soaked in moral allegories and kabbalistic mysteries."[58] A comparison of *Kavvanot ha-aggadot* and Froben's *Sefer Ḥasidim* leads to the conclusion that Luzzatto was indeed a kabbalist and that he played a key role in the production of the latter title.

There is a literary affinity between the two introductions in Froben's *Sefer Ḥasidim* and the introduction in *Kavvanot ha-aggadot*. That Luzzatto is explicitly credited with the latter suggests that he wrote both of the former.[59] All three contain lengthy passages written in short phrases, divided with superscript points, in staccato verse.[60] They employ the same verbal tropes: describing their accompanying texts as "precious fruits," a reference to Song of Songs 4:13; identifying the subject of their accompanying texts with the expression "on this path the axis [of the book] revolves"; and lamenting the present lack of industry among Jewish students with the rabbinic expression that they "did not achieve sufficient study."[61] Moreover, just as R. Abraham b. Moses ha-Cohen lauded his composition of the table of contents in the partners' *Sefer Ḥasidim* edition, laudatory statements in the first introduction suggest that Luzzatto may have composed this edition's table of contents as well. Above all, it is clear from the lengthy extracts from *Sefer Ḥasidim* in his *Kavvanot ha-aggadot* that Luzzatto read *Sefer Ḥasidim* attentively and revered it as a canonical text of a piece with classical rabbinic works, as we will discuss in chapters 5 and 6.

Aside from Zifroni and Luzzatto, a diverse cast of characters—Jewish and Christian—played bit parts in Froben's Hebrew printing enterprise. R. Elijah b. Moses Loans (or Lunschitz, 1564–1636), who may have been an investor in Froben's Talmud project, served as a proofreader in Froben's shop.[62] Zifroni mentioned Elijah in the letters preserved by Buxtorf. Elijah was a celebrated mystic who lived and taught throughout the Rhine Valley and is known to have composed kabbalistic works, including *Rinat dodim* (1600), a commentary on the Song of Songs, and *Mikhlol yofi* (1695), a commentary on Ecclesiastes.[63] Elijah also worked with Froben's contemporary, the Basel printer Konrad Waldkirch, and his name appears in some of Waldkirch's Hebrew titles.[64]

Froben also worked with R. Jacob b. Samuel Bunim Koppelman (1555–1594). Koppelman was the author of three Yiddish titles Froben printed at Freiburg: a translation of the ritual guide *Sefer ha-yir'ah* (also known as

Hayyei olam, 1583) by the medieval halakhist R. Jonah b. Abraham Gerondi; a translation of the medieval fable anthology *Mishlei shu'alim* (1583) by R. Berekhiah b. Natronai ha-Nakdani; and a rhymed translation of the Five Scrolls (1584). Koppelman was a native of Freiburg and a student of R. Mordecai Jaffe (1530–1612), one of Poland's leading halakhists in the late sixteenth century.[65] Jaffe was known for his interest in printing and his use of it to publicize his views and make money, something he may have passed on to his student Koppelman.[66] Yet, we do not know whether Koppelman played any role other than author/translator in Froben's print shop, though it is possible, given his ties to Freiburg, that he helped Froben and Zifroni prepare his translations for the press.

Among the Christians working with Froben was Marco Marini of Brescia, whose oversight and "correction" was stipulated in Froben and Simon's Talmud contract. Anthony Grafton has uncovered a letter from the summer of 1577 in which Froben asked Marini to "castigate" (*castigandi*) the Talmud—that is, prepare a text without objectionable elements so that it might be acceptable to the Church.[67] Marini did just that for at least some of the Talmud volumes; his name appears on several title pages, though not all.[68] As a Hebraist who had learned the language from a converted Jew in Brescia, he has been identified as one of a group of late-sixteenth-century Catholic scholars who collected and transcribed rabbinic texts for use in conversionary sermons.[69] In 1580, Froben also published Marini's Hebrew grammar, *Sefer Gan Eden*.[70] Marini's name is not found in any other Froben title, however.

Along with the Catholic Marini, Froben was assisted by a number of Protestant scholars. They included Vulcanius, Immanuel Tremellius, and Pierre Chevalier. Vulcanius was an experienced print-shop worker who played the role of "corrector" in Froben's shop and subsequently was appointed professor of Greek at the University of Leiden. Correctors prepared the exemplar texts that other workers ("craftsmen," in Zifroni's terms) set in type. For ancient and medieval texts that existed in multiple manuscripts, correctors were responsible for synthesizing divergent traditions—a task that involved considerable philological and linguistic expertise—and censoring offensive elements. By the late sixteenth century, this role, like the print shop itself, became more professionalized, and correctors developed new tools and standards, regularly claiming credit for their ingenuity in paratexts.[71]

Vulcanius worked for Froben from 1575 to 1577, when he returned home to the Netherlands. He helped Froben lay the groundwork for the Talmud project, composing Froben's letters to Marini, for example, but left town before it began in earnest. His departure may have been the result of his own ambivalence about Froben's Talmud. In his correspondence, Vulcanius both praised and condemned his employer's efforts.[72]

Tremellius (1510–1580) was a converted Jew from Ferrara and a peripatetic professor of Hebrew. In a letter to the French Calvinist theologian Theodore Beza from 1579, Tremellius recounted that, while he was at the University of Heidelberg, sometime prior to 1577, Froben had invited him to correct and censor several volumes of his Talmud edition.[73] Tremellius agreed enthusiastically and subsequently provided Froben with thoroughly censored and annotated copies of selected tractates, presumably tractates that Marini had not himself censored. In the years that followed, rumors circulated that impugned Tremellius for participating in this venture. In his letter to Beza, Tremellius defended his involvement, explaining that, in Kenneth Austin's words, "He had eliminated so much of the book that it would not have appealed to Catholics . . . or to the Jews, since so little of the original text was left."[74] This was an assessment that Froben himself would offer in defending his Talmud before Pope Gregory XIII, and one with which the Jews of Poland apparently concurred.

Froben also engaged Tremellius's student at Heidelberg, Pierre Chevalier.[75] Chevalier moved from Geneva, where he was among the first generation of Geneva-trained Protestant ministers, to Basel to work for Froben as a corrector and censor. Chevalier took the position against the orders of the city's Company of Pastors, of which he was a member.[76] Yet his interest in the Talmud and ancient Jewish sources overtook his vocation. Chevalier corresponded with Vulcanius in 1577 and suggested that the Talmud should be printed with as little modification as possible because it was a valuable historical source.[77] Chevalier's reputation, like that of Tremellius, appears to have been tarnished by this stance.[78] Nonetheless, in 1587, Chevalier was appointed professor of Hebrew at the Genevan Academy.

The extent to which any of these Christian printing professionals helped produce any of Froben's non-Talmudic titles, including *Sefer Ḥasidim,* is not clear. One tantalizing suggestion comes from the writings of the humanist and Hebraist Isaac Casaubon (1559–1614), Chevalier's student in Geneva.[79]

Casaubon owned a copy of Froben's *Sefer Ḥasidim,* and it is possible that he first encountered the title in Chevalier's classes, where his extant notes testify to their discussions of Jewish magic, a theme, we have already noted, that recurs in *Sefer Ḥasidim* passages.[80] Froben's *Sefer Ḥasidim,* moreover, was aggressively censored, in a manner similar to that of the text of Froben's Talmud edition, as we will observe in chapter 6. It is possible that Chevalier, who was employed by Froben in Basel in 1580, helped censor *Sefer Ḥasidim* as well, though his name is not attested in it, or in any of Froben's other titles.[81]

New Books for New Readers

Beyond the Talmud, Froben printed an eclectic list of titles at Basel and at Freiburg designed to appeal to the incipient diversity of early modern Hebrew and Yiddish readers. As he had with the Talmud, he appealed to the interests of the growing Jewish population in the Polish-Lithuanian Commonwealth. His first non-Talmudic title in Basel, printed in the summer of 1579, was an octavo liturgy for daily worship modeled on an edition produced in Mantua in 1558.[82] As we noted earlier, prayer books were the books most often printed and owned by Jews during the sixteenth century. The fact that this liturgy followed the Ashkenazic rite, and that it was printed in octavo format, made it attractive to non-elite Jews of the Polish-Lithuanian Commonwealth, where that rite was used.

In 1580, along with *Sefer Ḥasidim,* Froben printed *Ir gibborim,* an anthology of homilies by R. Ephraim Solomon b. Aaron of Luntshits, a rabbi in Lemberg and Prague who had achieved popular acclaim for his peripatetic preaching in Poland.[83] Froben received the manuscript for this title from a leading rabbi in Prague, R. Mordecai b. Moses ha-Levi, who also underwrote the cost of its printing.[84] R. Menchem Recanati's *Sefer ta'amei ha-miẓvoth* (1581), like the partners' edition of the thirteenth-century Italian kabbalist's *Piskei halakhot,* appealed to Polish readers clamoring for esoterica. *Sefer ta'amei ha-miẓvoth* contextualized the performance of the Jewish commandments in kabbalistic terms, drawing on precedents in the literature of the Zohar.[85]

Froben also produced Hebrew books for Christian Hebraists, including his *editio princeps* of Marco Marini's *Sefer Gan Eden,* a Hebrew primer with Bible excerpts and grammatical explanations in Latin translation. This title, perhaps more than any other, was intended for Christians seeking to grasp the *Hebraica veritas*.[86] Froben also creatively repackaged Hebrew works originally intended for Jews for Hebraists. His edition of the concordance *Me'ir nativ* (1581) was printed in three identical versions, one with the Latin subtitle *Concordantiae Bibliorum Hebraicae*. This Latin paratext signaled to Hebraist readers that the book was of use to them, even if it possessed the same text as the other two all-Hebrew versions.[87] Even more dramatically, Froben printed an anthology of the Hebrew chronicles *Seder olam rabbah* and *Seder olam zuta* (1580) in two versions, one with Hebrew alone and one in both Hebrew and Latin. By repurposing the pages from the exclusively Hebrew edition and juxtaposing them with the text of a 1578 translation by the French Benedictine Gilbert Génébrard, Froben avoided having to reset the Hebrew type. Aside from appealing to two different readerships, this adaptation, by using existing material meant for Jewish readers in an edition for Christians, economized and generated additional profit, a strategy pioneered by Daniel Bomberg.

As noted previously, Froben printed a number of Yiddish titles by Koppelman during his stay in Freiburg. Jean Baumgarten has noted that the emergence of Yiddish printing during the late sixteenth century led to a significant "expansion" of the Jewish reading public, and printers like Froben recognized the potential profit in this market.[88] The first printed Yiddish book was the biblical concordance *Mirkeves hamishne* by the aforementioned Helicz brothers in 1534. Thereafter, Yiddish printing spread to the existing centers of Hebrew printing, especially Venice and Mantua, and new Yiddish presses emerged close to the Yiddish-speaking regions of Germany and Poland-Lithuania, including Freiburg.[89] Indeed, the growth of Yiddish printing during the later sixteenth century mirrors the growth of printing in other European vernaculars during this time, as printers recognized that the markets for scholarly books were saturated and they could profit by appealing to non-scholarly or non-elite readers.[90]

Froben settled in Freiburg in 1583. His move may have been the result of a falling-out with Protestants in Basel, who were upset by his overtures to the Pope.[91] But his stay there lasted only a short while; in 1585, he returned to Basel, retired from printing, and transferred ownership of his press to his son Hieronymous and his son-in-law, Johann Meir. Hieronymous and Johann returned the business to printing non-Hebrew humanistic works.

Ambrosius, no longer printing controversial books, became an officer of one of the city's men's clubs and rejoined the Protestant Church of Saint Jakob. Zifroni returned to Italy and, in 1588, wrote Ambrosius's brother-in-law, the Basel humanist Theodore Zwinger, of his desire to return to Basel to print Hebrew books there. This wish was not to be. Zifroni spent the rest of his life in Venice printing Hebrew books at the Di Gara Press.[92]

Conclusion

Although Jews established themselves as printers of Hebrew books during the incunabular period and in the early sixteenth century, their primacy in the field gave way, amid the fires of the Counter-Reformation, to Christians such as Ambrosius Froben. Christians had always been involved in the production and maintenance of Hebrew books, as attested by the *Sefer Ḥasidim* passages with which this chapter began, but Christians and Christian power pervaded mid- and late-sixteenth-century Hebrew-book production in new ways. Christians chose the titles, corrected texts, and formed a market of readers. Basel was fertile ground for a new Hebrew printing enterprise supplying books to emergent communities of Jewish and Christian readers. It was situated at the crossroads of Protestant and Catholic Europe: Italy, Germany, and Poland. The blessing Froben received from the city's university, one denied to his father, signified the rise of Hebraism as a force in European culture. But Froben needed learned and skilled Jews to do the work of preparing the books he hoped to sell. He turned to the cradle of Hebrew printing, Italy, and there found Zifroni and Luzzatto. These men left their mark on many of Froben's titles, especially *Sefer Ḥasidim*, as the next chapters will show.

CHAPTER 5

Froben's *Sefer Ḥasidim*

PARATEXTS

Copied from a very ancient book, corrected and expurgated many times over. Because of this thing, you shall clear out the old and replace it with the new.

Title page, *Sefer Ḥasidim* (Basel, 1580)

. . . . .

FROBEN'S *Sefer Ḥasidim* edition was, for all intents and purposes, a copy of its Bolognese forerunner. Like the partners' edition, it was an octavo, an inexpensive and portable format meant to appeal to readers of even limited means. Significant portions of R. Abraham b. Moses ha-Cohen's introduction were reused, without attribution, in one of its two introductions. The layout of Froben's *Sefer Ḥasidim* text follows the partners' edition: the same passages appear together on the same page; the same words appear on the same lines. That text also carries over the partners' modifications and censoring, including the use of expressions and terms introduced by the partners but not found in manuscripts, such as "converted from the law" (*hemir et ha-dat*) or "foreigners" (*nokhri'im*).[1] Yet, despite its obvious dependence on the partners' edition, the title page of Froben's edition claimed it was "copied from a very ancient book." In reality, that book was only forty years old.

Froben and his team thus did not start from scratch. By the time they began their work, *Sefer Ḥasidim* was a book with a stable text and a known author, R. Judah he-Ḥasid. The partners created that book with the goal of inspiring popular religious devotion among an increasingly heterogeneous Italian Jewry. Froben and his team took the partners' book and transformed it, adding new paratexts and emendations, repackaging it as a work of rabbinic lore (*aggadah*) for young Jewish students (*talmidim*). This chapter and the next explore that transformation. This chapter focuses on the ways in which key paratexts in Froben's edition—its title page, two introductions, and table of contents—repackaged and re-presented *Sefer Ḥasidim* for the Hebrew readers of the late sixteenth century. The next chapter focuses on how Froben's team modified the partners' *Sefer Ḥasidim* text in light of their interest in *aggadah* and in hopes of avoiding the condemnation of the Counter-Reformation Church.

"The House of God . . . the Gateway to Heaven"

Over the course of the sixteenth century, title pages evolved from spare and laconic to elaborate and verbose. We noted the simplicity of the partners' *Sefer Ḥasidim* title page in chapter 3. By the end of the century, printers became aware that, in the early modern bookshop, where books were sold unbound, an enticing title page was an effective way of attracting the eyes of purchasers.[2] They filled them with comely images and bombastic text. Froben's *Sefer Ḥasidim* title page was no exception; it was stuffed to the gills with information and ornamentation, testifying to the book's value and virtue (figure 6). It identified the book's ideal readership: students, a new market that late-sixteenth-century Hebrew printers and writers were keen to reach. It advertised the book's author and the provenance of its text, linking it to R. Judah he-Ḥasid and Froben's venerable print shop. And it touted the superiority and accuracy of Froben's team's editing, while denigrating the partners' edition for its infelicities.

The title page of Froben's *Sefer Ḥasidim* concludes with the words pronounced by the biblical patriarch Jacob upon waking from his angelic night vision: "This is none other than the house of God; this is the gate of heaven" (Genesis 28:17). The verse is a chronogram: the sum of the numerical values of the first letter of each word corresponds to the Hebrew year of the book's printing.[3] It is also a play on words: The Hebrew word for "gate" (*sha'ar*) can also refer to a book's title page. References to gates and doorways, especially images of portals and porticoes with biblical verses (including this one, regularly) and promotional text, became hallmarks of Hebrew and Yiddish title pages in the late sixteenth century, and they remain common today.[4] Such imagery instilled (or reflected) the perception that printed books, in Elisheva Carlebach's words, were "synecdoches for the palace of the deity."[5]

Despite invoking the "gate of heaven," the title page of Froben's *Sefer*

Ḥasidim did not feature an image of a gate or portico. Instead, it was ornamented with two striking rectangular frames of interwoven vines, flowers, and geometric forms.[6] One frame contained the title *Sefer ha-Ḥasidim* and a second, below it, contained a description of the book:

> For the Lord's remnant people [Joel 3:5 and Jeremiah 31:1]. For the singular treasures of the generation. These ones who walk among [the ministering angels] who stand [Zachariah 3:7].[7] Corrected with pleasant and honorable literal scriptural interpretations.[8] With good and learned ethical teachings. For students.
>
> Authored by the father and head of the pious, the holy one, our rabbi, Judah he-Ḥasid, may he be remembered for life in the world to come.
>
> Copied from a very ancient book, corrected and expurgated many times over. Because of this thing, you shall clear out the old and replace it with the new [Leviticus 26:10]. This [holy] vessel they brought to the treasury.[9]
>
> Printed in the city of Baselea, the grand,
>
> May her glory be exalted and her sovereignty extolled,
>
> By order of the prince, Ambrosio Frobenio, may he and his descendants live, in his house.
>
> All the work was completed [1 Kings 7:49] in the month of Kislev, the year 341 [1580], meaning [i.e., equivalent to the numerical value of the verse], "This is none other than the abode of God, and this is the gateway to heaven" [Genesis 28:17].

This description, like much early modern Hebrew prose, and that of Hebrew paratexts in particular, is redolent with biblical allusions. The opening phrase "For the people of the Lord, the remnants" was a locution recalling the prophecies of Joel and Jeremiah that a pious few would survive the trials of divine retribution and exile.[10] *Sefer Ḥasidim* was intended for these *ḥasidim*, but not them alone; it was, as the first paragraph concludes, "for students" (*talmidim*) in particular. Who were these students?

As the market for scholarly books became saturated, Hebrew printers sought new non-elite readerships, as we began to discuss in chapter 4. One such group comprised the novices thronging the *yeshivot* and *ḥavurot* of early modern Italy and Poland. *Sefer Ḥasidim* was one of several of Froben's titles intended for these students. In his introduction to *Kavvanot ha-aggadot*, for example, Luzzatto wrote that the purpose of his book was to explicate misunderstood traditions for "students" who lacked familiarity with rabbinic lore (*aggadah*).[11] R. Jacob b. Samuel Bunim Koppelman, Froben's Yiddish translator and collaborator at Freiburg, adapted the language of the Passover Haggadah in the introduction to his commentary on the medieval philosopher R. Joseph Albo's *Ikkarim* (1584). It was a book for "the one who does not know how to ask, and they are the young students (*ha-talmidim ha-ketanim*) who don't know their right from their left."[12] A few decades earlier, in the introduction to his halakhic code, the *Shulḥan Arukh* (1565), R. Joseph Karo wrote, "The young students [*ha-talmidim ha-ketanim*] will meditate upon it [the *Shulḥan Arukh*] always and repeat its language orally [Deuteronomy 6:7], so that it might become like what one studies in childhood [*girsah de-yankuta*], ordered in their mouths as a practical guide from childhood."[13]

In early modern Italy and Poland, students like these frequently studied in *yeshivot* where new, independent approaches to Jewish learning were being put into practice. From late antiquity, the heart of the *yeshivah* curriculum had been the exposition of the legal passages (*halakhah*) of the Babylonian Talmud in the presence of a reputed master.[14] The sixteenth century, however, witnessed dramatic changes in *yeshivah* methods and curriculum. Foremost among them was the introduction of *pilpul* (Talmudic dialectics) and new texts, such as the *Shulḥan Arukh* and kabbalistic works.[15] Karo's *Shulḥan Arukh* revolutionized halakhic study, allowing students to discern rulings for themselves without having to sort through competing precedents in an increasingly unwieldy halakhic library.[16] The availability of printed kabbalistic texts, as well as study guides and abridgments, meant that students had access to the most esoteric works of Jewish tradition without the permission or oversight of reputed experts. Some students, relying on these newly printed works, even rejected Talmud study in favor of studying Kabbalah exclusively.[17]

The sixteenth century also witnessed the rising prominence of *ḥavurot* as fixtures of Jewish communal life, especially in Italy.[18] The proliferation of *ḥavurot* mirrored the parallel growth of confraternities among sixteenth-century Christians and their visibility in Italian civic life.[19] These institutions served varied purposes, from dowering brides to collecting charity, from caring for the dying to practicing early morning pietistic rituals. One important role of *ḥavurot*—which overlapped at times with *yeshivot*—was the education of young boys and men, who were called, interchangeably, *talmidim, baḥurim,* or *ne'arim* (youths, adolescents).[20] In such *ḥavurot,* students and teachers were confined, studying, and residing together, unable to leave except for rare interludes. Aside from the study of texts, which occupied much of the day, students also received frequent instruction on moral matters and proper comportment. The purpose of such an environment was as much to instill religious discipline as to cultivate scholarship—and to protect young men from "the temptations of the street."[21] In this context, then, Froben and his team likely hoped their new edition of *Sefer Ḥasidim* would be included in the emergent *yeshivah* and *ḥavurah* curricula as a moral and religious guide. The book taught, Luzzatto would write in his second introduction, "homilies, ethical teachings, good and upright virtues, and proper conduct"—grist for the *yeshivah* and *ḥavurah* mill.

Another innovative feature of the title page was the statement "Authored (*ḥiber*) by the father and head of the pious, the holy one, our rabbi, Judah he-Ḥasid, may he be remembered for life in the world to come," with "Judah" printed in enlarged type. In chapter 3, we noted that modern norms of authorial attribution were emerging but had yet to crystalize in the early sixteenth century. The partners thus identified Judah as *Sefer Ḥasidim*'s author (*meḥaber*) but did so only in the book's introduction. The partners' names, instead, featured prominently on the title page, for they were responsible for the book, in the Foucauldian sense. By the century's end, however, authors' names became ubiquitous on printed title pages. Like other late-sixteenth-century printers, Froben and his team recognized the value of linking books to venerated personages and accompanying those attributions with honorifics and biographical information.[22] Hence, they described Judah evocatively for potential purchasers to see as "the father and head of the pious, the holy one." Doing so bestowed authority and credibility on the book.

Alongside Judah, the title page also declaimed that this new *Sefer Ḥasidim* edition was printed "By order of the prince, Ambrosio Frobenio, may he and his descendants live, in his house." Froben used this phrase on the title pages of many of his Hebrew works, including the volumes of his Talmud edition, in contrast to the Latin phrase, "*Per* [through] *Ambrosium Frobenium,*" which appeared on his Latin titles of the same years.[23] This difference can be explained by the fact that, while Froben was trained to print in Latin, he had readily informed the Basel Council that he lacked the expertise to print in Hebrew. With the phrase "by order of" (*ba'miẓvat*), Froben signaled that he stood at a remove from the printing of his Hebrew books. The work was undertaken by trained professionals such as Zifroni and Luzzatto. The late-sixteenth-century print shop was thus more stratified than its predecessors, marked by a division of labor in which print-shop owners like Froben delegated editorial responsibilities to expert employees. For this reason, the foregoing analysis assumes Zifroni, with Luzzatto's assistance, and not Froben himself, was the primary actor responsible for the production of the second printed edition of *Sefer Ḥasidim*.[24]

Yet, Froben did not efface his responsibility for the book. As much as the title page made Judah out to be its author and alluded to the involvement of others in its production, Froben was the book's printer, and the title page made that clear. The book was produced "in his shop" (literally "in his house," *ba-veito*), a phrase reminiscent of the Latin "*ex officina*" used on his Latin title pages. No doubt, Froben sought to capitalize on his printing house's reputation as one of Basel's most venerable. But, perhaps more importantly for Jewish readers, Froben linked his shop to those of its distinguished Italian predecessors by Italianizing (in Hebrew characters) his name ("Ambrosio Frobenio") and that of his native city ("Baselea"), a point first noted by Joseph Prijs.[25] As we discussed earlier, until the early seventeenth century, the print shops of Italy produced nearly half of all Hebrew printed books, more than any other region. Even after Italian presses were eclipsed by those of Amsterdam and Poland, sixteenth-century Italian books had set the standards of Hebrew typography for successive generations.[26] Zifroni had trained in Italy, and Froben relied on the patronage and assistance of Italian scholars and religious authorities, not least of all the Pope. Froben thus portrayed his print shop as an extension of his Italian precursors, and his title page was meant to entice readers by affirming the standards of Hebrew printing that had been established in Italy earlier in the century.

As we noted previously, the title page also claimed, falsely, that Froben's new edition of *Sefer Ḥasidim* was "copied from a very ancient book." The phrase "very ancient book" (*sefer yashan noshan*) was a stock expression used by Hebrew printers, harkening back to the book of Leviticus, which prophesied that the righteous would "eat old grain long stored [literally 'very ancient,' *yashan noshan*], and you shall have to clear out the old to make room for the new" (26:10). In their paratexts, early modern printers frequently humble-bragged about their discoveries of hitherto unavailable sources, the superiority of their editorial and philological skills, and their industriousness and persistence in the face of innumerable challenges and roadblocks. Such statements generally involved a certain amount of dissimulation. Aldus Manutius, the famed Venetian printer of classical texts, regularly claimed to have located lost manuscripts, which he carefully collated into superior editions, yet he more often than not exaggerated his efforts. As Martin Lowry has shown, Aldus often made use of well-known and readily available exemplars, and his editing could be "subjective or arbitrary."[27]

Editing was another selling point that late-sixteenth-century printers touted on their title pages. As we noted in chapter 3, there was widespread concern among early modern printers and readers that printed books, in contrast to manuscripts, were marred by error and falsehood. In response, printers used paratexts to convince readers of their titles' bona fides.[28] The title page of Froben's *Sefer Ḥasidim* did just that, proclaiming that Froben's edition, unlike its predecessor, was "corrected [*mugah*] and expurgated [*mezukkak*] many times over." Luzzatto echoed these comments a page later, in his first introduction:

> I arrived at and found upright sayings, written with the finger of God [Exodus 31:18, Deuteronomy 9:10], fit words; expurgated, refined, corrected, and approved, this one canceling out all earlier editions [Genesis Rabbah 12:13]. This one comes to displace that one. Rabbi Yossi's statement is already well-known, from the second chapter of [Babylonian Talmud] *Ketubot* [regarding the biblical verse], "Do not let injustice reside in your tent" [Job 11:14]: "This refers to a person who retains an uncorrected book in his house."

In this introduction, Luzzatto took the rabbinic dictum that one may not possess an "uncorrected book [*sefer she-eino mugah*]" and applied it to the partners' edition, comparing it to the "injustice [*avlah*]" in the verse from Job.[29] While, in its original Talmudic context, R. Yossi's statement in *Ketubot* referred specifically to a Torah scroll (*sefer*), it served Luzzatto's purpose to read the statement more expansively, as a reference to all books (*sefarim*), and to the partners' edition of *Sefer Ḥasidim* specifically, with its manifold errors.[30] Printers of new editions frequently impugned their predecessors for their lack of diligence and expertise in textual preparation and correction. Luzzatto thus played a familiar tune when he wrote that the partners' edition was "not expurgated [*mezukkak*] appropriately and corrected [*mugah*] properly," and, as a result, "this one comes to displace that one."[31] Froben's edition was superior because it had been "expurgated, refined, corrected, and approved [*mezukkak, meẓuraf, mugah, u-me'ushar*]."

These four verbs—"expurgated, refined, corrected, and approved"—were terms editors and correctors regularly employed to describe the Sisyphean effort to produce authoritative texts free from error. Amnon Raz-Krakotzkin has asserted that the meanings of these verbs lie on a continuum from "the editing and emendation"—the production of the most accurate and intelligible text—to "censorship"—the elimination of elements deemed objectionable. Though today we might think of them as at cross-purposes, in the early modern print shop these processes were considered one and the same: To produce a text free from error, one had to assemble the most accurate text from preexisting sources, correct textual defects and corruptions, and eliminate elements that might cause offense. The governing principle behind these processes, Brian Richardson has written, was creating "something beautiful to behold, imparting 'nitidezza' or 'pulitezza' or purging stains." Texts thus could be improved by removing features that did not align with contemporaneous ideals of style, syntax, belief, or conduct without rendering them inauthentic or unauthoritative.[32] Yet even if, from the perspective of the print shop, "correction" (*hagahah*) and "expurgation" (*zikuk*) were interrelated, one wonders how Jewish readers in the early modern bookshop understood these terms, especially because the latter implied that texts were being "improved" in accordance with the sensibilities of Christian powers.

Raz-Krakotzkin has suggested that some Jews perceived censorship as a credit to Hebrew books. These Jews, primarily print-shop professionals who worked closely with Christians, were part of a vanguard seeking a less adversarial relationship between Judaism and Christianity. The modification of Hebrew books in accordance with Christian considerations, in this telling, presaged the "secularization" of the modern era.[33] Yet, Simon zur Gemze's testimony of Jewish readers' disappointment with Froben's Talmud suggests that many early modern Jews perceived the censoring of Hebrew texts as undesirable. For them, censorship eliminated essential features of venerable and canonical works. (Of course, the case of Froben's Talmud also illustrates how even a censored book might still run afoul of Christian sovereigns.)

It is also likely that, by the late sixteenth century, many Jewish readers were resigned to censorship as a necessary evil. Following the Hebrew book burnings of the 1550s and the Council of Trent, censorship made the circulation of Hebrew books possible in Catholic domains and decreased the likelihood of their confiscation and destruction.[34] Perhaps, then, Jews may have read the words "corrected and expurgated" on Froben's title page as a kind of insurance policy. At a time when printed books remained suspicious, such a statement confirmed both the book's quality and its orthodoxy (in the eyes of Christian sovereigns). Readers would be less likely to fall prey to "injustice"—in the words of the Talmud, quoted by Luzzatto—whether that injustice was a corrupt text or the retaliation of their Christian rulers.

Philosophy and Canonicity

The two introductions in Froben's *Sefer Ḥasidim* edition, both composed by Luzzatto, served different purposes. The first introduction made the case for the superiority of the new edition on account of the partners' edition's manifold errors (figure 7). The second introduction, our primary focus here, was lengthier, and in it Luzzatto made a number of interrelated claims (figure 8): First, wading into the ongoing conflict over the compatibility of philosophy and Judaism, Luzzatto portrayed *Sefer Ḥasidim* as an antidote to rationalism and a vindication of Jewish ritual and particularism. Second, he described *Sefer Ḥasidim* as a canonical text akin to better-known works of the rabbinic tradition (Talmud, *midrash*, the recently printed Zohar, 1558).[35] Third, Luzzatto argued *Sefer Ḥasidim* should be appreciated as a work of *aggadah* (rabbinic lore), a long-marginalized genre that was generating renewed interest in the late sixteenth century. Finally, he, like Abraham had in his introduction, asserted that R. Judah he-Ḥasid was *Sefer Ḥasidim*'s author (*meḥaber*), but he too suggested Judah's achievement entailed joining together preexisting sources, not fashioning a new text out of whole cloth.

In chapter 2, we explored how the question of the legitimacy of philosophy animated Jewish life in the sixteenth century. The partners, with their diverse list of titles, sought to reach readers on all sides of this debate. Luzzatto, in his second introduction, came down hard against philosophy. He portrayed *Sefer Ḥasidim* as an anti-Maimonidean, anti-rationalist work, which could restore to the Jewish people a sense of their "spiritual uniqueness" by teaching them the proper fulfillment of the commandments. He did this by quoting extensively, without attribution, from the late-medieval

Aragonese philosopher Hasdei Crescas's treatise *Or Adonai* (written in 1410 but printed for the first time in Ferrara in 1555).[36]

Crescas was one of Maimonides's lesser-known late-medieval critics.[37] In his view, Maimonides had taught that the basic philosophical principles undergirding Jewish law and practice were the same as those of Aristotelian physics and metaphysics. In his words: "Upon their [the philosophers'] weak principles he erected pillars and foundations to support the secrets of the Torah in the book that he called *Guide of the Perplexed*."[38] To remedy this error, Crescas sought to explain the "root-principles and cornerstones upon which the Torah in its totality rests" without recourse to a foreign philosophical tradition.[39]

Maimonides, according to Crescas, had also asserted that the benefit of living according to the Jewish system of commandments (*miẓvoth*) was that they created the necessary context, both psychological and political, for philosophical study. As the spiritual inheritance of the Jewish people, moreover, they were a particularistic path to universal knowledge. Crescas attacked this view as both "excessively intellectual," to paraphrase Hava Tirosh-Samuelson, and a denigration of Judaism itself, because he interpreted Maimonides as positing that the commandments were merely a means to an end.[40]

In *Or Adonai*, by contrast, Crescas asserted that the commandments were ends in themselves and ultimately led to human perfection and union with God. In his words: "Since it is the performance of the commandments that leads to... perfection, but there can be no performance of them without an understanding of them, the following dictum in the Mishnah is to be understood in its literal sense: 'and the study of Torah is the equivalent of all.'"[41] The practice and study of Judaism, for Crescas, elevated humankind to its highest instantiation. At the same time, Crescas wrote, "The final end is the acquisition of the good and the eternal attachment to the radiance of the Divine Presence."[42] The Hebrew term for "Divine Presence," *Shekhinah*, originated in rabbinic literature and there referred to God's numinous presence in "spatio-temporal" terms.[43] Maimonides intellectualized the concept of *Shekhinah*, transforming it into a synonym for the "acquired intellect," that is, the substance of true knowledge transferred from God to the individual in the process of cognition. According to Zev Harvey, Crescas rejected Maimonides's definition, believing that illumination by the "radiance of the

Divine Presence" was not merely a cognitive experience, but rather a spiritual one, in which the individual's soul united with God in an act of love and devotion through the performance of the commandments.[44] Thus, the commandments permitted the Jewish people to attain a status unavailable to all others; as Crescas wrote: "It was therefore necessary, when the kindness of the blessed and exalted One determined to perfect us, the congregation of the community of Israel, that He increase our acts"—meaning, the *mizvoth*.[45]

A lengthy quotation from the newly printed *Or Adonai* in Luzzatto's second introduction emphasized both the Jewish people's particularity and the significance of the commandments. "We must praise the God of Israel," Luzzatto began, and then quoted Crescas:

> In the magnitude of His kindness and the abundance of His goodness, God was provident over all from the realm of His abode, and chose the house of Jacob in whose midst to rest His glory, that they [the Israelites] might love and be in awe of Him, serve Him, and cleave unto Him. For to live thus is the pinnacle of human happiness, in pursuit of which many have become perplexed and have walked in darkness, to prepare the way for us, the way of life, a way that would be so very distant without them—Who could find it?—unless there shone upon it the true light that is called "the radiance of the Divine Presence."[46]

Jews expressed their love for God, united with God, and attained perfection and immortality by enacting the commandments, what Luzzatto and Crescas called "the way for us, the way of life." A similar claim appeared in *Sefer Ḥasidim*, §300:

> [God] gave [humankind] freedom to do good or evil and desired that they shall do His will without seeking a reward. Regarding those who love the pleasures of the world and those who fear for providential punishment, the Holy Blessed One says, "Do My will in order that it will be good for you and your children forever, and there are words of rebuke if you do not do My will." However, regarding one who does [God's bidding] out of love, he does not specify [literally "say"] their reward, because their reward is infinite.

For Luzzatto, *Sefer Ḥasidim* represented an access point through which Jews could reacquaint themselves with the meaning of the commandments, learn to love and serve God, and thereby acquire their transcendent reward. Within its pages, those commandments were distilled down to their essence. *Sefer Ḥasidim*, Luzzatto wrote,

> includes the root of the commandments and their branches and the branches of their branches in straightforward explanations, pleasant and honorable, with every luscious fruit [Song of Songs 4:13], and ethical teachings and rebuke for the collective and the individual. With awe-inspiring and marvelous tales that happened in the days of the pious ones.[47]

According to this description, *Sefer Ḥasidim* was composed of the two essential genres of rabbinic literature: *halakhah* (law—"the commandments") and *aggadah* (lore—"awe-inspiring and marvelous tales"), the normative and the narrative.[48] Its lore in particular was meant to arouse religious devotion.[49] Contemplating *Sefer Ḥasidim* and following its guidance allowed Jews to fulfill their destiny, their "perfection," among the nations.

But, for Luzzatto, *Sefer Ḥasidim* was more than a religious how-to book. It was, in the parlance of rabbinic Judaism, a "scroll of secrets" (*megilat s'tarim*), a canonical text, once oral but then written down in times of persecution. The concept of the "scroll of secrets" appeared in *Or Adonai*, where Crescas offered a précis of the traditional origin story of Judaism's dual concept of Scripture, the Written Torah (*Torah she-bikhtav*, the Hebrew Bible), and the Oral Torah (*Torah she-ba'al peh*, rabbinic literature). Drawing on the Talmud and medieval sources, Crescas explained that, in ancient times, the Oral Torah had been transmitted person to person verbally, but it was ultimately written down to prevent its loss in the face of persecution.[50] Luzzatto quoted Crescas's retelling of this origin story in his second introduction (here in bold), interspersing his own interpolations (here in regular type):

> **When troubles rained down on Israel**, and the exiles multiplied, forgetfulness became frequent, **the number of disciples who were insufficiently diligent in their studies increased, disputes proliferated, and several of these men allowed themselves to write down what was transmitted to them [orally]. They called these writings a "scroll of secrets."**[51]

A "scroll of secrets" was thus an *aide memoire*, a necessary expedient that prevented the substance of the Oral Torah from being forgotten among the Jewish people.

Notably, Crescas had identified the Greeks—pioneers of philosophy and persecutors of Jews—as the source of Israel's troubles. His original text read, "When, however, the Greeks rose to ascendancy and troubles rained down on Israel..." Luzzatto revised this statement, replacing the trauma of Hellenism's rise with "exiles" and "forgetfulness," more general crises that perhaps referred to recent events, such as the cataclysmic Spanish expulsion, the Counter-Reformation book burnings, and even the ongoing attraction of Aristotelian rationalism. Luzzatto argued that, in the face of these storms, *Sefer Ḥasidim* could help the Jewish people recover their religious commitments and their uniqueness among the nations. Reading it would allow Jews to remember all they had forgotten due to the exigencies of the times.[52]

Sefer Ḥasidim was as canonical as any of the great works of rabbinic tradition, Luzzatto asserted further. It was, like the stone tablets of the biblical covenant, "written with the finger of God" (*katuv ba-eẓba' Elohi[m]*, Exodus 31:18 and Deuteronomy 9:10)[53] and,

> Everyone who accustoms himself and his family to reading in it every day one portion thereby fulfills the lifelong obligation [as encapsulated in the teaching], "A man must divide his years into thirds..." [Babylonian Talmud, *Kiddushin* 30a]. From what source do we derive all that is in it [this teaching]? "Turn it and turn it, for everything is in it" [Mishnah, *Avot* 5:22].[54]

Here, Luzzatto cited the Babylonian Talmud's dictum that a person should reserve thirds of his life for studying the Written Torah, the Mishnah, and the Talmud (the latter two being the foremost works of the Oral Torah). Luzzatto equated *Sefer Ḥasidim* with those three venerable literatures. This was, no doubt, a touch of hyperbole, and similar claims appeared in other sixteenth-century Hebrew paratexts. Yet, when read alongside Luzzatto's assertion that *Sefer Ḥasidim* was a "scroll of secrets," and his assertions about *Sefer Ḥasidim*'s ancient origins, Luzzatto's analogy here suggests that he believed *Sefer Ḥasidim* was part of the Jewish canon of Torah. And, further, *Sefer Ḥasidim*, like these canonical texts, possessed a capacious meaning worthy, in the words of the Mishnah, of being "turned and turned again," through ongoing interpretation.[55]

Luzzatto's claim that *Sefer Ḥasidim* was a "secret scroll," the written remains of a formerly oral canonical tradition, is reminiscent of claims made about Kabbalah during the medieval and early modern periods. Kabbalah, too, was understood by its adherents as a corpus of traditions first transmitted orally and then written down in the face of forgetting.[56] During the mid- and late sixteenth century, a fierce debate emerged about whether kabbalistic texts, especially the literature of the Zohar, could be printed and circulated beyond a limited elite. Advocates for printing argued that the promulgation of these mystical texts was necessary because, in the oft-quoted language of the Psalms, "It is a time to act for the Lord, for they have violated Your teaching" (119:126).[57] Just as the sages permitted the writing down of the Oral Torah ("acting for the Lord") in the face of the exigencies of ancient history ("they have violated Your teaching"), so, too, it was permitted to print the Kabbalah in the face of early modern persecution.[58] In fact, some advocates argued, the Kabbalah was as much a part of the Oral Torah as were the other works of ancient rabbinic provenance.[59] It should not be a surprise, therefore, that Luzzatto deployed similar rhetoric in commending *Sefer Ḥasidim* to readers. He was, as his descendent Samuel David Luzzatto wrote, a "true Kabbalist," who popularized passages from the Zohar in his *Kavvanot ha-aggadot.*[60] *Sefer Ḥasidim,* Luzzatto believed, had a place in the Jewish canon alongside other printed rabbinic and kabbalistic works.

Aggadah and Authorship

While Luzzatto wrote that *Sefer Ḥasidim* contained both *halakhah* and *aggadah,* he was particularly interested in its *aggadah* and highlighted its relevance for readers in his second introduction. Since antiquity, rabbinic tradition generally understood that the Oral Torah was composed of both *halakhah* and *aggadah*—the latter a catchall for tales, homilies, exegesis, and historical accounts from antiquity. The Talmud, among other works, jumbled these genres together, yet the curriculum of the *yeshivah,* as it developed, privileged training students in the explication of *halakhah* and relegated *aggadah* to the margins.

In the sixteenth century, some scholars sought to rebalance the scales in favor of *aggadah.* Foremost among them was the Spanish exile R. Jacob ibn Ḥabib (1460–1516), author of the compendium of *aggadah* and commentary *Ein Ya'akov* (1516). Jacob believed *aggadah* possessed the spiritual succor necessary for Jews to withstand the temptations of philosophy.[61] The Maharal of Prague (R. Judah Loew ben Bezalel, d. 1609), similarly, believed that the *aggadah* was a source of esoteric wisdom and authored two books explicating aggadic passages from the Babylonian Talmud.[62] By contrast, Azariah de' Rossi, in his magnum opus, *Me'or einayim* (1573–1575), was dismissive.

In the sixteenth century, Christian missionaries and polemicists had begun to call attention to *aggadah* as proof of Jewish blindness and folly.[63] Among the more infamous passages they cited was the story from the Babylonian Talmud (*Gittin* 56b) that a gnat had flown into Roman emperor Titus's ear and caused him to go mad. Such stories, Christian critics argued, confirmed that Jews were fated to remain benighted. De' Rossi sought to nullify these attacks, as his medieval predecessor R. Moses Naḥmanides (1197–1270) had, by denying the *aggadah* any normative or historical value. In this way, it could be a source of moral teaching and even entertainment, though it did not possess the status of truth.[64]

Over and against de' Rossi, and in the face of recent "exiles" and "forgetfulness," Luzzatto, like ibn Ḥabib, believed that *aggadah* could provide spiritual succor and reinforce Jewish religious commitment. His *Kavvanot ha-aggadot* was a companion volume to ibn Ḥabib's, a digest of aggadic passages in the Babylonian Talmud, accompanied by Luzzatto's allegorical commentaries and cross-references to other works, including *Sefer Ḥasidim*.[65] With *Kavvanot ha-aggadot* in hand, Luzzatto argued, Jewish students would come to know "the true, hidden meaning of the Torah" (*sodot* or *sitrei Torah*) and the "root of faith" (*shoresh ha-emuna*).[66] In his book, Luzzatto juxtaposed *aggadot* from the Babylonian Talmud with those of the Palestinian Talmud, late antique *midrash* (exegesis) collections, the Zohar, and *Sefer Ḥasidim*. By including the newly printed Zohar and *Sefer Ḥasidim* with the other, better-known canonical works, he once again signaled that these works were of a piece, all part of the rabbinic canon, all relevant to the spiritual challenges of the day.

In his second introduction to *Sefer Ḥasidim*, Luzzatto emphasized the significance of the *aggadah* in *Sefer Ḥasidim*. As opposed to its halakhic content, "the axis around which *Sefer Ḥasidim* revolved" was the book's aggadic passages: the "rationales for the commandments [*ta'amei ha-mitẓvot*] or pleasant, literal scriptural exegesis [*peshatim ne'imim*], homilies [*d'rashot*], ethical teachings [*musarim*], good and upright virtues [*middot tovot va-y'sharot*], and proper conduct [*derekh ereẓ*]." It was meritorious, Luzzatto wrote, "with respect to the statements of the tales [*ma'asim*] and the occurrences [*ha-korot*] that are recounted . . . to explicate [*lidrosh*] them intelligently and with good sense."[67] Luzzatto, here, obliquely countered de' Rossi's argument that *aggadah* was not worthy of extended consideration. For Luzzatto, all this material was worthy of "explication" (*drishah*), like all Torah.

Luzzatto further challenged de' Rossi's dismissal of *aggadah* while praising the book's table of contents (which we will have occasion to discuss in greater detail later). Luzzatto wrote:

> Within [a short] time, one who inquires in the table of contents [in this edition] will come to the source of the book itself... Therefore, we chose a long and a short way to make references, including laws that are put forward and the tales.... For whatever way we may extract the pearl from the sand, there is no harm and no reason for fear, as the *Guide* [*of the Perplexed*] says in its introduction.[68]

Luzzatto's reference to extracting "the pearl from the sand" was an adaptation of a statement found in de' Rossi's *Me'or einayim*, which itself was an allusion to Maimonides's "parable of the pearl" at the outset of his *Guide of the Perplexed*. In the *Guide*, Maimonides articulated a theory of scriptural interpretation that asserted that the words of Scripture were written in code, their true meaning purposefully obscured by a deceptive artifice:

> The internal meaning of the *words of the Torah* is a *pearl* whereas the external meaning of all parables *is* worth *nothing*, and their comparison of the concealment of the subject by its parable's external meaning to a man who let drop a pearl in his house, which was dark and full of furniture. Now this pearl is there, but he does not see it and does not know where it is. It is as though it were no longer in his possession, as it is impossible for him to derive any benefit from it until, as has been mentioned, he lights a lamp—an act to which an understanding of the meaning of the parable corresponds.[69]

For Luzzatto, *Sefer Ḥasidim* was just such a pearl lost in a dark house, a book possessing profound yet occluded meaning. Its oral transmission and then its status as a "secret scroll" led to its acquiring textual distortions. According to Luzzatto, it was full of "stammering, distorted, and stiff language. Sometimes [there are passages] transmitted many times repetitiously. [There are] verbal corruptions that came [into the text] at various points."[70]

There was, however, a subtle discrepancy between the imagery in Maimonides's parable—a pearl lost in a dark house—and Luzzatto's analogy of *Sefer Ḥasidim* to a pearl "extracted" from sand. This discrepancy resulted from the fact that Luzzatto, in referring to the pearl, was in fact quoting, without attribution, from de' Rossi's *Me'or einayim*. In *Me'or einayim*, de' Rossi made the pearl a metaphor for the dubious stories found in *aggadah*. According to de' Rossi,

> Our sages saw no reason to divert themselves from the study of the Torah to which they were completely committed and to waste part of their time in giving mental application to detailed investigation of the facts either for their own edification or for our instruction. If they did want to give us any information about these things, they were content to extract for the purposes of the moment anything valuable they could take from the dross. When they would happen to relate some aspect of these matters, they, as it were, set their sights on attaining the worthwhile purpose to which they were aspiring. Such is the way the author of the *Guide* accounts for the fifth cause [of contradictory statements] in his introduction.[71]

De' Rossi thus explained that the sages of antiquity wrote *aggadah* to assist their students in understanding the meaning of Scripture. They followed the method described by Maimonides in his *Guide*, in which the teacher is "lax... using any means that occur to him or gross speculation" to make complex premises simpler for the student.[72] Similarly, the sages of antiquity, de' Rossi explained, created the *aggadah* only as an expedient to help students understand the message of Scripture and to promote its understanding among the masses, because, and here we come to the sentence in question, "In whatever way you extract the pearl from the sand, there is no harm nor reason to fear should one grope and turn it around to one's heart's content."[73] Luzzatto thus turned de' Rossi's statement on its head. If the religious meaning of Scripture was a pearl for de' Rossi, obscured by fanciful aggadic elements ("sand"), for Luzzatto, *aggadah*, and the aggadic passages of *Sefer Ḥasidim* in particular, were pearls, obscured by textual distortions ("sand"). Only through proper editing and "correction" (*hagahah*), which Zifroni and Luzzatto had undertaken themselves, was it possible to uncover the religious treasure hidden within *Sefer Ḥasidim*.

But if *Sefer Ḥasidim* were a work of *aggadah*, as Luzzatto claimed, how could R. Judah he-Ḥasid have been its "author" (*meḥaber*)?

We have already noted that the title page of Froben's edition, unlike that of the partners' edition, stated explicitly that Judah was *Sefer Ḥasidim*'s author. In his second introduction, Luzzatto clarified what that meant:

> For our reward is with us, and our actions [are] before God [Isaiah 40:10] with respect to the statements of the tales and the occurrences that are recounted... the words themselves and their meaning, to expound on them intelligently and with good sense. Indeed, what the mighty, pious author of blessed memory added are pure and refined words.[74]

Luzzatto wrote here that *Sefer Ḥasidim* was composed of both "statements of the tales and the occurrences . . . the words themselves and their meaning" and "pure and refined words" that "the mighty, pious author [*meḥaber*] of blessed memory added [*hosif*]." The former was the *aggadah*, preexisting canonical material originating in antiquity, like that of the Talmud or the Zohar. The latter were Judah's more recent compositions. Authorship, for Luzzatto, thus involved the joining of preexisting authoritative texts to an author's words. Judah's identity was not concealed or effaced in this patchwork, as it might have been in a medieval manuscript, yet he was not a solitary genius fashioning *Sefer Ḥasidim* out of whole cloth, in the way we might imagine an author today.

Earlier, we noted that, during the sixteenth century, recognizably modern notions of authorship began to emerge partly as a consequence of printers' efforts to win credibility for their publications. Thus, Judah's name appears in both the partners' and Froben's editions of *Sefer Ḥasidim*, in contrast to their manuscript antecedents. Froben's edition, however, made this attribution more prominent by placing Judah's name on the title page in enlarged type. In the partners' edition, Judah's role was overshadowed by that of the partners, who had their names, not Judah's, emblazoned on the title page. Luzzatto reaffirmed *Sefer Ḥasidim*'s ascription to Judah in his second introduction, but rather than depicting the book as solely Judah's creation in the way we might imagine a modern author, Luzzatto described Judah's role as that of an anthologizer and adapter of preexisting work. There was precedent for this: Canonical works of *aggadah* and Kabbalah, such as *Pirkei de-Rabbi Eliezer* and the Zohar, joined ancient materials with newly composed elements and ascribed the totality to named individuals from antiquity.[75] In his second introduction, Luzzatto placed *Sefer Ḥasidim* among these venerable anthologies. What differed, of course, was that, unlike R. Eliezer b. Hyrcanus and R. Shimon bar Yoḥai, the purported ancient authors of *Pirkei de-Rabbi Eliezer* and the Zohar respectively, Judah was an undeniably medieval figure engaged in creating a work of rabbinic tradition. In this way, while the title page of Froben's edition unambiguously proclaimed Judah's authorship of *Sefer Ḥasidim*, unlike the partners' title page, Luzzatto's second introduction walked back that claim somewhat, reasserting older notions of literary creativity as compilatory and anthological.

A Navigable Book

The table of contents in Froben's *Sefer Ḥasidim* edition, to which we have already referred, was four pages long; it followed Luzzatto's second introduction (figure 9). It is unclear who composed this table; it is similar in style and organization to others in Froben's books, and, as Froben's editor and corrector, Zifroni certainly would have had the skill and authority to do so. (He too, we noted in chapter 4, considered himself an "author," *meḥaber*, after all.) On the other hand, Luzzatto wrote about the table's import in his second introduction, as we have seen, and perhaps this signaled that he himself had composed it. Regardless, this table was structured differently than R. Abraham b. Moses ha-Cohen's table in the partners' edition. We have already observed that Abraham's table summarized all 1,178 passages in the partners' edition. It was not so much a finding aid as a digest of the text. Its entries highlighted the moral and ethical content of *Sefer Ḥasidim* and paid scant attention to its narratives.

The table of contents in Froben's edition is, by comparison, sparse. It contains only 130 entries. They are generally no more than one sentence long and cite a selection of passages, making no attempt at comprehensiveness. Sometimes the table skips large groups of passages; other times, it cites a series one by one, and, at still other times, the table groups consecutive passages by theme, as in the following selection:

> That the soul in death is just as it is in life, also that the dead wear [clothes], and permission is granted to be visible to those who desire [it], and the wicked stand outside, etc. [§]1,132[.]
>
> When a living person might dream of the dead, the reason is that the intellect is not dead. Further, there, all matters [relating to] death[.] [From §1,133] until [§]1,139[.]
>
> A [halakhic] problem: Why did they say a man should not fraternize with his [female] relatives [even] after—the [time of the] Second Temple—they blinded the eyes of the evil inclination? [§]1,138[.]
>
> That one should set the Book of Leviticus as the start of a boy's education when one reads to him, there [at §]1,140[.][76]

As this excerpt demonstrates, the table manifests a certain lack of precision. Occasionally, it reverses the order of passages: Here, the sequence of entries begins with §1,132, then skips to §1,139, then regresses to §1,138, and afterward returns to numerical order with §1,140.[77] Similarly, sometimes its numbering does not correspond to that of the text. In the quoted text, the concept that "permission is granted to be visible to those who desire [it], and the wicked stand outside" is in fact contained in the preceding passage, §1,131, not in §1,132. In addition, the table frequently summarizes large sections of consecutive passages by theme, as it does in the second entry.

In Ann Blair's and Peter Stallybrass's terms, this table of contents was designed to promote "consultation" or "nonlinear" reading. A reader searching for passages on a particular topic, such as repentance or marriage, could easily find them by skimming and looking up citations. As Luzzatto wrote in his second introduction:

> We did not want to change its [the book's] meaning and damage it with the table of contents that predecessors established [Deuteronomy 19:14]. Full of errors, their "faces covered with nettles" and "all grown over with thistles" [Proverbs 24:31]. We also saw that there was no benefit to lengthening the book with them—as they said, "One should always teach the short way" [Babylonian Talmud, *Pesaḥim* 3a], and the converse does greater damage than benefit. For maybe they will rely on the short summaries, which instruct about the essence of the book, and may never come to knowledge of the essence of the idea?[78]

Luzzatto did not restrain his criticism of Abraham's table of contents. It was so "full of errors" that it was "all grown over with thistles" and "covered with nettles." Even more tellingly, Luzzatto argued that Abraham's table obscured the true meaning of *Sefer Ḥasidim* because readers were more likely to consult its "short summaries" (*kelalim keẓarim*)—trusting that they accurately reflected the content of each passage—and bypass the text itself.[79]

Luzzatto's criticisms of the table of contents in the partners' edition recall R. Abraham Mintz of Padua's attack on R. Abraham b. Moses ha-Cohen, discussed in chapter 3, whom he believed relied overmuch on the newly printed reference aids of the sixteenth century rather than on a careful and thorough reading of texts. Luzzatto touted the new table of contents in Froben's edition because it was not meant to replace the text but, instead, facilitate the text's exploration and elucidate its meaning: "Within [a short] time," Luzzatto wrote, "one who inquires in the references [in this edition] will come to the essence of the book itself."

Stallybrass has also shown how early modern reference aids often served political or religious agendas. Reference aids in printed Bibles directed readers to verses that affirmed the theological positions of particular communities and factions. They therefore functioned as interpretive matrices, determining which parts of a text readers consulted and how they understood the meaning of the text as a whole.[80] This was certainly the case with the table of contents in Froben's edition, which privileged *aggadah*—and a particular type of *aggadah*, the *ma'aseh* (plural *ma'asim*, *ma'asiyot*).

Over a third of the table's entries employ the term *ma'aseh* explicitly to highlight the presence of *ma'asim* in *Sefer Ḥasidim* passages. While I have chosen to translate this term as "tale," its meaning is not self-evident. It is a noun derived from the Hebrew verb "to do" or "to make" (with the root *ayin-shin-hey*). As such, it may be accurately translated as an "action," "event," or "incident."[81] In Tannaitic texts (rabbinic texts dating from roughly the first two centuries CE), a *ma'aseh* was an "incident" or a "story," often about a sage, from which a Jewish legal principle was derived. Thus, in this early Talmudic stratum, a *ma'aseh* was an aggadic, nonlegal exemplum, linked to *halakhah*.[82]

By the medieval period, however, as Lucia Raspe and Erika Timm have shown, the term *ma'aseh* began to take on a more general meaning: simply a "tale" with no associated halakhic content.[83] In the sixteenth century, *ma'asim* (also, *ma'asiyot*) and the Yiddish cognate *mayses* (singular *mayse*) came to denote a new genre of popular literature as well as printed anthologies of tales in Hebrew and Yiddish, such as the *Ki-bukh* (c. 1555) and *Maysebukh* (1602).[84] These titles were meant first and foremost to entertain and often featured vivid depictions of daily life, as well as hagiographies of sages. Some of the *mayses* were based on sources from antiquity, while others were entirely new compositions. Indeed, in his *Kavvanot ha-aggadot*, Luzzatto anthologized a number of ancient *ma'asim* (including some that were subsequently contained in the *Maysebukh*).[85] It is not surprising, therefore, given both Luzzatto's interest in *aggadah* and the popularity of *ma'asim* among sixteenth-century Hebrew readers, that the table of contents in Froben's edition highlighted these elements.

Moreover, the table often emphasized *ma'asim* at the expense of the legal, ethical, and theological content of *Sefer Ḥasidim* passages. For example, the fifth entry in the table of contents reads:

> A tale of a woman who came to the house of study of R. Meir and said, "One of you betrothed me through sexual relations," etc. [§]22[.][86]

In fact, the passage summarized in the previous entry contains a much more complex discussion of the responsibilities of someone suspected of committing a sin:

> (a) One who sinned in a particular matter, and others are suspected, must say, "I am he, for I sinned," in order that everyone will not sin on his account by suspecting those who are innocent.
>
> (b) If he is in the company of other people, and a thing is done that is not proper, and it was not known who the sinner is, it is necessary that he should say, "I am he, for I sinned," even if he did not sin. And through me the sinner will confess and not be humiliated, like the tale of R. Meir:
>
> (c) There is a tale about a certain woman who came to the house of study of R. Meir. She said to them, "One of you betrothed yourself to me through sexual intercourse!" R. Meir stood up and wrote a bill of divorce and gave it to her.
>
> (d) Even one who confesses for others can say, "we sinned," and dirty himself with them, since "all Israel is bound to one another" [*Sifre* to Numbers, *Beḥukotai* 7:5].
>
> (e) If he saw people sinning and did not protest, he must confess even though he [himself] did not sin. When he confesses, he should remember all his sins as they are. If he does not repent on account of some of his sins, he should say, "You are our Creator, and You know our urges. Overpower the urge of our hearts and circumcise our foreskins, that our necks will no longer be stiff."[87]

Only one part of §22 contains a *ma'aseh*, section (c). The preceding and succeeding sections enumerate guidelines for how a pious person should comport himself after committing a sin or when he is in the presence of someone who commits a sin. By contrast, the table of contents in the partners' edition has a more accurate summary of this passage: "He who sinned in one matter, and the masses are suspicious, must say, 'I am he,' in order that the innocent will not be suspected." In this way, the table of contents in Froben's edition actualized the literary arguments Luzzatto made about *Sefer Ḥasidim* in his second introduction: It invited readers to those passages that were primarily aggadic and narrative in nature, leaving aside other literary elements.

While Froben's *Sefer Ḥasidim* was primarily directed at Jewish readers, it was printed during a period of Christian interest in Hebrew learning in general and *aggadah* in particular, and its table of contents also highlighted passages in *Sefer Ḥasidim* that were of interest to these readers. Nearly a quarter of the entries in the table, for example, refer to the afterlife, angels, or demons. These themes were of particular interest to Hebraists, who mined Jewish sources for occult wisdom.[88] Given its overall brevity, the table gives especially detailed descriptions of passages related to, for example, ghosts, such as, "The tale of a foreign woman [*nokhrit*] who died and returned and said that she saw in that world a Jewess whose hand was defiled with the fat with which she made a fire too close to [the start of Sabbath] eve" (§270).[89] Or, "On Hoshana Rabba eve, the souls go out from their graves to pray, and there [are also in this passage] matters [concerning] the dead and martyrs" (§452).[90] While these themes account for only a small portion of the book's overall content, a reader of the table of contents would not be faulted for thinking that the occult was *Sefer Ḥasidim*'s major preoccupation.

Similarly, the table of contents also highlighted passages concerning the relationships of Jews to non-Jews and to Jewish converts to Christianity. It called attention to such passages as the one discussed in chapter 3 (§188): "The tale of one whose son converted, and his father and his mother wanted to give him money to cause him to return to their house" and (§859): "The tale that happened to a certain apostate [*mumar*], when there was a fire on the Sabbath, [who] said, 'Give me your book and I will rescue them [*sic*] from the fire.'" Christian Hebraists maintained an abiding interest in Jewish attitudes toward Christians and Christianity, composing, in Ronnie Po-Chia Hsia's terms, "ethnographies" meant to highlight those elements of Jewish tradition and custom that they perceived as anti-Christian.[91] Johannes Buxtorf the Elder, for example, recorded extracts from Hebrew texts and his own observations of Jewish daily life in his notebook as part of a larger scholarly project demonstrating the contemptibility of Judaism and superiority of Christianity.[92] In their preoccupation with magic and anti-Christian animus, these ethnographies called attention to Jewish concepts and practices that most validated Christians' polemical predisposition to perceiving Jews and Judaism as superstitious and inherently hostile.[93]

By featuring the magical and ethnographic elements in *Sefer Ḥasidim*, the table of contents showed how printers of a book primarily for Jews could attract a secondary readership among Christians. The concerns and interests of Christian readers could shape the construction of paratexts that directed readers to passages validating their presuppositions about Judaism. (Of course, these same passages might be of interest to Jews, for different reasons.) In this, Froben and his team were successful in attracting the interest of at least one Hebraist, Isaac Casaubon, whom, we noted earlier, owned a copy. His marginalia in that book indicate that he took a special interest in *Sefer Ḥasidim*'s *ma'asim.*[94]

Conclusion

The title page, introductions, and table of contents of Froben's *Sefer Ḥasidim* edition indicate that it was part of a surge of late-sixteenth-century Hebrew books for Jewish students (*talmidim*). With his paratexts containing quotations from Crescas's *Or Adonai* and de' Rossi's *Me'or einayim,* Luzzatto endowed the book with an antique pedigree and imposed on it a canonical veneer. As Luzzatto presented it, R. Judah he-Ḥasid compiled and composed *Sefer Ḥasidim,* joining his words to those of ancient sources. Like the Zohar, it was a canonical text containing an antidote to Maimonidean rationalism and spiritual succor in the face of the persecutions of the late sixteenth century.

Unlike the partners' edition, Froben's *Sefer Ḥasidim* was produced in a Christian-owned print shop, in a city where the settlement of Jews was curtailed. This shop was emblematic of the heterogeneous world of late-sixteenth-century printing, where Jews and Christians labored side by side to produce new editions of Hebrew texts.[95] The paratexts in Froben's *Sefer Ḥasidim* were reflective of this heterogeneous social location. While Froben and his team emphasized that their book was produced primarily for Jews, they also made sure that it would be of interest to Hebraists, an intention that is even more apparent in Zifroni's textual emendations, to which we will now turn.

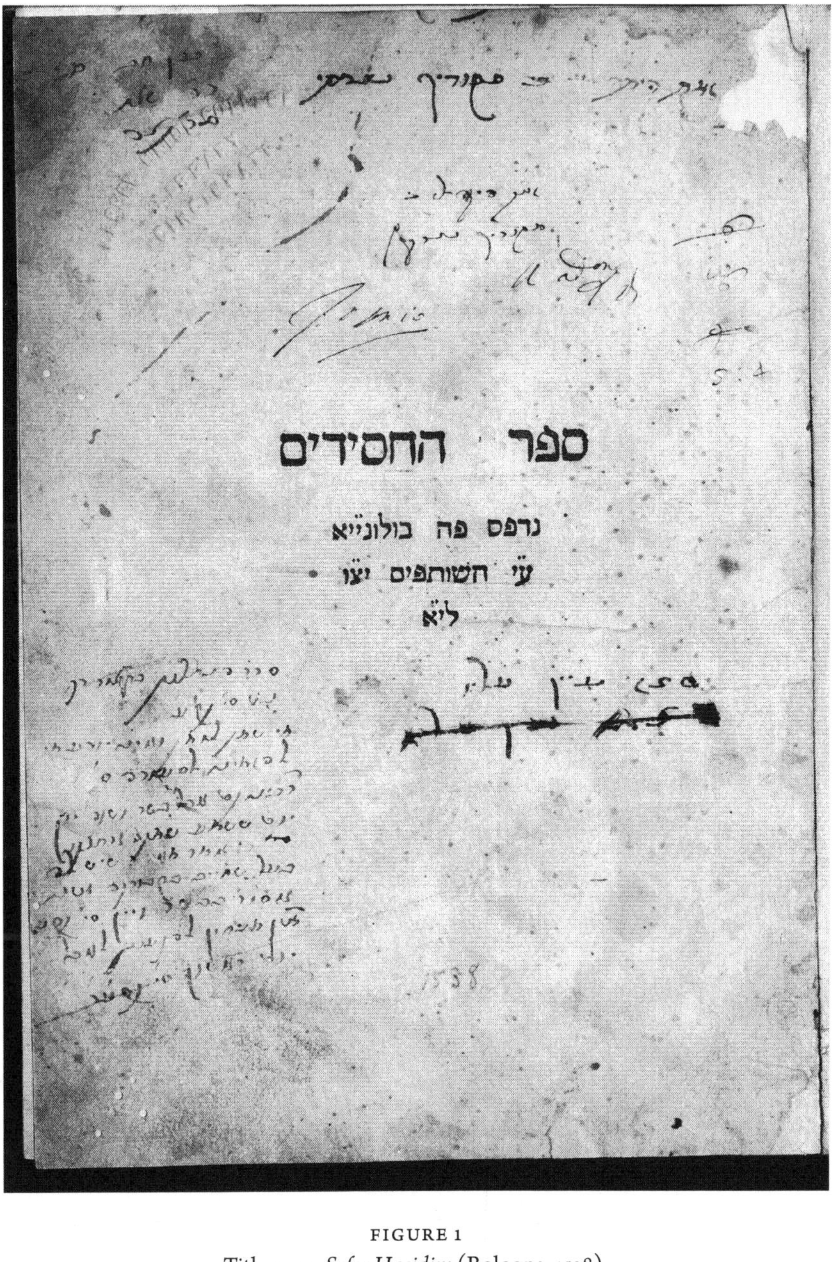

FIGURE 1

Title page, *Sefer Ḥasidim* (Bologna, 1538).

Courtesy of the Klau Library, Cincinnati,
Hebrew Union College-Jewish Institute of Religion.

FIGURE 2

Title page, Bomberg's Babylonian Talmud, *Tractate Berakhot* (Venice, 1520).

Courtesy of the Klau Library, Cincinnati,
Hebrew Union College-Jewish Institute of Religion.

-9746-

יתברך

ספר החסידים

FIGURE 3

Introduction, *Sefer Ḥasidim* (Bologna, 1538).

Courtesy of the Klau Library, Cincinnati, Hebrew Union College-Jewish Institute of Religion.

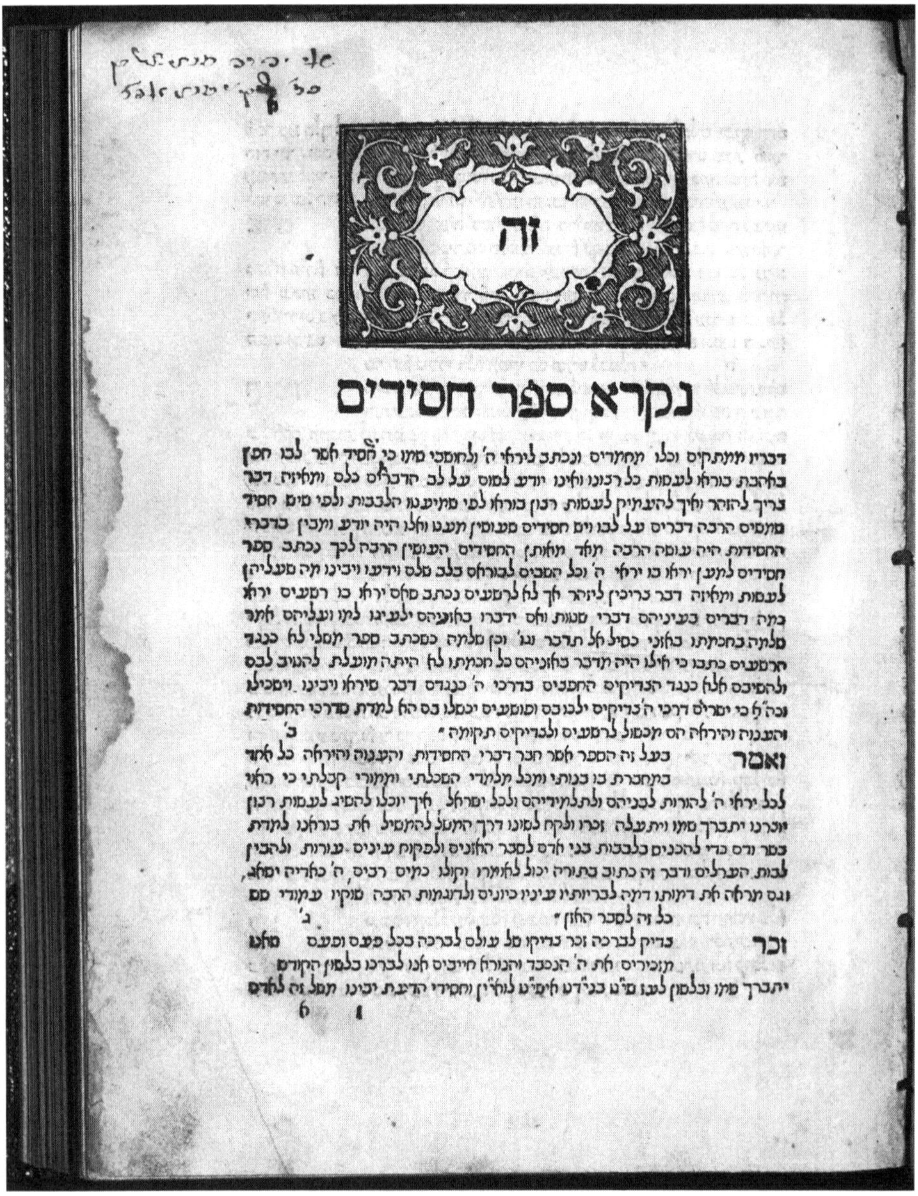

זה

נקרא ספר חסידים

FIGURE 4

Page 1a, *Sefer Ḥasidim* (Bologna, 1538).

Courtesy of the Klau Library, Cincinnati,
Hebrew Union College-Jewish Institute of Religion.

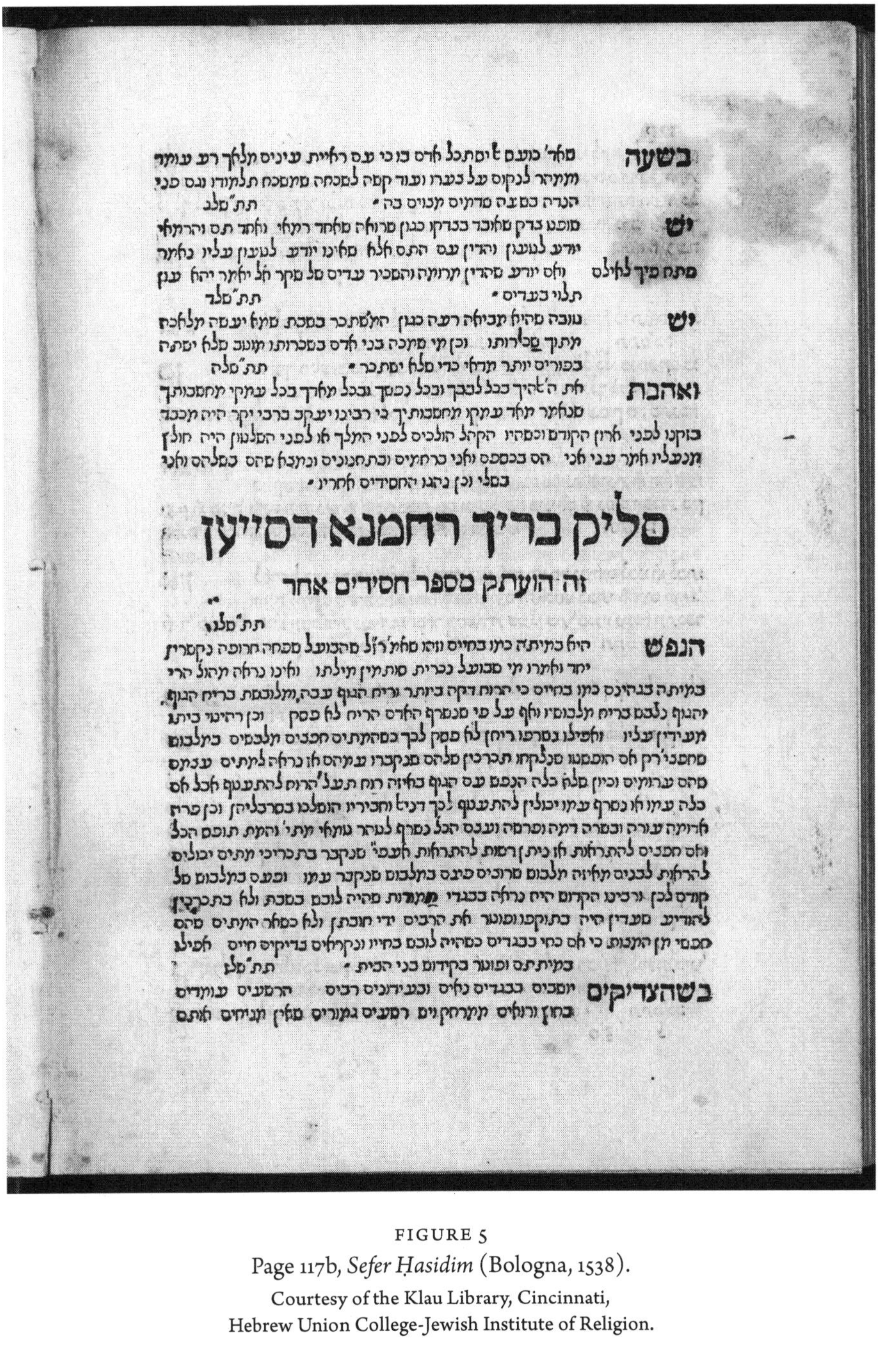

בשעה

יש

פתח פיך לאלם

יש

ואהבת

סליק בריך רחמנא דסייען

זה הועתק מספר חסידים אחר

הנפש

בשהצדיקים

FIGURE 5

Page 117b, *Sefer Ḥasidim* (Bologna, 1538).

Courtesy of the Klau Library, Cincinnati,
Hebrew Union College-Jewish Institute of Religion.

ספר החסידים

לעם ה' השרידים · לסגולי הדור היחידים · המהלכים
האלה בין העומדים · מתוקן בפשטים נעימים
ונכברים · עם מוסרי דרכים טובים
ולמודים · לתלמידים ·

חברו אב וראש לכל החסידים · הקדוש רבינו יהודה החסיד זלה"ה :

הועתק מספר ישן נושן יותר ומוחזק מבעתים : ובגלל
הדבר הזה ישן מפני חדש תוציאו : וכלי זה
אל בית האוצר הביאו :

נדפס בעיר בסיליאה הגדולה

ירום הודה ותנשא מלכותה

במצות השר אמברוסיאו פרוביניאו יגן וכביתו :

ותשלם כל המלאכה בחדש כסלו שנת שמ"א לאין זה כי אם בית אלהים
וזה שער השמים :

FIGURE 6

Title page, *Sefer Ḥasidim* (Basel, 1580).

Courtesy of the Klau Library, Cincinnati,
Hebrew Union College-Jewish Institute of Religion.

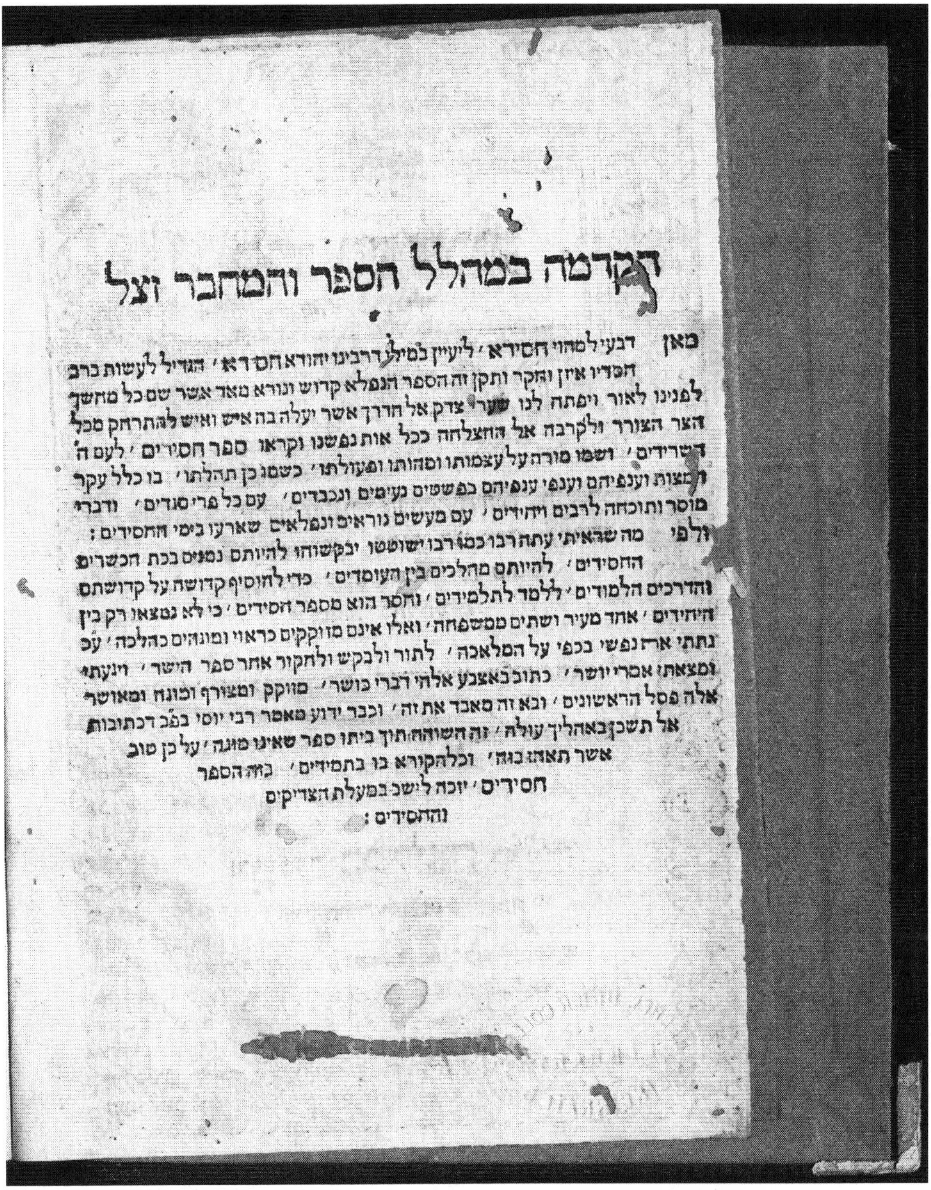

הקדמה במהלל הספר והמחבר זצ״ל

מאן דבעי למהוי חסידא ׳ ליעיין במילי דרבינו יהודא חסידא ׳ הגדיל לעשות כרב חסדיו אזן וחקר ותקן זה הספר הנפלא קדוש ונורא מאד אשר שם כל מחשך לפנינו לאור ויפתח לנו שערי צדק אל הדרך אשר יעלה בה איש ואיש להתרחק מכל הצר הצורר ולקרבה אל ההצלחה ככל אות נפשנו וקראו ספר חסידים ׳ לעם ה׳ השרידים ׳ ושמו מורה על עצמותו ומהותו ופעולתו ׳ כשמו כן תהלתו ׳ בו כלל עקר המצות וענפיהם וענפי ענפיהם במשפטים נעימים ונכבדים ׳ עם כל פריסודים ׳ ודברי מוסר ותוכחה לרבים ויחידים ׳ עם מעשים נוראים ונפלאים שארעו בימי החסידים :

ולפי מה שראיתי עתה רבו כמו רבו ישוטטו יבקשוהו להיותם נמנים בכת הכשרים החסידים ׳ להיותם מהלכים בין העומדים ׳ כדי להוסיף קדושה על קדושתם והדרכים הלמודים ׳ ללמד לתלמידים ׳ נחסר הוא מספר חסידים ׳ כי לא נמצאו רק בין היחידים ׳ אחד מעיר ושתים ממשפחה ׳ ואלו אינם מזוקקים כראוי ומוגהים כהלכה ׳ ע״כ נתתי את נפשי בכפי על המלאכה ׳ לתור ולבקש ולחקור אחר ספר הישר ׳ ויגעתי ומצאתי אמרי יושר ׳ כתוב באצבע אלהי דברי כושר ׳ מזוקק ומצורף ומכוון ומאושר אלה פסל הראשונים ׳ ובא זה מאבד את זה ׳ וכבר ידוע מאמר רבי יוסי בפ״ב דכתובות אל תשכן באהליך עולה ׳ זה השוהה תוך ביתו ספר שאינו מוגה ׳ על כן טוב אשר תאחז בזה ׳ וכל הקורא בו בתמידים ׳ בזה הספר חסידים ׳ יזכה לישב במעלת הצדיקים והחסידים :

FIGURE 7

First introduction (unpaginated), *Sefer Ḥasidim* (Basel, 1580).

Courtesy of the Klau Library, Cincinnati,
Hebrew Union College-Jewish Institute of Religion.

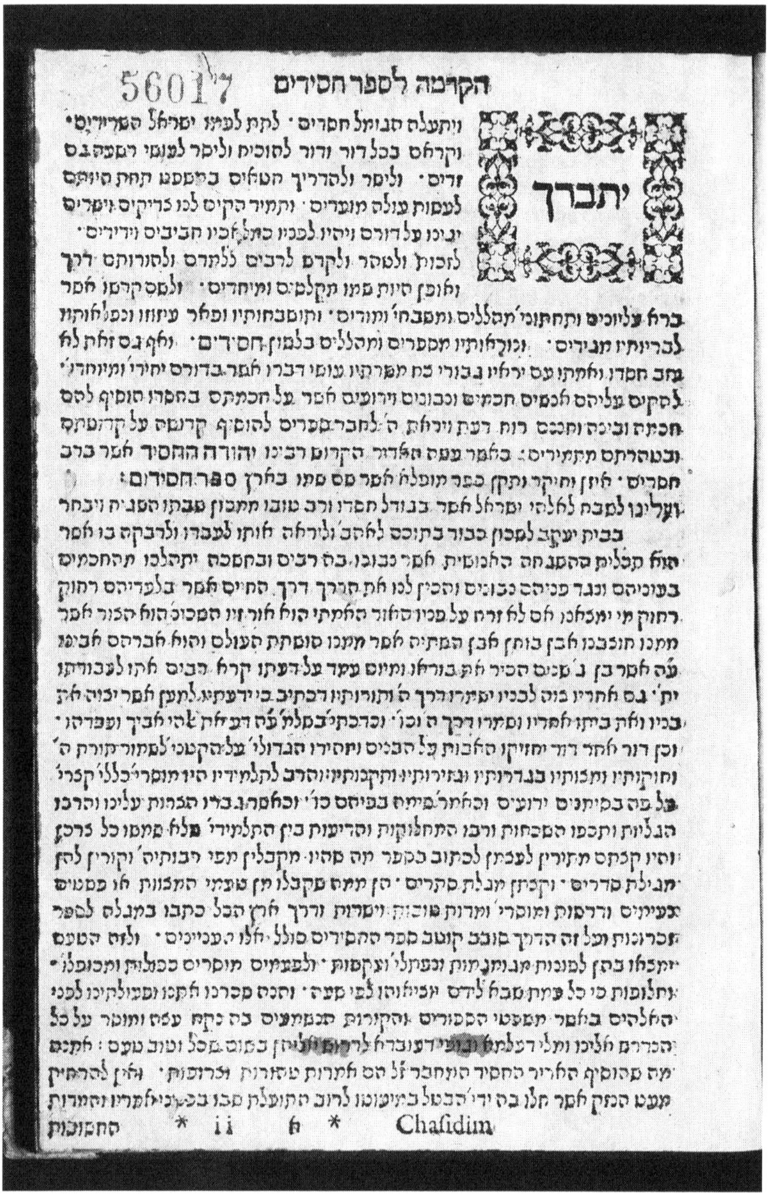

הקדמה לספר חסידים

56017

Chasidim

FIGURE 8

Second introduction, first page (unpaginated), *Sefer Ḥasidim* (Basel, 1580).

Courtesy of the Klau Library, Cincinnati,
Hebrew Union College-Jewish Institute of Religion.

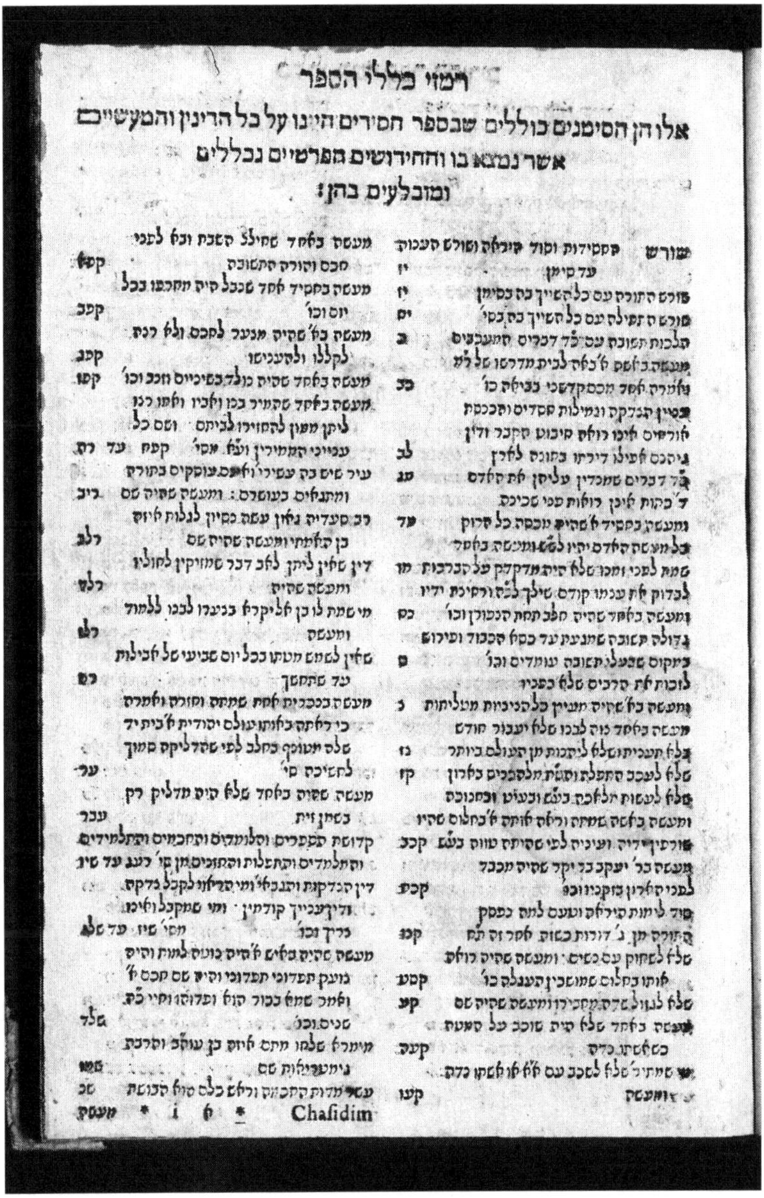

רמזי כללי הספר

אלו הן הסימנים כוללים שבספר חסידים היינו על כל הדינין והמעשיים אשר נמצא בו והחידושים הפרטיים נכללים ומובלעים בהן:

Chafidim

FIGURE 9

Table of contents, first page (unpaginated), *Sefer Ḥasidim* (Basel, 1580).

Courtesy of the Klau Library, Cincinnati,
Hebrew Union College-Jewish Institute of Religion.

ספר חסידים א

זה נקרא ספר חסידים

דבריו ממתקים וכלו מחמדים ונכתב ליראי ה׳ ולחושבי שמו כי חסיד אשר לבו חפץ באהבת בוראו לעשות כל רצונו ואינו יודע לשום על לב הדברים כלם ומאיזה דבר צריך להזהר ואיך להעמיק לעשות רצון בוראו לפי שמיעטו הלבבות ולפי שיש חסיד שמשים הרבה דברים על לבו ויש חסידים שעושין מעט ואילו היה יודע ומבין בדברי החסידות היה עושה הרבה מאד מאותן החסידים העושין הרבה לכך נכתב ספר חסידי׳ למען יראו בו יראי ה׳ וכל השבים לבוראם בלב שלם וידעו ויבינו מה שעליהן לעשות ומאיזה דבר צריכין ליזהר אך לא לרשעים נכתב׳ שאם יראו בו רשעים יהיו נראים כמה דברי׳ בעיניהם דברי שטות ואם ידברו באוניהם ילעיגו למו ועליהם אמר שלמה בחכמתו באזני כסיל אל תדבר וגו׳ וכן שלמה כשכתב ספר משלי לא כנגד הרשעים כתבו כי אילו היה מדבר באוניהם כל חכמתו לא היתה מועלת להטיב לבם ולהשיבם לא כנגד הצדיקים החפצים בדרכיה׳ כנגדם דבר שיראו ויבינו וישכילו וכדכתיב כי ישרים דרכי ה׳ צדיקים ילכו בם ופושעים יכשלו בם הא למדת שדרכי החסידות והענוה והיראה הם מכשול לרשעים ולצדיקים תקומה:

ב ואמר בעל זה הספר אשר חבר דברי החסידו׳ והענוה והיראה כל אחד במחברת בו בנותי ומכל מלמדי השכלתי וממורי קבלתי כי ראוי לכל יראי ה׳ להורות לבניהם ולתלמידיהם ולכל ישרא׳ איך יוכלו להשיג לעשות רצון יוצרנו יתברך שמו ויתעלה זכרו ולקח לשונו דרך המשל להמשיל את בוראנו למדת בשר ודם כדי להכניס בלבבות בני אדם ולסבר האזנים ולפקוח עינים עורות ולהבין לבות הערלי׳ ודבר זה כתוב בתורה וקולו כמים רבים ה׳ כאריה ישאג וגם מראה את דמותו לבריותיו עיניו כיונים ולדוגמות הרבה שוקיו עמודי שש כל זה לסבר האזן:

ג זכר צדיק לברכה זכר צדיקו של עולם לברכה בכל פעם ופעם שאנו מזכירים את ה׳ הנכבד והנורא חייבים אנו לברכו בלשון הקודש יתברך שמו וחסירי הדעת יבינו משל זה לאדם אשר בנו הלך לדרך מרחקי׳ או אוהבו כאשר מזכירו הוא אומ׳ בני לשלו׳ יפקד היום הזה׳ יהיה טוב עליו׳ ומה אדם שמת אומר מנוחתו כבוד׳ הקב״ה שהוא חי וקיים יתברך שמו של יוצרינו על אחת כמה וכמה שיש לברכו על הזכרת שמו שהוא חי וקיים ית׳ שמו הנכבד׳ ועל זה אמרו כל השומע הזכרה מפי חבירו צריך לנדותו׳ ואם

לא a i א א Chaſidim

FIGURE 10

Page 1a, *Sefer Ḥasidim* (Basel, 1580).

Courtesy of the Klau Library, Cincinnati, Hebrew Union College-Jewish Institute of Religion.

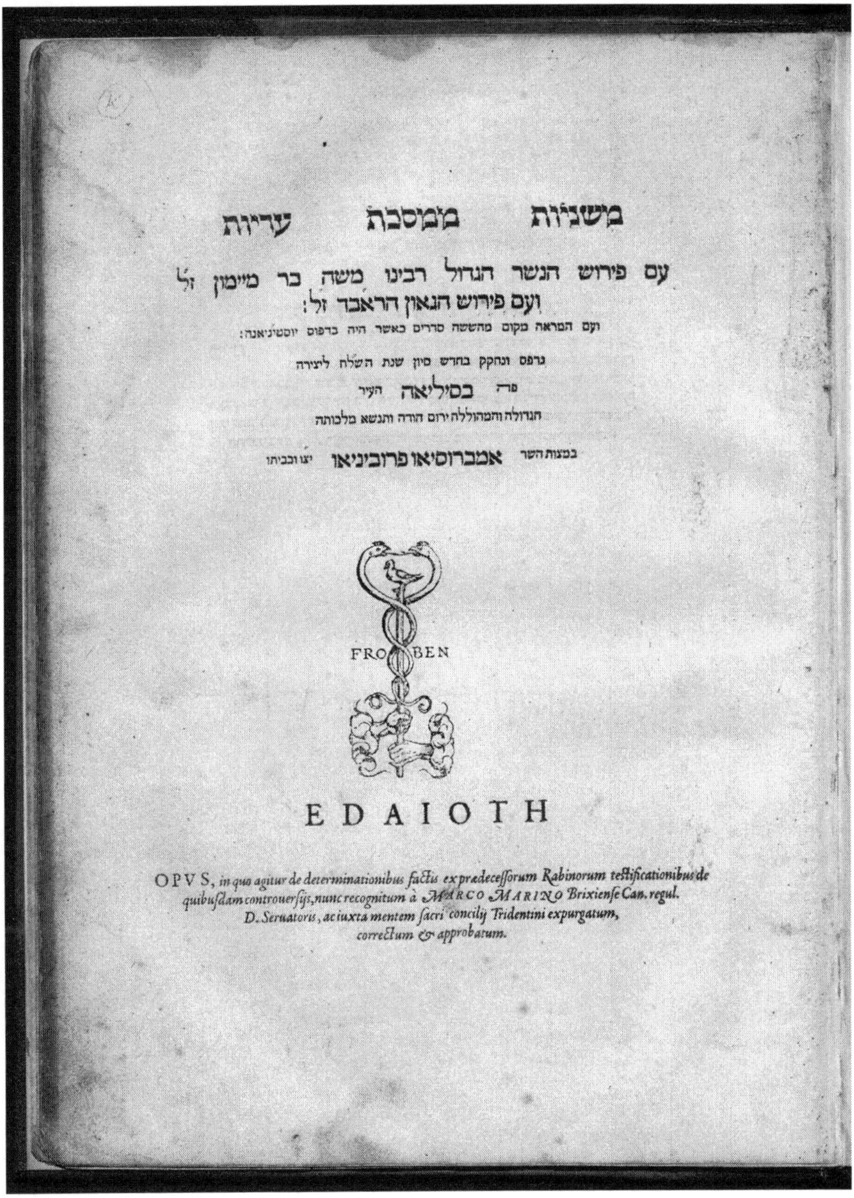

משניות ממסכת עדיות

עם פירוש הנשר הגדול רבינו משה בר מיימון ז״ל

ועם פירוש הגאון הראבד ז״ל:

ועם הוראה מקום מהששה סדרים כאשר היה בדפוס יוסטיניאנה:

נדפס ונחקק בחדש סיון שנת השלח ליצירה

פה בסיליאה העיר

הגדולה והמהוללה ירום הודה ותנשא מלכותה

במצות השר אמברוסיאו פרוביניאו יצו וכביתו

FROBEN

EDAIOTH

OPVS, in quo agitur de determinationibus factis ex prædecessorum Rabinorum testificationibus de quibusdam controuersijs, nunc recognitum à MARCO MARINO Brixiense Can. regul. D. Seruatoris, ac iuxta mentem sacri concilij Tridentini expurgatum, correctum & approbatum.

FIGURE 11

Title page, *Mishnayot mi-masekhet eduyot* (Basel, 1578).

Courtesy of the Klau Library, Cincinnati, Hebrew Union College-Jewish Institute of Religion.

CHAPTER 6

Froben's *Sefer Ḥasidim*

TEXT

And He gave unto Moses, when He had made an end of speaking
with him upon Mount Sinai, the two tables of the testimony,
tables of stone, written with the finger of God.

Exodus 31:18

. . . . .

IN HIS FIRST INTRODUCTION to Froben's *Sefer Ḥasidim* edition, we noted in chapter 5 that R. Jacob Luzzatto analogized *Sefer Ḥasidim* to the stone tablets "written with the finger of God" (*katuv ba-eẓba' Elohim*) that Moses brought down from Mount Sinai.[1] The analogy served Luzzatto's larger goal of presenting *Sefer Ḥasidim* as a canonical book, akin to classic collections of *aggadah*. The typography of the edition reinforced that association: its *Sefer Ḥasidim* text was printed in a square typeface (figure 10). The partners, by contrast, used a semicursive typeface (commonly called "Rashi-script"). The square typeface had, by the late sixteenth century, become synonymous with canonical texts, including the Bible and the Talmud, as well as the liturgy and medieval classics, such as Maimonides's *Mishneh Torah*. On the other hand, printers used the semicursive for noncanonical works, such as commentaries.[2] Printing *Sefer Ḥasidim* in a square typeface signaled to readers that the book was in fact written like the works of Scripture and rabbinic tradition, "with the finger of God."

As we noted in chapter 4, Froben did not possess the skill or expertise to oversee the printing of Hebrew books himself, and so he delegated that work to Zifroni and other professionals. Thus, while Zifroni's name is not present in Froben's *Sefer Ḥasidim* edition, it is reasonable to conclude that Froben's senior deputy bore editorial responsibility for the book. Its *Sefer Ḥasidim* text was, as we noted earlier, based on the partners' edition, but in addition to its typography, Zifroni transformed that text in three principal ways: First, he censored it more aggressively, substantially altering the meaning of several passages. Second, he eliminated Yiddish and Judeo-French terms and phrases. Third, he introduced punctuation and explanatory glosses. With these innovations, Zifroni drove home Luzzatto's point that *Sefer Ḥasidim* was a canonical work of *aggadah* from antiquity. Zifroni's innovations further epitomized the changing contexts of late-sixteenth-century Hebrew printing—the increased surveillance of the Counter-Reformation Church and the emergence of a market for Hebrew books among non-scholarly readers and Christian Hebraists.

Shaved-Heads and Sadducees

While Zifroni certainly collaborated with Luzzatto on Froben's *Sefer Ḥasidim* edition, it is unclear who else may have joined in this project; in fact, its censoring could have been accomplished with the help of Christians. When it was printed, in the autumn of 1580, Pierre Chevalier may still have been in residence at Froben's shop assisting with the completion of the Talmud edition. Some of the modifications in *Sefer Ḥasidim* are reminiscent of those in the Talmud, a point we will consider later in this chapter. Yet, unlike several of the Talmud volumes, the book contained no Christological glosses and no censor's mark (figure 11). One would imagine that a Christian censor such as Chevalier, who had introduced the former into the text of the Talmud, would have done the same in *Sefer Ḥasidim*. Zifroni was certainly capable of applying the methodologies of "correction" and "expurgation" established in Froben's Talmud to *Sefer Ḥasidim*. He, we noted earlier, called himself a "corrector" (*megihah*), and as the partners' edition demonstrates, Jewish printers were willing to censor Hebrew books, even before the Church imposed this practice. Thus, for the purposes of the following analysis, we will assume that Zifroni undertook the censoring of Froben's *Sefer Ḥasidim* edition.

In the aftermath of the book burnings of the 1550s, as we discussed in chapter 4, the Counter-Reformation Church established a formal policy of censorship and expurgation with the Tridentine Index of 1564. This policy was part and parcel of a broader anti-Jewish persecutory program involving exorbitant taxation, ghettoization, and expulsion—as was the case for Bologna's Jews in 1569. Zifroni crafted Froben's edition of *Sefer Ḥasidim* in the shadow of this policy, and consequently he censored the text much more aggressively than the partners had. In their edition of *Sefer Ḥasidim,* the partners had removed elements objectionable to Christians while preserving the meaning of the text and occasionally, in Ruth Langer's terms, even "transform[ing] the intent of" the text.[3] Generally, the partners' interventions involved replacing individual words with alternatives; they did not alter whole sentences and did not delete words or phrases. Zifroni, by contrast, did. His efforts may be summarized as follows: In some passages, he substituted less-objectionable variants for problematic words or phrases, such as *nokhri* for *goy,* just as the partners had. Yet, in other passages, Zifroni went further: He anachronized, substituting terms that could be understood as references to Christians with others that applied to groups from antiquity—crucially, groups that no longer existed. He also universalized, transforming statements that applied exclusively to Christians into statements that applied to all people. And, finally, in some cases, Zifroni eliminated problematic words, phrases, and sentences altogether.

As we noted in chapter 3, the partners' effort to remove objectionable content—like most censorship in the sixteenth century—was haphazard. The production of Froben's edition involved a further winnowing of the suspect elements remaining in its source text.[4] Moreover, it is clear that Zifroni was concerned about the presence of words the partners had previously read as neutral or inoffensive. One example was §221 (table 5), which describes strategies medieval Jews employed to avoid persecution at the hands of crusading armies.[5] Zifroni modified this passage in the following ways: He used (1) the acronym for "idol worship" (*avodat elilim*) in place of the acronym for *avodah zarah*; (2) "servants of pagan idol worship" (*meshartei avodat elilim*), rather than "priests" (*komerim*); and (3) "house of their prayer" (*beit tefillatam*), rather than "house of *avodah zarah*." Additionally, he eliminated the phrase "priests and shaved-heads" (*komerim ve-galaḥim*) altogether.

As discussed earlier, the partners apparently were untroubled by the expression *avodah zarah*; this term appeared throughout their edition. While in antiquity *avodah zarah* referred to pagan ritual practices, in the Middle Ages it came to apply to Christianity and Christians as well.[6] By the late sixteenth century, Christian censors sought to remove all mention of it from Jewish books. Thus, the first principle of expurgation in the convert-censor Domenico Gerosolimitano's *Sefer ha-Zikkuk* (1596) was: "Any instance of *avodah zarah,* which is not meant explicitly as idol worship—namely the *avodah zarah* that existed prior to Christianity—one should write in its place the acronym *ayin-kaf-vav-mem* [pronounced *akum*], meaning, 'worshippers of the stars and constellations.'"[7]

According to Federica Francesconi, Domenico understood *avodah zarah* as an expression of "the idea that Jews claimed superiority over Christianity": Jews practiced the true religion, while Christians practiced little more than pagan idolatry.[8] This pejorative understanding led to elimination of the entire tractate entitled *Avodah Zarah* from Froben's Talmud edition. Similarly, in *Sefer Ḥasidim,* Zifroni replaced *avodah zarah* with alternatives that referred unmistakably to pagan idol worship. This task was made easier because, in their edition, the partners frequently employed the Hebrew acronym *ayin-zayin* in place of the full Hebrew expression. To transform this acronym into an unambiguous reference to idolators, the editors simply had to replace the Hebrew character *zayin* with an *aleph,* resulting in the acronym for *avodat elilim* (pagan idol worship).

With this modification, Zifroni no longer needed to replace another Hebrew term, "foreigner" (*nokhri*), that was found throughout the partners' edition. By the medieval period, Christians perceived this term as a synonym for *goy,* with all its negative associations.[9] Indeed, Domenico equated *goy* and *nokhri,* writing, "names *goy, goyim, nokhri, nokhrit,* if understood as implying any disgrace, slander, and insult to that very *goy,* should be erased, and in its place [should be written the acronym] *akum.*"[10] In many instances, Zifroni indeed replaced *nokhri* with nonpejorative alternatives, a decision that indicated his sensitivity to negative perceptions and his willingness to second-guess the partners. In §221, however, Zifroni avoided having to make a substitution by transforming *avodah zarah* into *avodat elilim,* so that the "foreigners" referred to in the text became unmistakably pagan. Zifroni traded on the ambiguity of the term *nokhri* and assumed that context would prevent Christian readers from taking offense.

Zifroni replaced the word for "priests" (*komerim*) with *m'shartei avodat elilim* (servants of pagan idol worship). In the Bible, the term *komerim* was regularly used to refer to practitioners of idolatrous cults (2 Kings 23; Hosea 10:25), in contrast to the *kohanim* (also "priests") of the Lord.[11] By the Middle Ages, this term, like *avodah zarah,* came to refer to Christian religious figures—an equivalence underscored in the passage by the linkage of *komerim*

Partners' Edition	Froben Edition
(a) "Among the nations, they shall not be reckoned…" [Numbers 23:9]. "All who see shall recognize that they are a stock the Lord has blessed" [Isaiah 61:9]. How so? (b) Jews shall not say, if soldiers come to them, that they will make a sign of ***avodah zarah*** on their clothes, and they shall not make themselves like those who are **priests**. They shall not place on their homes a sign of **idolatry**, and they shall not shave the top of the head **like priests and shaved-heads**, so that the foreigners might think that they are foreigners. (c) If the foreigners pass by and chance upon them, the Jews, and the foreigners go into **a house of *avodah zarah***, they, the Jews, shall not go with them, that they might think that they are foreigners, as it says, "If we forgot the name of our God and spread forth our hands to a foreign god, God would surely search it out" [Psalms 44:21–22], and it is written, "Then Jehu and Jehonadav son of Rehab came into the temple of Baal, and they said to the worshippers of Baal, 'Search and make sure that there are no worshippers of the Lord among you, but only worshippers of Baal'" [2 Kings 10:23], for they were fearful lest worshippers of the Lord were with them out of fear of the king.	(a) "Among the nations, they shall not be reckoned…" [Numbers 23:9]. "All who see shall recognize that they are a stock the Lord has blessed" [Isaiah 61:9]. How so? (b) Jews shall not say, if soldiers come to them, that they will make a sign of **idol worship** on their clothes, and they shall not make themselves like those who are **servants of pagan idol worship**. They shall not place on their homes a sign of **idol worship**, and they shall not shave the top of the head, so that the foreigners might think that they are foreigners. (c) If the foreigners pass by and chance upon them, the Jews, and the foreigners go into **a house of their prayer**, they, the Jews, shall not go with them, that they might think that they are foreigners, as it says, "If we forgot the name of our God and spread forth our hands to a foreign god, God would surely search it out" [Psalms 44:21–22], and it is written, "Then Jehu and Jehonadav son of Rehab came into the temple of Baal, and they said to the worshippers of Baal, 'Search and make sure that there are no worshippers of the Lord among you, but only worshippers of Baal'" [2 Kings 10:23], for they were fearful lest worshippers of the Lord were with them out of fear of the king.

TABLE 5

with *galaḥim* (shaved-heads), a disparaging epithet for tonsured Christian monks. Once again, Zifroni substituted a reference to pagan religious practitioners for a reference to Christians, directing the reader's focus away from Christianity and toward the religions of antiquity.

The third modification in §221 was subtler and more sophisticated. In section (c), the partners' text discourages Jews from entering a church to avoid persecution because they might be mistaken for Christians. There, the church is called a house of *avodah zarah*. Zifroni, however, substituted *beit tefillatam* (house of their prayer). Rather than replacing a word that might be read as a reference to Christianity with a word whose definition was restricted to paganism, he subtly humanized the antagonists in the story. They were no longer servants of an alien cult; rather, they were people who offer *tefillot*, prayers—like Jews. At the same time, the aural similarity of the words *tefillah* (prayer) and *tiflah* (frivolity) perhaps allowed Jewish readers to perceive, subtly, a vestige of the passage's old polemical reading.[12]

Another passage, §698 in the partners' edition (§697 in Froben's edition), evinces more concerted censorship, including multiple deletions (table 6).[13] Once again, this passage deals with the Christian persecution of Jews:[14]

Partners' Edition	Froben Edition
(a) "Whose mouths speak lies, and whose oaths are false" [Psalms 144:8]. (b) One time, they decreed **forced apostasies upon the Jews to cause them to abandon their law, to baptize them in water,** and to leave the Lord, the God of Israel, to acquire **the foreign faith**. And the Jews busied to flee from their place. (c) There were many lords who showed themselves to be comrades, and they said, "Come to us, and we will shield you from your enemies." They [the Jews] came unto them, and they killed them. Therefore, they said, **"A Jew should not fraternize with a foreigner."**	(a) "Whose mouths speak lies, and whose oaths are false" [Psalms 144:8]. (b) One time, they decreed upon the Jews **to cause them to abandon their law**, and to leave the Lord, the God of Israel, to acquire **a foreign faith**. And the Jews busied to flee from their place. (c) There were many lords who showed themselves to be comrades, and they said, "Come to us, and we will shield you from your enemies." They [the Jews] came unto them, and they killed them. Therefore, they said, **"A Jew should not fraternize with an Egyptian or someone similar to them."**

TABLE 6

In Froben's edition, Zifroni made several deletions and modifications: He eliminated the term "forced apostasies" (*shemadot*) and the phrase "to baptize them in water" (*le-hatbilam ba-mayim*).[15] He modified the phrase "the foreign faith" (*emunat ha-nokhri'ah*) to read "a foreign faith" (*emunat nokhri'ah*). And he modified the statement "a Jew should not fraternize with a foreigner" (*al yityaḥed Yehudi im nokhri*) to read "a Jew should not fraternize with an Egyptian or someone similar to them" (*al yityaḥed Yehudi im Miẓri ve-domeihem*).

The first deletions concern the Hebrew term *shemadot* (forced apostasies). As discussed earlier, the root of *shemad* denotes "destruction" and "cutting off."[16] In antiquity, it came to signify the forced conversion of Jews at the hands of the Roman emperor Hadrian (c. 135 CE) and other subsequent instances of forced conversion.[17] Despite the fact that Church doctrine had long maintained that baptism could not be coerced, forced baptism occurred throughout the medieval and early modern periods, infamously during the Crusades.[18] The ambivalence of Christians toward forced conversion and the negative associations with the root of *shemad*—that a person who had been forcefully converted had been "destroyed" or "cut off"—triggered Christian indignation.

It was relatively easy to remove the offensive word *shemad* from the text without altering its essential meaning. "They decreed forced apostasy upon the Jews to cause them to give up their law" became, in Froben's edition, "They decreed upon the Jews to cause them to give up their law." Thus, Zifroni eliminated the judgment signified by the word *shemad*, but the events recorded remained the same.

Similarly, Zifroni deleted the phrase "to baptize them in water" (*le-hatbilam ba-mayim*). This modification did not radically transform the story; the concept that Jews were forcefully converted remained in place. Nonetheless, by deleting the phrase in question, Zifroni eliminated the only direct reference to Christianity in the passage. Further, in transforming "the foreign faith" (*emunat ha-nokhri'ah*) to "a foreign faith" (*emunat nokhri'ah*) by eliminating the definite article—the Hebrew letter *hey*—Zifroni introduced ambiguity. He presented Judaism as not in direct conflict with a single specific group. As a result, readers no longer had to assume that the antagonists in the passage were Christians; they just as well could have been ancient pagan persecutors.

Zifroni modified the last sentence of section (c), the moral of the tale, to emphasize this ambiguity. In the partners' edition, the moral was that a Jew should not "fraternize with a foreigner" (*nokhri*). The term "foreigner" was the partners' innovation; manuscript witnesses read *goy*.[19] However, in Froben's version of this passage, Zifroni replaced *nokhri* with the phrase *Miẓri ve-domeihem* (an Egyptian or someone similar to them). This was an example of the phenomenon of anachronization: transforming a term of opprobrium in the present into a reference to a people or peoples of the past. Introducing the word *domeihem* (someone similar to them) further increased ambiguity. Readers no longer had to assume that the antagonists in question were Christians; in fact, they could be one of a number of ancient groups.

On one level, we might infer that this sort of modification impeded readers from associating the persecutors in the passage with Christians. At the same time, one wonders whether the word *domeihem*, in fact, implicitly preserved the possibility that Jewish readers might continue to read this passage as a critique of Jewish-Christian fraternizing. Could Jewish readers have understood this passage as implying that the people in their own day who were "similar to" the enslaving Egyptians were indeed Christians? This may have been a possibility, given that the Hebrew term *Miẓri* (Egyptian) was aurally similar to *Noẓri* (Christian).[20]

Froben's *Sefer Ḥasidim* is rife with examples of this kind of anachronization: Zifroni substituted Arameans, Egyptians, and Epicureans from antiquity for plausible references to Christians and Christianity. One notable example concerns a passage cited earlier, §429, about Christian clergy and Hebrew books (table 7). The second half of the passage, quoted in full in chapter 3, raises the question of Jews' relationships with individuals identified as *minim* (sectarians):

Partners' Edition	Froben's Edition
(c) If there is a Bible that a **sectarian** wrote and did not inscribe it with his name or the **name of an *avodah zarah*** or the name of a holy thing, do not store it with Jewish books [i.e., books written by Jews], "For the rod of wickedness shall not rest upon the lot of the righteous" [Psalms 125:3]. (d) If there is a **sectarian** who wants to make **a hymn to *avodah zarah***, or a **foreigner** wants to make [a hymn in honor of] a sin, and he says to a Jew, "Sing me a pleasant melody with which to praise your God," do not sing to him, so that [his transgression] will not occur on your account.	(c) If there is a Bible that a **Sadducee** wrote and did not inscribe it with his name or the **name of pagan idol worship** or the name of a holy thing, do not store it with Jewish books [i.e., books written by Jews], "For the rod of wickedness shall not rest upon the lot of the righteous" [Psalms 125:3]. (d) If there is a **Sadducee** who wants to make a **hymn to pagan idol worship**, or a **foreigner** wants to make [a hymn in honor of] a sin, and he says to a Jew, "Sing me a pleasant melody with which to praise your God," do not sing to him, so that [his transgression] will not occur on your account.

TABLE 7

As expected, in Froben's edition, Zifroni substituted *avodat elilim* (pagan idol worship) for the phrase *avodah zarah*. Interestingly, he did not change the word *nokhri*.[21] He did, however, substitute *Ẓadoki* (Sadducee) for *min* (sectarian).

As we discussed in chapter 3, the word *min* was not original to this passage; the partners introduced it in place of *galaḥ* (shaved-head/monk), likely believing that *min* was preferable to the original because, in rabbinic texts, it referred to sectarians generally. However, by the medieval period, *min* (plural *minim*) had become a derogatory designation for Christians.[22] Zifroni sought greater specificity and historical distance, and so Sadducees, a Jewish sect from the Second Temple period, took the place of *minim*. Once again, with these replacements, Zifroni made the antagonists in question deviant Jews and not Christians.[23] To paraphrase Raz-Krakotzkin, he transformed the "polemical dimension" of the text, reshaping a Jewish polemic against Christianity in the present into an artifact of an ancient Jewish dispute.[24]

In the context of this passage in particular, Zifroni's decision to replace *min* with Sadducee also hints at his appreciation for the literary qualities of the text. Section (c) employs a quotation from the book of Psalms—"For the rod of wickedness shall not rest upon the lot of the righteous" (125:3)—as a proof text for the claim that one should not store non-Jewish books beside Jewish books. It equates non-Jewish books with "the rod of wickedness" and Jewish books with "the lot of the righteous." This is also a play on words, because the term "righteous" (*ẓaddikim*) is etymologically related to Sadducee (*Ẓadoki*). In this way, Zifroni's modifications often harmonized with the text to such an extent that, in many cases, they did not appear out of place at all.[25]

Zifroni also universalized troubling terms, transforming references to Christians into those that could be applied to all people. For example, §699 in the partners' edition (§698 in Froben's) describes another instance of persecution (table 8).

Partners' Edition	Froben's Edition
(a) Two are sitting, and ***goyim*** demand to kill one of them. If one is a scholar, and the other is a layman, it is commanded that the layman say, "Kill me and not my friend." (b) [This is] like Rabbi Reuven ben Istrobli, who demanded that they kill him and not Rabbi Akiva, since the masses needed Rabbi Akiva.	(a) Two are sitting, and **enemies** demand to kill one of them. If one is a scholar, and the other is a layman, it is commanded that the layman say, "Kill me and not my friend." (b) [This is] like Rabbi Reuven ben Istrobli, who demanded that they kill him and not Rabbi Akiva, since the masses needed Rabbi Akiva.

TABLE 8

In the version of this passage in Froben's edition, Zifroni substituted the ambiguous term "enemies" (*oyevim*) for *goyim*. By replacing a troubling term with a generic one, Zifroni made it possible for the antagonists in the tale to be anyone—Jew or Christian—with a nefarious plot. In this way, he again eliminated the polemical dimension of the passage; it became a tale about a person's proper conduct when faced with a life-or-death encounter. And yet, these two terms also possessed an aural similarity; one could be mistaken for the other. In this way, Zifroni both demonstrated sensitivity to the literary dimensions of the text he was adapting and clandestinely preserved a vestige of the original, controversial reading.

Modifications like these—from anachronization to universalization to the introduction of ambiguity writ large—raise the question of whether Jewish readers did, in fact, continue to identify Christians as antagonists in such passages. European Jews lived as members of a minimally tolerated minority in a society thoroughly suffused with Christian power and symbols. Conversion was a goal of both the Catholic and Protestant churches, one undertaken with varying degrees of coercion throughout the sixteenth century. While the manifest content of these censored passages explicitly disavowed their applicability to Christianity—as in the statement, "A Jew should not fraternize with an Egyptian or someone similar to them"—that same content could be read with a wink and a nod by those inclined to interpret the passage's guidance in light of present persecution. This was all the more true when Zifroni's chosen substitutions possessed an aural similarity to what they replaced. Jews could read between the lines, which affirms the philosopher Leo Strauss's statement: "Persecution, then, cannot prevent independent thinking."[26]

Yet, if reading "between the lines" remained possible for Jews even after extensive modifications like those described here, and presumably Christians were aware of this possibility, then what was the purpose of this form of censorship? First, modifications like those described can be understood as an attempt to blot out the textual evidence of blasphemy. Elisheva Carlebach has noted the keen interest of Christian Hebraists in the perceived "inner, or 'secret,' life of Jews," including their assumed covert anti-Christian animus.[27] Thus, even though late-sixteenth-century Christian sovereigns and scholars believed in the merit of censoring explicit instances of (perceived) blasphemy in Hebrew texts, they nonetheless expected that their Jewish readers would persist in implicit blasphemy.

Second, Raz-Krakotzkin has asserted that early modern censorship in Hebrew books was an attempt to "create an alternative definition of the Jew... formulated more positively and not based on confrontation with the other."[28] While self-understanding may necessarily involve comparison to an Other, real or imagined, to say that early modern Jewish identity was "based on confrontation with" Christianity is perhaps too extreme.[29] Raz-Krakotzkin is no doubt correct, however, that the Christians who imposed policies of censorship on Hebrew books during the Counter-Reformation understood Jews as perceiving themselves in confrontation with Christianity. It is possible to see Zifroni's anachronization and universalization as an attempt to lessen that perceived confrontation and thereby normalize Christianity in the minds of Jewish readers, at least rhetorically.

Third, Zifroni's modifications served another purpose, one unrelated to censorship. The technique of anachronization, while certainly diminishing the explicit polemical dimension of some passages, also retrojected *Sefer Ḥasidim* into ancient Palestine. Gone were the realia of medieval Europe—its priests and monks and chivalric romances—and, in its place, Zifroni invoked Sadducees, Egyptians, and other ancient groups. These modifications bolstered Luzzatto's claim that *Sefer Ḥasidim* was an ancient canonical book, of a piece with more familiar rabbinic works.

Over and above modifications like these, Froben's edition of *Sefer Ḥasidim* was marked by a much more thorough form of censorship that made it considerably harder for Jewish readers to intuit passages' original content, to read between the lines: the deletion of whole sentences in the text. One example of this technique is found in §191 (table 9).[30]

Partners' Edition	Froben's Edition
(a) A Jew who converts, we give him a nickname, as it says, "They that make them shall be like unto them" [Psalms 115:8]. "Like unto them" one should name him; for example, if his name is Abraham, he may be called "Aphram," and so forth. (b) And this is the case even for a righteous man, and they stray after him, for example Simon Cephas, whom they called *Peter Ḥamor*.	(a) A Jew who converts, we give him a nickname, as it says, "They that make them shall be like unto them" [Psalms 115:8]. "Like unto them" one should name him; for example, if his name is Abraham, he may be called "Aphram," and so forth.

TABLE 9

This passage focuses once again on the conversion of a Jew to Christianity and begins by explaining the custom of nicknaming the convert.[31] In section (b), it draws on an obscure medieval tradition about Simon Cephas (known to Christians as the Apostle Peter) that originated in a number of *Toledot Yeshu* manuscripts.[32] *Toledot Yeshu* (*The Life Story of Jesus*) was a medieval treatise, extant in a great many witnesses, that mocked Jesus and his circle. One version of these texts depicts Simon as a pious and ascetic Jew, a composer of liturgical poetry (*piyyutim*), who sought to prevent Christians from throwing off the yoke of *halakhah* and deifying Jesus. Yet, despite his best intentions, he became, in Wout van Bekkum's words, "a sign of faith for the Christians."[33] The passage describes Simon similarly as a "righteous man" (*ẓaddik*) who nonetheless caused the apostasy of Jews. Because of this, he earned the nickname *Peter Ḥamor* (firstborn ass). This nickname is a play on, first, the Greek name "Peter," meaning "rock" (in Aramaic, "Cephas"), that Jesus gave to Simon in Matthew 16:18; and, second, the biblical tradition of redeeming the firstborn ass, called *peter ḥamor* (Exodus 13:3). Zifroni, not surprisingly, eliminated section (b) entirely.

He made similar deletions in the first portion of the next passage, §192 (table 10).[34]

Partners' Edition	Froben's Edition
Why weren't the names of the angels revealed in the Torah? Lest they make them into gods. Because one day in the year, they make a feast day for Michael and spread lies about him.	Why weren't the names of the angels revealed in the Torah? Lest they make them into gods.

TABLE 10

In the partners' edition, this passage condemns the Christian practice of celebrating saints' days.[35] Zifroni truncated this passage for Froben's edition, leaving only the introductory question and answer: "Why weren't the names of the angels revealed in the Torah? Lest they make them into gods." Zifroni's rationale for these changes likely stemmed from the probability that readers might interpret the implied subject of the section—the unspecified "they"—as Christians. After all, Christians celebrated the Feast of Saint Michael (Michaelmas) and venerated him as the celestial guardian of the Church.[36]

Such substantial truncating was, from Zifroni's perspective, likely warranted because of the extent of the charges against the antagonists, presumably Christians. Christians might be troubled by the application of the term *yom eid* (feast day) to their festivals. In rabbinic texts the word *eid* was used exclusively for idolatrous observances, in contrast to Jewish *ḥagim*.[37] The censor Domenico, in his handbook, called this term "language of derision" (*lashon ḥerpah*) and prescribed that it be "erased completely."[38] By the same token, Christian readers would have rejected the assertion that they transformed angelic figures into gods and that they would be denounced at the end of days by the very angel they venerated. Zifroni's abbreviated version of this passage, in lacking the direct reference to Christian practice, universalized a statement—"lest they make them into gods"—that had previously referred to Christians. In the new formulation, the text eliminated all references to Michael, a revered figure for Christians (and for Jews), and thus warned all readers that they could be the very "they" who fell into the trap of confusing angels with the Divinity.[39]

Many of the censorship techniques that Zifroni undertook in Froben's edition of *Sefer Ḥasidim* are familiar to students of Froben's Talmud. In that work, Marco Marini and his colleagues replaced anti-Christian terms with neutral or anachronistic alternatives: *meshummad* with *mumar*, for example, and *min* with *Ẓadoki* (Sadducee) or *apikoros* (heretic). They eliminated full passages that depicted Jesus.[40] But they were even more assiduous. Marini and his colleagues deleted, modified, or glossed passages that contained terms and descriptions they considered immodest or vulgar or distressing; laws and practices that applied differently to Jews and non-Jews; and passages that depicted God anthropomorphically.[41] In one case, the censor of tractate *Eduyot* contradicted the Mishnah's statement that "the duration of the sentence of the wicked in hell [*gehenom*] is twelve months," inserting a gloss (*hagahah*) in the margin of the text: "But for the completely wicked, and pagan idol worshippers [*ovdei elilim*], the duration of their sentence in hell is forever and ever." The Mishnah's statement was ripe for correction, of course, because it contradicted the Church's teaching on the eternity of hell, and also perhaps because it could be perceived as an inducement to immorality, lessening the perceived gravity of the crimes of "the wicked."[42]

Yet the eagerness with which Marini and others deleted, adapted, and glossed problematic passages in Froben's Talmud should not lead one to assume their efforts were comprehensive. Joseph Prjis has noted that Aramaicized variations of the proscribed word *Talmud* found their way into several tractates.[43] The censorship of the Froben Talmud, like much late-sixteenth-century censorship, was intensive but far from comprehensive. The same can be said for Froben's edition of *Sefer Ḥasidim*. Aside from editorial oversights—the persistence of short words such as *goy* that were usually removed—there are some cases in which Zifroni made no changes to passages that we might have reasonably assumed he would have modified.

One example of this apparent inconsistency is §802 (numbered §805 in the partners' edition). This passage describes King Ahasuerus of Persia as an *arel* (literally "uncircumcised man," plural *arelim*) who rapes the newly crowned Queen Esther. The term *arel* was used in rabbinic literature to refer to non-Jews.[44] Elsewhere in Froben's *Sefer Ḥasidim*, Zifroni substituted the words "enemy" and "Egyptian" for *arel*.[45] It is likely that Zifroni chose not to replace *arel* in this section because it referred to a non-Christian Gentile from antiquity and could not be confused with a reference to non-Jews in the present. In his handbook, Domenico stated categorically: "Any insult that denigrates the foreskin, it is necessary to specify [that it refers to a case] in the past."[46] Upon this justification, Domenico argued, certain references to non-Jews as *arelim* could remain in Hebrew texts.

De-Vernacularization

Zifroni's technique of anachronizing passages made *Sefer Ḥasidim* appear more ancient than it was. He furthered this perception by eliminating the linguistic traces of its medieval origins, that is, words and phrases in Judeo-French and Yiddish. His effort is evident in passages such as §419, which discusses the practice of swearing oaths. In the partners' edition (table 11), this passage included a reference to *la'az*, the Judeo-French vernacular spoken in medieval Ashkenaz.[47] In this passage, a group of non-Jews accuses a Jew of a crime he did not commit and forces him to swear an oath that he is innocent. Subsequently, the Jew regrets the oath and seeks the advice of a sage on how best to atone for his misdeed. R. Judah he-Ḥasid and his circle condemned the practice of oath-swearing, even though it was an especially common (and necessary) feature of medieval commerce.[48] In the partners' edition, the sage advises the Jew, "Accept upon yourself that you will not

Partners' Edition	Froben's Edition
(a) There was a Jew, the ***goyim*** libeled him and said to him, "You did such-and-such to us. You have to swear this is not the case." He swore truthfully. (b) He said to a sage, "I regret that I swore—even though I swore truthfully, and I was forced to swear against my will, so that they would not kill me—since my mother and father never swore, even truthfully." (c) The sage said to him, "If you wish to atone for this, accept upon yourself that you will not mention God's name, not truthfully and not in vain, **not in *la'az*, and not in any language**, like one is accustomed to say thusly, 'The Lord help me!' [Psalms 109:26]. You may not say this unless you are reading the [biblical] verse. Even, you do not engage in commerce, unless you are able to do so without an oath, so that it will not result in your [swearing] an oath."	(a) There was a Jew, the ***foreigners*** libeled him and said to him, "You did such-and-such to us. You have to swear this is not the case." He swore truthfully. (b) He said to a sage, "I regret that I swore—even though I swore truthfully, and I was forced to swear against my will, so that they would not kill me—since my mother and father never swore, even truthfully." (c) The sage said to him, "If you wish to atone for this, accept upon yourself that you will not mention God's name, not truthfully and not in vain, **and not in any language**, like one is accustomed to say thusly, 'The Lord help me!' [Psalms 109:26]. You may not say this unless you are reading the [biblical] verse. Even, you do not engage in commerce, unless you are able to do so without an oath, so that it will not result in your [swearing] an oath."

TABLE 11

mention God's name (*shem shamayim*), not truthfully and not in vain, not in *la'az*, and not in any language."

Zifroni made two significant adjustments to this passage: First, as would be expected, in section (a), he substituted *nokhri'im* (foreigners) for *goyim*. Secondly, and more interestingly, in section (c), he deleted the phrase, "not in *la'az*." Why delete it? The modification did not affect the passage's lesson, that swearing by God's name should be avoided regardless of one's language, because Zifroni retained the phrase, "not in any language." Rather, by eliminating the preceding phrase "not in *la'az*," Zifroni removed from the text the linguistic residue of the medieval European milieu from which *Sefer Ḥasidim* emerged.

Passage §3 contains an even bolder example of this technique and is especially significant because it appears on the first pages of both editions (table 12). These first pages would no doubt have been the books' most-read. This passage discusses the proper way for a pious person to mention the name of God:

Partners' Edition	Froben's Edition
(a) Every time that we mention the Lord, the honored and awesome, we are obligated to bless Him in Hebrew [with the words] "May His name be blessed" **and, in the language of *la'az*, "*saint bendit et saint lui.*"** (b) When he mentions him, he says, "My son, may peace be commended to him, may this day be good for him: '***Bon jour et tel je a notre sire le comande.***'"	(a) Every time that we mention the Lord, the honored and awesome, we are obligated to bless Him in Hebrew [with the words] "May His name be blessed." (b) When he mentions him, he says, "My son, may peace be commended to him, may this day be good for him."

TABLE 12

In the partners' edition, the text enumerates pious formulas in both Hebrew and *la'az*. There, the Judeo-French phrase is a translation of the Hebrew, literally "the Holy Blessed One and Holy [be] He."[49] In Froben's edition, Zifroni removes that clause. The passage goes on to describe what one might say when speaking about a child or friend who has traveled far away. There, the Judeo-French phrase may be translated as, "A good day and such, to our Lord I commend him."[50] Here again, Zifroni eliminated all the vernacular, leaving only the Hebrew.

Further, in the partners' edition, the subsequent passage, §4, repeats the idea discussed in §3, that a person who invokes God's name should follow with the words "May His name be blessed" in Hebrew or "*notre sire*" (our Lord) in *la'az*. It proceeds to tell the story of a pious bridegroom who "heard one of the singers during the dancing" at his wedding "mention the Lord in his song, '*le devin Dé*.'" This Old French expression may be translated as "the Godly God."[51] This pious bridegroom excommunicated the singer "each and every time" he sang God's name without following it with the required formula.

In Froben's edition, on the other hand, Zifroni combined §3 and §4 and eliminated the first half of §4, that is, the discussion of invoking God's name with the proper response, "May His name be blessed" in Hebrew and "*notre sire*" in *la'az*.[52] He then proceeded directly to the story of the pious bridegroom but removed the reference to the blasphemous vernacular song lyrics. The final sentences of the story read, "He heard one of the singers during the dancing mention the Lord in his song. This very pious man excommunicated him for each and every time [he said God's name]."

With revisions like these, Zifroni once again buttressed the historical argument about *Sefer Ḥasidim*'s provenance that Luzzatto proffered in his second introduction. The presence of *la'az* in the text—especially on the first pages—revealed that *Sefer Ḥasidim* was of a recent vintage. Luzzatto, in his second introduction, asserted that during *Sefer Ḥasidim*'s manuscript transmission, "verbal corruptions came [into the text] at various points," as did "stammering, distorted, and stiff language." In response, he explained, these features "were removed according to reason" in the process of preparing the new edition.[53] It is possible that Luzzatto here referenced not merely standard-issue corruptions but also the traces of medieval Ashkenazic culture that proliferated in the partners' edition—*la'az* and the like. Luzzatto thus may implicitly have been characterizing Zifroni's interventions not as editorial manipulation or pseudepigraphy but as the "recovery" of *Sefer Ḥasidim*'s true ancient form.

Conceiving of print shop adaptations and modifications like these as a recovery of the past, rather than anachronism, reflected the Renaissance interest in the "revival of antiquity."[54] Brian Richardson, we noted earlier, described a similar phenomenon in sixteenth-century editions of classical texts. Their editors frequently claimed to have removed generations of scribal corruptions and emendations, restoring texts to their pristine original condition. Linguistic features that did not align with Renaissance ideals of grammar, syntax, and diction could be removed by editors and correctors without rendering texts inauthentic.[55] This was one feature of what Grafton has called an early modern "culture of correction."[56] By removing from the text of *Sefer Ḥasidim* expressions in *la'az*, and by inserting into it references to the culture of Greco-Roman Palestine, Zifroni, in characteristic Renaissance fashion, purified *Sefer Ḥasidim* of what he and Luzzatto likely believed were late accretions, recovering its original form as a work of antiquity.

Punctuation and *Perushim*

Zifroni also contributed to Froben's *Sefer Ḥasidim* by enhancing its readability with punctuation, textual emendations, and explanatory glosses. His changes made the text easier to grasp for nonexpert readers. Many of these improvements are found in Zifroni's rendering of the passage numbered §802 in the partners' edition:

(a) "One should not be the bearer of bad news" [Babylonian Talmud, *Megillah* 15a] precisely when you can say, "There is nothing to learn from it." But, there are cases where if one were to share the bad news, one could be a remedy—to speak, as in the case of [the verse], "A fugitive brought the news to Abram the Hebrew" [Genesis 14:13] [that Lot had been taken captive]. If he had not told [this news], he would have sinned more. Thus, if one does not tell about the sickness of one's friend, one will not inquire about a [potential] cure, just as [in the case of the verse], "Some time afterward, Joseph was told, 'Your father is ill'" [Genesis 48:1], so that he would bring his sons with him [to see their grandfather]. Thus, Rabban Yohanan b. Zakkai [said] to Rabbi Hanina ben Dosa that he should pray for his son—so that he might be cured [literally "remedied"], he told him.[57] Or to testify on behalf of [a man's] wife, so that she might remarry, and to make a remedy for the orphans.[58]

(b) If this is the case, why did Hathach not tell [the bad news] to Mordecai?[59] For, in his [Hathach's] eyes, it was bad that she did not want to come before the king and give herself over to death, to go to King Ahasuerus. Further, he said that if she gave herself over to the king for sexual intercourse, she would be prohibited to Mordecai.[60] For until this point, she was raped by him, and now she presented herself to the foreskinned-one.

This passage is based on a vignette in the Babylonian Talmud, Tractate *Megillah*, that uses the story of Queen Esther to teach the lesson, "One should not be a bearer of bad news" (*ein meshivin al ha-kalkalah*).[61] This passage modified this teaching, arguing that one, in fact, can bear bad news if doing so might lead to a positive outcome (literally a "remedy," *takkanah*).

The partners' Hebrew version of this passage is marked by an absence of punctuation (a feature that could not be accurately represented in the English translation here); the version in Froben's edition (numbered §805), on the other hand, includes punctuation throughout (as it does in this translation).[62] In the partners' edition, sentences and clauses run together; conjunctions, such as the conjunctive *vav* or the word *ve-khen*, imply distinctions. The absence of punctuation dividing sentences and clauses was a hallmark of medieval Latin and Hebrew manuscripts, such as those of *Sefer Ḥasidim*.[63] When punctuation was used, it generally was meant to assist in the oral declamation of a text.[64] With the advent of Hebrew printing, punctuation began to serve, according to Sinai Turan, a "syntactic-analytic" function, visually dividing statements and clauses within a text.[65]

Unlike in the partners' edition, where the passage appears as a single block of unpunctuated text, in Froben's edition a colon divides the passage midway into two thematic sections, (a) and (b). Section (a) articulates the general principle that one can share bad news if it will lead to a positive outcome and offers examples from the Bible and Talmud where this occurred. Section (b) provides the counterexample of Hathach, King Ahasuerus's eunuch, who did not share his bad news. While the distinction between these sections can be inferred without the colon, the colon shows the reader that the passage has moved to a new focus and that the example in section (b) differs from what preceded it.

In addition, Zifroni added superscript points (˙) to break this passage into smaller syntactic units. In many cases, they appeared prior to implied forms of punctuation: conjunctions and disjunctions. Yet these points also indicated where quotations end and where new ideas begin, such as at the end of the biblical verses in section (a). Punctuation also helped emphasize particular statements, such as the rhetorical question, "If this is the case, why did Hathach not tell [the bad news] to Mordecai?" In the partners' edition, this question ran directly into the text that followed it. The use of a superscript point in the way we would use a question mark added to the question's rhetorical power, allowing it to stand on its own. By and large, the punctuation in Froben's edition functioned this way: While not radically affecting the meaning of passages, it would have helped readers—especially novice readers—parse the text with greater precision.

Froben's editors also eased comprehension of this passage with the addition of key letters and words. In the partners' edition, the verb in the Aramaic expression, "there is nothing to learn from it" (literally "we don't learn/gain [anything] from it," *lo nafka lan mina*) lacks a final *aleph*. Zifroni corrected this error. More tellingly, in the partners' edition, the circumstances under which a person may "testify on behalf of a man's wife" are left to be inferred by the reader; thus, the last sentence of section (a) reads: "Or to testify on behalf of [a man's] wife, so that she might remarry, and to make a remedy for the orphans." In Froben's edition, Zifroni added two Hebrew words, so that the sentence read, "Or to testify **about** the [**man's**] **death** [*al ha-met*] on behalf of his wife, so that she might remarry, and to make a remedy for the orphans." These two words clarify that the testimony in question is related to the case of an *agunah,* a woman whose husband has disappeared and who is prohibited from remarrying until his death has been affirmed by witnesses in court.

Zifroni also added an extra word at the end of section (b), clarifying that Esther knowingly gave herself over (sexually) to Ahasuerus when she petitioned him to save the Jews of Persia. In the partners' edition, the last sentence of the passage read: "Now she presented herself to the foreskinned-one [*le-arel*]." Zifroni emended the sentence to read: "Now she presented herself to the foreskinned one **willingly** [*le-arel* ***be-razon***]." By adding the word "willingly," moreover, Zifroni made the wording of this story accord with its source in the Babylonian Talmud.

Taken together, the addition of punctuation and the occasional choice word did not alter the meaning of passages but did assist the reader's comprehension. These innovations could have made the text more accessible to any reader, but they would have been particularly useful for Christian Hebraists who had learned Hebrew as adults.

Froben's edition also featured occasional explanatory glosses with examples of implied or unclear phenomena. The subject of §107 (table 13) was the medieval custom of interrupting the reading of the Pentateuch in the synagogue to have a grievance heard by the community's leaders (*ikuv ha-kri'ah* or *bittul ha-tamid*):[66]

Partners' Edition	Froben's Edition
Anyone who prevents a Torah scroll from being inserted into the holy ark and thus wants to force and prod the congregation that they might do his bidding, the leaders of the community should say: "This is not legal, what you are doing!" In the future, the Torah will cry out and announce about his soul: "This man, so-and-so, may not come to such-and-such a place in peace."	Anyone who prevents a Torah scroll from being inserted into the holy ark, **for instance the petitioner in the synagogue before the ark**, and thus wants to force and prod the congregation that they might do his bidding, the leaders of the community should say: "This is not legal, what you are doing!" In the future, the Torah will cry out and announce about his soul: "This man, so-and-so, may not come to such-and-such a place in peace."

TABLE 13

The addition of the bolded phrase distinguishes Froben's version of this passage. Zifroni added this text to clarify that the situation to which the passage referred was precisely that of *ikuv ha-kri'ah*, when an aggrieved person interrupted the service.

Other passages include explanatory glosses preceded by the Hebrew letter *pey*, an abbreviation for the word *perush* (explanation, plural *perushim*). Often, these clarify the meaning of a biblical or Talmudic proof text. Thus, §57 describes the gravity of the sin of humiliating someone publicly and equates it with murder.[67] The passage concludes by adducing a tradition from the Palestinian Talmud: A "murderer who came to a city, and [the people of the city] show him honors, must say 'I am a murderer.' As it says [in Scripture], 'And this is the case [*davar*] of the murderer'" (Deuteronomy 19:4).[68]

This Talmudic proof text is a *midrash* on the meaning of the word *davar* in the biblical verse; it can be understood as "case," "word," or "speech." While "case" may be a more appropriate reading in the original biblical context, the Talmud understands the word as "speech": The murderer must make a speech admitting his guilt if he finds himself honored by the inhabitants of his new city. The passage takes this *midrash* a step further, arguing that the biblical verse does not refer to a murderer per se, but to someone who has humiliated his fellow, a sin it equates with murder. The connection between the verse and this conclusion seems tenuous in the partners' text. The reader must intuit the relationship between the biblical verse and the conclusion the Talmud draws from it. To clarify this linkage, Zifroni added the following gloss at the end of the passage: "Explanation: A speech [*dibbur*] that he will speak [*she-yidabber*] before them, and he will confess to the murder." The gloss explains that the word *davar* in the verse should be understood precisely as "speech" (*dibbur*), and not as "case," and that the verse is an injunction requiring the slanderer/murderer to confess his guilt publicly.

Explanatory *perushim* like the one quoted here, along with added punctuation, demonstrate Zifroni's intent to make the meaning and message of *Sefer Ḥasidim* more accessible, especially to readers who were less familiar with the mechanics of midrashic interpretation and the syntax of medieval Hebrew. These glosses differed from those occasionally found in the margins of Froben's Talmud edition. Those sometimes presented Christian counter-readings, as we saw earlier, or explained the allegorical meaning of aggadic passages. Joseph Prijs has suggested that the latter glosses presaged interpretations found in *Kavvanot ha-aggadot* and may have been composed by Luzzatto.[69] Here, in Froben's edition of *Sefer Ḥasidim*, however, the glosses helped clarify the literal meaning of the text and facilitated its comprehension.

Conclusion

The years between the printing of the partners' edition of *Sefer Ḥasidim* in 1538 and Froben's edition in 1580 witnessed dramatic events in the history of the Hebrew book. In the autumn of 1553, the Roman Inquisition, directed by Cardinal Giampietro Carafa (later Pope Paul IV), confiscated and burned the Talmud and other Hebrew books in the Campo de' Fiori. Other cities of the Papal States followed suit in the next months, and as late as 1559 there was a Talmud burning in the northern Italian city of Cremona.[70] In 1554, Pope Julius III promulgated the bull *Cum sicut nuper*, formally initiating a policy of pre- and post-publication censorship of Hebrew books.[71] In the following decades, the Church developed a network of knowledgeable censors—many of whom were converts from Judaism, like Domenico Gerosolimitano—who vetted and authorized Hebrew books before and after printing. At the same time, new Hebrew presses were established in northern Italy, central Europe, and Poland, as well as in Constantinople and Salonica. Some, especially those in Germany, sought to produce Hebrew books for Christian readers. Indeed, as we noted earlier, the emergence of a market for Hebrew books among both Protestants and Catholics was a consequence of Reformation-era interest in uncovering the *Hebraica veritas* (the root meaning of Scripture in its Hebrew original).[72]

Froben's edition of *Sefer Ḥasidim* testifies to these events. On the one hand, the obvious fact that it was produced in the city of Basel by a Christian printer is emblematic of the expansion of Hebrew printing northward from Italy and the growing interest of Christians in Hebrew and Jewish literature. Froben and his team intended their *Sefer Ḥasidim* to attract the interest of Jewish students (*talmidim*) seeking deeper knowledge of the neglected *aggadah*. Zifroni and Luzzatto's editorial decisions, from the two introductions to the emendations in the text, were meant to make its *aggadah* more accessible, just as Luzzatto had hoped *Kavvanot ha-aggadot* would do for the *aggadah* of the Talmud.

At the same time, we might have assumed that the censorship in Froben's

Sefer Ḥasidim edition would have been even more meticulous than it was, given the Talmud burnings of the 1550s and the promulgation of *Cum sicut nuper* in 1559, as well as the failure of Froben's Talmud. What we find, on the one hand, are more aggressive forms of censorship than those we observed in the partners' edition: the replacement of perceived anti-Christian words and phrases with anachronisms, the universalizing of passages that hitherto referred only to Christians, and the elimination, without a trace, of complete sentences. Zifroni carried out this process in the same manner as had the partners of Bologna, in the sense that objectionable words and phrases remained. This haphazardness was, as observed earlier, a hallmark of early modern censorship. The text of *Sefer Ḥasidim* was not mechanically scoured and every offending word highlighted and expunged, in the fashion of twenty-first-century censors using digital technologies.[73] Rather, Zifroni read the text carefully, but not scrupulously, and selectively adapted or emended its contents.

Raz-Krakotzkin has argued that the censorship of Hebrew books in the late sixteenth century was marked by a creative interplay of Jewish and Christian print-shop workers, through which Jewish texts were rewritten to eliminate polemical elements and to make them fit within the "limits of discourse" defined by the Church. The overall effect, he argues, was more beneficial than deleterious, for the softening of long-standing polemics was a prelude to the "secularization" and "modernization" of Jewish culture.[74] Piet van Boxel has rejected this view, arguing that neither the Church nor its censors "had the intention of reformulating the censored passages or of conveying new knowledge."[75] Van Boxel has argued, moreover, that these efforts extended only as far as eliminating the "presence of inadmissible vocabulary" and generally left texts mangled and readers aware of lacunae.[76] He asserts that censorship was not a step in a larger editorial process, and that editors and censors performed very different tasks: Unlike editors, censors were intent on removing any and all offending passages without regard for syntax, style, or content.[77]

The analyses in this chapter indicate that late-sixteenth-century Hebrew censorship was more aggressive than it had been earlier in the century, and that the meaning of texts changed when polemics were eliminated. Sometimes a reader could intuit the original meaning, and sometimes new meanings were created that were at variance with the original. Van Boxel is correct that this reflected the increased surveillance of Jews that went hand-in-hand with the Counter-Reformation-era persecution of early modern Jewry. The neutralization of the polemical dimension of Hebrew texts was not a form of "secularization," as Raz-Krakotzkin would have us believe. Rather, it was Christian society once more imposing its will upon Jews and Judaism, forcing Jews to accept Christian interpretations of Hebrew texts about Christians, and perceiving Jews and their texts as preoccupied with anti-Christian animus.

At the same time, Raz-Krakotzkin is correct that censorship was part of larger editorial processes. In his introductions, Luzzatto linked *haggahah* (correction) and *zikkuk* (expurgation). Zifroni prepared a text of *Sefer Ḥasidim* by engaging in parallel creative processes of editing, correcting, glossing, and censoring, alongside or in partnership with Luzzatto, who composed the accompanying paratexts that depicted *Sefer Ḥasidim* as an ancient text relevant to specific early modern concerns. In this way, *Sefer Ḥasidim* differed from the subjects of van Boxel's study, rabbinic Bibles, which were censored by Church officials prior to their printing. In Froben's *Sefer Ḥasidim,* by contrast, the removal of perceived anti-Christian invective was undertaken by Jewish actors responding to the concerns of the Church, not external actors imposing the Church's will on a text. Yet Christian readers were only one constituency with a stake in the book's content. For their book to be commercially successful, Froben and his team had to make their edition attractive to Jewish readers first and foremost. They did so by presenting *Sefer Ḥasidim* as a canonical text uniquely suited to the religious and educational concerns of late-sixteenth-century Jewry.

Epilogue

I saw a small treatise, which said at its head: "This is *Sefer ha-Ḥasidim,* which was set down by R. Samuel the Prophet, father of our R. Judah he-Ḥasid."

GEDALIAH b. Joseph ibn Yaḥya,
Sefer shalshelet ha-kabbalah
(Venice, 1587)

. . . . .

IN 1587, the Di Gara press of Venice—another Christian-owned Hebrew press where Zifroni worked following his departure from Basel—printed Gedaliah b. Joseph ibn Yaḥya's *Sefer shalshelet ha-kabbalah,* one of a spate of sixteenth-century Hebrew historiographic titles. Gedaliah was the son of R. Joseph b. David ibn Yaḥya, the author of *Torah or,* which the partners of Bologna printed the same year as *Sefer Ḥasidim.* He was a student of R. Obadiah Sforno in Bologna and a close reader of Azariah de' Rossi's *Me'or einayim.*[1] He divided *Sefer shalshelet ha-kabbalah* into three parts: a chronicle of Jewish history from Adam to the present, a treatise on astrology and magic, and a timeline of non-Jewish sages and rulers from antiquity to the present. In the first part, amid a précis of the Jewish people's eminent scholars and their literary achievements, Gedaliah remarked that he once happened upon a "small treatise" (*ḥibbur katan*) called "*Sefer ha-Ḥasidim.*"

The Hebrew noun Gedaliah used to describe *Sefer Ḥasidim* was *ḥibbur,* derived from the root *ḥet-bet-resh,* like *meḥaber* (author), and again connoting something "joined" or "composed." According to Gedaliah, Samuel "set down" (*y'sado*) this *ḥibbur.* That verb, from the root *yod-samekh-dalet,* is roughly equivalent to the verb "to author" (*ḥiber*), though it perhaps conveys even more finality and responsibility. Samuel established *Sefer Ḥasidim*'s text for perpetuity, though that process might have entailed the joining of preexisting texts within a single work. The fact that, sometime between 1549 and 1587, the years that Gedaliah was writing *Sefer shalshelet ha-kabbalah,* he felt confident enough in Samuel's authorship to ascribe *Sefer Ḥasidim* to him, speaks to the vagaries of both medieval manuscript transmission and printed book production during the sixteenth century.[2]

By the time Gedaliah finished writing *Sefer shalshelet ha-kabbalah* in 1587, three printed *Sefer Ḥasidim* editions had appeared: the partners' *editio princeps,* Froben's edition, and a reprinting of the partners' edition in Krakow in 1581. All three identified Judah as *Sefer Ḥasidim*'s author. For this reason, it is likely that Gedaliah's "small treatise" was a manuscript, one that circulated in Italy, where Gedaliah resided throughout his life. The fact that Gedaliah quoted from this manuscript—rather than the available printed editions—when discussing *Sefer Ḥasidim* testifies to the persistence of manuscripts during the first century of Hebrew printing. David McKittrick and Yaacob Dweck have shown how manuscripts continued to be written and read alongside printed books throughout the early modern period and beyond.[3] For Jews, who maintained the practice of reading from a handwritten Torah scroll in synagogue, manuscripts retained religious authority, and, as Dweck has shown, for some genres of texts, especially polemics, they became the preferred mode of communication.

Thus, from Gedaliah's statement that Samuel "set down" *Sefer Ḥasidim,* we can infer that at least one *Sefer Ḥasidim* manuscript circulating in sixteenth-century Italy was ascribed to a specific individual, Samuel, not Judah. None of the extant *Sefer Ḥasidim* manuscripts possesses any formal statement of attribution like the statement Gedaliah cited. Yet, in the Parma manuscript, copied in Ashkenaz around 1300, and in the manuscript formerly known as JTS Boesky 45, copied in Italy in the fourteenth or fifteenth century and closely related to the Parma manuscript, the name "Samuel" does appear at the very beginning, following the heading "The Secret of the God-fearers." Marcus has contended that this "Samuel" was intended to ascribe this first subsection of these manuscripts (the purported *Sefer ha-yir'ah,* meaning *The Book of the God-Fearers,* i.e., §§153–162 of the partners' edition) to R. Samuel he-Ḥasid.[4] Since the name "Samuel" appears here on its own, however, unaccompanied by any customary formula of attribution—like the one quoted by Gedaliah—it is not clear that this name was meant as an attribution at all, let alone an attribution to R. Samuel he-Ḥasid rather than some other Samuel.

Nonetheless, Gedaliah's testimony suggests that there was a tradition linking R. Samuel he-Ḥasid to a title known as *Sefer Ḥasidim*, or parts of such a work, and that that tradition was as old as the sixteenth century, if not older. In light of this tradition, the partners' attribution of their *Sefer Ḥasidim* edition to Judah suggests that they either deliberately contradicted the prevailing view or that the tradition associating *Sefer Ḥasidim* with Samuel was not widely known. The latter is more likely than the former, given that modern notions of authorial attribution were coming into existence in the early sixteenth century and that the partners described Judah as *Sefer Ḥasidim*'s author as if that claim were uncontested. They offered no evidence in support and did not seek to refute rival attributions. In fact, Samuel's name is not found in their edition. Their attribution of the book to Judah quickly took hold. Zifroni and Luzzatto retained it in Froben's edition, and generations of *Sefer Ḥasidim* printers thereafter continued to tout Judah's authorship. Only recently have scholars begun to raise questions.

Attribution was one technique the partners employed to fashion *Sefer Ḥasidim* into a book. However, it became a *sefer*, in the sense of a sacred book, as a result of Zifroni and Luzzatto's efforts. In many Jewish communities today, the word *sefer* is freighted with meaning. While modern Hebrew has secularized it, as we discussed in chapter 1, for speakers of Jewish English, the word *sefarim* (or *seforim*) can also refer to handwritten scrolls and to printed codices of canonical texts. Such volumes are often decorated to look like medieval manuscript codices, with leather (or more likely faux leather) bindings and gold embossing.

No doubt the medieval writers and copyists (the distinction between these two roles remains, after the foregoing analysis, unclear) who wrote down the passages of *Sefer Ḥasidim* believed they possessed some sanctity (*kedushah*). Otherwise, they would not have labored to communicate them with fine materials and care. Yet, for these writers, were these manuscripts *sefarim*, sacred books, despite the word *sefer* in their titles?

From the perspective of the passages of *Sefer Ḥasidim* themselves, it seems such works would have been considered not *sefarim* but *kuntresim* (singular *kuntres*, "notebook"). In medieval Ashkenaz, and in the early modern period as well, *kuntresim* were used for notetaking in the *yeshivah*, recording a teacher's lessons, and drafting texts of different genres, including commentaries, journals, and letters. Famously, the Tosafists referred to their copies of Rashi's

Talmud commentary as *kuntresim*.[5] As we noted earlier, several *Sefer Ḥasidim* passages distinguish between *kuntresim*, which possess a lower level of sanctity, and *sefarim*, which possess a higher level. One *Sefer Ḥasidim* passage, for example, counseled that "a man should not rest a *kuntres* on a *sefer* when ruling the *kuntres* with lines, because there is no sanctity [*kedushah*] in it."[6] *Kuntresim* sometimes contained passages from the Written and Oral Torah, and thereby accrued some sanctity, but they were of a more ephemeral nature and thus were not of the same caliber as *sefarim*. Perhaps the preprint writers of *Sefer Ḥasidim*, those who "gathered" or "gleaned" its various passages and composed stories of pietists and sages, ghosts and monks, considered the works they produced as *kuntresim*, records of teachings and tales shared in the Ashkenazic *yeshivah*. Zifroni and Luzzatto, by printing Froben's *Sefer Ḥasidim* edition in square type, and by contextualizing it as a canonical work of *aggadah*, made the case that *Sefer Ḥasidim* was not merely a *kuntres* but was, rather, a *sefer*, one destined for the bookshelf alongside works of Torah, both Scripture and rabbinic tradition.

Sefer Ḥasidim's forceful prescriptions against intermingling texts of differing sanctity within the same codex, against "adding" to preexisting works, and against alluding to one's own name indicate that such practices were part and parcel of manuscript culture. Medieval writers did not mechanically copy preexisting material; they adapted it and fashioned it into new works. Intermingling, reuse, and adaptation continued in the early modern print shop. The differences in the ways that the partners, on the one hand, and Zifroni and Luzzatto, on the other, presented and re-presented, adapted and manipulated, *Sefer Ḥasidim* passages, and contextualized their editions with paratexts, demonstrates their creativity. They did not merely "reproduce" an author's "discourse" for the "public," as Kant described the role of the publisher; they actively created new discourses in response to their own interests and the interests of potential readers.[7]

On the bookshelf, encased in leather, ornamented with gold, *Sefer Ḥasidim*, like other *sefarim*, gives off an impression of fixity and timelessness. It appears to exist today more or less as it always has. That impression, of course, as this monograph has taken pains to show, is an illusion. Scholars of digitization have identified the phenomenon of "screen essentialism," whereby readers of online texts grant them "an uncritical endorsement" as a result of what they perceive as "the computer's power to reproduce the real, uncompromised and undistorted by its own materiality."[8] Today's "screen essentialism" is, to some degree, matched in the Jewish community by a "print essentialism," which imputes to printed *sefarim* a greater confidence in their religious authority than it does to digital editions.

We have chronicled how early modern printers worked to imbue their books with confidence and credibility in times marked by a concomitant "manuscript essentialism," an enduring faith in the handwritten word. Printers created the book known as *Sefer Ḥasidim*—at least as it was known until the late nineteenth century. The story of its first two editions demonstrates how the textual and material forms of religious literature, while often portrayed by adherents as unchanging, are, in fact, historically contingent. *Sefer Ḥasidim,* Luzzatto claimed, was, like the tablets handed down by God on Mount Sinai, "written with the finger of God," set in stone. In reality, with their "inky fingers," in Anthony Grafton's turn of phrase, Luzzatto and Zifroni themselves, along with their print-shop colleagues and their predecessors in Bologna, brought *Sefer Ḥasidim* down from the mountain, for readers, Jewish and Christian, to read and revere.[9]

Notes

Introduction

1. The literature on *Sefer Ḥasidim* is voluminous. Some of the classic studies are: Y. N. Simhoni, "Ha-ḥasidut ha-ashkenazit be-yemei ha-beinayim," *Hatsefirah* (1917): 12–32, reprinted in Ivan G. Marcus, *Dat v'hevrah bamishnatam shel Ḥasidei Ashkenaz* (Jerusalem: Mercaz Shazar, 1999), 47–80; Jacob Freimann, introduction to *Sefer Ḥasidim: Al pi nusaḥ ketav ha-yad be-Parma*, ed. Jehuda Wistinetzki (Frankfurt: Wahrmann, 1924); Yitzhak Baer, "Ha-megamah ha-dadit- ha-ḥevrutit shel 'Sefer Ḥasidim,'" *Zion* 3 (1938); Gershom Sholem, *Major Trends in Jewish Mysticism* (New York: Schocken, 1946), 80–118; Haym Soloveitchik, "Three Themes in the *Sefer Ḥasidim*," *AJS Review* 1 (1976); Ivan G. Marcus, *Piety and Society: The Jewish Pietists of Medieval Germany* (Leiden: Brill, 1981); Joseph Dan, *Ḥasidut Ashkenaz be-toledot ha-maḥshavah ha-Yehudit* (Tel Aviv: Open University of Israel, 1990); Tamar Alexander-Frizer, *The Pious Sinner: Ethics and Aesthetics in the Medieval Hasidic Narrative* (Tübingen: Mohr Siebeck, 1991); Ephraim Kanarfogel, *Jewish Education and Society in the High Middle Ages* (Detroit, MI: Wayne State University Press, 1992); and Elisheva Baumgarten, *Practicing Piety in Medieval Ashkenaz: Men, Women, and Everyday Religious Observance* (Philadelphia: University of Pennsylvania Press, 2014). A summary of recent research on *Sefer Ḥasidim* and its world may be found in David I. Shyovitz, *A Remembrance of His Wonders: Nature and the Supernatural in Medieval Ashkenaz* (Philadelphia: University of Pennsylvania Press, 2017), 4–7.

2. On various rabbinic titles and honorifics, as well as the question of ordination, see Robert Bonfil, *Rabbis and Jewish Communities in Renaissance Italy*, trans. Jonathan Chipman (Oxford: Littman Library of Jewish Civilization, 1990), 35–99.

3. On the history and challenges associated with the term "early modern," see Randolph Starn, "The Early Modern Muddle," *Journal of Early Modern History* 6, no. 3 (2002).

4. On *Sefer Ḥasidim*'s influence, see Joseph Dan, *Ḥasidut Ashkenaz be-toldot ha-maḥshavah ha-Yehudit*, 3 vols. (Tel Aviv: ha-Universiṭṭah ha-Petuḥah, 1990); Eric Zimmer, *Olam ke-Minhago Noheg: Eraḳim be-Toldot ha-Minhagim, Hilkhotehem ve-Gilgulehem* (Jerusalem: Merkaz Zalman Shazar, 1996); Edward Fram, "German Pietism and Sixteenth- and Early Seventeenth-Century Polish Rabbinic Culture," *Jewish Quarterly Review* 96, no. 1 (2006).

5. Lucien Febvre and Henri-Jean Martin, *L'apparition du livre* (Paris: A. Michel, 1958); English edition: *The Coming of the Book: The Impact of Printing, 1450–1800*, trans. David

Gerard (London: Verso, 2010); Elizabeth L. Eisenstein, *The Printing Revolution in Early Modern Europe*, 2 vols. (New York: Cambridge University Press, 2005).

6. This question was the subject of an important debate between Eisenstein and Adrian Johns. See "AHR Forum: How Revolutionary Was the Print Revolution?" *American Historical Review* 107, no. 1 (February 2002). See also David McKittrick, *Print, Manuscript, and the Search for Order*, 1450–1830 (Cambridge: Cambridge University Press, 2003); Wolfgang Behringer, "Communications Revolutions: A Historiographical Concept," *German History* 24, no. 3 (2006); Sabrina Alcorn Baron and Eric N. Lindquist, eds., *Agent of Change: Print Culture Studies after Elizabeth L. Eisenstein* (Amherst: University of Massachusetts Press, 2007); and Andrew Pettegree, *The Book in the Renaissance* (New Haven, CT: Yale University Press, 2010).

7. David B. Ruderman, *Early Modern Jewry: A New Cultural History* (Princeton, NJ: Princeton University Press, 2010), 15, 100–103. Here, Ruderman is drawing on Ann Blair's characterization of the Renaissance provoking an "explosion of knowledge." Ann Blair, *The Theater of Nature: Jean Bodin and Renaissance Science* (Princeton, NJ: Princeton University Press, 1997), 68. Two recent explorations of the effect of printing on Jewish culture are Joshua Teplitsky, *Prince of the Press: How One Collector Built History's Most Enduring and Remarkable Jewish Library* (New Haven, CT: Yale University Press, 2019) and Andrea Gondos, *Kabbalah in Print: The Study and Popularization of Jewish Mysticism in Early Modernity* (Albany: SUNY Press, 2020).

8. Roger Chartier, *The Order of Books: Readers, Authors, and Libraries in Europe between the Fourteenth and Eighteenth Centuries* (Stanford, CA: Stanford University Press, 1994), 13.

9. Sigurður Gylfi Magnússon and István M. Szijártó, *What Is Microhistory?: Theory and Practice* (New York: Taylor & Francis, 2013), 22. On the complexities of microhistory and its relationship to cultural and social history, see Francesca Trivellato, "Microstoria/Microhistoire/Microhistory," *French Politics, Culture & Society* 33, no. 1 (Spring 2015) and the full volume of the *Journal of Medieval and Early Modern Studies* 47, no. 1 (January 2017), especially, "Microhistory Today: A Roundtable Discussion."

10. Edoardo Grendi is generally credited with coining the term; see Edoardo Grendi "Micro-Analyse et Histoire Sociale," trans. Pierre Savy, *Écrire l'histoire* 3 (2009): 70–72, originally published as Edoardo Grendi, "Micro-analisi e storia sociale," *Quaderni Storici* 12, no. 35 (2) (1977): 505–20 and Edoardo Grendi, "Ripensare la microstoria?" *Quaderni Storici* 29, no. 86 (2) (1994): 539–49.

11. Carlo Ginzburg, *The Cheese and the Worms: The Cosmos of a Sixteenth-Century Miller*, trans. John Tedeschi and Anne Tedeschi (Baltimore: Johns Hopkins University Press, 1980), xx, originally published as *Il formaggio e i vermi* (Turin: Giulio Einaudi, 1976). Ginzburg has acknowledged that features present in the microcosm cannot automatically be assumed present in the macrocosm. Determining the applicability of information gleaned about either realm for the other "constitutes both the greatest dif-

ficulty and the greatest potential benefit of microhistory." Carlo Ginzburg, "Microhistory: Two or Three Things That I Know About It," *Critical Inquiry* 20, no. 1 (1993): 33.

12. On the question of technological determinism, see Elizabeth L. Eisenstein, "An Unacknowledged Revolution Revisited," *American Historical Review* 107, no. 1 (2002).

13. The earliest printed Hebrew book that includes a date of publication is an edition of Rashi's commentary on the Pentateuch, printed in 1475 by Abraham b. Garton b. Isaac in Reggio di Calabria. See A. M. Habermann, *Ha-sefer ha-ivri be-hitpatḥuto: Mesimanim le-otiyot u-me-megillah le-sefer* (Jerusalem: Rubin Mass, 1968), 75–76. Undated Hebrew works were printed in Rome and elsewhere prior to that year; see Marvin J. Heller, introduction to *The Sixteenth Century Hebrew Book: An Abridged Thesaurus*, vol. 1 (Leiden: Brill, 2004), xiii–xvi; and Habermann, *Ha-sefer ha-ivri be-hitpatḥuto*, 74–143.

14. Printed books prior to 1501 are differentiated from those afterward, as they more closely resemble manuscripts. These early printed books are called "incunabula," and the period from 1455 to 1501 is designated the "incunabular period." Controlling for the fact that Hebrew printing began in 1475, and thus the incunabular period lasted for only twenty-five years and not a full century, we can say that five times more Hebrew books were printed in the sixteenth century than in the fifteenth. For these figures, see Heller, introduction to *The Sixteenth Century Hebrew Book*, xiii; Joseph R. Hacker and Adam Shear, introduction to *The Hebrew Book in Early Modern Italy* (Philadelphia: University of Pennsylvania Press, 2011), 2, 198n4; and Anat Gueta, "Ha-sefarim ha-mudpasim shel shenot ha-shin ke-makor le-ḥeker ḥaye ha-ru'ah shel ha-ḥevrah ha-yehudi" (PhD diss., Bar Ilan University, 2002). On Hebrew incunabula, see A. K. Offenberg, *A Choice of Corals: Facets of Fifteenth-Century Hebrew Printing*, Biblia Humanistica & Reformatorica 52 (Nieuwkoop, Netherlands: De Graaf, 1992), 42–58.

15. On Bomberg's press, see Aron Freiman, "Daniel Bomberg und seine hebräische Druckerei in Venedig," *Zeitschrift für hebräische Bibliographie* 10 (1909): 32–36; A. M. Habermann, *Hamadpis Daniel Bombergi ve-reshimat sifrei beit defuso* (Safed: Museum of Printing Art, 1978); Avraham Rosenthal, "Daniel Bomberg and His Talmud Editions," in *Gli Ebrei e Venezia: Secoli XIV–XVIII*, ed. Gaetano Cozzi (Milan: Edizioni Communità, 2012); and Bruce Nielsen, "Daniel van Bombergen, a Bookman of Two Worlds," in *The Hebrew Book in Early Modern Italy*, eds. Hacker and Shear.

16. Shifra Baruchson, *Sefarim ve-kor'im: Tarbut ha-keri'ah shel Yehude Iṭalyah be-shilhe ha-Renesans* (Ramat-Gan: Bar Ilan University Press, 1993); Gueta, "Ha-sefarim ha-mudpasim shel shenot ha-shin."

17. Brian Richardson, *Printing, Writers, and Readers in Renaissance Italy* (Cambridge: Cambridge University Press, 1999), 21. See also Ann Blair, who places the upper limit of the figure at 1,250 copies; Ann Blair, "Information in Early Modern Europe" in *Information: A Historical Companion*, eds. Ann Blair, Paul Duguid, Anja-Silvia Goeing, and Anthony Grafton (Princeton, NJ: Princeton University Press, 2021), 69. On the limitations the size of a typical print run imposed on the success of a book, see Adam

Teller, "Culture and Money: The Economic Dimension of Cultural History and What It Can Teach Us," *Jewish Quarterly Review* 104, no. 2 (Spring 2014): 279–80.

18. Baruchson, *Sefarim ve-kor'im*, 29; Ziporah (Shifra) Baruchson, "Money and Culture: Financing Sources and Methods in Hebrew Printing Shops in Cinquecento Italy," *La Bibliofilia* 92 (1990): 35.

19. Blair, "Information in Early Modern Europe," 71.

20. Shifra Z. Baruchson-Arbib, "The Prices of Hebrew Printed Books in Cinquecento Italy," *La Bibliofilia* 97, no. 2 (1995): 157.

21. Baruchson-Arbib, "The Prices of Hebrew Printed Books in Cinquecento Italy," 160.

22. As noted in chapter 4, Froben printed (or intended to print) 1,100 copies of the Babylonian Talmud shortly before he began work on *Sefer Ḥasidim*.

23. On the Zohar, Daniel Abrams has been especially forthright: "The 'Book of the *Zohar*' [as it is known today] *is a late invention* that should not be attributed to the process or intention of its composition at the end of the thirteenth century and the beginning of the fourteenth century." Emphasis in original. Daniel Abrams, *Kabbalistic Manuscripts and Textual Theory: Methodologies of Textual Scholarship and Editorial Practice in the Study of Jewish Mysticism* (Jerusalem: Magnes Press, 2010), 227. See also Boaz Huss, *The Zohar: Reception and Impact*, trans. Yudith Nave (London: Littman Library of Jewish Civilization, 2016); Andrea Gondos, *Kabbalah in Print: The Study and Popularization of Jewish Mysticism in Early Modernity* (Albany: SUNY Press, 2020). Yakov Z. Mayer's study of the Bomberg *editio princeps* of the Palestinian Talmud and the editorial practices its printers employed is especially illuminating. Yakov Z. Mayer, "Me-tarbut k'tav ha-yad le-tarbut ha-defus" (PhD diss., Tel Aviv University, 2018).

24. Princeton University *Sefer Ḥasidim* Project Database, Trustees of Princeton University, accessed March 3, 2021, https://etc.princeton.edu/sefer_hasidim/index.php. These manuscripts have also recently been cataloged by Ivan G. Marcus, *Sefer Hasidim and the Ashkenazic Book in Medieval Europe* (Philadelphia: University of Pennsylvania Press, 2018), 90–103. Marcus also has cataloged nearly twenty *Sefer Ḥasidim* manuscripts that postdate the appearance of the first printed edition in his *Sefer Hasidim and the Ashkenazic Book*, 103–21.

25. Jehuda Wistinetzki, ed., *Sefer Ḥasidim nusaḥ ketav ha-yad be-Parma*, republished by Freimann, *Sefer Ḥasidim: Al pi nusaḥ ketav ha-yad be-Parma*. A facsimile was published by Ivan Marcus, *Kitve-yad ivriyim me-otsrot sifriyat ha-Palatina be-Parma* (Jerusalem: Beit ha-sefarim ha-le'umi, 1985).

26. Schäfer began questioning the fetishization of the *Urtext* in rabbinic literature scholarship in the 1980s; see Peter Schäfer, "Research into Rabbinic Literature: An Attempt to Define the Status Quaestionis," in *Rabbinic Texts and the History of Late-Roman Palestine* (Oxford: Oxford University Press, 2010), 150, originally published in *Journal of Jewish Studies* 37, no. 2 (1986), where he wrote powerfully, "Are there texts

that can be defined and clearly delimited, or are there only basically 'open' texts, which elude temporal and redactional fixation?" Schäfer subsequently began several research projects demonstrating the inherent instability of Hebrew manuscripts, ancient and medieval, including the Princeton University *Sefer Ḥasidim* Project.

27. This terminology draws on that of Schäfer, Israel Ta-Sh'ma, and David Konstan.

28. Ivan G. Marcus, *Sefer Hasidim and the Ashkenazic Book in Medieval Europe*, 7.

29. Marcus, *Sefer Hasidim and the Ashkenazic Book*, 4–5, 32. In the Muslim world, Jews adopted the practice of producing the single-authored treatise beginning in the tenth century; see Rina Drory, *Models and Contacts: Arabic Literature and Its Impact on Medieval Jewish Culture* (Leiden: Brill, 2000), 136–43.

30. This is admittedly but one definition of "book" that I discuss in greater detail in chapter 1. On the various definitions of that word in the context of the history of Hebrew printing, see Yaacob Dweck, "What Is a Jewish Book?" *AJS Review* 34, no. 2 (November 2010).

31. The question of the fixity of the printed word is fraught and has been much discussed since Eisenstein's *The Printing Press as an Agent of Change*. See the sources cited in note 6. In the case of *Sefer Ḥasidim*, however, the fixed form of the printed text persisted until the nineteenth century. The printers of the second edition introduced important changes, also discussed in following chapters, but preserved the overall structure established in the Bologna edition.

32. On the persistence of manuscripts after printing, see Yaacob Dweck, *The Scandal of Kabbalah: Leon Modena, Jewish Mysticism, Early Modern Venice* (Princeton: Princeton University Press, 2012), 32–58.

33. As Joseph Dan has noted, the number of Ashkenazi *ḥasidim* at any one time during the medieval period was very limited, and their distinctive ritual, ethical, and theological concepts were known only to an intimate circle of scholars. Joseph Dan, "Ashkenazi Ḥasidim, 1941–1991: Was There Really a Hasidic Movement in Medieval Germany?" in *Gershom Scholem's Major Trends in Jewish Mysticism Years After: Proceedings of the Sixth International Conference on the History of Jewish Mysticism*, eds. Peter Schäfer and Joseph Dan (Tübingen: Mohr, 1992), 94–101. Haym Soloveichik has gone further, arguing that the distinctive ideas of *Sefer Ḥasidim* had next to no influence on subsequent generations of Jewish scholars; Haym Soloveitchik, "Piety, Pietism and German Pietism: Sefer Ḥasidim and the Influence of *Ḥasidei Ashkenaz*," *Jewish Quarterly Review* 92, no. 3 (2002). I have found that the title *Sefer Ḥasidim* is not widely cited, even among Ashkenazic authorities. Among the handful of examples are *Tosafot* on the Babylonian Talmud, *Kiddushin* 60b, *lemma: ki ha-hi* and Isaac b. Moses, *Sefer or zaru'a, hilkhot tefilin*, vol. 1, no. 576, Bar Ilan Responsa Project.

34. The number fifty is a based on Yeshayahu Vinograd's listings in his *Oẓar ha-sefer ha-Ivri* (Jerusalem: Ha-Makhon le-bibliyografyah memuḥshevet, 1993), the holdings of the National Library of Israel, and Ivan Marcus's catalog of editions in his *Sefer*

Hasidim and the Ashkenazic Book in Medieval Europe, 119–23. There are discrepancies among these listings, but the sheer multiplicity of editions conveys a sense of the demand for *Sefer Ḥasidim*, especially among Eastern European Jews, where most were printed. The fifty editions produced prior to the printing of the Parma manuscript in 1891 thus share a common ancestor: the 1538 Bologna edition. My own survey of the vast majority of these editions has demonstrated that they all possess the same textual hallmarks—such as the same censorings, the same numeration, the same subsections, the same organization, and the same headings—introduced by the printers of the first edition and modified in the second edition.

35. Edward Fram, "German Pietism and Sixteenth- and Early Seventeenth-Century Polish Rabbinic Culture," *Jewish Quarterly Review* 96, no. 1 (Winter 2006): 51.

36. Alexandra Gillespie, *Print Culture and the Medieval Author: Chaucer, Lydgate, and Their Books, 1473–1557* (Oxford: Oxford University Press, 2006), 83–94. Note how various scholarly enterprises outside the print shop served to "repackage" the Bible during the early modern period; see Jonathan Sheehan, *The Enlightenment Bible* (Princeton, NJ: Princeton University Press, 2005).

37. Emphasis in original. Craig Kallendorf, *Printing Virgil: The Transformation of the Classics in the Renaissance* (Leiden: Brill, 2019), 14.

38. Pamela H. Smith, "Why Write a Book? From Lived Experience to the Written Word in Early Modern Europe," *Bulletin of the German Historical Institute* 47 (Fall 2010).

39. Simon Schaffer and Steven Shapin, *The Leviathan and the Air Pump: Hobbes, Boyle, and the Experimental Life* (Princeton, NJ: Princeton University Press, 2011).

40. Adrian Johns, *The Nature of the Book: Print and Knowledge in the Making* (Chicago: University of Chicago Press, 1998), 42. Johns has argued that Elizabeth Eisenstein failed to pay close attention to the internal dynamics of the print shop and, therefore, failed to notice how printers worked actively to win authority and credibility for their works and the new medium of printing.

41. Johns, *The Nature of the Book*, 42.

42. Emphasis in original. Gérard Genette, *Paratexts: Thresholds of Interpretation*, trans. Jane E. Lewin (Cambridge: Cambridge University Press, 1997), 1.

43. Genette, *Paratexts*, 2.

44. Genette, *Paratexts*, 407; Duncan and Smyth, *Book Parts* (Oxford: Oxford University Press, 2019).

45. Brian Richardson, *Print Culture in Renaissance Italy: The Editor and the Vernacular Text, 1470–1600* (Cambridge: Cambridge University Press, 1994), 1, 182–83.

46. Anthony Grafton, *The Culture of Correction in Renaissance Europe* (London: British Library, 2011), 26.

47. See *Jewish Encyclopedia*, 2nd ed., s.v. "Title-Page," which notes that formal title

pages began to appear in Hebrew printed books in the mid-1510s. My own survey of the digitized printed Hebrew books in the National Library of Israel collection confirms this claim. However, Marvin Heller has noted that a small number of incunabula contained decorated first pages; see Marvin J. Heller, *Further Studies in the Making of the Early Hebrew Book* (Leiden: Brill, 2013), 3–34.

48. Michel Foucault, "What Is an Author?" in *The Book History Reader*, eds. David Finkelstein and Alistair McCleery, 2nd ed. (London: Routledge, 2006), 284–85. Foucault dates this change to the period of the great revolutions "at the end of the eighteenth century and the beginning of the nineteenth century," though it would be more accurate to see this as a process that began with the advent of print and continued into the nineteenth century.

49. Lisa Jardine, *Erasmus, Man of Letters: The Construction of Charisma in Print* (Princeton, NJ: Princeton University Press, 1993), 5.

50. Ann M. Blair, *Too Much to Know: Managing Scholarly Information Before the Modern Age* (New Haven, CT: Yale University Press, 2010), 117.

51. Adam Shear, *The Kuzari and the Shaping of Jewish Identity, 1167–1900* (Cambridge: Cambridge University Press, 2008), 160.

52. Annabel M. Patterson, *Censorship and Interpretation: The Conditions of Writing and Reading in Early Modern England* (Madison: University of Wisconsin Press, 1984), 45.

53. Patterson, *Censorship and Interpretation*, 40. See also Leo Strauss, *Persecution and the Art of Writing* (Glencoe, IL: Free Press, 1952).

54. Hannah Marcus, *Forbidden Knowledge: Medicine, Science, and Censorship in Early Modern Italy* (Chicago: University of Chicago Press, 2020), 2.

55. Amnon Raz-Krakotzkin, *The Censor, the Editor, and the Text: The Catholic Church and the Shaping of the Jewish Canon in the Sixteenth Century* (Philadelphia: University of Pennsylvania Press, 2007), 180–94.

56. Alexander Marx, "Aldus and Hebrew Type," *Papers of Bibliographical Society of America* (1919): 64–67.

57. On Christian Hebraism, see chapter 4, as well as Jerome Friedman, *The Most Ancient Testimony: Sixteenth-Century Christian-Hebraica in the Age of Renaissance Nostalgia* (Athens: Ohio University Press, 1983); Allison P. Coudert and Jeffrey S. Shoulson, eds., *Hebraica Veritas? Christian Hebraists and the Study of Judaism in Early Modern Europe* (Philadelphia: University of Pennsylvania Press, 2004); Anthony Grafton and Joanna Weinberg, *"I Have Always Loved the Holy Tongue": Isaac Casaubon, the Jews, and a Forgotten Chapter in Renaissance Scholarship* (Cambridge, MA: Belknap Press of Harvard University Press, 2011); and Stephen G. Burnett, *Christian Hebraism in the Reformation Era* (1500–1660) (Leiden: Brill, 2012).

58. De' Rossi will be discussed in greater detail in chapter 5, but see Joanna Weinberg,

introduction to *The Light of the Eyes* (New Haven, CT: Yale University Press, 2001), 1–6, and the sources cited therein. On Lampronti, see Debra Glasberg Gail, "Scientific Authority and Jewish Law in Early Modern Italy" (PhD diss., Columbia University, 2016).

59. See the topics covered in Finkelstein and McCleery, eds., *The Book History Reader*. A new encyclopedic volume seeks to rectify this Christo- and Euro-centric bias by expanding the perspective to include the Islamic world and East Asia. Here too, however, Hebrew books are given short shrift. See Blair, Duguid, Goeing, and Grafton, eds., *Information: A Historical Companion*.

Sefer Ḥasidim in the Middle Ages

1. These are topics discussed in *Sefer Ḥasidim* (Bologna, 1538), §281, §431, §429, and §918. These passages all have many parallels within the Bologna *editio princeps* and in the manuscripts.

2. In the original German, Kant calls such a person a "Schriftsteller" (writer) and then glosses the term parenthetically, as Gregor does in her translation, as "autor" (author).

3. Immanuel Kant, *The Metaphysics of Morals*, trans. Mary Gregor (Cambridge: Cambridge University Press, 1991), 106, originally published as *Die Metaphysik der Sitten* (1794).

4. On the enduring significance of Kant's definition, see Dweck, "What Is a Jewish Book?" 367–71; Ronald Hendel, "What Is a Biblical Book?" in *From Author to Copyist: Essays on the Composition, Redaction, and Transmission of the Hebrew Bible in Honor of Zipi Talshir*, ed. Cana Werman (State College, PA: Penn State University Press, 2015), 283–84.

5. Kant, *The Metaphysics of Morals*, 107. Kant also discussed this theory in Immanuel Kant, "Of the Injustice of Counterfeiting Books" (1785), in *Essays and Treatises on Moral, Political, and Various Philosophical Subjects* (London: William Richardson, 1799). On Kant's conception of intellectual property, see Riccardo Pozzo, "Immanuel Kant on Intellectual Property," *Trans/Form/Ação* 29, no. 2 (2006) and Adrian Johns, *Piracy: The Intellectual Property Wars from Gutenberg to Gates* (Chicago: University of Chicago Press, 2010), 54–55.

6. The two versions of this passage are primarily differentiated by the presence of the introductory sentences detailing the wise man's instructions to his son. The version quoted is found in the Bologna printed edition §97, Ms. Ambrosiana X 111 §97, Ms. Cambridge Add. 379 §97, Ms. Oxford Bodleian Opp. 340 §45, and Ms. Vatican 285 §154. The second abbreviated version is found in the Bologna printed edition §916, Ms. Parma §647, and Ms. JTS (formerly) Boesky 45.

7. Wistinetski, ed., *Sefer Ḥasidim al pi nusah k'tav yad be-Parmah*.

8. Abraham Epstein, "R. Shmu'el he-Ḥasid b'R. Kalonimus ha-zaken," *Ha-goren* 4

(1903): 92. Epstein was not the first scholar to propose this chronology, however; that distinction goes to Epstein's contemporary, the Jerusalemite rabbi and bibliophile Solomon Wertheimer. On this history, see Ivan G. Marcus, "The Recensions and Structure of '*Sefer Ḥasidim*,'" *Proceedings of the American Academy for Jewish Research* 45 (1978): 139–40.

9. Freimann, "Introduction," in Wistinetski, ed., *Sefer Ḥasidim: Al pi nosaḥ ketav yad asher be-Parma*, 19.

10. Haym Soloveitchik, "Piety, Pietism and German Pietism," 465; Johann Maier, "I '*Sefer Hasidim*': Il manoscrito Parmenese 3,280 e Edizione di Bologna, 1,538. Observazioni critiche," in *Manoscritti, frammentti e libri ebraici nell'Italia dei secoli XV–XVI*, ed. Giuliano Tamani and Angelo Vivian (Rome: Carucci, 1991), 129–36; Saskia Dönitz, "Assessing the Manuscripts of *Sefer Ḥasidim*," *Jewish History* 34 (2021).

11. In a 1978 article, for example, Marcus carried on Freimann's topical analysis, suggesting that "the Parma manuscript and ed. Bologna have not preserved editions of an original *Sefer Ḥasidim*, now lost, but contain at least three recensions of the book itself," and that "the topical structure" of these recensions "represents the original structure of Judah the Pietist's *Sefer Ḥasidim*." Ivan G. Marcus, "The Recensions and Structure of '*Sefer Ḥasidim*,'" 151. Marcus's recent work, stressing the openness of *Sefer Ḥasidim*, is a significant departure from his own scholarship.

12. Several of the manuscripts that postdate the Bologna edition do appear to have been copied directly from the Bologna edition, such as Ms. Hamburg Staats- und Universitätsbibliothek, Cod. Heb. 303 and Ms. Hebrew Union College 269.

13. Note that the definite article (*hey*) in this form of the title also appears on the title page of the Bologna printed edition.

14. Ms. Ambrosiana X 111 is composed of §§1–152 of the Bologna edition; Ms. Moscow Günzburg 103/4 is composed of §§1–152 (lacking §113); Ms. Nîmes Bibliothèque Municipale 26 is composed of §§1–62; and Ms. Oxford Bodleian Mich. 155 is composed of §§1–16.

15. Ms. Oxford Bodleian App. Opp. 340 (it lacks §§103–116).

16. SH I or *Sefer Ḥasidut* introduces both the longer Ms. Cambridge Add. 379 and the Ms. Bodleian Opp. Add. 34. See Soloveitchik, "Piety, Pietism and German Pietism," 464; Marcus, *Sefer Hasidim and the Ashkenazic Book*, 38; Judah Galinsky, "The Impact of *Ḥasidei Ashkenaz* in Northern France: The Evidence of *Sefer Ḥasidut* and *Ḥayyei Olam*," *Jewish History* (2021).

17. Seven of the seventeen *Sefer Ḥasidim* manuscripts with discernible titles employ the term *likkutim* and related phrases.

18. Presumably, at least some scribes would have chosen to copy a "complete" version of *Sefer Ḥasidim* if they had had access to one.

19. *Sefer Ḥasidim*, Cambridge University Library, Ms. Add. 379.2, Cambridge, England, fol. 74. This manuscript was copied in thirteenth or fourteenth century Ashkenaz; see

Stefan C. Reif, *Hebrew Manuscripts at Cambridge University Library* (Cambridge: Cambridge University Press, 1997), 222–23.

20. Marcus identified "thematic notebooks"—groupings of passages on topics relating to "the Sabbath" or "charity," for example—and Soloveitchik noted the presence of extracts from other known medieval works.

21. The word "this" (*zeh*) is set within an ornamental woodcut frame. The words "called *Sefer Ḥasidim*" are below the frame and above the first block of text, set in a square typeface.

22. This is the same as what is identified as *Sefer Ḥasidim* 2 (*bet*) in the Parma manuscript.

23. Marcus, in his early work, offered a different scheme for dividing the Bologna edition: He perceived the text as divided into three self-contained "recensions," which he called SHB I, SHB II, and SHB III. Each of these recensions was composed of a series of topical "notebooks," that is, gatherings of passages on a particular theme, such as "reverence" or "atonement." Marcus argued that the topical notebooks in SHB I and SHB III appear roughly in the same order. SHB II shared themes with SHB I and SHB III but is, in his words, more "fragmentary." He then telegraphed this thematic ordering onto the Parma manuscript, demonstrating that parts of the Parma manuscript followed the same structure. Marcus, "The Recensions and Structure of 'Sefer Ḥasidim,'" 146–47.

24. Following the paragraphing of the Bologna edition, these include §§18–21, 23, 33–34, 43, and 51–52. The excerpts are taken from *Mishneh Torah* "Laws of Prayer," "Laws of Repentance," "Laws of Torah Study," and "Laws of Mental Dispositions."

25. Soloveitchik has commented that these Maimonidean passages "are interwoven with the words of *SH I*, and the mix that results seems so natural, the transitions so seamless, that one is hard-pressed to detect where one ends and the other begins." Soloveitchik, "Piety, Pietism and German Pietism," 462.

26. The quotation from *Megillat setarim* (which, unfortunately, is no longer extant) is found in §§604–605; the quotation from *Hilkhot ha-Rif* (tractate *Rosh HaShanah* 4a, section 5) is §606; and the quote from *Emunot ve-De'ot* (5:4–5) is §§613–614.

27. §§765–766. On the implications of this responsum for scholarship on the history of the *Ḥasidei Ashkenaz*, see Ephraim Kanarfogel, "'R. Judah he-Hasid and the Rabbinic Scholars of Regensburg: Interactions, Influences, and Implications," *Jewish Quarterly Review* 96, no. 1 (2006).

28. Marcus is not entirely clear on which passages make up *Sefer ha-yir'ah*. In his early work, he identified §§153–166 as *Sefer ha-yir'ah*; see Marcus, *Piety and Society*, 136. However, more recently, Marcus has suggested that *Sefer ha-yir'ah* was §§153–161; see Marcus, *Sefer Hasidim and the Ashkenazic Book*, 39. The latter division seems more probable because §162 of the Bologna edition, as noted earlier, begins with the enlarged

heading "*Sefer ha-Ḥasidim*," indicating that it originates from a different source from that which precedes it.

29. A. J. Minnis, *Medieval Theory of Authorship: Scholastic Literary Attitudes in the Later Middle Ages* (Philadelphia: University of Pennsylvania Press, 1988), 10–11, 114. Minnis describes how this concept of authorship changed in the course of the thirteenth century with the popularization of Aristotle's theories of causation and the emergence of the Aristotelian prologue, in which the copyist would sketch biographical details of an author's life. These medieval innovations, however, very often applied to the canonical authors of antiquity rather than to noncanonical texts and recent compositions. On the medieval conception of authorship in Jewish texts, see Moshe Halbertal, *Concealment and Revelation: Esotericism in Jewish Thought and Its Philosophical Implications*, trans. Jackie Feldman (Princeton, NJ: Princeton University Press, 2007), 39; and Abrams, *Kabbalistic Manuscripts and Textual Theory*, 366.

30. Gerald L. Burns, "The Originality of Texts in a Manuscript Culture," *Comparative Literature* 32, no. 2 (Spring 1980): 113–129, especially 125; and Israel Ta-Shma, "The 'Open' Book in Medieval Hebrew Literature: The Problem of Authorized Editions," *Bulletin of the John Rylands University Library of Manchester* 73, no. 3 (Autumn 1993).

31. The Parma manuscript and the manuscript formerly known as JTS Boesky 45, which is closely related to it, has the name "Samuel" at the top of the first column. Yet the presence of "Samuel" is hardly a formal statement of attribution. These manuscripts do not, for example, employ any of the standard Hebrew attribution formulae. However, Marcus took this as an assertion that the first portion of the Parma manuscript—the beginning of the so-called *Sefer ha-yir'ah*—was written by Judah's father, R. Samuel he-Ḥasid. Jehuda Wistinetzki, in his note below the text in the 1891 edition of the Parma manuscript, wrote, "I am not able to discern or comprehend this word." It is possible that Gedaliah ibn Yaḥya, however, the author of the sixteenth-century Hebrew chronicle and bibliography, *Sefer shalshelet ha-kabbalah*, saw this very manuscript and understood the name "Samuel" on the first page in the same way as Marcus did; see Marcus, *Piety and Society*, 139–40. In *Sefer shalshelet ha-kabbalah*, Gedaliah wrote, "I saw a small composition (*ḥibbur katan*) that says at its start, 'This is *Sefer ha-Ḥasidim* which was established [*yasado*] by our Rabbi Samuel the prophet, the father of our Rabbi Judah he-Ḥasid.'" Gedaliah ibn Yaḥya, *Sefer shalshelet ha-kabbalah* (Venice, 1587), 54. Gedaliah's attribution of *Sefer Ḥasidim* to Samuel will be discussed further in the epilogue.

32. *Sefer Ḥasidim* (Bologna, 1538), §367; Wistinetski, ed., *Sefer Ḥasidim*, §1,052.

33. Marcus, *Sefer Hasidim and the Ashkenazic Book*, 30. In perhaps the boldest refutation of this long-standing consensus, David Shyovitz has suggested scholars refocus their attentions from authorship to "author function," following Foucault, exploring the ways attribution contextualizes and informs readers' understandings of a specific work. This is exactly the kind of work this monograph sets out to do in chapters 3 and 5. Shyovitz, "Was Judah He-Ḥasid the 'Author' of *Sefer Ḥasidim*?" *Jewish History* (April 2021).

34. *Peirush al ha-Torah le-Yehudah he-Ḥasid,* Ms. Günzberg Hebrew 82, Russian State Library, Moscow, Russia, 63v; see also Isaak S. Lange, ed., *Peirushei al ha-Torah* (Jerusalem: Lange, 1974), 17.

35. Shyovitz, "Was Judah He-Ḥasid the 'Author' of *Sefer Ḥasidim?*"

36. See Isaac b. Moses, *Sefer or zaru'a, hilkhot shaliaḥ ẓibbur,* vol. 1, no. 114, Bar Ilan Responsa Database; Meir Ha'Kohen, *Hagahot Maimoniyot, Hilkhot avodah zarah* (Warsaw, 1888), 7:2, Bar Ilan Responsa Database.

37. See Isaac b. Moses, *Sefer or zaru'a, hilkhot tefilin,* vol. 1, no. 576, Bar Ilan Responsa Database; Peretz b. Elijah, *Hagahot al sefer mitẓvot katan,* §195, Bar Ilan Responsa Database.

38. Yitzhak F. Baer, "The Socioreligious Orientation of '*Sefer Ḥasidim,*'" in *Binah: Studies in Jewish Thought,* vol. 2, ed. Joseph Dan (New York: Praeger, 1989), originally published as "Ha-megama ha-datit ha-ḥevratit shel Sefer Ḥasidim," *Zion* 3 (1937).

39. *Sefer Ḥasidim* (Bologna, 1538), §1. The phrase "execute profoundly" is Soloveitchik's translation of the Hebrew *le-ha'amik la'asot*; Soloveitchik, "Three Themes in the '*Sefer Ḥasidim,*'" 313.

40. Soloveitchik, "Three Themes in the '*Sefer Ḥasidim,*'" 314–17.

41. Wistinetski, ed., *Sefer Ḥasidim,* §44. On this teaching and others relating to prayer, see Baumgarten, *Practicing Piety in Medieval Ashkenaz,* 24.

42. Wistinetski, ed., *Sefer Ḥasidim,* §5. The next passage attacks the actions of a sage (*talmid ḥakham*) who came and taught the shepherd the traditional liturgy. The lessons did not stick, however. The shepherd forgot what he learned from the sage but was afraid to say the words he had previously been accustomed to reciting. The text concludes that the shepherd should continue to say his old prayer.

43. Wistinetski, ed., *Sefer Ḥasidim,* §973. See Scholem, *Major Trends in Jewish Mysticism,* 221; and Soloveitchik, "Three Themes in the '*Sefer Ḥasidim,*'" 329.

44. Baumgarten, *Practicing Piety in Medieval Ashkenaz,* 148–55.

45. Wistinetski, ed., *Sefer Ḥasidim,* §985. On this passage, see Baer, "The Socioreligious Orientation of '*Sefer Ḥasidim,*'" 63; and Ivan Marcus, "A Jewish-Christian Symbiosis: The Culture of Early Ashkenaz," in *Cultures of the Jews,* ed. David Biale (New York: Schocken, 2002), 485.

46. Wistinetski, ed., *Sefer Ḥasidim,* §815; *Sefer Ḥasidim* (Bologna), §15.

47. Hebrew Bible quotations are usually those of the NJPS translation; here, I deviate and cite the Jewish Publication Society (1914) translation, as it is closer to the literal sense of the verse and accords better with the exposition.

48. Wistinetski, ed., *Sefer Ḥasidim,* §648. For a counterpoint, see Baer's discussion of this passage; Baer, "The Socioreligious Orientation of '*Sefer Ḥasidim,*'" 65.

49. *Sefer Ḥasidim* (Bologna, 1538), §929; Wistinetski, ed., *Sefer Ḥasidim*, §664. See Kanarfogel, "R. Judah He-Hasid," 36.

50. Wistinetski, ed., *Sefer Ḥasidim*, §§1,592–93; *Sefer Ḥasidim* (Bologna), §§762–63.

51. Wistinetski, ed., *Sefer Ḥasidim*, §43. The passage quoted at the start of this chapter invokes the teaching that a person should fast regularly, over and above the statutory fasts of the Jewish calendar. See also *Sefer Ḥasidim* (Bologna), §225. The parallel in Ms. Parma is less stringent: "No forty days should pass" without a fast; Wistinetski, ed., *Sefer Ḥasidim*, §280. On extra-statutory fasting, see Baumgarten, *Practicing Piety in Medieval Ashkenaz*, 72–85.

52. Wistinetski, ed., *Sefer Ḥasidim*, §1,556. When another Jew accuses this *ḥasid* of transgression by purposefully endangering his life, the *ḥasid* invokes the midrashic interpretation of Isaiah 53:5: His behavior was intended to prevent the Messiah himself from suffering on account of the *ḥasid*'s sins. Isaiah 52–53 is the *locus classicus* of the suffering servant motif that is associated with the Messiah in later Jewish and Christian interpretation. See Marc Brettler and Amy-Jill Levine, "Isaiah's Suffering Servant: Before and after Christianity," *Interpretation: A Journal of Bible and Theology* 73, no. 2 (2019). This passage in *Sefer Ḥasidim*, Ms. Parma, was discussed by Scholem, *Major Trends in Jewish Mysticism*, 246.

53. Wistinetski, ed., *Sefer Ḥasidim*, §2; *Sefer Ḥasidim* (Bologna), §155. On the motif of the wondrousness of the body in *Sefer Ḥasidim* in contrast to the negation of the body, see Shyovitz, *A Remembrance of His Wonders*, 73–113.

54. *Sefer Ḥasidim* (Bologna), §57.

55. Wistinetski, ed., *Sefer Ḥasidim*, §815; *Sefer Ḥasidim* (Bologna), §300.

56. Wistinetski, ed., *Sefer Ḥasidim*, §202; *Sefer Ḥasidim* (Bologna), §199.

57. *Sefer Ḥasidim* (Bologna), §142. See Marcus, "A Jewish-Christian Symbiosis," 486.

58. *Sefer Ḥasidim* (Bologna), §429. This passage is discussed in chapter 3 as well and is found in several manuscripts.

59. *Sefer Ḥasidim* (Bologna), §427. This passage is also found in several manuscripts.

60. *Sefer Ḥasidim* (Bologna), §464; Wistinetski, ed., *Sefer Ḥasidim*, §1,465. This translation is that of Shyovitz, *A Remembrance of His Wonders*, 154, and his discussion of the werewolf in *Sefer Ḥasidim*, 153–57.

61. Wistinetski, ed., *Sefer Ḥasidim*, §397. Again, for a translation and discussion of this passage, see Shyovitz, *A Remembrance of His Wonders*, 156.

62. *Sefer Ḥasidim* (Bologna), §452; Wistinetski, ed., *Sefer Ḥasidim*, §1,543.

63. Soloveitchik, "Piety, Pietism and German Pietism."

64. Ivan G. Marcus, *Rituals of Childhood* (New Haven, CT: Yale University Press, 2015), 11–13.

65. Elisheva Baumgarten, "Appropriation and Differentiation: Jewish Identity in Medieval Ashkenaz," *AJS Review* 42, no. 1 (2018).

The Partners of Bologna

1. Kenneth R. Stow, *Alienated Minority: The Jews of Medieval Latin Europe* (Cambridge, MA: Harvard University Press, 2009), 71.

2. Joseph Delmedigo, *Sefer meẓaref leḥokhma* (Odessa, 1865), 21a. Joseph claims to be quoting directly from a manuscript, and manuscripts containing the story exist, including one in the National Library of France, Ms. 722; see *Encyclopedia Judaica*, 2nd. ed. (Detroit, MI: Macmillan, Keter Publishing House, 2007), s.v. "Kalonymus."

3. On these southward migrations, see Erika Timm, "The Migration of German Jews into Italy and the Emergence of Local Rites of Seliḥot Recitation," in *The Jews of Europe Around 1400: Disruption, Crisis, and Resilience*, eds. Lukas Clemens and Christoph Cluse (Weisbaden, Germany: Harrassowitz, 2018).

4. On the basis of literary evidence, Mauro Perani and Bracha Rivlin suggest that Jews resided in Bologna as early as the fourth century CE. Attilio Milano points to the earliest extant Jewish residence permits, from the mid-fourteenth century, as the earliest evidence for Jews in the city. On this and the history of Jewish life in Bologna more generally, see Milano's article in *Encyclopedia Judaica*, s.v. "Bologna"; Mauro Perani and Bracha Rivlin, *Vita religiosa ebraica a Bologna nel cinquecento: Gli statuti della Confraternita dei Solerti* (Florence: Giuntina, 2000), 73–82; and Ariel Toaff, "Bologna ebraica negli studi recenti," in *La cultura ebraica a Bologna tra medioevo e rinascimento*, ed. Mauro Perani (Florence: Giuntina, 2002), 13–28.

5. Louis Finkelstein, *Jewish Self-Government in the Middle Ages* (New York: Jewish Theological Seminary of America, 1924), 86–87.

6. Bernard Cooperman, "Political Discourse in a Kabbalistic Register: Isaac De Lattes's 'Plea for Stronger Communal Government,'" in *Be'erot Yitzhak: Studies in Memory of Isadore Twersky*, ed. Jay Michael Harris (Cambridge, MA: Harvard Center for Jewish Studies, 2005), 47. The figure of around 1,000 individuals is standard. Moses Shulvass put the number of Jews in Rome during the first half of the sixteenth century at between 1,500 and 1,800. He estimated that about 1,000 Jews resided in Venice, and perhaps as many as 2,000 Jews resided in Mantua and Ferrara, respectively; Moses A. Shulvass, *The Jews in the World of the Renaissance*, trans. Elvin I. Kose (Leiden: Brill, 1973), 15–28. On the total population of Bologna, see Jan de Vries, *The City: European Urbanization, 1500–1800*, 2nd ed. (Cambridge, MA: Harvard University Press, 1997), 276.

7. Shulvass, *Jews in the World of the Renaissance*, 6.

8. Despite losing Florence, the Medici still controlled the papacy, and thus their Jewish banker clients were welcomed into Bologna, which had been integrated into the Papal States through the War of the League of Cambrai (1508–1516). See Stefanie B.

Siegmund, *The Medici State and the Ghetto of Florence: The Construction of an Early Modern Jewish Community* (Stanford, CA: Stanford University Press, 2006), 98; Isaiah Sonne, "*Le-toldot kehillat Bologna ba-teḥilat ha-meah ha-16*," *Hebrew Union College Annual* 16 (1941): 78.

9. Cooperman, "Political Discourse in a Kabbalistic Register," 47.

10. Sonne, "Le-toldot kehillat Bologna," 37–38; Bonfil, *Rabbis and Jewish Communities*, 192–206; Bernard Cooperman, "Theorizing Jewish Self-Government in Early Modern Italy," in *Una manna buona per mantova: Studi in onore di Vittore Colorni*, ed. Mauro Perani (Florence: L. S. Olschki, 2004), 365–80. On interethnic conflict among Italian Jews in sixteenth-century Italy, see Serena Di Nepi, *Surviving the Ghetto: Toward a Social History of the Jewish Community in 16th-Century Rome*, trans. Paul M. Rosenberg (Leiden: Brill, 2020), 28–33; Bernard D. Cooperman, "Ethnicity and Institution Building among Jews in Early Modern Rome," *AJS Review* 30, no. 1 (April 2006); and Cooperman, "Political Discourse," 48–51.

11. Perani and Rivlin, *Vita religiosa ebraica a Bologna*, 74.

12. My translation. Alexander Marx, "R. Yosef ish Arli be-tor moreh ve-rosh yeshivah be-Siena," in *Sefer yovel: Likhvod Levi Gintzburg, ḥelek ivri*, vol. 2 (New York: American Academy for Jewish Research, 1946), 278–79n46.

13. See Perani and Rivlin, *Vita religiosa ebraica a Bologna*, 75.

14. On the relationship between the University of Bologna and the city's presses, see the following passage, as well as Carl F. Bühler, *The University and the Press in Fifteenth-Century Bologna* (Notre Dame, IN: Mediaeval Institute, University of Notre Dame, 1958).

In the years that followed, Bologna was one of only five Italian cities where presses operated continuously to the end of the sixteenth century. According to Neil Harris, during the fifteenth and early sixteenth centuries, it was largely a peripatetic enterprise; no sooner did a printer print a book in a given locale than he decided to pull up stakes and move elsewhere; see Neil Harris, "The History of the Book in Italy," in *The Oxford Companion to the Book*, vol. 1, eds. Michael F. Suarez, S. J. Woudhuysen, and H. R. Woudhuysen, 259 (Oxford: Oxford University Press, 2010). The fact that forty-seven presses were known to have operated in Bologna prior to 1500, many producing but one title, demonstrates the instability of the business of printing books during this period; Bühler, *The University and the Press*, 43. By the turn of the seventeenth century, printing spread northward, and the Italian peninsula lost its dominance in book production.

15. All three were humanists from prominent Bolognese families with close ties to the city's illustrious university. Azzoguidi had two brothers who were faculty members, and Malpigli was a faculty member himself; see Bühler, *University and the Press*, 15–16. The fact that this press was also founded by three men is not merely a coincidence. Establishing a press during the fifteenth and early sixteenth centuries was an expensive endeavor, and press founders required significant starting capital, and thus collaboration.

16. On financing the publication of a book in Renaissance Italy, see Richardson, *Printing, Writers and Readers*, 25–35.

17. Friedberg, *Toldot ha-defus*, 28; David Werner Amram, *The Makers of Hebrew Books in Italy: Being Chapters in the History of the Hebrew Printing Press* (Philadelphia: Julius H. Greenstone, 1909), 48.

18. On Kimḥi's polemics against Christianity and the Christological interpretation of Scripture, see Frank Talmage, "R. David Kimḥi as Polemicist," *Hebrew Union College Annual* 38 (1967).

19. Friedberg, *Toldot ha-defus*, 29; Amram, *Makers of Hebrew Books*, 42. Abraham the Dyer was assisted by the corrector Joseph of Strasbourg, who wrote the book's colophon. Amram suggests that this Joseph was likely the same "Meister Joseph" of the earlier Bologna press.

20. Perhaps this was a consequence of the region's political instability. Bologna, and Romagna more generally, was the site of repeated struggles between warring European powers, especially during the War of the League of Cambrai (1508–1516). For an overview, see Sonne, "Le-toldot kehillat Bologna," 35–37.

21. Treves, introduction to *Maḥzor ke-fi minhag kehillat kodesh Roma* (1540).

22. Throughout the introduction and in the colophon to the book, Treves himself emphasizes his wish to remain anonymous. According to Alexander Marx, however, the publishers of a subsequent edition of the *maḥzor* identified Treves as the editor and author of its commentary when they reissued it in 1550. Alexander Marx, "R. Joseph of Arles and Rabbi Yochanan Treves," in *Studies in Memory of Moses Schorr*, ed. Louis Ginzburg and Abraham Weiss (New York: Professor Moses Schorr Memorial Committee, 1944), 194.

23. On the title page to *Sefer or amim* (1536–1537), they called themselves "the insignificant, the partners, may they succeed and live, one and the same, makers of silk-work." On the title page to *Sefer Torah or* (1537–1538), they called themselves "the partners, may they succeed and live, makers of silk-work."

24. This was signified by their use of the title *moreinu harav*. The various rabbinic titles used during this period, and the distinctions between them, are nuanced and difficult to render in English. On rabbinic titles and honorifics, as well as the question of ordination, see Bonfil, *Rabbis and Jewish Communities*, 35–99.

25. Richardson, *Printing, Writers and Readers*, 33.

26. Bruce Nielsen, "Daniel Van Bombergen, a Bookman of Two Worlds," in *The Hebrew Book in Early Modern Italy*, eds. Hacker and Shear, 56–75; Avraham Rosenthal, "Daniel Bomberg and His Talmud Editions," in *Gli Ebrei e Venezia: Secoli XIV–XVIII*, ed. Gaetano Cozzi (Milan: Edizioni Communità, 2012), 375–416; A. M. Habermann, *Ha-madpis Daniel Bombergi*; Freiman, "Daniel Bomberg und seine hebräische Druckerei," 32–36.

27. On the role of privileges in premodern Christian Europe with an instructive comparison to the more generous legal structures governing Jewish settlement in the Islamic world, see Mark R. Cohen, *Under Crescent and Cross: The Jews in the Middle Ages* (Princeton, NJ: Princeton University Press, 2008).

28. See references throughout Shlomo Simonsohn, *The Apostolic See and the Jews: Documents, 1522–1538* (Toronto: Pontifical Institute of Mediaeval Studies, 1990). On Jews and papal taxation, see Kenneth R. Stow, *Taxation, Community and State: The Jews and the Fiscal Foundations of the Early Modern Papal State* (Stuttgart: Anton Hiersemann, 1982).

29. Paul F. Grendler, *The Roman Inquisition and the Venetian Press* (Princeton, NJ: Princeton University Press, 1977), 90–93.

30. This report is found in the Biblioteca Apostolica Vaticana, Ms. Vaticani latini 3928 130v–131r, and reproduced in Tamburini, *Ebrei Saraceni Cristiani*, 108–10 (though the page numbers cited by Tamburini are incorrect).

31. On the relationship of converts from Judaism to their former identities and communities, see Elisheva Carlebach, *Divided Souls: Converts from Judaism in Germany, 1500–1750* (New Haven, CT: Yale University Press, 2001).

32. Biblioteca Apostolica Vaticana, Ms. Vaticani latini 3928, 130v. I thank my dear friend Marie-Thérèse Daniëls-Dirven for assistance with Latin translations.

33. Biblioteca Apostolica Vaticana, Ms. Vaticani latini 3928, 131r.

34. On Pier Luigi, see George B. Parks, "The Pier Luigi Farnese Scandal: An English Report," *Renaissance News* 15, no. 3 (1962).

35. Vatican Apostolic Archives, Brevia Lat., vol. 27, 272r–273r, published in Simonsohn, *The Apostolic See and the Jews: Documents, 1522–1538*, 2,114 (document 1,903).

36. Shlomo Simonsohn, *The Apostolic See and the Jews: History* (Toronto: Pontifical Institute of Mediaeval Studies, 1991), 284.

37. Archivio Apostolico Vaticano, Ms. Armadio XLI, vol. 8, 179r–179v, published in Simonsohn, *The Apostolic See and the Jews: Documents*, 1522–1538, 2,054 (document 1,812).

38. Archivio Storico del Tribunale della Penitenzieria Apostolica, Registri matrimonialium et diversorum 95, published in Tamburini, *Ebrei Saraceni Cristiani*, 113–15. On the role of the Apostolic Penitentiary, see Tamburini, *Ebrei Saraceni Cristiani*, 13–19.

39. Archivio Storico del Tribunale della Penitenzieria Apostolica, Registri matrimonialium et diversorum 95; Tamburini, *Ebrei Saraceni Cristiani*, 114.

40. This book may have been a grammar about which Sforno wrote to his brother Ḥananel a decade earlier. In the letter, Sforno stated he hoped to write a book "with a Latin translation," meant to "demonstrate the virtue of the Hebrew language over every other people's language." Sforno refers to Hebrew idiomatically as the "Holy

Language" (*lashon ha-koshesh*) and to Latin as "Christian" (*nozrit*). The letter is one of a series found in Ms. Parma 2399, published by Joseph Laras, "Letters from Rabbi Obadiah Sforno" [in Hebrew], *Sinai* 62 (1968): 262–67. The letter is undated, but Laras suggests that because Sforno's brother lived in Bologna, Sforno must have written the letter from outside the city. Though this is not a given, if it was written prior to his arrival in Bologna, that would have been prior to 1527. Interestingly, Sforno comments that he was preparing the grammar "at the request of the Lord of Fusignano," namely, the humanist Celio Calcagnini; see Saverio Campanini, "Un intellettuale ebreo del rinascimento: 'Ovadya Sforno a Bologna e i suoi rapporti con i Cristiani,'" in *Verso l'epilogo di una convivenza: Gli ebrei a Bologna nel XVI secolo*, ed. Maria Giuseppina Muzzarelli (Florence: Giuntina, 1996), 111. On the concept of the superiority of the Hebrew language in the early modern period, see Adam Shear, *The Kuzari and the Shaping of Jewish Identity, 1167–1900* (Cambridge: Cambridge University Press, 2008), 98–103.

41. Amram, *The Makers of Hebrew Books*, 190; Habermann, *Ha-madpis Daniel Bombergi*.

42. On Bomberg's privileges, see Christopher L. C. E. Witcomb, *Copyright in the Renaissance: Printers and the Privilegio in Sixteenth-Century Venice and Rome* (Leiden: Brill, 2004), 43–45. On the operation of his press, see Habermann, *Ha-madpis Daniel Bombergi*, 14–15.

43. Fabio Giusberti and Francesca Roversi Monaco, "Economy and Demography," in *A Companion to Medieval and Renaissance Bologna*, ed. Sarah Rubin Blanshei (Leiden: Brill, 2018), 167.

44. Maria Giuseppina Muzzarelli has noted that the relationship between Bologna's Jews and the silk trade demands further investigation; Maria Giuseppina Muzzarelli, "Ebrei a Bologna nel XVI Secolo," in *Bologna Nell'Età Moderna (Secoli XVI–XVIII)*, ed. Adriano Prosperi (Bologna: Bononia University Press, 2008), 872.

45. The phrase is Carlo Poni's, and, though anachronistic, it evocatively describes the mechanized, large-scale manufacturing undertaken by Bolognese silk makers in the sixteenth century. Carlo Poni, "Per la storia del distretto industriale serico di Bologna (secoli XVI–XIX)," *Quaderni Storici* 73 (April 1990): 93–94.

46. Stephen R. Epstein, *Freedom and Growth: The Rise of States and Markets in Europe, 1300–1750* (London: Routledge, 2000), 67.

47. Carlo Poni, *La seta in Italia: Una grande industria prima della Rivoluzione Industriale* (Bologna: Il Mulino, 2009), 444.

48. Poni, *La seta in Italia*, 7.

49. Poni, *La seta in Italia*, 74; and Poni, "Per la storia del distretto industriale serico di Bologna," 93–94.

50. Giusberti and Roversi Monaco, "Economy and Demography," 169–70.

51. Giusberti and Roversi Monaco, "Economy and Demography," 167. See also Luca Molà, *The Silk Industry of Renaissance Venice* (Baltimore: Johns Hopkins University

Press, 2000), 15–17; and Paola Massa Piergiovanni, "Technological Typologies and Economic Organisation of Silk Workers in Italy, from the XIVth to the XVIIIth Centuries," *Journal of European Economic History* (1993): 553.

52. Trade in *strazzaria* was a lucrative business in which Italian Jews in other locales also participated; see Benjamin Ravid, "The Venetian Government and the Jews," in *The Jews of Early Modern Venice*, ed. Robert C. Davis and Benjamin Ravid (Baltimore: Johns Hopkins University Press, 2001). Prominent Jews were members of the Drapers and Strazzaroli guild; see Alberta Toniolo, "Els mercats de les sedes: Paper I Herència dels Sefardites a Bolognya en l'Edat Moderna," *Revista d'Història Medieval* 4 (1993): 35.

53. Archivio Apostolico Vaticano, Ms. Amadio XXIX, vol. 84, 67v, published in Simonsohn, *The Apostolic See and the Jews: Documents, 1522–1538*, 1,771 (document 1,441).

54. Archivio Apostolico Vaticano, Ms. Amadio XXIX, vol. 78, 171r, published in Simonsohn, *The Apostolic See and the Jews: Documents*, 1,719 (document 1,373).

55. Alberta Toniolo, "Los Sefarditas Españoles y la sedería Italiana en la Primera Edad Moderna," *Revista de Historia Industrial* 12 (1997): 65.

56. Carlo Poni, "The Circular Silk Mill: A Factory before the Industrial Revolution in Early Modern Europe," *History of Technology* 21 (1999): 78.

57. My translation. Poni, *La seta in Italia*, 447–48.

58. Poni, "The Circular Silk Mill," 78.

59. Compare Piergiovanni, "Technological Typologies," 543, with Richardson, *Printing, Writers and Readers*, 25–26; and Baruchson, "Money and Culture," 24.

60. Richardson, *Printing, Writers and Readers*, 25–35; Baruchson, "Money and Culture," 24, 33.

61. Grafton, *The Culture of Correction*, 58.

62. Ruderman, *Early Modern Jewry*, 17, 159.

63. On printing in Italy, see Harris, "The History of the Book in Italy."

64. Ruderman, *Early Modern Jewry*, 100. Ruderman's comments are based on a number of important articles by Elhanan Reiner, especially "The Ashkenazi Elite at the Beginning of the Modern Era: Manuscript Versus Printed Book," in *Polin: Studies in Polish Jewish History*, vol. 10, *Jews in Early Modern Poland*, ed. Gershon David Hundert (London: Littman Library of Jewish Civilization, 1997). See also Joseph Davis, "The Reception of the Shulḥan 'Arukh and the Formation of Ashkenazic Jewish Identity," *AJS Review* 26, no. 2 (2002).

65. Recanati's *Piskei halakhot* (1538) was a first edition; the text was extant only in manuscript prior to the partners' publication. Selections from Adret's responsa had been printed previously (in Rome and in Constantinople), but this edition was considered the most comprehensive. See *Encyclopedia Judaica*, 2nd ed., s.v. "Recanati,

Menahem ben Benjamin." On *Tefillot Latini*, see Umberto Cassuto, "Les traductions judéo-italiennes du Rituel," *Revue des Études Juives* 89, nos. 177–178 (1930).

66. Siegmund, *The Medici State and the Ghetto of Florence*, 401.

67. Sonne, "Le-toldot kehillat Bologna," 49; and *Encyclopedia Judaica*, 2nd ed., s.v. "Adret, Solomon ben Abraham."

68. Simha Emanuel, "Piskei R. Menaḥem mi-Recanati," *Jewish Law Annual* 25 (2008): 164.

69. On the blurring of communal boundaries in early modern Italy, see Cooperman, "Ethnicity and Institution Building"; and Kenneth R. Stow, "Ethnic Rivalry or Melting Pot: The 'Edot' in the Roman Ghetto," *Judaism* 41 (Summer 1992).

70. *Tefilah: Mireshit ve-ad aḥarit ha-shanah* (Bologna, 1537).

71. The *siddur* is not paginated, but *Seder ma'arekhet Eliyahu* begins in the morning prayers after the hymn *Adon olam*. On the printing of this ritual, see Samuel David Luzzatto, ed., *Mavo le-maḥzor b'nai Roma* (Tel Aviv: D'vir, 1966), 125. On R. Eliyahu b. Menaḥem and the *Seder ha-ma'arakhah*, see Avraham Grossman, *Hakhmei Tzarfat ha-rishonim: Koroteihem, darkham be-hanhagat ha-tzibur, ve-yetziratam ha-ruḥanit* (Jerusalem: Magnes Press, 2001), 84–104.

72. On Abraham's arrival in Bologna around 1503, see Yakov Boksenboim, *Parashiyot: Me-ḥayai Yehude Iṭalyah ba-meah ha-16* (Tel Aviv: Tel Aviv University, 1986), 8, 210n276. In a responsum, R. Joshua b. Shaltiel calls Abraham the "head and overseer of the community of Bologna"; Boksenboim, *Parashiyot*, 218. According to Marx and Sonne, Abraham served as the "rabbi of Bologna" for fifteen years. See Alexander Marx, "A Jewish Cause Celebre in Sixteenth Century Italy (the Pesakim of 1519)," in *Studies in Jewish History and Booklore*, ed. Alexander Marx (New York: Jewish Theological Seminary, 1944), 131–33; and Isaiah Sonne, "Le-toldot kehillat Bologna," 48–50. A more recent analysis of the Italian rabbinate by Robert Bonfil, however, argues that Jewish communities in Italy did not have communally appointed rabbis until the second half of the sixteenth century. Nonetheless, Bonfil suggests that Abraham was widely respected among Italian rabbis, and Jews more generally; Bonfil, *Rabbis and Jewish Communities in Renaissance Italy*, 53. Most famously, Abraham is known to have been one of the major participants in the Finzi-Norsa controversy of 1519—a debate, among other things, over whether the rabbis in one locale had authority over the Jews of other locales—which involved many of Italy's rabbis.

73. Archivio Apostolico Vaticano, Ms. Armadio XXIX, vol. 84, 162v–163v, published in Simonsohn, *The Apostolic See and the Jews: Documents*, 1,593 (document 1,272).

74. Archivio Apostolico Vaticano, Ms. Armadio XXIX, vol. 84, 162v.

75. Cooperman, "Political Discourse," 48–52. See also Bonfil, *Rabbis and Jewish Communities*, 193–196.

76. My translation. Boksenboim, *Parashiyot*, 210.

77. Cooperman, "Theorizing Jewish Self-Government in Early Modern Italy," 11.

78. Maria Giuseppina Muzzarelli, "Ferrara, ovvero un porto placido e sicuro tra XV è XVI secolo," in *Vita e cultura ebraica nello stato Estense*, ed. Euride Fregni and Mauro Perani (Bologna: Edizioni Fattoadarte, 1993), 245–46.

79. Attilio Milano, *Storia degli Ebrei in Italia* (Torino: Einaudi, 1992), 637.

80. Giuseppina Muzzarelli, "Ferrara, ovvero un porto placido e sicuro," 245.

81. We know Abraham wrote the introduction because it is phrased in the first person and he writes there, "I, the insignificant, the poorest among the greats who signed at the conclusion of this book . . ." *Sefer Ḥasidim* (Bologna, 1538), 121b. In fact, his is the only name signed at the conclusion of the book, at the end of the colophon, which itself is written in the first person. Isaiah Sonne called Abraham a "partner" in the firm; Sonne, "L'toldot kehilat Bologna," 49. It is difficult to gauge whether or not this assertion is correct. The fact that Abraham, and not the partners themselves, wrote the introduction and colophon is suggestive of this conclusion but is not definitive. See also Amram, *The Makers of Hebrew Books in Italy*, 234.

82. *Sefer Ḥasidim* (Bologna, 1538).

83. Zeev Gries, "Le-demuto shel ha-mabi le-defus ha-yehudi be-shalhey yemey ha-benayim," *Iggeret ha-Akademiah ha-Leumit ha-Yisraelit le-mada'im* 11 (1992): 7–11.

84. Baruchson, "Money and Culture," 24, 33.

85. Jacob b. Asher, *Arba'ah turim: Orah ḥayyim, hilkhot birkot ha-shakhar ve-sha'ar ha-berachot* (Vilna, 1923), §46 and §268.

86. These are Ms. Oxford, Bodleian; Ms. Mich. 155; and Ms. Oxford, Bodleian, Or., 608. See Adolf Neubauer, ed., *Catalogue of the Hebrew Manuscripts in the Bodleian Library and in the College Libraries of Oxford* (Oxford: Clarendon Press, 1886), 677, 256; and Malachi Beit-Arié, ed., *Catalogue of the Hebrew Manuscripts in the Bodleian Library: Supplement of Addenda and Corrigenda to Vol. 1* (Oxford: Clarendon Press, 1994), 359.

87. *Sefer Ḥasidim* (Bologna, 1538), introduction.

88. Sonne, "Le-toldot kehillat Bologna," 49–50. Recanati's *Piskei halakhot* (1538) was a first edition; the text was extant only in manuscript prior to the partners' publication.

89. Sonne uses the Hebrew verb *tappel*; "L'toldot kehilat Bologna," 42.

90. On Sforno, see Maria Giuseppina Muzzarelli, "Ebrei, famiglie e citta: Gli Sforno di Bologna," *Zakhor* 3 (1999): 73; Campanini, "Un intellettuale," 99–127; and Andrew D. Berns, "Ovadiah Sforno's Last Will and Testament," *Journal of Jewish Studies* 68, no. 1 (2017).

91. Campanini, "Un intellettuale," 104.

92. Campanini suggests that Sforno's grammar was not printed because the market for Hebrew grammars was already "saturated" with Johannes Reuchlin's *De rudimentis*

Hebraicis (Pforzheim, 1506) and Abraham de Balmes's *Mikneh Avram* (Venice, 1523). Campanini, "Un intellettuale," 111. It is also possible that the partners used the notion of a Hebrew grammar by a Jewish scholar known for his commerce with churchmen as a pretext to entice the Holy See to approve their request for a *condotta*. Such a book might assist the Church in its mission to the Jews by giving Catholic scholars access to Jewish wisdom that could be deployed in support of conversionary arguments. Gerolama, wife of Pier Luigi Farnese, likely would have approved of this project. It is clear from the partners' list, however, that the partners were interested in supplying books only to Jewish, not Christian, readers.

93. Obadiah Sforno, *Opusculum nuper editum contra nonnullas Peripateticoru[m] opinio[n]es, demo[n]strative docens presertim circa creationem & universi novitatem & divinam de mortalibus curam & humanaru[m] animarum immortalitatem: Quas ipsi turpiter respuunt religio[n]is penitus irride[n]tes, quare illud merito Lumen gentium appello* (Bologna, 1538). On Giaccarelli, see Dinora Pulega, "La tipographia bolognese dei Giaccarelli," *L'Archiginnasio* (1940).

94. On de' Rossi as an historian, see Salo W. Baron, "Azariah de' Rossi: A Biographical Sketch," in *History and Jewish Historians: Essays and Addresses*, eds. Salo W. Baron, Arthur Hertzberg, and L. A. Feldman (Philadelphia: Jewish Publication Society, 1964), 167–73; Yosef H. Yerushalmi, "Clio and the Jews: Reflections on Jewish Historiography in the Sixteenth Century," in *Essential Papers on Jewish Culture in Renaissance and Baroque Italy*, ed. David Ruderman (New York: New York University Press, 1992); and Joanna Weinberg, translator's introduction to *The Light of the Eyes* by Azariah de' Rossi, ed. and trans. Joanna Weinberg (New Haven, CT: Yale University Press, 2001), xiii–xlv.

95. De' Rossi, *Light of the Eyes*, 30, 707. De' Rossi, like many but not all of the city's Jews, subsequently fled to Ferrara; see Daniel Carpi, "Geirush ha-yehudim mimedinat ha-kenisiyah be-yemei ha-apiphior Pius ha-ḥamishi u-mishpatei ha-ḥakirah neged yehudei Bologna (1566–1569)," in *Scritti in memoria di Enzo Serani*, eds. Daniel Carpi, Attilio Milano, and Umberto Nahon (Jerusalem: Fondazione Sally Mayer, 1970), 145–65.

96. Joseph b. David ibn Yaḥya, *Torah or* (Bologna, 1538). On the devices printers used to advertise their titles, see chapters 2 and 4, as well as Richardson, *Print Culture in Renaissance Italy*; Richardson, *Printing, Writers and Readers*; Grafton, *The Culture of Correction*; and Genette, *Paratexts*.

97. On the ascription of the acrostic poem to de' Rossi, see Azariah de' Rossi, *Sefer me'or einayim*, ed. David Cassel (Vina: Romm, 1866), 144; and Israel Davidson, *Thesaurus of Mediaeval Hebrew Poetry*, vol. 3 (New York: K'tav, 1970), 253. It is possible, however, that this poem was written by another Azariah, not the well-known Azariah de' Rossi. Yet the timing and other circumstantial data lend this ascription a significant degree of probability.

98. See Isaac Abravanel, *Mirkevet ha-mishneh* (Sabbioneta, 1551). Joanna Weinberg has analyzed a commonplace book de' Rossi wrote during this period and has noted that it contains a number of poems by other writers. Copying poetry was a common educational technique in the early modern period; see Weinberg, *Light of the Eyes,* xiv–xv. For an anthology of de' Rossi's poetry, see the appendix to the Cassel edition of *Me'or einayim*; de' Rossi, *Sefer me'or einayim,* 137–44.

99. The physician Amatus Lusitanus describes the meeting in his book *Centuriae medicinales*; see Weinberg, *Light of the Eyes,* xv. According to Weinberg, de' Rossi's meeting with Lusitanus likely occurred in Ferrara, which would indicate that de' Rossi had multiple stays in Bologna: one in the 1530s, when he may have been involved in the partners' press, and one in the 1560s, which concluded with his expulsion.

100. Weinberg, *Light of the Eyes,* xvi. There was no formal, institutionalized censorship of Hebrew books in Italy prior to the 1550s.

101. Weinberg estimates that de' Rossi was born around 1511, meaning that he could have only been referring to the years (generously) between 1525 and 1550. During this period, Hebrew presses also operated in Venice (Bomberg), Rimini (Soncino), and, briefly, Rome; for a list of Italian presses, see Amram, *Makers of Hebrew Books.* The nature of this censorship will be discussed in greater detail later on.

102. Bonfil suggests that "these were the main questions which interested people during that period"; perhaps we should revise "people" to "scholars." Bonfil, *Rabbis and Jewish Communities,* 284–94.

103. Adret, *Teshuvot she'elot meha-eshel ha-gadol* (Bologna, 1538–1539), 74b–76a or §§415–417.

104. Adret, *Teshuvot she'elot,* 76a–85b or §418. On Bedersi, see *Encyclopedia Judaica,* s.v. "Jedaiah ben Abraham Bedersi."

105. Joseph b. David Yaḥya, *Sefer Torah or* (Bologna, 1538), introduction, 2b–3a.

106. Yaḥya, *Sefer Torah or,* 5b.

107. Yaḥya, *Sefer Torah or,* 4a. See Mishnah, *Sanhedrin* 10:1.

108. In his defense of Judaism, Joseph adopts the extreme particularism of Judah HaLevi. *Torah or* has not received sufficient scholarly attention. For a summary, see Israel Zinberg, *A History of Jewish Literature: Italian Jewry in the Renaissance Era,* trans. Bernard Martin (New York: K'tav, 1974), 57–59.

109. It is notable that *Torah or* and *Or amim* are linked by the fact that their titles contain the Hebrew word for "light" (*or*)—a reference to enlightenment and revelation.

110. Obadiah Sforno, *Sefer or amim* (Bologna, 1537), 2b–3a.

111. Sforno, *Sefer or amim,* 11b.

112. Giada Coppola, "Obadiah Sforno and the Individual Human Soul," *Yearbook of the Maimonides Centre for Advanced Studies* (2020): 103; Mauro Zonta, "The Autumn

of Medieval Jewish Philosophy," in *"Herbst Des Mittelalters"? Fragen zur Bewertung des 14. und 15. Jahrhunderts*, eds. Jan A. Aertsen and Martin Pickavé (Berlin: De Gruyter, 2004): 475. Zev Harvey has even suggested that Sforno was hired to teach a class on Averroes at the University of Bologna; see Coppola, "Obadiah Sforno and the Individual Human Soul," 104. On *Or amim*, Averroes, Maimonides, and the harmonization of religion and philosophy, see Symon Lee Foren, "Reconciling Philosophy and Scripture in Renaissance Italy: Obadiah Sforno's Hebrew and Latin Versions of the Light of the Nations" (PhD diss, University of Oxford, 2020). *Or amim* is the subject of a large international research project led by Giuseppe Veltri at the University Hamburg, entitled, "Between Two Worlds: The Tractate 'Light of the Nations' of 'Ovadyah Sforno (ca. 1475–1550)." The goal of the project is to produce a critical edition of *Or amim*, drawing on both the Hebrew and Latin editions, as well as a translation. Already the project has generated a dramatic reassessment of Sforno's thought, as evinced in the articles cited and the conference "Lost and Found in Translation: Obadiah Sforno and His World," January 18–19, 2017, at the University of Hamburg.

113. See, for example, the work of another Jew of Bologna, R. Vitale da Pisa. His *Minḥat kena'ot* was written two years after Sforno's *Or amim* and, as suggested by Alessandro Guetta, was a response to the partners' publication of Bedersi's *Ketav ha-hitnaẓelut*. Alessandro Gueta, "Religious Life and Jewish Erudition in Pisa: Yehiel Nissim da Pisa and the Crisis of Aristotelianism," in *Cultural Intermediaries: Jewish Intellectuals in Early Modern Italy*, ed. David Ruderman (Philadelphia: University of Pennsylvania Press, 2004), 103n7.

The literature on the popularization of Kabbalah is extensive: See Simcha Assaf, "Le-pulmus al ha-defus sifrei kabbalah," in *Mekorot u-meḥkarim* (Jerusalem: Mosad HaRav Kook, 1946), 238–46; Isaiah Tishby, "Ha-pulmus al Sefer ha-Zohar be-me'ah ha-shesh esrei b'Italia," in *Studies in Kabbalah and Its Branches: Research and Sources*, vol. 1 (Jerusalem: Magnes Press, 1982); Moshe Hallamish, "Te'udah le-toldot ha-pulmus al ha-kabbalah b'Italia bereishit ha-me'ah ha-17," *Bar Ilan Annual* 22 (1988); Jacob Elbaum, *Petiḥut ve-histagrut: Ha-yeẓirah ha-ruḥanit ha-sifrutit be-Polin u-ve-arẓot Ashkenaz be-shilhei ha-me'ah ha-shesh esrei* (Jerusalem: Magnes Press, 1990), 146–49, 356–76; Boaz Huss, *Ke-zohar ha-raki'a: Perakim be-hitkablut ha-Zohar u-ve-havnayat erko ha-simli* (Jerusalem: Ben-Zvi Institute, 2008); Dweck, *The Scandal of Kabbalah*; and Roni Weinstein, *Kabbalah and Jewish Modernity* (Oxford: Littman Library of Jewish Civilization, 2016).

114. An excellent example of the angst this provoked is found in Leon Modena's *Ari nohem*; see Dweck, *The Scandal of Kabbalah*, 61–100.

115. Toaff, "Bologna ebraica," 25.

116. Works that fifteenth- and sixteenth-century Italian Jews knew and owned; Bonfil, *Rabbis and Jewish Communities*, 278.

117. Moshe Idel, *Kabbalah in Italy, 1280–1510* (New Haven, CT: Yale University Press,

2011), 112. Note that prior to is being printed in the years 1558–1560, the title "Zohar" was associated with a heterogeneous corpus of manuscripts, not unlike *Sefer Ḥasidim*. Hence, when speaking about the period prior to 1558, I have chosen to refer to the "literature of the Zohar" (texts that were associated with that appellation) rather than "the Zohar," since that work as we know it was born in early modern print shops. On this point, see Abrams, *Kabbalistic Manuscripts and Textual Theory*.

118. Idel, *Kabbalah in Italy*, 113; Simcha Emanuel, "Piskei R. Menachem mi'Recanati," *Jewish Law Annual* 25 (2008).

119. Lucien Febvre and Henri-Jean Martin, *The Coming of the Book: Impact of Printing, 1450–1800*, trans. David Gerard (London: Verso, 2010), 84–86; Richardson, *Printing, Writers and Readers*, 132–33. On deceptive marketing, see Helen Smith, "'Imprinted by Simeon Such a Signe': Reading Early Modern Imprints," in *Renaissance Paratexts*, eds. Helen Smith and Louise Wilson (Cambridge: Cambridge University Press, 2011), 17–33.

120. See, for example, his interpretation of the sacrifices in his introduction, as well as his interpretation of the hand-washing ritual on the first page of the *maḥzor*. This was also noted by Heller, *Thesaurus of the Sixteenth Century Hebrew Book*, 251. Interestingly, the Zohar had yet to be printed at this time and thus was only available in manuscript. The title *Kimḥa de-Avishuna* means "flour derived from burned grain" (*grano arso* or *freekeh*), namely the most refined flour. On this phrase, see Marcus Jastrow, *A Dictionary of the Targumim*, s.v. "Avishuna, av'shuna"; and Babylonian Talmud, *Megillah* 7b.

121. Yoḥanan, introduction to *Maḥzor ke-fi minhag kehillat kodesh Roma*.

122. Toaff, "Bologna ebraica," 25.

123. *Sefer Ḥasidim* (Bologna, 1538), introduction, unpaginated.

124. The translation is Haym Soloveitchik's in his "Three Themes in the *Sefer Ḥasidim*," *AJS Review* 1 (1976): 312.

125. Treves's view is based on a passage in the Babylonian Talmud, *Hagiga* 5b, and on Tosafot to *Avodah Zarah* 22b.

126. Yoḥanan's elevation of prayer to the status of scriptural recitation may be perceived as a reflection of the postprint textualization of Jewish culture. This process was alluded to by Talya Fishman, *Becoming the People of the Talmud: Oral Torah as Written Tradition in Medieval Jewish Cultures* (Philadelphia: University of Pennsylvania Press, 2011), 220. It is unlikely, further, that the partners' *maḥzor* was any more accurate than other printed books, as errors were an unavoidable feature of early modern printing. See chapter 3 and chapter 5 for a fuller discussion.

Yoḥanan's critique of printed liturgies and his concern for Italian Jewry's spiritual welfare is reminiscent of the later efforts of Polish rabbis to ameliorate printed errors in the liturgy by producing an "authorized daily prayerbook." According to Stefan Reif, the project, completed in 1617 by Shabbetai Sofer of Przemysl, came about when a coalition of Polish rabbis agreed to eliminate "non-standard Hebrew" in the liturgy and to encourage more worshippers to understand the meaning of the prayers. Stefan C. Reif, *Judaism and Hebrew Prayer: New Perspectives on Jewish Liturgical History* (Cambridge: Cambridge University Press, 1993), 231–32; and Stefan Reif, *Shabbethai Sofer and His Prayer-Book* (Cambridge: Cambridge University Press, 1979).

127. In point of fact, Cassuto explains, the printers actually summarized and reprinted older translations of the prayers that existed in manuscript; see Cassuto, "Les traductions judéo-italiennes," 274.

128. For a summary of the research, see Howard Adelman, "Italian Jewish Women," in *Jewish Women in Historical Perspective*, ed. Judith R. Baskin (Detroit, MI: Wayne State University Press, 1998), 150–168; Howard Adelman, "The Educational and Literary Activities of Jewish Women in Italy during the Renaissance and Counter-Reformation," in *Shlomo Simonsohn Jubilee Volume*, ed. Daniel Carpi (Tel Aviv: Tel Aviv University Press, 1993); and Robert Bonfil, *Jewish Life in Renaissance Italy*, trans. Anthony Oldcorn (Berkeley: University of California Press, 1994), 132–33.

129. The phrase "men who are like women" refers to men who could not read Hebrew; see Chava Weissler, *Voices of the Matriarchs* (Boston: Beacon Press, 1998), 36–65. Weissler also reflects on the power relationship between men as the producers of this literature and women as the consumers.

130. Bonfil has asserted that the institution of "communally-appointed rabbi" emerged first in Verona in 1539; see Bonfil, *Rabbis and Jewish Communities*, 153–56. See also Meir Benayahu, *Marbiẓ Torah: Samkhuyotav, tafkidav ve-hetko be-mosedot ha-kehillah* (Jerusalem: Mosad HaRav Kook, 1953).

131. Alexander Marx, "Glimpses of the Life of an Italian Rabbi of the First Half of the Sixteenth Century (David ibn Yaḥya)," *Hebrew Union College Annual* 1 (1924): 615.

132. David B. Ruderman, introduction to *Preachers of the Italian Ghetto* (Berkeley: University of California Press, 1992), 3. This term seems to have come from Cecil Roth, *Jewish Life in Renaissance Italy* (Philadelphia: Jewish Publication Society, 1959), 35. See also Marc Saperstein, "Italian Jewish Preaching: An Overview," in *Preachers of the Italian Ghetto*, 29, where he describes the outpouring of sermon collections printed in Italy and the Ottoman Empire during the last decades of the sixteenth century and the beginning of the seventeenth. On the significance of sermons in the Sephardic world during this period, see Joseph Hacker, "Ha-derashot ha-sephradit be-me'ah ha-16 bein sifrut le-makor histori," *Pe'amim* 26 (1986), especially after 113.

The Partners' *Sefer Ḥasidim*: Paratexts and Text

1. See *Sefer Ḥasidim* (Bologna, 1538), §142, 281.

2. On *kuntres*, see J. H. Chajes, "Accounting for the Self: Preliminary Generic-Historical Reflections on Early Modern Jewish Egodocuments," *Jewish Quarterly Review* 95, no.

1 (2005): 7–8; and Malachi Beit-Arié, *Hebrew Codicology* (Jerusalem: Israel Academy of Sciences and Humanities, 1981), 44–45n77. For more on this distinction, see the epilogue.

3. On Jewish English, see Sarah Bunin Benor, "Do American Jews Speak a 'Jewish Language'?: A Model of Jewish Linguistic Distinctiveness," *Jewish Quarterly Review* 99, no. 2 (2009), where Benor explains why Jewish English is a language and not a dialect. The inherent association of sanctity with the word *sefer* is even more manifest in Yiddish, see *Jewish English Lexicon*, s.v. "sefer," https://jel.jewish-languages.org/words/484 (accessed February 23, 2022). On modern Hebrew, see *Milon Even-Shoshan*, s.v. "sefer."

4. The final phrase of the passage "it is forbidden to add to the book" is only found in the Bologna printed edition. The other manuscripts, such as Ms. Parma and Cambridge University Library Ms. Add. 379, read, "for there is no honor for the book in this" or "for he damages the book."

5. See *Sefer Ḥasidim* (Bologna, 1538), §136.

6. On the significance of format, see McKittrick, *Print, Manuscript, and the Search for Order*, 88. See also Martin Lowry, *The World of Aldus Manutius: Business and Scholarship in Renaissance Venice* (Ithaca, NY: Cornell University Press, 1979).

7. Martin Davies, *Aldus Manutius: Printer and Publisher of Renaissance Venice* (London: British Library, 1995), 40–55.

8. See *Jewish Encyclopedia*, s.v. "Title-Page" by Joseph Jacobs and Judah David Eisenstein, which notes that formal title pages start to appear in Hebrew printed titles beginning in the mid-1510s. My own unscientific survey of the digitized printed Hebrew books in the National Library of Israel collection confirms this claim. However, Marvin Heller has noted that a small number in incunabula contain decorated first pages, see Marvin J. Heller, "Behold, You Are Beautiful, My Love: The Use of Ornamental Frames in Hebrew Incunabula," in *Further Studies in the Making of the Early Hebrew Book* (Leiden: Brill, 2013), 3–34.

9. Richardson, *Printing, Writers, and Readers*, 132.

10. The title page of the first volume of the Bomberg Talmud edition of 1520 reads: "Tractate Berakhot with Rashi's commentary and Tosafot" in large type, with the words "And the judgements of Tosafot (piskei Tosafot), the commentary of the Mishnahs and Rebbeinu Asher, printed by Daniel Bomberg of Antwerp in the year 480 [1520] according to the abbreviated calculation here in" in smaller type spread over three lines below it, and "Venice" in larger type, on the bottom line, *Tractate Berakhot*... (Venice, 1520).

11. *Sefer Ḥasidim* (Bologna, 1538), introduction, unpaginated.

12. *Sefer Ḥasidim* (Bologna, 1538), §1.

13. David Stern, *The Jewish Bible: A Material History* (Seattle: University of Washington Press, 2018), 140.

14. On the way typeface affects meaning, see Armando Petrucci, *Public Lettering: Script, Power, and Culture,* trans. Linda Lappin (Chicago: University of Chicago Press, 1993).

15. Duncan and Smyth, *Book Parts,* 42. Over the course of the sixteenth and seventeenth centuries, printers gradually abandoned the colophon, and its functions were replaced by elaborate front matter.

16. *Sefer Ḥasidim* (Bologna, 1538), §367.

17. *Sefer Ḥasidim* (Bologna, 1538), introduction.

18. See, for example, Exodus 36:10: "And he coupled [or joined, *ḥeber*] five curtains one to another; and the other five curtains he coupled one to another."

19. Perhaps the foremost example of this conceptual transformation is the fact that R. Joseph Karo is known as, simply, the *Meḥeber* ("the composer") as a result of his composition of the halakhaic code the *Shulḥan Arukh.* Even here, however, Karo's authorship maintains a certain premodern quality because the act of composing a legal code is by its nature compilatory. Nonetheless, in that the work became associated with Karo and only with Karo (even though the addition of R. Moses Isserles's glosses were what earned it authority throughout the Jewish world) demonstrates how the *ḥibur* ("composition") came to signify possessive authorship.

20. Kant, *The Metaphysics of Morals,* 106.

21. Eisenstein, *Printing Press,* 121.

22. Jardine, *Erasmus, Man of Letters,* 5.

23. Johns, in particular, focuses on hagiographic narratives about printers and the press itself; *The Nature of the Book,* 324–79.

24. Marx, "A Jewish Cause Celebre in Sixteenth Century Italy," 175 (translation my own based on Marx's transcription).

25. Mintz was a supporter of Norsa, and Abraham was a supporter of Finzi. Mintz's letter was written long before the founding of the partners' printing house, sometime prior to 1519, and so Mintz could not have been referring to Cohen's work in preparing reference aids to the partners' volumes.

26. Etienne Molinier, *Mystère de la croix* (1635), quoted in Blair, *Too Much to Know,* 120.

27. Blair, *Too Much to Know,* 117, 8–9.

28. On medieval indices, see Mary A. Rouse and Richard H. Rouse, "La Naissance des Index," *Histoire de l'édition française* 1 (1982): 77–85.

29. Blair, *Too Much to Know,* 133.

30. Peter Stallybrass, "Books and Scrolls: Navigating the Bible," in *Books and Readers in Early Modern England,* eds. Jennifer Andersen and Elizabeth Sauer (Philadelphia: University of Pennsylvania Press, 2002), 44.

31. Stallybrass, "Books and Scrolls," 60.

32. Ms. Cambridge Add. 379.2 is described in Reif, *Hebrew Manuscripts at Cambridge University Library*, 223. I was able to study this manuscript in microfilm at the Jewish Theological Seminary of America's microfilms collection, reel 155. The ink of the manuscript, as noted by the Princeton University *Sefer Ḥasidim* Project, is smudged and difficult to decipher at many points, but much of the table of contents is legible.

33. Reif, *Hebrew Manuscripts at Cambridge University Library*, 223.

34. The entry for §37 in the manuscript table of contents is admittedly smudged and near illegible. Yet, it was possible to make out some of its letters and deduce its content with knowledge of the first words of the passage. I have not been able to determine why some passages have enlarged, centered headings and others do not.

35. On the fraught question of whether one can kill a louse, especially on the Sabbath, and the medieval scientific notion of the spontaneous generation of organisms, see Ahuva Gaziel, "Spontaneous Generation in Medieval Jewish Philosophy and Theology," *History and Philosophy of the Life Sciences* 34, no. 3 (2012).

36. See Blair, *Too Much to Know*, 71–74, 85–93. Notes like these not only benefited the note-taker but also formed the basis of the period's reference works, which were, for all intents and purposes, anthologies of cross-referenced reading notes.

37. Blair, *Too Much to Know*, 133. See also Grafton, *The Culture of Correction*, 26; and Richardson, *Printing, Writers, and Readers*, 151.

38. *Sefer Ḥasidim* (Bologna, 1538), introduction.

39. This is a phrase of biblical origin (Psalms 23:5), whose history in postbiblical literature is worth further study. Most famously, of course, it became the title of R. Joseph Karo's legal code (1565).

40. *Sefer Ḥasidim* (Bologna, 1538), 16.

41. These were important concerns for the *Ḥasidei Ashkenaz*, whose self-understanding was tied to their experience of mockery and social alienation; see Marcus, *Piety and Society*, 92.

42. On the significance of *ma'asim* (cases or tales) in *Sefer Ḥasidim*, see chapter 4.

43. The tradition of Solomon's 1,000 wives is found in Babylonian Talmud, *Bava Metzia* 86b.

44. Joseph Dan, "Rabbi Judah the Pious and Caesarius of Heisterbach: Common Motifs in Their Stories," in *Studies in Aggadah and Folk-Literature* 22 (1971): 27.

45. *Sefer Ḥasidim* (Bologna, 1538), 121.

46. The only exception is §1,177, which appears in the Parma manuscript as §237, and in several other *Sefer Ḥasidim* manuscripts as well.

47. Marcus, *Sefer Hasidim and the Ashkenazic Book*, 90–103. Three more manuscripts, copied outside of Italy, are presently found in the collections of Italian libraries, indicating that they may have circulated in Italy during the early modern period. They

include Ms. Parma, Biblioteca Palatina H3266; Ms. Milan, Ambrosiana X.III sup; and, of course, the famous "Parma manuscript," Ms. Parma, Biblioteca Palatina, Heb. Ms. 3280 (De Rossi 1133).

48. The literature on early modern censorship is voluminous. For theoretical treatments focusing on England and the Continent, see Debora Shuger, *Censorship and Cultural Sensibility: The Regulation of Language in Tudor-Stuart England* (Philadelphia: University of Pennsylvania Press, 2013); Patterson, *Censorship and Interpretation*; and Cyndia Susan Clegg, *Press Censorship in Jacobean England* (New York: Cambridge Unversity Press, 2001). On France, see Robert Darnton, *Censors at Work: How States Shaped Literature* (New York: W. W. Norton, 2015). On Italy, see Gigliola Fragnito, *La bibbia al rogo: La censura ecclesiastica e i volgarizzamenti della scrittura: 1471–1605* (Bologna: Il Mulino, 1997); Gigliola Fragnito, ed., *Church, Censorship, and Culture in Early Modern Italy*, trans. Adrian Belton (Cambridge: Cambridge University Press, 2001); and Marcus, *Forbidden Knowledge.*

49. Kenneth R. Stow, "The Burning of the Talmud in 1553, in Light of Sixteenth-Century Catholic Attitudes toward the Talmud," *Bibliothèque d'Humanisme et Renaissance* 34, no. 3 (1972); and Raz-Krakotzkin, *The Censor, the Editor, and the Text.* See also Piet van Boxel, *Jewish Books in Christian Hands: Theology, Exegesis and Conversion Under Gregory XIII (1572–1585)* (Vatican: Biblioteca Apostolica Vaticana, 2002), 30–37; and Grendler, *The Roman Inquisition and the Venetian Press.*

50. Joseph R. Hacker, "Sixteenth-Century Jewish Internal Censorship of Hebrew Books," in *The Hebrew Book in Early Modern Italy*, eds. Hacker and Shear, 111. See also Finkelstein, *Jewish Self-Government in the Middle Ages*, 92–95.

51. William Popper, *The Censorship of Hebrew Books* (New York: Knickerbocker, 1899), 21–29. See also Amram, *The Makers of Hebrew Books in Italy*; and R. N. N. Rabinowicz, *Ma'amar al hadpasat ha-Talmud* (Munich: A. Huber, 1877).

52. Popper, *The Censorship of Hebrew Books*, 28.

53. Nurit Pasternak, "Marchion in Hebrew Manuscripts: State Censorship in Florence, 1472," in *The Hebrew Book in Early Modern Italy*, eds. Hacker and Shear, 30.

54. Patterson, *Censorship and Interpretation*, 7.

55. It is worth noting the different political circumstances of English writers and printers under the watchful eyes of the monarch, and Hebrew printers, especially Jewish printers, whose existence was entirely dependent on the sufferance of Catholic sovereigns. While the writers and printers of England, as producers of books, were vulnerable to persecution, Jewish printers, as a subject, tolerated minority ,were even more vulnerable.

56. As the partners' privilege of 1536 makes clear; see Filippo Tamburini, *Ebrei, saraceni, cristiani*, 110.

57. On the censorship of Hebrew books in general, see Popper, *The Censorship of Hebrew*

Books; Isaiah Sonne, *Expurgation of Hebrew Books––the Work of Jewish Scholars: A Contribution to the History of the Censorship of Hebrew Books in Italy in the Sixteenth Century* (New York: The New York Public Library, 1943); Raz-Krakotzkin, *The Censor, the Editor, and the Text*; and Piet van Boxel, "Hebrew Books and Censorship in Sixteenth-Century Italy," in *Jewish Books and Their Readers: Aspects of the Intellectual Life of Christians and Jews in Early Modern Europe*, eds. Scott Mandelbrote and Joanna Weinberg (Leiden: Brill, 2016). Domenico Gerosolimitano (1555–1621), the convert censor who composed the well-known *index expurgatorius* (*Sefer ha-Zikkuk*, begun in 1596 and updated thereafter), studied the partners' edition of *Sefer Ḥasidim* and prescribed nearly a hundred modifications to both Abraham's table of contents and the text itself. Many of these involve erasing and/or replacing offensive terminology, but in several cases he prescribed eliminating full passages or sections of passages. See Gila Prebor, "'*Sefer ha-Zikkuk*' shel Dominico Yerushalmi," *Italia* 18 (2008): 83–85.

58. My translation. Freimann, introduction to *Sefer Ḥasidim*, 360. For their *condotta*, Archivio Apostolico Vaticano, Ms. Armadio XLI, vol. 8, 179r, and see chapter 2.

59. Ruth Langer, *Cursing the Christians?: A History of the Birkat Haminim* (Oxford: Oxford University Press, 2011), 115.

60. Patterson, *Censorship and Interpretation*, 45.

61. I have located numerous censored passages that reference Christians or Christianity in the partners' edition: 188, 191, 193, 194, 198, 199, 202, 203, 204, 205, 206, 209, 219, 220, 221, 270, 280, 289, 427, 428 (misnumbered as 429), 429, 430, 438, 804, 862, 869, and 906.

62. Note that the phrase "he ate unfit flesh" appears in all the texts mentioned here. It can be translated literally as "he put out my bowl for unfit flesh," which rhymes in the original Hebrew. "Unfit flesh" refers to meat from an animal that has been slaughtered incorrectly or carrion.

63. Jastrow, *A Dictionary of the Targumim*, s.v. "shamad"; Carlebach, *Divided Souls*, 12.

64. Compare Chaim Milikowsky, who argues, "The *meshummad* is one who transgresses the commandments, not because it is not in his power to stand up to the temptation, but rather because he rejects them. In rabbinic literature the meaning of *meshummad* is not one who converts from Judaism to another religion, rather one who renounces Judaism" (Chaim Milikowsky, "Gehenom u-poshei yisrael al pi 'Seder Olam,'" *Tarbiz* 55, no. 3 [1986]: 332 [my translation]), to Solomon Zeitlin: "A Jew who was forced to adopt another religion was called *meshumad*... Hence, until the time of the Hadrianic persecutions an apostate was called *mumar*. After this period, when the persecutions against the Jews... began... a Jew who was forced to adopt another religion was called *meshumad* signifying that he had to adopt another religion because of the threat of destruction" (Solomon Zeitlin, "Mumar and Meshumad," *Jewish Quarterly Review* 54, no. 1 [July 1963]: 86). Ruth Langer, who provides the most detailed treatment, acknowledges that rabbinic texts tend to "struggle to differentiate among

the various categories of marginal people in their world." Langer, *Cursing the Christians?* 52. She includes the *meshummad* among them.

65. Langer, *Cursing the Christians?* 48. This was, of course, a not uncommon occurrence in R. Judah he-Ḥasid's time. On conversion and apostasy in the eleventh century, see Robert Chazan, *European Jewry and the First Crusade* (Berkeley: University of California Press, 1996), 99–136; Ephraim Kanarfogel, *Peering Through the Lattices: Mystical, Magical, and Pietistic Dimensions in the Tosafist Period* (Detroit, MI: Wayne State University Press, 2000), 234; and David Malkiel, *Reconstructing Ashkenaz: The Human Face of Franco-German Jewry, 1000–1250* (Stanford, CA: Stanford University Press, 2008), 114–47.

66. Langer, *Cursing the Christians?* 77.

67. Carlebach, *Divided Souls*, 244n3.

68. Langer, *Cursing the Christians?* 45.

69. The phenomenon of convert-censors has been explored by Carlebach, *Divided Souls*, 9; and Raz-Krakotzkin, *The Censor, the Editor, and the Text*, 111–12.

70. My translation. Prebor, "Sefer ha-Zikkuk," 53, rule 1.

71. My translation, according to Prebor's transcription of Ms. Vatican 273; Prebor, "Sefer Ha-Zikkuk," 53. See also Raz-Krakotzkin, *The Censor, the Editor, and the Text*, 111–12.

72. Langer, *Cursing the Christians?* 98.

73. Emphasis in original. Ishay Rosen-Zvi and Adi Ophir, "Goy: Toward a Genealogy," *Diné Israel* 28 (2011): 120.

74. Rosen-Zvi and Ophir, "Goy," 69.

75. My translation, according to Prebor's transcription of Ms. Vatican 273; Prebor, "Sefer Ha-Zikkuk," 53. See also Raz-Krakotzkin, *The Censor, the Editor, and the Text*, 121.

76. On the practice of reusing book bindings, see Andreas Lehnardt and Judith Olszowy-Schlanger, eds., *Books within Books: New Discoveries in Old Book Bindings* (Leiden: Brill, 2014). Note that it has been asserted that anxieties about the use and reuse of Christian paraphernalia and the need to aggressively differentiate from Christians and Christianity were essential to the psyche of the *Ḥasidei Ashkenaz*. Jacob Katz, *Exclusiveness and Tolerance: Studies in Jewish-Gentile Relations in Medieval and Modern Times* (New York: Oxford University Press, 1961), 95–99.

77. Ms. Parma §1,348 (Wistinetzki, *Sefer Ḥasidim*, 332); (former) Ms. Boesky 45 §§549–550; Cambridge University Add. 379 §431. Interestingly, the version of this passage in the Boesky manuscript was censored and several words were covered over with ink, but that ink has faded and it is now possible to read the original script.

78. *Milon Even-Shoshan*, s.v. "galaḥ."

79. See Jastrow, *A Dictionary of the Targumim*, s.v. "pasul," and the examples cited therein.

80. Langer, *Cursing the Christians?* 70–78. For Rashi's gloss, see Babylonian Talmud, *Sanhedrin* 100b.

81. Langer, *Cursing the Christians?* 84–93.

82. Prebor, "Sefer ha-Zikkuk," 53.

83. Patterson, *Censorship and Interpretation*, 40.

84. On the history of this term in rabbinic literature and in the medieval period, see Moshe Halbertal and Avishai Margalit, *Idolatry*, trans. Naomi Goldblum (Cambridge, MA: Harvard University Press, 1992) 3–4, 202–13.

85. Prebor, "Sefer ha-Zikkuk," 53, rule 1.

86. Mss. Parma §1,348, (former) Boesky 45 §§549–550, and Cambridge University Add. 379 §428.

87. My translation. Prebor, "Sefer ha-Zikkuk," 54, rule 17.

88. Note that these illegitimate non-Jewish festivals are called *eidim* and are contrasted in rabbinic literature with the legitimate Jewish festivals, called *ḥagim*. See Jastrow, *A Dictionary of the Targumim*, s.v. "eid"; and Babylonian Talmud, *Avodah Zarah* 2a.

89. I express my gratitude to Jessica Kirzane for helping me parse this phrase and translate it accurately.

90. See Mishnah, *Sanhedrin* 7:6; and Babylonian Talmud, *Sanhedrin* 106a.

91. Shai Alleson-Gerberg, "Nittel Nacht: An Inverted Christmas with Toledot Yeshu," TheTorah.com, https://www.thetorah.com/article/nittel-nacht-an-inverted-christmas-with-toledot-yesh. See also Marc Shapiro, "Torah Study on Christmas Eve," *Journal of Jewish Thought and Philosophy* 8, no. 2 (1999); and Marcus, "A Jewish-Christian Symbiosis," 480.

92. Jewish folk traditions connecting Jesus and excreta originate in the Babylonian Talmud (*Gittin* 57a), circulated widely in Ashkenaz and were known to Christians. See Marcus, "A Jewish-Christian Symbiosis," 479.

93. Shuger, *Censorship and Cultural Sensibility*, 2.

94. Prebor, "Sefer ha-Zikkuk," 21.

95. Raz-Krakotzkin, *The Censor, the Editor, and the Text*, 15.

96. Gillespie, *Print Culture and the Medieval Author*, 83–94.

Ambrosius Froben of Basel

1. On Jewish-Christian collaboration in the production of holy books, and the quoted passage in particular, see Annett Martini, "Ritual Consecration in the Context of Writing the Holy Scrolls: Jews in Medieval Europe Between Demarcation and Acculturation," *European Journal of Jewish Studies* 11, no. 2 (2017).

2. This passage is especially rich and merits its own sustained scholarly treatment. It was censored in the partners' version; in its manuscript parallels, the "priest" is called a "shaved-head" (*galaḥ*) and a *goy*. Then there is the first *ḥasid*'s proof text. In its original context, Isaiah 52:1 is a reassurance: "the uncircumcised and the unclean" will "never enter you again," meaning Israel, personified as a woman, defiled by her enemies. The *ḥasid* reads the verse as an instruction not to permit non-Jews near his sacred books. He may also be expressing unease at non-Jews being called "the uncircumcised and the unclean"—terms that medieval Christians found offensive. Yet the verse, of course, is also found in Christian Bibles, and Christian readers would not have perceived the verse as addressed to them.

3. *Sefer Ḥasidim* (Bologna, 1538), §429 (see this book's chapter 3).

4. Raz-Krakotzkin, *The Censor, the Editor, and the Text*, 102.

5. Over three decades, Bomberg printed more than two hundred Hebrew titles. Once Bomberg's monopoly lapsed, the Venetian Senate forbade Jews from printing their own books, which continued to be produced at Christian-owned shops. Similar regulations emerged elsewhere in Italy.

6. Froben has received significant attention from bibliographers and historians for his Talmud edition; his other Hebrew (and Yiddish) titles, by contrast, have merited far less notice. See R. N. N. Rabbinovicz, *Ma'amar al hadpasat ha-Talmud* (Munich: 1877), 65–70; Heinrich Pallmann, *Ambrosius Froben von Basel als Drucker des Talmud* (Leipzig: Stadt-Bibliothek Frankfurt am Main, 1882); Achilles Nordmann, "Geschichte der Juden in Basel seit dem Ende der Zweiten Gemeinde bis zur Einführung der Glaubens- und Gewissensfreiheit: 1397–1875," *Basler Zeitschrift für Geschichte und Altertumskunde* 13 (1914): 23–32; Ernst Staehelin, "Des Basler Buchdruckers Ambrosius Froben Talmudausgabe und Handel mit Rom," *Basler Zeitschrift für Geschichte und Altertumskunde* 30 (1930); Joseph Prijs, *Die Basler hebräischen Drucke, 1492–1866: Im Auftrag der öffentlichen Bibliothek der Universität Basel* (Olten: Urs Graf, 1965), 175–88; Stephen G. Burnett, "German Jewish Printing in the Reformation Era (1530–1633)," in *Jews, Judaism, and the Reformation in Sixteenth-Century Germany*, eds. Dean Philip Bell and Stephen G. Burnett (Leiden: Brill, 2006); Fausto Parente, "The Index, the Holy Office and the Condemnation of the Talmud and Publication of Clement VIII's Index," in *Church, Censorship and Culture in Early Modern Italy*, ed. Gigliola Fragnito (Cambridge: Cambridge University Press, 2001), 171–74; and the contributions to the session on the "World of Ambrosius Froben" at the Renaissance Society of American conference (March 2018) by Theodor Dunkelgrün and Michela Andreatta. Dunkelgrün and Andreatta, along with Anthony Grafton, are currently leading an international research collaboration on the Froben Talmud. Two exceptions to the focus on the Talmud are Habermann, *Ha-sefer ha-ivri*; and Marvin J. Heller, "Ambrosius Froben, Israel Zifroni and Hebrew Printing in Freiburg-im-Breisgau," in *Studies in the Making of the Early Hebrew Book* (Leiden: Brill, 2008).

7. For a resume of sixteenth-century Hebrew presses in Italy, see Amram, *The Makers of Hebrew Books in Italy*. On Germany, see Burnett, "Christian Hebrew Printing." On Poland, see Magda Teter and Edward Fram, "Apostasy, Fraud, and the Beginnings of Hebrew Printing in Cracow," *AJS Review* 30, no. 1 (2006).

8. This process mirrors what occurred among non-Jewish vernacular printers; see Richardson, *Print Culture in Renaissance Italy*, 182–83.

9. According to the Universal Short Title Catalogue, the first book printed at Basel was a Latin Bible printed by Berthold Ruppel in 1468. "Basel, home to a distinguished university and a renowned group of humanist scholars, published mostly for these academic and ecclesiastical markets." Pettegree, *The Book in the Renaissance*, 36, and 30–36 more generally.

10. Earle Hilgert, "Johann Froben and the Basel University Scholars, 1513–1523," *Library Quarterly* 41, no. 2 (April 1971).

11. See Hilgert, "Johann Froben," 151, on Wolfgang Capito's influence in this area; and Burnett, "German Jewish Printing," 510.

12. Burnett, *Christian Hebraism in the Reformation Era*, 261. On the trade in books between Protestant Basel and Catholic Italy, see also Pettegree, *The Book in the Renaissance*, 117.

13. On Froben, see Charles William Heckethorn, *The Printers of Basle in the XV & XVI Centuries: Their Biographies, Printed Books and Devices* (London: T. Fisher Unwin, 1897); and Valentina Sebastiani, *Johann Froben, Printer of Basel: A Biographical Profile and Catalogue of His Editions* (Leiden: Brill, 2018). Erasmus lived in Froben's home intermittently beginning in the 1510s and died there in 1536. See, especially, Nicholas Naquin, "On the Shoulders of Hercules: Erasmus, the Froben Press and the 1516 Jerome Edition in Context" (PhD diss., Princeton University, 2013); Jardine, *Erasmus, Man of Letters*; and Eileen Bloch, "Erasmus and the Froben Press: The Making of an Editor," *Library Quarterly* 32, no. 2 (April 1965).

14. Among them were editions of the biblical wisdom books in Hebrew and Latin translation and Münster's Hebrew and Aramaic dictionaries and grammars. See Joseph Prijs's bibliography in *Die Basler Hebräischen Drucke*, 9–55; and Marvin J. Heller, *Printing the Talmud: A History of the Earliest Printed Editions of the Talmud* (New York: I. M. HaSefer, 1993), 242–43.

15. Burnett, "German Jewish Printing," 509–10.

16. The quotation from Galatinus is from his *De arcadis*, quoted in Stow, "The Burning of the Talmud in 1553," 449.

On sixteenth-century Church debates over the permissibility of the Talmud, see Salo Wittmayer Baron, "The Council of Trent and Rabbinic Literature," in *Ancient and Medieval Jewish History*, ed. Leon Feldman (New Brunswick, NJ: Rutgers University Press, 1972), 358; Stow, "The Burning of the Talmud"; Parente, "The Index, the Holy

Office and the Condemnation of the Talmud"; Raz-Krakotzkin, *The Censor, the Editor, and the Text*, 32–57; and van Boxel, *Jewish Books in Christian Hands.*

17. Stow, "The Burning of the Talmud," 451.

18. Piet van Boxel, "Robert Bellarmine Reads Rashi: Rabbinic Bible Commentaries and the Burning of the Talmud," in *The Hebrew Book in Early Modern Italy*, eds. Hacker and Shear, 121–23; and van Boxel, *Jewish Books in Christian Hands*, 7–39.

19. The revision was entitled *Moderatio Indicis Librorum Prohibitorum*; see Parente, "The Index, the Holy Office and the Condemnation of the Talmud," 167.

20. Raz-Krakotzkin, *The Censor, the Editor, and the Text*, 58.

21. Quoted in Parente, "The Index, the Holy Office and the Condemnation of the Talmud," 169. See also Raz-Krakotzkin, *The Censor, the Editor, and the Text*, 60–64.

22. Van Boxel, *Jewish Books in Christian Hands*, 31–36.

23. Piet van Boxel, in particular, has studied these manuals. See van Boxel, *Jewish Books in Christian Hands*, 39–56.

24. Van Boxel, *Jewish Books in Christian Hands*, 36.

25. Henri Estienne II, *Francofordiense emporium* (1574), quoted and translated in John L. Flood, "'Omnium Totius Orbis Emporiorum Compendium": The Frankfurt Fair in the Early Modern Period," in *The History of the Book in the West: 1455–1700*, ed. Ian Gadd (London: Routledge, 2007), 328.

26. Pettegree, *The Book in the Renaissance*, 79–82; and Joshua Teplitsky, *Prince of the Press: How One Collector Built History's Most Enduring and Remarkable Jewish Library* (New Haven, CT: Yale University Press, 2019), 111–17.

27. My translation. The contract is reproduced in Pallmann, *Ambrosius Froben*, 49.

28. It has been estimated that, by mid-century, Polish Jewry numbered 50,000. See Bernard D. Weinryb, *The Jews of Poland: A Social and Economic History of the Jewish Community in Poland from 1100 to 1800* (Philadelphia: Jewish Publication Society of America, 1972), 309–20; and Adam Teller, "Culture and Money: The Economic Dimension of Cultural History and What It Can Teach Us," *Jewish Quarterly Review* 104, no. 2 (2014): 279–80, 280n4.

29. See, among many, Katz, *Tradition and Crisis*; Weinryb, *The Jews of Poland*, 107–75; Jacob Elbaum, *Petiḥut ve-histagrut: Ha-yiẓirah ha-ruḥanit ha-sifrut be-Polin uve-artzot Ashkenaz be-shilhei ha-me'ah ha-shesh esreh* (Jerusalem: Magnes Press, 1990); and Gershon David Hundert, *Jews in Poland-Lithuania in the Eighteenth Century* (Berkeley: University of California Press, 2004).

30. Teter and Fram, "Apostasy, Fraud, and the Beginnings of Hebrew Printing."

31. Bernhard (Chaim) Friedberg, *Toldot ha-defus ha-Ivri be-Polaniyah* (Tel Aviv: publisher not identified 1950).

32. Marie Buňatová, "Trade Contacts Between Prague Jews and Northern Italy and

Their Engagement in the Italian Commodity Trade in the 16th and Early 17th Centuries," *Judaica Bohemiae* 54, no. 1 (2019): 8; Magda Teter, *Jews and Heretics in Catholic Poland: A Beleaguered Church in the Post-Reformation Era* (Cambridge: Cambridge University Press, 2005), 105–106; Pavel Sládek, "A Sixteenth-Century Rabbi as a Published Author: The Early Editions of Rabbi Mordecai Jaffe's *Levushim*," in *Connecting Histories: Jews and Their Others in Early Modern Europe*, eds. Francesca Bregoli and David B. Ruderman (Philadelphia: University of Pennsylvania Press, 2019), 62–63.

33. Of course, the Bible contains some material in Aramaic as well, such as substantial portions of the book of Daniel.

34. Jakob Burckhardt, *The Civilization of the Renaissance in Italy*, trans. S. G. C. Middlemore (London: Penguin, 2004), 121.

35. The former view is that of Friedman, *The Most Ancient Testimony*, 116. The latter view is described by Coudert and Shoulson in their introduction to *Hebraica Veritas?* 6. See also Stephen G. Burnett, *From Christian Hebraism to Jewish Studies: Johannes Buxtorf (1564–1629) and Hebrew Learning in the Seventeenth Century* (Leiden: Brill, 1996); Burnett, *Christian Hebraism in the Reformation Era*; Allison P. Coudert, *The Impact of the Kabbalah in the Seventeenth Century: The Life and Thought of Francis Mercury van Helmont (1614–1698)* (Leiden: Brill, 1999); Ruderman, *Early Modern Jewry*, 173–80; Carlebach, *Divided Souls*, 200–21; Richard I. Cohen, Natalie B. Dohrman, Adam Shear, and Elchanan Reiner, eds., *Jewish Culture in Early Modern Europe: Essays in Honor of David B. Ruderman* (Pittsburgh, PA: Hebrew Union College Press, 2014), 123–88; and Eva de Visscher, *Reading the Rabbis: Christian Hebraism in the Works of Herbert of Bosham* (Leiden: Brill, 2014).

36. See sources quoted by Grafton, *The Culture of Correction*, 133.

37. While a crucial page from the notes from the May session of the Basel Council meeting is missing, we do know that Froben's petition was raised at that meeting and that Froben went on to print the Talmud, meaning, as Nordmann has written, that the council approved his request. Nordmann, "Geschichte der Juden in Basel . . . ," 28.

38. Pallmann cites Simon's letter to Froben in Pallmann, *Ambrosius Froben*, 49; this is my translation. Problems about packaging and shipping indicate just how complicated the process of producing and transmitting books was. Darnton—in his concept of the "communications circuit"—has emphasized the many parties involved in this process. Robert Darnton, "What Is the History of Books?" *Daedalus* 111, no. 3 (Summer 1982): 67. Underappreciated but crucially important were the paper manufacturers, press workers, and shippers. They held the fate of a title in their hands.

39. This information is found in one of two letters from Ambrosius Froben to Pope Gregory XIII that are conserved in the Archive of the Congregation for the Doctrine of the Faith, *Index*, II/i, f. 80r. It is quoted in Parente, "The Index, the Holy Office and the Condemnation of the Talmud," 174.

40. On repossession in early modern Europe, see Daniel Lord Smail, *Legal Plunder:*

Households and Debt Collection in Late Medieval Europe (Cambridge, MA: Harvard University Press, 2016).

41. Staehelin, "Des Basler Buchdruckers Ambrosius Froben," 26.

42. On Santoro, see Piet W. van Boxel, "Cardinal Santoro and the Expurgation of Hebrew Literature," in *The Roman Inquisition, the Index and the Jews*, ed. Stephan Wendehorst (Brill: Leiden, 2004), 19–34. Marini's name only appears in some of the Talmud volumes.

43. See Grafton, *The Culture of Correction*, 11.

44. For biographical information about this group, see Amram, *The Makers of Hebrew Books in Italy*. Adelkind is especially notable for his long association with Bomberg, as well as other Venetian Hebrew printers, and his involvement in the copyright infringement dispute with R. Meir Katzenellenbogen. See A. M. Habermann, *Ha-madpis Cornelio Adelkind u-beno Daniel u-reshimat ha-sefarim she-nidpesu al yedeihem* (Jerusalem: Rubin Mass, 1980).

45. My translation. Cited in Nordmann, "Geschichte der Juden in Basel," 29.

46. According to Nordmann, the *Ratsprotokolle* of the Basel Council do not record the council's decision on Froben's petition. We can assume, however, that it was accepted because Zifroni (along with R. Jacob Luzzatto) was engaged in the production of the Talmud by the summer of 1578. See Nordmann, "Geschichte der Juden in Basel," 29.

47. A. M. Habermann, "Ha-madpis Yisrael ha-Zifroni u-beno Elishama," in *Perakim b'toldot ha-madpisim ha-ivri'im v'inyanei sefarim*, ed. A. M. Haberman (Jerusalem: Rubin Mass, 1978), 217.

48. He is frequently referred to with the honorific *ma'alat k'vod Torato* and is called a "sage" (*ḥakham*) by his interlocutors; Habermann, "Ha-madpis Yisrael ha-Zifroni," 271–89.

49. Habermann, "Ha-madpis Yisrael ha-Zifroni," 218; Elisheva Carlebach, "Precious Time: Jewish Wall Calendars in the Valmadonna Collection," in *The Writing on the Wall: A Catalogue of Judaica Broadsides from the Valmadonna Trust Library*, eds. Sharon Liberman Mintz, Shaul Seidler-Feller, and David Wachtel (London: Valmadonna Trust Library, 2015), 23.

50. The tractate is not dated, but this date is assumed based on Joseph Prijs's sequencing of these volumes in his bibliography in Joseph Prjis, *Die Basler hebräischen Drucke, 1492–1866: Im Auftrag der Öffentlichen Bibliothek der Universität Basel* (Olten, Switzerland: Urs Graf-Verlag, 1964), 199.

51. This expression was used regularly during the sixteenth century to indicate the identity of the corrector-editor who oversaw the production of a work, in contrast to the *madpis* (printer) and the *meivi l'beit ha'dfus* (publisher), who enabled a work's printing, whether by underwriting the costs or by providing manuscripts, though it should be noted that these terms are notoriously imprecise. *Hukam al ha-malakhah*

is a variation of the same term used to describe R. Raphael Talmi, the artisan who assisted the partners with their edition.

52. Menaḥem ibn Zarah, *Ẓeidah le-derekh* (Sabbionetta, 1567), 1b; and Menaḥem ibn Zarah, *Ḥamishah ḥumshei Torah ve-ḥamesh megillot* (Sabbionetta, 1567), 1b. On Zifroni's role in preparing texts and paratexts, see Habermann, "Ha-madpis Yisrael ha-Zifroni," 231–32; and Carlebach, "Precious Time," 23.

53. Prijs, *Die Basler Hebräischen Drucke*, 178.

54. Jacob b. Isaac Luzzatto, *Sefer kavvanot ha-aggadot* (Basel, 1580), 162b. See also Marvin J. Heller, "And the Work, the Work of Heaven, was Performed on Shabbat," in *Studies in the Making of the Early Hebrew Book* (Leiden: Brill, 2008).

55. Luzzatto, *Sefer kavvanot ha-aggadot*, 162b.

56. All three titles appeared on the title page, but different copies privilege and enlarge different titles. It is not entirely clear to me why Froben used multiple titles. One supposition is that because the work discussed *aggadot* that Christian theologians condemned—such as Babylonian Talmud, *Berakhot* 3a, which describes God's "wailing like a lion" over the destruction of the Temple—Froben hoped that if one version of the book were condemned, others might continue to circulate. On Christian responses to similar texts from Babylonian Talmud, *Berakhot*, see Stow, "The Burning of the Talmud," 445–46.

See the colophon to Menaḥem b. Benjamin Recanati, *Sefer ta'amei ha-miẓvoth* (Basel, 1581). See also Samuel Joseph Fuenn, *Keneset Yisrael* (Warsaw: 1887), who ascribes a number of other works to him.

57. Solomon Molcho, *Sefer ha-mefo'ar* (1569), cited in Moritz Steinschneider, *Catalogus librorum Hebraeorum in Bibliotheca Bodleiana*, vol. 1 (Berlin: A. Friedlaender, 1852–1860), 1,229.

58. My translation. Samuel David Luzzatto, *Autobiografia di S. D. Luzzatto preceduta da alcune notizie storico-letterarie sulla famiglia Luzzatto* (Padua: Crescini, 1882), 10.

59. Habermann asserted that Zifroni composed both introductions, without offering evidence in support of his view. A. M. Habermann, *Perakim be-toldot ha-madpisim ha-ivri'im v'inyanei sefarim* (Jerusalem: Rubin Mass, 1978), 237. Perhaps he assumed this because, throughout his career, Zifroni was known for writing paratexts; see chapter 5.

60. *Kavvanot ha-aggadot* (Basel, 1880), 4b.

61. These are phrases borrowed from Hasdai Crescas's *Or Adonai* (Ferrara, 1555), a literary feature that is discussed at length in chapter 5. The rabbinic expression "did not achieve sufficient study" (*lo shimshu et rabeihem kol ẓorkhan*) is found in multiple places in rabbinic literature, for instance in Palestinian Talmud, *Hagiga* 10b, where it is used to describe the first disputes that emerged between the houses of Hillel and Shammai.

62. Habermann, "Ha-madpis Yisrael ha-Zifroni," 275.

63. *Jewish Encyclopedia*, s.v. "Loans, Elijah ben Moses Ashkenazi or Loanz."

64. Waldkirch also published Elijah's compositions; see Eliezer Landshuth, *Sefer amudei ha-avodah* (Berlin, 1884), 16. See also Joanna Weinberg, "Johann Buxtorf Makes a Notebook," in *Canonical Texts and Scholarly Practices: A Global Comparative Approach*, eds. Anthony Grafton and Glenn W. Most (Cambridge: Cambridge University Press, 2016), 286.

65. *Encyclopedia Judaica*, s.v. "Koppelman, Jacob ben Samuel Bunim."

66. See Pavel Sládek, "A Sixteenth-Century Rabbi as a Published Author."

67. Quoted in Grafton, *The Culture of Correction*, 134.

68. Compare the title pages of *Masekhet arakhin* and *Masekhet kritut*, where Marini's name is present, to those of *Berakhot* and *Shabbat*, for example.

69. Burnett, "German Jewish Printing," 511; van Boxel, *Jewish Books in Christian Hands*, 54.

70. I have not found censors' marks in Froben's non-Talmudic publications, however.

71. Grafton, *The Culture of Correction*, 79–142.

72. On Vulcanius, see the papers collected in Hélène Cazes, ed., *Bonaventura Vulcanius, Works and Networks: Bruges 1538–Leiden 1614* (Leiden: Brill, 2010).

73. This letter is discussed in Kenneth Austin, *From Judaism to Calvinism: The Life and Writings of Immanuel Tremellius (c. 1510–1580)* (Aldershot, UK: Ashgate, 2007), 169–72. The chronology Tremellius recounts is intriguing. If Froben approached Tremellius before his departure from Heidelberg in 1577, he did so prior to making his contract with Simon zur Gemze in 1578, meaning that either Froben and Simon had discussed and planned their collaboration at least one year prior to the contract signing or that Froben had intended to publish the Talmud himself.

74. Austin, *From Judaism to Calvinism*, 172.

75. On Chevalier, see G. Lloyd Jones, *The Discovery of Hebrew in Tudor England: A Third Language* (Manchester, UK: Manchester University Press, 1983), 77–78.

76. See the petition dated January 1578 in Olivier Labarthe and Bernard Lescaze, eds., *Registres de la Compagnie des pasteurs de Genève: 1575–1582*, vol. 4 (Geneva: Librairie Droz, 1974), 104. See also Scott M. Manetsch, *Calvin's Company of Pastors: Pastoral Care and the Emerging Reformed Church, 1536–1609* (Oxford: Oxford University Press, 2013), 59–60.

77. Anthony Grafton, "'Pandects of the Jews': A French, Swiss and Italian Prelude to John Selden," in *Jewish Books and Their Readers: Aspects of the Intellectual Life of Christians and Jews in Early Modern Europe*, eds. Scott Mandelbrote and Joanna Weinberg (Leiden: Brill, 2016), 176–78.

78. Grafton, "'Pandects of the Jews,'" 177.

79. K. J. Drake, *The Flesh of the Word: The Extra Calvinisticum from Zwingli to Early Orthodoxy* (Oxford: Oxford University Press, 2021), 230n108.

80. Anthony T. Grafton and Joanna Weinberg, *"I Have Always Loved the Holy Tongue,"* 87. The bibliographer Joseph Prijs has asserted that Chevalier merely lent his name to the project but did not serve as a censor. Prijs quotes Buxtorf's statement that Chevalier was the "censor of the Talmud" in his *Lexicon Caladium*; see Prijs, *Die Basler Hebräischen Drucke*, 176.

81. Given Froben's interest in securing the favor of the pope and distributing his wares in Poland, it is reasonable to assume that he made sure the names of Protestants would not be mentioned in his books, despite their involvement in their production.

82. Prijs, *Die Basler Hebräischen Drucke*, 211.

83. Heller, *The Sixteenth Century Hebrew Book*, vol. 2, 699.

84. See the title page, on which Mordecai's role is declaimed.

85. Idel, *Kabbalah in Italy*, 124–27.

86. Marini, in 1593, also published a Hebrew-Latin dictionary, entitled *Arca Noe*, at Venice.

87. Marvin Heller discusses the three versions of this text in Heller, *The Sixteenth Century Hebrew Book*, vol. 2, 706.

88. Jean Baumgarten, *Introduction to Old Yiddish Literature* (Oxford: Oxford University Press, 2005), 56.

89. By the seventeenth century, Yiddish printing, like its Hebrew counterpart, declined in Italy and expanded in Poland, Bohemia, and Germany; Baumgarten, *Introduction to Old Yiddish Literature*, 67.

90. Richardson, *Print Culture in Renaissance Italy*.

91. This is the suggestion of Staehelin, "Des Basler Buchdruckers Ambrosius Froben," 35–36.

92. Staehelin, "Des Basler Buchdruckers Ambrosius Froben," 36.

Froben's *Sefer Ḥasidim*: Paratexts

1. A representative example is *Sefer Ḥasidim* (Basel, 1580), §188. See also the passages discussed in chapter 6. While it is theoretically possible that both the partners' and Froben's editions were derived from the same (censored) exemplar(s), no such manuscript has come down to us. None of the medieval manuscripts of *Sefer Ḥasidim* is as similar to Froben's edition as the partners' edition is.

2. According to Brian Richardson, late-sixteenth-century title pages tended to combine "the roles which nowadays we would expect to see shared among the title page, the title verso, the cover of a p aperback or the dust jacket of a hardback book, and sometimes also the contents page." Richardson, *Printing, Writers, and Readers in Renaissance Italy*, 133.

3. That total is 341, which is an abbreviated rendering of the year 5341, equivalent to the Gregorian year 1580–1581.

4. Daniel Bomberg was the first to use such an image, in the Rabbinic Bible of 1517; see Stern, *The Jewish Bible*, 144–48.

5. Elisheva Carlebach, *Palaces of Time: Jewish Calendar and Culture in Early Modern Europe* (Cambridge, MA: Harvard University Press, 2011), 86.

6. Froben's print shop used this second, more intricate frame regularly in 1580 and 1581; see R. Ephraim b. Aaron of Luntshits, *Ir gibborim* (1580); and R. Menaḥem b. Benjamin Recanati, *Sefer ta'amei ha-mitzvot* (1581). Such frames were a feature of Hebrew (and non-Hebrew) printing from the incunabular period. Heller, "Behold, You Are Beautiful, My Love."

7. This is an allusion to Zachariah 3:7, which describes the benefits accorded to the righteous, who may dwell among the ministering angels: "Thus said the Lord of Hosts: If you walk in My paths and keep My charge, you in turn will rule My House and guard My courts, and I will permit you to move about among these attendants."

8. I am unsure of whether to translate the verb *metukkan* here as "corrected," and thereby as a reference to the editing this edition underwent, in contrast to the first edition, or more simply, "made fit or proper," referring to the content of the book more generally. Perhaps, as Elisheva Carlebach has suggested, the verb was meant to be deliberately ambiguous.

9. This alludes to the pillaging of the Jerusalem Temple by Nebuchadnezzar, as described in Daniel 1:2: "The Lord delivered King Jehoiakim of Judah into his power, together with some of the vessels of the House of God, and he brought them to the land of Shinar to the house of his god; he deposited the vessels in the treasury of his god."

10. The verses are as follows: "But everyone who invokes the name of the Lord shall escape; for there shall be a remnant on Mount Zion and in Jerusalem, as the Lord promised. Anyone who invokes the Lord will be among the survivors" (Joel 3:5); and "'At that time—declares the Lord—I will be God to all the clans of Israel, and they shall be My people.' Thus said the Lord: 'The people escaped from the sword, Found favor in the wilderness; When Israel was marching homeward'" (Jeremiah 31:1–2). For other uses of this phrase, see Joseph Solomon Delmedigo, *Sefer meẓaref le-ḥokhmah* (Warsaw, 1892), 48; and Shabbatai ben Meir ha-Cohen Katz's introduction to the *seliḥot* for the victims of the massacres in *Seliḥot* (Amsterdam: Yohanan Levi, 1806). *Sefer Ḥasidim* (Basel, 1580), §1, makes a similar case: "It was written for God-fearers and ones who dwell on His name, for a pious person whose heart desired the love of his Creator to do all His will . . . but not for the wicked was it written, for if the wicked were to see it, they would perceive some things in it as nonsense."

11. *Kavvanot ha-aggadot* (Basel, 1880), introduction, unpaginated.

12. The translation is by Marvin J. Heller, "Ambrosius Froben, Israel Zifroni and Hebrew Printing," 148.

13. Joseph Karo, "hakdamah" (introduction) to *Shulḥan Arukh* (Jerusalem: Ketuvim, 1992), Bar Ilan Responsa Database.

14. While the literature on the history of Jewish scholarship is voluminous, there is no definitive history of the early modern *yeshivah*, though reflections on the *yeshivah* curriculum may be found in Mordechai Breuer, *Oholei Torah: Ha-yeshivah tavnitah ve-toldoteha* (Jerusalem: Zalman Shazar Center, 2003), 83–165. See also Katz, *Tradition and Crisis*, 185–99; Bonfil, *Rabbis and Jewish Communities*, 19–25; Elbaum, *Petiḥut ve-histagrut*; Eric Zimmer, *Gaḥaltan shel ḥakhamim: Perakim be-toldot ha-rabbanut be-Germanyah ba-me'ah ha-shesh-esreh u-va-me'ah ha-sheva esreh* (Be'er Sheva, Israel: Ben Gurion University of the Negev, 1999); and Marjorie Lehman, *The En Yaaqov: Jacob ibn Habib's Search for Faith in the Talmud Corpus* (Detroit, MI: Wayne State University Press, 2012), 3–5, 100–15.

15. See Elbaum, *Petihut ve'histagrut*; Bonfil, *Rabbis and Jewish Communities*; and Elchanan Reiner, "Temurot be-yeshivot polin ve-ashkenaz be-me'ot ha-16-17 ve-ha-viku'aḥ al ha-pilpul," in *Studies in Jewish Culture in Honor of Chone Shmeruk*, eds. Israel Bartal, Ezra Mendelssohn, and Chava Turniansky (Jerusalem: Zalman Shazar Center for Jewish History, 1993).

16. Elchanan Reiner, "The Ashkenazi Elite at the Beginning of the Modern Era: Manuscript versus Printed Book," in *Polin: Studies in Polish Jewish History*, vol. 10, *Jews in Early Modern Poland*, ed. Gershon David Hundert (London: Littman Library of Jewish Civilization, 1997), 85–98; Joseph Davis, "The Reception of the *Shulḥan 'Arukh*," 252–76; Joseph A. Skloot, "Blood and Guts in Jewish Law: The Laws of the Forbidden and the Permitted and Religious Norms in Rabbi Moses Isserles' Glosses on the Shulḥan Arukh" (paper, "Norms and Normativity in History" conference, Paris-Sorbonne University, March 2010).

17. Elchanan Reiner, "A Biography of an Agent of Culture: Eliezer Altschul of Prague and His Literary Activity," in *Schöpferische Momente des europäischen Judentums in der frühen Neuzeit*, ed. Michael Graetz (Heidelberg: Universitätsverlag C. Winter, 2000), 246; Gondos, *Kabbalah in Print*, 59–65.

18. Elliot Horowitz, "Processions, Piety and Jewish Confraternities," in *The Jews of Early Modern Venice*, eds. Robert C. Davis and Benjamin Ravid (Baltimore: Johns Hopkins University Press, 2001), 231. Two confraternities devoted to Torah study emerged in Rome in 1539, and others emerged later in the century. Leon Modena stated that Venice had the most Jewish confraternities, as quoted in Horowitz, "Processions, Piety and Jewish Confraternities," 240. See also Elliot Horowitz, "Coffee, Coffeehouses, and the Nocturnal Rituals of Early Modern Jewry," *AJS Review* 14, no. 1 (Spring 1989): 30–38; Elliot Horowitz, "Yeshiva and *Hevra*: Educational Control and Confraternal Organization in Sixteenth-Century Italy," in *Sefer yovel li-Shelomo Simonson: Kovetz meḥkarim le-toldot ha-yehudim be-yemei ha-beinayim u-ve-tekufat ha-Renesans*, ed. Aharon Oppenheimer (Tel Aviv: Tel Aviv University, 2017); and Michela Andreatta, "The Printing of Devotion in Seventeenth-Century Italy: Prayer Books Printed for the Shomrim La-Boker Confraternities," in *The Hebrew Book in Early Modern Italy*, eds. Hacker and Shear.

19. Horowitz, "Processions, Piety and Jewish Confraternities," 230–236. Horowitz here also compares the *ḥavurot* to "boarding schools." See Natalie Zemon, "Some Tasks and Themes in the Study of Popular Religion," in *The Pursuit of Holiness in Late Medieval and Renaissance Religion*, eds. Charles Trinkaus and Heiko Oberman (Leiden: Brill, 1974), 314–36. She notes the distinction between confraternities for adults and adolescents.

20. Horowitz, "Yeshiva and *Hevra*," 142.

21. Horowitz, "Yeshiva and *Hevra*," 140, 127–130.

22. Richardson, *Printing, Writers and Readers*, 132.

23. Compare, for example, the title pages of *Masekhet megilah* and *Masekhet gitin* (Basel, 1578–1581) to his Felix Platter, *De corporis humani structura et vsu Felicis Plateri Bas. medici antecessoris libri III* (Basel, 1581), a title Froben printed multiple times during the 1570s and early 1580s, or Augustine of Hippo, *Primus [-decimus] tomus eximii patris, inter summa latinae ecclesiæ ornamenta ac lumina principis, D. Aurelii Augustini Hipponensis episcopi* (Basel, 1569, and successive reprintings).

24. Froben's remoteness from the production process of *Sefer Ḥasidim* is also implied by the lack of his printers' mark on the title page. This insignia—two snakes entwined around a staff held by two hands, with the letters "FRO" and "BEN" on either side of the staff—appeared prominently on the title pages of his Talmud volumes and his Latin titles. Yet it was absent from several of Froben's non-Talmudic titles, including *Sefer Ḥasidim*. This, however, may also be a consequence of the fact that unlike the folio-size Talmud volumes, many of these titles were printed in a smaller format, with consequently smaller title pages. To use the printers' mark on these smaller title pages would dramatically reduce the amount of usable space for promotional text. This speculation is affirmed by the fact that the printers' mark did appear on the title page of his edition of *Ir gibborim* (1580) and *Me'ir nativ* (1581), also folios.

25. Prijs, *Die Basler Hebräischen Drucke*, 184.

26. Gueta, "Ha-sefarim ha-mudpasim"; Shear and Hacker, eds., introduction to *The Hebrew Book in Early Modern Italy*, 8; Joshua Bloch, "Venetian Printers of Hebrew Books," in *Hebrew Printing and Bibliography: Studies by Joshua Bloch and Others, Reprinted from the Publications of the New York Public Library on the Occasion of the Seventy-Fifth Anniversary of the Jewish Division of the New York Public Library*, ed. Charles Berlin (New York: New York Public Library, 1976), 65–88; Heller, introduction to *The Sixteenth Century Hebrew Book*, vol. 1, xv–xvii.

27. Lowry, *The World of Aldus Manutius*, 236–41.

28. Johns, *The Nature of the Book*, 2. See also his second and third chapters in particular (58–265) on the techniques printers used to establish veracity.

29. Luzzatto's citation is not quite correct: The Babylonian Talmud (*Ketubot* 19b) does not ascribe this teaching to any particular tradent. The midrash collection *Yalkut Shimoni*, however, does ascribe it to Rabbi Yossi (§906).

30. This is a play on the Hebrew word *sefer*, which can refer both to a scroll and to a book more generally. On the status of uncorrected books more generally, see Maimonides, Mishneh Torah, *Laws of Tefillin, Mezuzah, and Torah Scrolls*, 7:12; and Joseph Karo, *Shulḥan Arukh, Yoreh Deah, Laws of Torah Scrolls*, 379:1.

31. This is an allusion to *Genesis Rabbah* 12:13.

32. Richardson, *Print Culture in Renaissance Italy*, 185. On the way this approach shaped the printing of the Palestinian Talmud, see Mayer, "Me-tarbut k'tav ha-yad le-tarbut ha-defus."

33. Raz-Krakotzkin has argued that Jewish editors and censors "collaborated" in censoring Hebrew texts, and that they perceived their work as part of a process of establishing "a separated Jewish space." Raz-Krakotzkin, *The Censor, the Editor, and the Text*, 84. For a critique of this view, see the next chapter.

34. Raz-Krakotzkin, *The Censor, the Editor, and the Text*, 181.

35. Two versions of the title *Sefer ha-Zohar* appeared near-simultaneously: a one-volume edition printed in Cremona in 1558 and a three-volume edition printed in Mantua between the years 1558 and 1560. Heterogeneous manuscripts associated with the name Zohar circulated in Europe during the preceding centuries, in a similar fashion to *Sefer Ḥasidim*.

36. It is clear that Luzzatto borrowed from the 1555 Ferrara edition of *Or Adonai* because one of the quotations he employed carried over an error found in that edition but not in subsequent editions. That error appears in the middle of Luzzatto's introduction and concerns the sentence, "They would call [such books] a 'scroll of orders' [*megillat sedarim*]." The proper rabbinic term for these books is *megiliot setarim*, literally "sequestered scrolls." I have not found instances of the expression "scroll of orders" in any ancient, medieval, or early modern Hebrew text—except in the Ferrara *editio princeps* of *Or Adonai* and Luzzatto's second introduction to Froben's *Sefer Ḥasidim*.

37. On Crescas's limited influence among his contemporaries and successors, see Daniel J. Lasker, "Chasdai Crescas," in *History of Jewish Philosophy*, eds. Daniel H. Frank and Oliver J. Leaman (London: Routledge, 1997).

38. Hasdai ibn Crescas, introduction to *Sefer or Adonai* (Ferrara, 1555), unpaginated. This translation is that of Roslyn Weiss in Roslyn Weiss, trans., *Light of the Lord (Or Hashem)* (Oxford: Oxford University Press, 2018), 23.

39. Crescas, introduction to *Sefer or Adonai* (unpaginated), trans. Weiss, *Light of the Lord*, 24.

40. Hava Tirosh-Rothschild [Samuelson], "Jewish Philosophy on the Eve of Modernity," in *History of Jewish Philosophy*, eds. Frank and Leaman, 500.

41. Crescas, introduction to *Sefer or Adonai* (unpaginated), trans. Weiss, *Light of the Lord*, 18.

42. Crescas, *Sefer or Adonai*, Book II, Part VI (unpaginated), trans. Weiss, *Light of the Lord*, 225.

43. See *Encyclopedia Judaica*, s.v. "Shekhinah"; and Babylonian Talmud, *Berakhot* 17a and 64a.

44. Harvey, "Hasdai Crescas's Critique," 187–88.

45. Crescas, introduction to *Sefer or Adonai* (unpaginated), trans. Weiss, *Light of the Lord*, 18. Hava Tirosh-Samuelson has argued that Crescas's emphasis on the performance of the commandments for their own sake had a clear anti-Christian message: "The road to personal immortality lies not in holding certain views but in the performance of specific acts which Israel alone is commanded to do." See Tirosh-Rothschild [Samuelson], "Jewish Philosophy," 502.

46. Jacob b. Isaac Luzzatto, "*Hakdamah le-Sefer Ḥasidim*," in *Sefer Ḥasidim* (Basel, 1580), first page (unpaginated section). This is a near-verbatim quotation from the introduction of the Ferrara edition of *Or Adonai*, trans. Weiss, *Light of the Lord*, 16–17.

47. Luzzatto, "*Hakdamah le-Sefer Ḥasidim*," second page (unpaginated section).

48. The essential relationship between law and lore in Jewish tradition has been explored by scholars over the centuries, though one of the more influential treatments of the last century is Robert M. Cover, "Nomos and Narrative," *Harvard Law Review* 97, no. 1 (1983).

49. On the significance of tales in rabbinic literature, see Jeffrey L. Rubenstein, *Talmudic Stories* (Baltimore: Johns Hopkins University Press, 2003), and the historiographic introduction in chapter 1.

50. See Babylonian Talmud, *Temurah* 14b; and Sherira Gaon, *Letter of Rav Sherira Gaon*, ed. D. Metzger (Jerusalem: Neve Asher Institute, 1998), §17–19, Bar Ilan Responsa Database. This tradition was also used to justify the printing of kabbalistic books during the early modern period.

51. Luzzatto, "*Hakdamah le-Sefer Ḥasidim*," first page (unpaginated section), quoted from Crescas, introduction to *Sefer or Adonai* (unpaginated), trans. Weiss, *Light of the Lord*, 20.

52. This argument would also be made about the Zohar in modern times; see Dweck, *The Scandal of Kabbalah*, 227.

53. The biblical quotation "written with the finger of God" is slightly abbreviated, the last word lacking its final *mem*. It is found in Jacob b. Isaac Luzzatto, "*Hakdamah ba-mehalel ha-sefer ve-ha-mehaber . . .*," in *Sefer Ḥasidim* (Basel, 1580), unpaginated.

54. Luzzatto, "*Hakdamah le-Sefer Ḥasidim*," second page (unpaginated section).

55. For this phrase's traditional meaning as a reference to Torah, see Maimonides's and Obadiah mi-Bartenura's commentaries on Mishnah, *Avot* 5:22.

56. Elliot R. Wolfson, "Beyond the Spoken Word: Oral Tradition and Written Transmission in Medieval Jewish Mysticism," in *Transmitting Jewish Traditions: Orality, Textuality, and Cultural Diffusion* (New Haven, CT: Yale University Press, 2000), 197; Halbertal, *Concealment and Revelation*, 69–76.

57. This is the NJPS translation, whose syntax accords better with the interpretation of the Babylonian Talmud, *Gittin* 60a.

58. Tishby, "Ha-pulmus al Sefer ha-Zohar," vol. 1, 140.

59. Dweck, *The Scandal of Kabbalah*, 10, 61.

60. Luzzatto, *Autobiografia di S. D. Luzzatto*, 10; see chapter 4.

61. Lehman, *The En Yaaqov*, 118.

62. Jacob Elbaum, "Rabbi Judah Loew's Attitude to the Aggadah," in *Midrash Unbound: Transformations and Innovations*, eds. Joanna Weinberg and Michael Fishbane (Oxford: Littman Library of Jewish Civilization, 2013), 400. It is worth noting that Elbaum and Veltri's analyses contradict that of Ben Zion Bokser, who depicts the Maharal's attitude as not that much different from Maimonides's. Ben Zion Bokser, *The Maharal: The Mystical Philosophy of Rabbi Judah Loew of Prague* (Northvale, NJ: Jason Aaronson, 1994), 181–82. Judah b. Bezalel Loew, *Be'er ha-golah* (Jerusalem: Maḥon Yerushalayim, 2000), 6:10, Bar Ilan Responsa Project.

63. Stow, "The Burning of the Talmud," 445–47. These include Talmudic stories about Onkelos the proselyte's conversion to Judaism (Baylonian Talmud, *Gittin* 56b) and the origin of *birkat ha'minim* (the blessing against heretics, Baylonian Talmud, *Berakhot* 28b). See Weinberg, "Johann Buxtorf Makes a Notebook," 283–85.

64. Weinberg, translator's introduction to de' Rossi, *The Light of the Eyes*, xxvi. Giuseppe Veltri, "Maharal against Azariah de' Rossi: The Other Side of Scepticism," in *Rabbinic Theology and Jewish Intellectual History: The Great Rabbi Loew of Prague*, ed. Meir Seidler (London: Routledge, 2013), 67, 70. On Naḥmanides's pronouncements in the disputation and his true opinions about the status of *aggadah*, see Shalem Yahalom, "Viku'ah Barcelona u'ma'amad ha'aggadah b'mishnat ha'Ramban," *Zion* 69, no. 1 (2004): 25–43.

65. Andrea Gondos has described the emergence of "digests" and "summaries" as a new genre of printed Hebrew book meant to "assist novice readers with the processing" of difficult rabbinic and kabbalistic works during the sixteenth century. Gondos, *Kabbalah in Print*, 82–85.

66. Jacob b. Isaac Luzzatto, "*Hakdamah*," in *Sefer kavvanot ha-aggadot* (Basel, 1580), first page (unpaginated section).

67. Luzzatto, "*Hakdamah le-Sefer Ḥasidim*," first page (unpaginated section).

68. Luzzatto, "*Hakdamah le-Sefer Ḥasidim*," second page (unpaginated section).

69. Emphasis in original. Moses Maimonides, *The Guide of the Perplexed*, trans. Shlomo Pines (Chicago: University of Chicago Press, 1963), 11. On this parable, see Josef Stern, *The Matter and Form of Maimonides' Guide* (Cambridge, MA: Harvard University Press, 2013), 18–63. Maimonides sent mixed signals as to the value of the exoteric meaning of Scripture. His "parable of the apple" indicates that the exoteric meaning of Scripture is true and of value, but not as profound as the esoteric meaning.

70. Luzzatto, "*Hakdamah le-Sefer Ḥasidim*," first page (unpaginated section).

71. De' Rossi, *The Light of the Eyes*, trans. Joanna Weinberg, 386. See Weinberg's footnotes for an explication of de' Rossi's rich allusions to ancient and medieval texts. It should be noted, in addition, that this passage appears within a larger apology for the sages, who, in contrast to classical Greek and Roman authors, paid scant attention to history and current events.

72. Maimonides, *The Guide of the Perplexed*, 17–18.

73. De' Rossi, *The Light of the Eyes*, trans. Joanna Weinberg, 386.

74. Luzzatto, "*Hakdamah le-Sefer Ḥasidim*," first page (unpaginated section).

75. Jacob Elbaum, "*Yalqut Shim'oni* and the Medieval Midrash Anthology," in *The Anthology in Jewish Literature*, ed. David Stern (New York: Oxford University Press, 2004), 161–62.

76. "*Kelalei remazei Sefer ha-Ḥasidim*," in *Sefer Ḥasidim* (Basel, 1580), last page (unpaginated section).

77. In such cases, there seems to be no reasonable explanation for why the order of the entries is reversed, except for carelessness.

78. Luzzatto, "*Hakdamah le-Sefer Ḥasidim*," second page (unpaginated section).

79. Luzzatto's criticism of the table of contents in the first edition also recalled that of the humanist and editor Konrad Pellikan a few decades earlier. According to Grafton, in addition to his philological and theological activities, Pellikan "became a specialist in making indexes," and nevertheless, "like other indexers before and after, he enjoyed ridiculing his readers for taking advantage of the shortcut provided." Grafton, *The Culture of Correction*, 16. Finding aids in early modern printed works were thus perceived as a double-edged sword: They could facilitate engagement with the text by directing readers more quickly to specific passages—and for this reason were especially desirable and worthy of extolling on title pages and in introductions—but they also deterred some readers from reading the full text.

80. Stallybrass, "Books and Scrolls," 60.

81. *Milon Even Shoshan*, s.v. "ma'aseh"; Jastrow, *A Dictionary of the Targumim*, s.v. "ma'aseh."

82. Rikva Shemesh, "On the Narrative Discourse in Tannaitic Language: An Exploration of the *ma'aseh* and *pa'am ahat* Discourse Units," *Hebrew Studies* 49 (2008); *Encyclopedia Judaica*, s.v. "ma'aseh."

83. Lucia Raspe, *Jüdische Hagiographie im Mittelalterlichen Aschkenas* (Tübingen: Mohr Siebeck, 2006), 47–50. See also Eli Yassif, *The Hebrew Folktale: History, Genre, Meaning*, trans. Jacqueline S. Teitelbaum (Indianapolis: Indiana University Press, 2009), 132, 492n64; Erika Timm, "Zur Frühgeschichte der Yiddischen Erzählprosa: Eine neuaufgefundene Maise-Handschrift," *Beiträge zur Geschichte der Deutschen Sprache und Literatur* 117 (1995); and Dan Ben-Amos, "Generic Distinctions in the Aggadah," in *Studies in*

Jewish Folklore: Proceedings of a Regional Conference of the Association for Jewish Studies, Chicago, May 1–3, 1977, ed. Frank Talmage (Cambridge, UK: Association for Judaic Studies, 1980), 62.

84. There is debate about when each of these titles was printed for the first time, though both occurred during the sixteenth century; see Isreal Zinberg, *A History of Jewish Literature*, vol. 4, trans. Bernard Martin (Cleveland: Press of Case Western Reserve University, 1974), 186.

85. Max Grünbaum, *Jüdischdeutsche Chrestomathie: Zugleich ein Beitrag zur Kunde der Hebräischen Literatur* (Leipzig: F. A. Brockhaus, 1882), 450.

86. "*Kelalei remazei Sefer ha-Ḥasidim*," in *Sefer Ḥasidim* (Basel, 1580), first page (unpaginated section).

87. This passage is based on Babylonian Talmud, *Sanhedrin* 11a.

88. Moshe Idel, "Man as the 'Possible' Entity in Some Jewish and Renaissance Sources," in *Hebraica Veritas?* eds. Coudert and S. Shoulson; Chaim Wirszubski, *Pico Della Mirandola's Encounter with Jewish Mysticism* (Cambridge, MA: Harvard University Press, 1989).

89. "*Kelalei remazei Sefer ha-Ḥasidim*," in *Sefer Ḥasidim* (Basel, 1580), first page (unpaginated section).

90. "*Kelalei remazei Sefer ha-Ḥasidim*," in *Sefer Ḥasidim* (Basel, 1580), second page (unpaginated section).

91. Ronnie Po-Chia Hsia, "Christian Ethnography of Jews in Early Modern Germany," in *The Expulsion of the Jews and After*, ed. Raymond Waddington (New York: Garland, 1994); see also Yaacov Deutsch, "Polemical Ethnographies: Descriptions of Yom Kippur in the Writings of Christian Hebraists and Jewish Converts in Early Modern Europe," in *Hebraica Veritas?* eds. Coudert and Shoulson, 204; Yaacov Deutsch, *Judaism in Christian Eyes: Ethnographic Descriptions of Jews and Judaism in Early Modern Europe*, trans. Avi Aronsky (New York: Oxford, 2012).

92. Weinberg, "Johann Buxtorf Makes a Notebook," 293.

93. Deutsch, "Polemical Ethnographies," 224.

94. Grafton and Weinberg, *"I Have Always Loved the Holy Tongue,"* 55–59.

95. Eisenstein, *The Printing Press as an Agent of Change*, 56; Burnett, *From Christian Hebraism to Jewish Studies*, 48–53; Raz-Krakotzkin, *The Censor, the Editor, and the Text*, 25; Grafton, *The Culture of Correction*, 78–142.

Froben's *Sefer Ḥasidim*: Text

1. Luzzatto, "*Hakdamah ba-mehalel ha-sefer ve-ha-mehaber* . . . ," unpaginated.

2. *Encyclopedia Judaica*, 2nd ed., s.v. "typography"; A. M. Habermann, *Ha'sefer ha'ivri b'hitpathuto*.

3. See chapter 2 and Langer, *Cursing the Christians?* 115.

4. It should be noted, however, that even the attempts of Froben's editors were imperfect. A number of passages remained that included offensive words, and even the word *goy*. See below.

5. Joseph Hacker discusses parallels to this passage from the Parma manuscript. See Joseph Hacker, "Al gezerat tat'nu (1096)," *Zion* 31, no. 1 (1966): 225–31. The concept of disguising oneself to avoid persecution also appears in the Babylonian Talmud, such as in the case of Rabbi Meir in *Avodah Zarah* 18a. The literature on the persecution of Jews during the medieval period and the Crusades, to which this passage alludes, is vast. A sampling includes: A. Neubauer and M. Stern, *Hebräische Berichte über die Judenverfolgungen während der Kreuzzüge* (Berlin: Simion, 1892); Shlomo Eidelberg, *The Jews and the Crusaders: The Hebrew Chronicles of the First and Second Crusades* (Madison: University of Wisconsin Press, 1977); Ivan Marcus, "From Politics to Martyrdom: Shifting Paradigms in the Hebrew Narratives of the 1096 Crusade Riots," *Prooftexts* 2 (1982): 40–52; Robert Chazan, *European Jewry and the First Crusade* (Berkeley: University of California Press, 1996); and Susan Einbinder, *Beautiful Death: Jewish Poetry and Martyrdom in Medieval France* (Princeton, NJ: Princeton University Press, 2002).

6. Halbertal and Margalit, *Idolatry*, 3–4, 202–213.

7. My translation, according to Prebor's transcription of Ms. Vatican 273; Prebor, "Sefer ha-Zikkuk," 53. See also Raz-Krakotzkin, *The Censor, the Editor, and the Text*, 121.

8. Federica Francesconi, "'This Passage Can Also Be Read Differently…': How Jews and Christians Censored Hebrew Texts in Early Modern Modena," *Jewish History* 26, no. 1 (June 12, 2012): 149.

9. Rosen-Zvi and Ophir, "Goy," 69.

10. My translation, according to Prebor's transcription; Prebor, "Sefer ha-Zikkuk," 53. See also Raz-Krakotzkin, *The Censor, the Editor, and the Text*, 121.

11. Margaret Barker, *The Mother of the Lord*, vol. 1, *The Lady in the Temple* (London: T & T Clark, 2012), 40.

12. I am grateful to Elisheva Carlebach for this insight.

13. At this point in Froben's edition, the sequence of passages falls one behind the Bologna edition due to the absence of §681, as the passage numbered §681 in the partners' edition is misnumbered as §421 in Froben's edition.

14. This case is one of Christians who failed to protect their Jewish neighbors from Crusaders; Stow, *Alienated Minority*, 108.

15. On baptismal water's negative associations among Ashkenazi Jews, see Einbinder, *Beautiful Death*, 32.

16. See above, as well as Jastrow, *A Dictionary of the Targumim*, s.v. "shemad."

17. My translation. Saul Lieberman, *Tosefta kifshuta*, vol. 3 (New York: Jewish Theo-

logical Seminary of America, 1962), 402n45, cited in Milikowsky, "Gehenom u-poshei Yisrael," 333n94. Note that this term differs from its cousins, the noun *meshummad* and the verb *nishtamed*, discussed in chapter 2. While those terms do not necessarily refer to "forced conversion," the noun in question does. See Langer, *Cursing the Christians?* 45n35.

18. The principle that baptism cannot be coerced dates to Pope Gregory the Great's (sixth-century) bull *Sicut Judaeis*. Christians debated both the efficacy of forced baptism and what precisely constituted illegal coercion throughout the medieval and early modern periods. *Encyclopedia Judaica*, 2nd ed., s.v. "Baptism, forced"; see also van Boxel, *Jewish Books in Christian Hands*, 29–30.

19. See Ms. Parma 3280 §250 and Ms. JTS (former) Boesky 45 §114.

20. I am indebted to Elisheva Carlebach for sensitivity to the aural dimension of these texts and this suggestion as well.

21. Why Froben's editors chose not to replace *nokhri* in this passage is unclear to me. Perhaps it was simply an oversight, though that is surprising because the passage was heavily edited.

22. See above and Langer, *Cursing the Christians?* 70–78.

23. While the identity and ideology of this group in antiquity is not clear, see Albert I. Baumgarten, *The Flourishing of Jewish Sects in the Maccabean Era: An Interpretation* (Leiden: Brill, 1997); Babylonian rabbis of late antiquity expressed hostility to them and accused them of insufficient loyalty to Jewish traditions; see Babylonian Talmud, *Eruvin* 68b.

24. For other references to Sadducees in Froben's edition, see §977 (compare to §982 in the partners' edition) and §433. It could be suggested, however, that for some Jewish readers the word "Sadducees" was a code for Christians, because Jesus himself, in the Talmud, was understood as a deviant Jew. Yet, on the literal level at least, and it was on this level that much early modern censorship occurred, Zifroni's intervention removed any direct reference to Christianity.

25. Froben's editors made other anachronizing replacements throughout their edition. In §280, Froben's editors replaced the word *komer* ("priest") with the appellation "*Arami*," which may be translated literally as "Syrian," but which referred to Roman pagans in rabbinic literature. See Jastrow, *A Dictionary of the Targumim*, s.v. "arami," and the sources cited therein, especially Palestinian Talmud, *Shevi'it* 4:2, in which a Roman pagan is juxtaposed with a Jewish Judean, "*yehudi yehudi o' arami arami.*" See also the Aramaic incantation reproduced in Dan Levene, "May These Curses Go Out and Flee," in *Magical and Religious Literature of Late Antiquity*, vol. 2, eds. Shaul Shaked and Siam Bhayro (Leiden: Brill, 2013), 98, where the term is once again juxtaposed with "*yehudi.*" Levene translates it as "pagan." Elsewhere, the term "Egyptian" (*Miẓri*) replaces *komer*; see §433 and §829 (compare to §832 in the partners' edition). Froben's editors also use the term *apikoros* ("heretic") as a replacement for *galaḥ*, as in §296,

where it is juxtaposed with "Sadducee." See Jastrow, *A Dictionary of the Targumim*, s.v. "apikoros," and the examples cited therein, especially Babylonian Talmud, *Hagigah* 5b.

26. Strauss, *Persecution and the Art of Writing*, 24.

27. Carlebach, *Divided Souls*, 201–12.

28. Raz-Krakotzkin, *The Censor, the Editor, and the Text*, 133.

29. On the self/Other dichotomy, see Jacques Derrida, "Deconstruction and the Other," in *Dialogues with Contemporary Continental Thinkers*, ed. Richard Kearney (Manchester, UK: University of Manchester Press, 1984), 117; Samuel Moyn, *Origins of the Other: Emmanuel Levinas between Revelation and Ethics* (Ithaca, NY: Cornell University Press, 2005).

30. In this passage, I have provided the JPS (1917) translation, which is closer to the syntax of the Hebrew.

31. The names Aphram and Avram are phonologically similar. Avram was, of course, the patriarch Abraham's name prior to his covenant with YHWH (Genesis 17:5). It is thus a reminder of the person's apostasy. I thank Elisheva Carlebach for this insight. According to Reuven Margoliot, the name Aphram is related to the word *efer* ("dust"). He cites the view of R. Chaim Joseph David Azulai (1724–1806), a noted commentator on *Sefer Ḥasidim*, in whose responsa, *Yosef ometz*, this passage appears. Azulai stated that a nickname given to an apostate should sound like the name by which he was known among non-Jews. *Sefer Ḥasidim* (Jerusalem, 1961), 11, Bar Ilan Responsa Project.

32. For a summary of these variations, see Peter Schäfer and Michael Meerson, introduction to *Toledot Yeshu: The Life Story of Jesus*, eds. Peter Schäfer, Michael Meerson, and Yaacov Deutsch (Tübingen: Mohr Siebeck, 2014), 113–19.

33. Wout van Bekkum, "The Poetical Qualities of the Apostle Peter in Jewish Folktale," *Zutot* 3, no. 1 (2003): 17; see also John Gager, "Simon Peter, the Founder of Christianity or the Savior of Israel?" in *Toledot Yeshu*, eds. Schäfer, Meerson, and Deutsch.

34. Again, the JPS (1917) translation preserves the syntax of the Hebrew.

35. On the meaning of this passage, see Dan, *Ḥasidut Ashkenaz be-toldot*, vol. 1, 86.

36. *Catholic Encyclopedia*, s.v. "St. Michael the Archangel"; and Rosemary Guiley, *Encyclopedia of Angels* (New York: Facts on File, 1996), s.v. "Michael."

37. See Jastrow, *A Dictionary of the Targumim*, s.v. "eid," and the citations therein, especially Babylonian Talmud, *Avodah Zarah* 7a.

38. My translation. Prebor, "Sefer ha-Zikkuk," 54.

39. Other examples of this sort of truncation include §277 and §864 (numbered §861 in Froben's edition).

40. Babylonian Talmud, *Sanhedrin* 43a; see Popper, *The Censorship of Hebrew Books*, 56.

41. On the extensive censoring of Froben's Talmud, see Rabbinovicz, *Ma'amar al hadpasat ha-Talmud*, 68–70; and Popper, *The Censorship of Hebrew Books*, 55–62.

42. *Tractate Eduyot* (Basel, 1578), end of chapter 2, page 6b (though this page lacks numeration).

43. Prijs, *Die basler hebräischen Drucke*, 179.

44. See Jastrow, *A Dictionary of the Targumim*, s.v. "arel," and the citations therein, especially Mishnah, *Nedarim* 3:11, which refers to the term's being used specifically for uncircumcised gentiles, and not uncircumcised Jews.

45. See §433 and §703. The latter term "Egyptian" is ironic, because Egyptians were known throughout antiquity for practicing circumcision; see Herodotus, *The History of Herodotus*, vol. 1, trans. G. C. Macaulay (London: Macmillan, 1904), book 2, ch. 35 (132).

46. My translation. Prebor, "Sefer ha-Zikkuk," 53.

47. The term *la'az* has frequently been mistaken as an acronym for the Hebrew expression *lashon am zar* ("the language of a foreign people"). On its use in the medieval period, see Kirsten A. Fudeman, "Glosses of Hebrew: Medieval French," in *Encyclopedia of Hebrew Language and Linguistics*, ed. Geoffrey Khan (Brill Online, 2016). There appears to be little scholarship on the *le'azim* in *Sefer Ḥasidim*, and further, their relation to the *le'azim* in other medieval Hebrew texts, such as Rashi's commentaries. On the linguistic peculiarities of *Sefer Ḥasidim* and its relationship to Middle High German, see Chaim Rabin, "Zemanim u-derachim be-po'al she-be-lashon 'Sefer Ḥasidim,'" *Papers of the Fourth World Congress of Jewish Studies* 2 (1968): 113–16; and Simha Kogot, "The Language of *Sefer Ḥasidim*," in *Studies in Medieval Jewish History and Literature*, vol. 2, ed. Isadore Twersky (Cambridge, MA: Harvard University Center for Jewish Studies, 1984), 95–109. The passages discussed later are clearly derived from French.

48. Samuel he-Ḥasid, Judah's father, may even have been exiled from Speyer because he sought to prevent his coreligionists from swearing oaths. See Ephraim Shoham-Steiner, "Mi-Shpeyer le Regensburg: N'dodei mishpahat he-Ḥasid mi-hevel ha-Rhine le-hevel Danube," *Zion* 81, no. 2 (2016): 168–69.

49. Cyril Aslanov, email message to author, November 3, 2016. I am especially grateful to Professor Aslanov for helping me transcribe and translate these phrases from *la'az*, here and in the following paragraphs. Professor Aslanov suggested to me that the partners' edition's text of this phrase is corrupt.

50. Aslanov, email message to author, November 3, 2016. The Judeo-French phrase is a translation of the Hebrew.

51. Aslanov, email message to author, November 3, 2016.

52. Interestingly, Froben's editors left a trace reminder of the existence of §4 by not renumbering the passages, so the sequence of passages moves from §3 to §5.

53. Luzzatto, "*Hakdamah le-Sefer Ḥasidim*," first page (unpaginated).

54. Jacob Burckhardt, *The Civilization of the Renaissance in Italy*, 120–184; more recently, Roberto Weiss, *The Renaissance Discovery of Classical Antiquity* (Oxford: Oxford University Press, 1988).

55. Richardson, *Print Culture in Renaissance Italy*, 185. On the way this approach shaped the printing of the Palestinian Talmud, see Mayer, "Me-tarbut k'tav ha-yad le-tarbut ha-defus."

56. Grafton, *The Culture of Correction in Renaissance Europe*.

57. This incident is found in Babylonian Talmud, *Berakhot* 34b.

58. This case, of course, refers to a "chained woman" (*agunah*), a woman whose husband has disappeared and whom Jewish law prohibits from remarrying until the husband's death has been ascertained.

59. This example is based on Esther 4:5–16 and Babylonian Talmud, *Megillah* 15a, which record the traditions about Hatach, one of Ahashuarus's eunuchs who functioned as a go-between for Mordecai and Esther.

60. This refers to the midrashic tradition that Esther and Mordecai were husband and wife; see Babylonian Talmud, *Megillah* 13a.

61. This expression is also found in Babylonian Talmud, *Avodah Zarah* 10b and *Yoma* 77a.

62. Indeed, though punctuation was not absent in the first printed edition of *Sefer Ḥasidim*, it was far more infrequent than in the second edition. Generally, the partners divided passages into sections with apostrophes and blank spaces. These sections were frequently quite long.

63. This kind of dividing punctuation became common first in liturgical texts, which had to be read aloud, but was not used in vernacular and nonreligious texts through the later medieval period. See Raymond Clemens and Timothy Graham, *Introduction to Manuscript Studies* (Ithaca, NY: Cornell University Press, 2007), 86; M. B. Parkes, *Pause and Effect: An Introduction to the History of Punctuation in the West* (Berkeley: University of California Press, 1993), 44–49; and Brian Richardson, *Manuscript Culture in Renaissance Italy* (Cambridge: Cambridge University Press, 2009), 11.

64. Clemens and Graham, *Introduction to Manuscript Studies*, 82.

65. Sinai (Tamas) Turan, "Pirkei mavo le-toldot ha-pisuk ha-ivri," *Tarbiz* 71, no. 3 (2002): 472–77.

66. On the practice of interrupting the Torah reading, see Finkelstein, *Jewish Self-Government in the Middle Ages*, 15–18.

67. For the Talmudic *locus classicus* of this idea, see Mishnah, *Sanhedrin* 4:5.

68. The source of this tradition is Palestinian Talmud, *Makkot* 2:6. It is also found in the Babylonian Talmud, *Makkot* 12a. In my translation of the biblical verse, I deviate from the JPS for greater clarity. The JPS reads "manslayer," not "murderer."

69. Prijs, *Die basler hebräischen Drucke*, 178.

70. Stow, "The Burning of the Talmud."

71. Van Boxel, "Hebrew Books and Censorship."

72. Burnett, "Christian Hebrew Printing in the Sixteenth Century."

73. Gudrun Wacker, "The Internet and Censorship in China: Gudrun Wacker," in *China and the Internet*, eds. Christopher R. Hughes and Gudrun Wacker (London: Taylor & Francis, 2003).

74. Raz-Krakotzkin, *The Censor, the Editor, and the Text*, 180–94.

75. Van Boxel, "Hebrew Books and Censorship," 90.

76. Van Boxel, "Hebrew Books and Censorship," 85.

77. Van Boxel, "Hebrew Books and Censorship," 80.

Epilogue

1. On Gedaliah's education and the dependence of *Shalshelet ha-kabbalah* on *Me'or einayim*, see Abraham David, "R. Gedalya Ibn Yahya's Shalshelet Hakabbalah (Chain of Tradition): A Chapter in Medieval Jewish Historiography," *Immanuel: A Semi-Annual Bulletin of Religious Thought and Research in Israel* 12 (1981).

2. On the dates of the composition of *Shalshelet ha-kabbalah*, see David, "R. Gedalya Ibn Yahya's Shalshelet Hakabbalah," 62.

3. McKittrick, *Print, Manuscript, and the Search for Order*, 17–20; Dweck, "What Is a Jewish Book?" 371–72; Dweck, *The Scandal of Kabbalah*, 29–58.

4. Ivan (Yisrael) Marcus, *Sefer Ḥasidim: k.y. Parmah H-3280* (Jerusalem: Dinur Center, 1985), 15.

5. On the etymology and meaning of *kuntres*, see J. H. Chajes, "Accounting for the Self," 7–8.

6. *Sefer Ḥasidim* (Bologna, 1538), §101. One commentary on this passage, David Greenhut's seventeenth-century *Perush kadmon*, suggests that a *kuntres* possesses no *kedushah* only when it contains no text of its own. When the writer fills it with text, especially quotations from sacred books, it can acquire *kedushah*.

7. Kant, *The Metaphysics of Morals*, 106.

8. Kathryn Sutherland, "Anglo American Editorial Theory," in *The Cambridge Companion to Textual Scholarship*, eds. Neil Freistat and Julia Flanders (Cambridge: Cambridge University Press, 2013), 55. The term "screen essentialism" was coined by Nick Montfort; see Matthew G. Kirschenbaum, *Mechanisms: New Media and the Forensic Imagination* (Cambridge, MA: MIT Press, 2012), 78–79.

9. Anthony Grafton, *Inky Fingers: The Making of Books in Early Modern Europe* (Cambridge, MA: Harvard University Press, 2020).

Bibliography

Abrams, Daniel. *Kabbalistic Manuscripts and Textual Theory: Methodologies of Textual Scholarship and Editorial Practice in the Study of Jewish Mysticism*. Jerusalem: Magnes Press, 2010.

Abravanel, Isaac. *Mirkevet ha-mishneh*. Sabbioneta, 1551.

Adelman, Howard. "Italian Jewish Women." In *Jewish Women in Historical Perspective*. Edited by Judith R. Baskin, 150–68. Detroit, MI: Wayne State University Press, 1998.

Adelman, Howard. "The Educational and Literary Activities of Jewish Women in Italy during the Renaissance and Counter-Reformation." In *Shlomo Simonsohn Jubilee Volume* [English side]. Edited by Daniel Carpi, 9–24. Tel Aviv: Tel Aviv University, 1993.

Adret, Shlomo ibn. *Teshuvot she'elot meha-eshel ha-gadol*. Bologna, 1538–1539.

Alexander-Frizer, Tamar. *The Pious Sinner: Ethics and Aesthetics in the Medieval Hasidic Narrative*. Tübingen: Mohr Siebeck, 1991.

Alleson-Gerberg, Shai. "Nittel Nacht: An Inverted Christmas with Toledot Yeshu." TheTorah. https://www.thetorah.com/article/nittel-nacht-an-inverted-christmas-with-toledot-yeshu.

Amram, David Werner. *The Makers of Hebrew Books in Italy: Being Chapters in the History of the Hebrew Printing Press*. Philadelphia: Julius H. Greenstone, 1909.

Andreatta, Michael. "The Printing of Devotion in Seventeenth-Century Italy: Prayer Books Printed for the Shomrim La-Boker Confraternities." In *The Hebrew Book in Early Modern Italy*. Edited by Joseph R. Hacker and Adam Shear, 156–70. Philadelphia: University of Pennsylvania Press, 2011.

Assaf, Simcha. "Le-pulmus al ha-defus sifrei kabbalah." In *Mekorot u-meḥkarim*. Edited by Simcha Assaf, 238–46. Jerusalem: Mosad HaRav Kook, 1946.

Austin, Kenneth. *From Judaism to Calvinism: The Life and Writings of Immanuel Tremellius (c. 1510–1580)*. Aldershot, UK: Ashgate, 2007.

Azulai, Chaim Joseph David. *Yosef ometz*. Jerusalem, 1961. Bar Ilan Responsa Project.

Baer, Yitzhak F. "Ha-megamah ha-dadit- ha-ḥevrutit shel 'Sefer Ḥasidim.'" *Zion* 3, no. 1 (1938): 1–50.

Baer, Yitzhak F. "The Socioreligious Orientation of 'Sefer Hasidim.'" In *Binah: Studies in Jewish Thought*. Vol. 2. Edited by Joseph Dan, 57–95. New York: Praeger, 1989.

Baile, David, ed. *Cultures of the Jews: A New History*. New York: Schocken Books, 2002.

Barker, Margaret. *The Mother of the Lord*. Vol. 1, *The Lady in the Temple*. London: T & T Clark, 2012.

Baron, Salo W. "Azariah de' Rossi: A Biographical Sketch." In *History and Jewish Historians: Essays and Addresses*. Edited by Salo W. Baron, Arthur Hertzberg, and L. A. Feldman, 167–73. Philadelphia: Jewish Publication Society, 1964.

Baron, Salo W. "Azariah De Rossi's Attitude to Life (Weltanschauung)." In *Jewish Studies in Memory of Israel Abrahams*, 12–52. New York: Press of the Jewish Institute of Religion, 1927.

Baron, Salo Wittmayer. "The Council of Trent and Rabbinic Literature." In *Ancient and Medieval Jewish History*. Edited by Leon Feldman, 352–71. New Brunswick, NJ: Rutgers University Press, 1972.

Baruchson, Shifra. *Sefarim ve-kor'im: Tarbut ha-keri'ah shel Yehude Iṭalyah be-shilhe ha-Renesans*. Ramat-Gan: Bar Ilan University Press, 1993.

Baruchson, Ziporah (Shifra). "Money and Culture: Financing Sources and Methods in Hebrew Printing Shops in Cinquecento Italy." *La Bibliofilia* 92 (1990): 23–39.

Baruchson-Arbib, Shifra Z. "The Prices of Hebrew Printed Books in Cinquecento Italy." *La Bibliofilia* 97, no. 2 (1995): 149–61.

Baskin, Judith R. "Women and Sexual Ambivalence in 'Sefer Ḥasidim.'" *Jewish Quarterly Review* 96, no. 1 (2006): 1–8.

Baumgarten, Elisheva, Elisabeth Hollender, and Ephraim Shoham-Steiner, eds. "Appropriation and Differentiation: Jewish Identity in Medieval Ashkenaz." *AJS Review* 42, no. 1 (2018): 39–63.

Baumgarten, Elisheva, Elisabeth Hollender, and Ephraim Shoham-Steiner. "Introduction: Sefer Ḥasidim—Book, Context, and Afterlife." *Jewish History* 34 (2021).

Baumgarten, Elisheva, Elisabeth Hollender, and Ephraim Shoham-Steiner, eds. *Practicing Piety in Medieval Ashkenaz: Men, Women, and Everyday Religious Observance*. Philadelphia: University of Pennsylvania Press, 2014.

Baumgarten, Elisheva, Elisabeth Hollender, and Ephraim Shoham-Steiner, eds. "Seeking Signs? Jews, Christians and Proof by Fire in Medieval Germany and Northern France." In *New Perspectives on Jewish-Christian Relations in Honor of David Berger*. Edited by Elisheva Carlebach and Jacob J. Schacter, 205–25. Leiden: Brill, 2015.

Baumgarten, Jean. *Introduction to Old Yiddish Literature*. Oxford: Oxford University Press, 2005.

Behringer, Wolfgang. "Communications Revolutions: A Historiographical Concept." *German History* 24, no. 3 (2006): 333–74.

Beit-Arie, Malachi. "Beit Ariyeh - Sefer Hasidim." In *Rashi 1040–1990: Hommage à Ephraïm E. Urbach*. Edited by Gabrielle Sed-Rajna, 559–66. Paris: Les Éditions du Cerf, 1993.

Beit-Arie, Malachi. "The Codicological Data-Base of the Hebrew Palaeography Project: A Tool for Localizing and Dating Hebrew Medieval Manuscripts." In *Hebrew Studies: Papers Presented at a Colloquium on Resources for Hebraica in Europe*. Edited by Diana Rowland Smith and Peter Shmuel Salinger, 165–97. London: The British Library, 1991.

Beit-Arie, Malachi. *Hebrew Codicology*. Jerusalem: Israel Academy of Sciences and Humanities, 1981.

Beit-Arie, Malachi. "Ideal Versus Reality: Scribal Prescriptions in Sefer Ḥasidim and Contemporary Scribal Practices in Franco-German Manuscripts." In *Rashi 1040–1990: Hommage à Ephraïm E. Urbach*. Edited by Gabrielle Sed-Rajna, 559–66. Paris: Editions du Cerf, 1993.

Beit-Arie, Malachi. *Unveiled Faces of Medieval Hebrew Books: The Evolution of Manuscript Production—Progression or Regression*. Jerusalem: Magnes Press, 2003.

Ben-Amos, Dan. "Generic Distinctions in the Aggadah." In *Studies in Jewish Folklore: Proceedings of a Regional Conference of the Association for Jewish Studies, Chicago, May 1–3, 1977*. Edited by Frank Talmage, 45–71. Cambridge, UK: Association for Jewish Studies, 1980.

Ben-Yaakov, Yitzhak. *Oẓar ha-sefarim*. Vilna, 1880.

Benayahu, Meir. *Marbiẓ Torah: Samkhuyotav, tafkidav ve-hetko be-mosedot ha-kehillah*. Jerusalem: Mosad HaRav Kook, 1953.

Bendowska, Magda, and Jan Doktór. "Sefer Ha-Zohar: The Battle for Editio Princeps." *Kwartalnik Historii Zydów* 2 (2012): 141–61.

Berger, Shlomo. "An Invitation to Buy and Read: Paratexts of Yiddish Books in Amsterdam, 1650–1800." *Book History* 7, no. 1 (2004): 31–61.

Berger, Shlomo. *Producing Redemption in Amsterdam: Early Modern Yiddish Books in Paratextual Perspective*. Leiden: Brill, 2013.

Berns, Andrew D. "Ovadiah Sforno's Last Will and Testament." *Journal of Jewish Studies* 68, no. 1 (2017): 1–33.

Blair, Ann. "Errata Lists and the Reader as Corrector." In *Agent of Change: Print Culture Studies after Elizabeth L. Eisenstein*. Edited by Sabrina Alcorn Baron and Eric N. Lindquist, 21–66. Amherst: University of Massachusetts Press, 2007.

Blair, Ann. "Information in Early Modern Europe." In *Information: A Historical Companion*. Edited by Ann Blair, Paul Duguid, Anja-Silvia Goeing, and Anthony Grafton, 61–85. Princeton, NJ: Princeton University Press, 2021.

Blair, Ann, Paul Duguid, Anja-Silvia Goeing, and Anthony Grafton, eds. *Information: A Historical Companion*. Princeton, NJ: Princeton University Press, 2021.

Blair, Ann M. *The Theater of Nature: Jean Bodin and Renaissance Science*. Princeton, NJ: Princeton University Press, 1997.

Blair, Ann M. *Too Much to Know: Managing Scholarly Information Before the Modern Age*. New Haven, CT: Yale University Press, 2010.

Blair, Ann M., and Anthony Grafton. *The Transmission of Culture in Early Modern Europe*. Philadelphia: University of Pennsylvania Press, 1990.

Bloch, Eileen. "Erasmus and the Froben Press: The Making of an Editor." *Library Quarterly* 32, no. 2 (1965): 109–20.

Bloch, Joshua, et al. *Hebrew Printing and Bibliography: Studies by Joshua Bloch and Others, Reprinted from the Publications of the New York Public Library on the Occasion of the Seventy-Fifth Anniversary of the Jewish Division of the New York Public Library.* Edited by Charles Berlin. New York: The New York Public Library, 1976.

Boksenboim, Yacov. *Parashiyot: Me-ḥayai Yehude Iṭalyah ba-meah ha-16.* Tel Aviv: Tel Aviv University, 1986.

Bokser, Ben Zion. *The Maharal: The Mystical Philosophy of Rabbi Judah Loew of Prague.* Northvale, NJ: Jason Aaronson, 1994.

Bonfil, Robert. *Jewish Life in Renaissance Italy.* Translated by Anthony Oldcorn. Berkeley: University of California Press, 1994.

Bonfil, Robert. *Rabbis and Jewish Communities in Renaissance Italy.* Translated by Jonathan Chipman. Oxford: Littman Library of Jewish Civilization, 1990.

Bonfil, Robert. "Torat ha-nefesh ve-ha-kedushah be-mishnat R. Ovadiah Sforno." In *Eshel Beer Sheva* 1 (1976): 200–57.

Breuer, Mordechai. *Oholei Torah: Ha-yeshivah tavnitah ve-toldoteha.* Jerusalem: Zalman Shazar Center, 2003.

Brown, Horatio F. *The Venetian Printing Press.* New York: G. P. Putnam's Sons, 1891.

Bühler, Carl F. *The University and the Press in Fifteenth-Century Bologna.* Notre Dame, IN: Mediaeval Institute, University of Notre Dame, 1958.

Buňatová, Marie. "Trade Contacts Between Prague Jews and Northern Italy and Their Engagement in the Italian Commodity Trade in the 16th and Early 17th Centuries." *Judaica Bohemiae* 54, no. 1 (2019): 5–30.

Bunin Benor, Sarah. "Do American Jews Speak a 'Jewish Language'?: A Model of Jewish Linguistic Distinctiveness." *Jewish Quarterly Review* 99, no. 2 (2009): 230–69.

Burckhardt, Jakob. *The Civilization of the Renaissance in Italy* [*Die Kultur der Renaissance in Italien*]. Translated by S. G. C. Middlemore. London: Penguin, 2004.

Burnett, Stephen G. *Christian Hebraism in the Reformation Era (1500–1660).* Leiden: Brill, 2012.

Burnett, Stephen G. "Christian Hebrew Printing in the Sixteenth Century: Printers, Humanism and the Impact of the Reformation." *Helmantica: Revista de Filología Clásica y Hebrea* 51, no. 154 (2000): 13–42.

Burnett, Stephen G. *From Christian Hebraism to Jewish Studies: Johannes Buxtorf (1564–1629) and Hebrew Learning in the Seventeenth Century.* Leiden: Brill, 1996.

Burnett, Stephen G. "German Jewish Printing in the Reformation Era (1530–1633)." In *Jews, Judaism, and the Reformation in Sixteenth-Century Germany.* Edited by Dean Philip Bell and Stephen G. Burnett, 503–27. Leiden: Brill, 2006.

Burns, Gerald L. "The Originality of Texts in a Manuscript Culture." *Comparative Literature* 32, no. 2 (Spring 1980): 113–29.

Buxtorf, Johann. *De abbreviaturis hebraicis, liber novus et copiosus...* Basel, 1613.

Buxtorf, Johann. *Tiberias sive Commentarius Masoreticus.* Basel, 1620.

Campanini, Saverio. "Un intellettuale Ebreo del Rinascimento: 'Ovadya Sforno a Bologna e i suoi rapporti con i Cristiani." In *Verso l'Epilogo di una convivenza: Gli Ebrei a Bologna nel XVI Secolo.* Edited by Maria Giuseppina Muzzarelli, 99–127. Florence: Giuntina, 1996.

Carlebach, Elisheva. *Divided Souls: Converts from Judaism in Germany, 1500–1750*. New Haven, CT: Yale University Press, 2001.

Carlebach, Elisheva. *Palaces of Time: Jewish Calendar and Culture in Early Modern Europe*. Cambridge, MA: Harvard University Press, 2011.

Carlebach, Elisheva. "Precious Time: Jewish Wall Calendars in the Valmadonna Collection." In *The Writing on the Wall: A Catalogue of Judaica Broadsides from the Valmadonna Trust Library*. Edited by Sharon Liberman Mintz, Shaul Seidler-Feller, and David Wachtel, 20–31. London: Valmadonna Trust Library, 2015.

Carpi, Daniel. "Geirush ha-yehudim mimedinat ha-kenisiyah be-yemei ha-apiphior Pius ha-ḥamishi u-mishpatei ha-ḥakirah neged yehudei Bologna (1566–1569)." In *Scritti in memoria di Enzo Serani*. Edited by Daniel Carpi, Attilio Milano, and Umberto Nahon, 145–65. Jerusalem: Fondazione Sally Mayer, 1970.

Cassuto, Umberto. "Les traductions Judéo-Italiennes du rituel." *Revue des Études Juives* 89, no. 177–78 (1930): 260–80.

Cazes, Hélène, ed. *Bonaventura Vulcanius, Works and Networks: Bruges 1538 - Leiden 1614*. Leiden: Brill, 2010.

Chajes, J. H. "Accounting for the Self: Preliminary Generic-Historical Reflections on Early Modern Jewish Egodocuments." *Jewish Quarterly Review* 95, no. 1 (2005): 1–15.

Chartier, Roger. *The Order of Books: Readers, Authors, and Libraries in Europe between the Fourteenth and Eighteenth Centuries*. Translated by Lydia G. Cochrane. Stanford, CA: Stanford University Press, 1994.

Chazan, Robert. *European Jewry and the First Crusade*. Berkeley: University of California Press, 1996.

Clegg, Cyndia Susan. *Press Censorship in Jacobean England*. New York: Cambridge University Press, 2001.

Clemens, Raymond, and Timothy Graham. *Introduction to Manuscript Studies*. Ithaca, NY: Cornell University Press, 2007.

Cohen, Mark R. *Under Crescent and Cross: The Jews in the Middle Ages*. Princeton, NJ: Princeton University Press, 2008.

Cohen, Richard I., Natalie B. Dohrman, Adam Shear, and Elchanan Reiner, eds. *Jewish Culture in Early Modern Europe: Essays in Honor of David B. Ruderman*. Pittsburgh, PA: Hebrew Union College Press, 2014.

Cooperman, Bernard. "Legitimizing Rhetorics: Jewish 'Heresy' in Early Modern Italy." *Études Épistémè* 31 (2017): 1–17.

Cooperman, Bernard. "Political Discourse in a Kabbalistic Register: Isaac De Lattes' 'Plea for Stronger Communal Government'." In *Be'Erot Yitzhak: Studies in Memory of Isadore Twersky*. Edited by Jay Michael Harris, 47–68. Cambridge, MA: Harvard Center for Jewish Studies, 2005.

Cooperman, Bernard. "Theorizing Jewish Self-Government in Early Modern Italy." In *Una manna buona per Mantova: Studi in onore di Vittore Colorni*. Edited by Mauro Perani, 365–80. Florence: L. S. Olschki, 2004.

Cooperman, Bernard D. "Ethnicity and Institution Building Among Jews in Early Modern Rome." *AJS Review* 30, no. 1 (2006): 119–45.

Coppola, Giada. "Obadiah Sforno and the Individual Human Soul." *Yearbook of the Maimonides Centre for Advanced Studies* (2020): 101–24.

Coudert, Allison P. *The Impact of the Kabbalah in the Seventeenth Century: The Life and Thought of Francis Mercury van Helmont (1614–1698)*. Leiden: Brill, 1999.

Coudert, Allison P., and Jeffrey S. Shoulson, eds. *Hebraica Veritas? Christian Hebraists and the Study of Judaism in Early Modern Europe*. Philadelphia: University of Pennsylvania Press, 2004.

Cover, Robert M. "Nomos and Narrative." *Harvard Law Review* 97, no. 1 (1983): 2–68.

Crescas, Hasdai ibn. *Light of the Lord (or Hashem)*. Translated by Roslyn Weiss. Oxford: Oxford University Press, 2018.

Crescas, Hasdai ibn. *Sefer or Adonai*. Ferrara, 1555.

Dan, Joseph. "Ashkenazi Hasidim, 1941–1991: Was There Really a Hasidic Movement in Medieval Germany." In *Gershom Scholem's Major Trends in Jewish Mysticism 50 Years After: Proceedings of the Sixth International Conference on the History of Jewish Mysticism*. Edited by Peter Shäfer and Joseph Dan, 87–101. Tübingen: Mohr, 1992.

Dan, Joseph. "The Emergence of Mystical Prayer." In *Studies in Jewish Mysticism*. Edited by Joseph Dan and Frank Talmage, 85–120. New York: K'tav, 1982.

Dan, Joseph. *Ḥasidut Ashkenaz betoldot ha-maḥshavah ha-yehudit*. Vol. 1. Tel Aviv: Open University of Israel, 1990.

Dan, Joseph. *R. Judah he-Ḥasid*. Jerusalem: Zalman Shazar, 2006.

Dan, Joseph. "Rabbi Judah the Pious and Caesarius of Heisterbach: Common Motifs in Their Stories." *Scripta Hierosolymitana* 22 (1971): 18–27.

Darnton, Robert. *Censors at Work: How States Shaped Literature*. New York: W. W. Norton, 2015.

Darnton, Robert. "What Is the History of Books?" *Daedalus* 111, no. 3 (1982): 65–83.

David, Abraham. "R. Gedalya ibn Yahya's Shalshelet Hakabbalah (Chain of Tradition): A Chapter in Medieval Jewish Historiography." *Immanuel: A Semi-Annual Bulletin of Religious Thought and Research in Israel* 12 (1981): 60–76.

Davidson, Israel. *Thesaurus of Mediaeval Hebrew Poetry*. Vol. 3. New York: K'tav, 1970.

Davis, Joseph. "The Reception of the Shulhan 'Arukh and the Formation of Ashkenazic Jewish Identity." *AJS Review* 26, no. 2 (2002): 252–76.

Davis, Natalie Zemon. "Some Tasks and Themes in the Study of Popular Religion." In *The Pursuit of Holiness in Late Medieval and Renaissance Religion*. Edited by Charles Trinkaus and Heiko Oberman, 307–36. Leiden: Brill, 1974.

Derrida, Jacques. "Deconstruction and the Other." In *Dialogues with Contemporary Continental Thinkers*. Edited by Richard Kearney, 105–26. Manchester, UK: University of Manchester Press, 1984.

De Visscher, Eva. *Reading the Rabbis: Christian Hebraism in the Works of Herbert of Bosham*. Leiden: Brill, 2014.

De Vries, Jan. *The City: European Urbanization, 1500–1800*. 2nd ed. Cambridge, MA: Harvard University Press, 1997.

De' Rossi, Azariah. *The Light of the Eyes*. Translated by Joanna Weinberg. New Haven, CT: Yale University Press, 2001.

De' Rossi, Azariah. *Sefer me'or einayim*. Edited by David Cassel. Vilna: Romm, 1866.

Delmedigo, Jospeh Solomon. *Sefer meẓaref le-ḥokhmah*. Warsaw, 1892.

Deutsch, Yaacov. *Judaism in Christian Eyes: Ethnographic Descriptions of Jews and Judaism in Early Modern Europe*. New York: Oxford, 2012.

Deutsch, Yaacov. "Polemical Ethnographies: Descriptions of Yom Kippur in the Writings of Christian Hebraists and Jewish Converts in Early Modern Europe." In *Hebraica Veritas? Christian Hebraists and the Study of Judaism in Early Modern Europe*. Edited by Allison P. Coudert and Jeffrey S. Shoulson, 202–33. Philadelphia: University of Pennsylvania Press, 2004.

Dönitz, Saskia. "Assessing the Manuscripts of Sefer Ḥasidim." *Jewish History* 34, no. 1–3 (2021).

Drory, Rina. *Models and Contacts: Arabic Literature and Its Impact on Medieval Jewish Culture*. Leiden: Brill, 2000.

Duncan, Dennis, and Adam Smyth. *Book Parts*. Oxford: Oxford University Press, 2019.

Dweck, Yaacob. *The Scandal of Kabbalah: Leon Modena, Jewish Mysticism, Early Modern Venice*. Princeton, NJ: Princeton University Press, 2012.

Dweck, Yaacob. "What Is a Jewish Book?" *AJS Review* 34, no. 2 (2010): 367–75.

Efraim b. Aaron of Luntshits. *Ir gibborim*. Freiburg-im-Breisgau, 1580.

Eidelberg, Shlomo. *The Jews and the Crusaders: The Hebrew Chronicles of the First and Second Crusades*. Madison: University of Wisconsin Press, 1977.

Einbinder, Susan L. *Beautiful Death: Jewish Poetry and Martyrdom in Medieval France*. Princeton, NJ: Princeton University Press, 2002.

Eisenstein, Elizabeth L. *The Printing Press as an Agent of Change: Communications and Cultural Transformations in Early-Modern Europe*. Vol. 1 and 2. Cambridge: Cambridge University Press, 1979.

Eisenstein, Elizabeth L. *The Printing Revolution in Early Modern Europe*. 1st ed. Cambridge: Cambridge University Press, 1983.

Eisenstein, Elizabeth L. *The Printing Revolution in Early Modern Europe*. 2nd ed. New York: Cambridge University Press, 2005.

Eisenstein, Elizabeth L. "An Unacknowledged Revolution Revisited." *American Historical Review* 107, no. 1 (2002): 87–105.

Elbaum, Jacob. *Petiḥut ve-histagrut: Ha-yeẓirah ha-ruḥanit ha-sifrutit be-Polin u-ve-arẓot Ashkenaz be-shilhei ha-me'ah ha-shesh esrei*. Jerusalem: Magnes Press, 1990.

Elbaum, Jacob. "Rabbi Judah Loew's Attitude to the Aggadah." In *Midrash Unbound: Transformations and Innovations*. Edited by Joanna Weinberg and Michael Fishbane, 389–406. Oxford: Littman Library of Jewish Civilization, 2013.

Elbogen, Ismar. *Jewish Liturgy: A Comprehensive History*. Translated by Raymond R. Scheindlin. Philadelphia: Jewish Publication Society, 1993.

Emanuel, Simcha. "Piskei R. Menachem Mi'Recanati." *Jewish Law Annual* 25 (2008): 139–98.

Epstein, Abraham. "R. Shmu'el he-Ḥasid b'R. Kalonimus ha-zaken." *Ha-goren* 4 (1903).

Epstein, Stephen R. *Freedom and Growth: The Rise of States and Markets in Europe, 1300–1750*. London: Routledge, 2000.

Febvre, Lucien, and Henri-Jean Martin. *The Coming of the Book: The Impact of Printing, 1450–1800*. Translated by David Gerard. London: Verso, 2010.

Finkelstein, David, and Alistair McCleery, eds. *The Book History Reader*. London: Routledge, 2006.

Finkelstein, Louis. *Jewish Self-Government in the Middle Ages*. New York: Jewish Theological Seminary of America, 1924.

Fishman, Talya. *Becoming the People of the Talmud: Oral Torah as Written Tradition in Medieval Jewish Cultures*. Philadelphia: University of Pennsylvania Press, 2011.

Fishman, Talya. "Rhineland Pietist Approaches to Prayer and the Textualization of Rabbinic Culture in Medieval Northern Europe." *Jewish Studies Quarterly* 11, no. 4 (2004): 313–31.

Flood, John L. "'Omnium Totius Orbis Emporiorum Compendium': The Frankfurt Fair in the Early Modern Period." In *The History of the Book in the West: 1455–1700*. Edited by Ian Gadd, 321–62. London: Routledge, 2007.

Foren, Symon Lee. "Reconciling Philosophy and Scripture in Renaissance Italy: Obadiah Sforno's Hebrew and Latin Versions of the Light of the Nations." PhD diss., University of Oxford, 2020.

Foucault, Michel. "What Is an Author?" In *The Book History Reader*. Edited by David Finkelstein and Alistair McCleery, 281–91. London: Routledge, 2006.

Fox, Adam. *Oral and Literate Culture in England, 1500–1700*. Oxford: Clarendon Press, 2000.

Fragnito, Gigliola, ed. *Church, Censorship and Culture in Early Modern Italy*. Translated by Adrian Belton. Cambridge: Cambridge University Press, 2001.

Fragnito, Gigliola, ed. *La bibbia al rogo: La censura ecclesiastica e i volgarizzamenti della Scrittura: 1471–1605*. Bologna: Il Mulino, 1997.

Fram, Edward. "German Pietism and Sixteenth- and Early Seventeenth-Century Polish Rabbinic Culture." *Jewish Quarterly Review* 96, no. 1 (2006): 50–59.

Fram, Edward. *My Dear Daughter: Rabbi Benjamin Slonik and the Education of Jewish Women in Sixteenth-Century Poland*. Cincinnati, OH: Hebrew Union College Press, 2007.

Francesconi, Federica. "'This Passage Can Also be Read Differently...': How Jews and Christians Censored Hebrew Texts in Early Modern Modena." *Jewish History* 26, no. 1–2 (2012): 139–60.

Freiman, Aron. "Daniel Bomberg und seine Hebräische Druckerei in Venedig." *Zeitschrift für hebräische Bibliographie* 10 (1909): 32–36.

Freimann, Jacob. Introduction to *Sefer Ḥasidim: 'Al pi nosaḥ ketav yad asher be-Parma*. 2nd ed. Edited by Jehuda Wistinetzki. Frankfurt-am-Main: M. A. Wahrmann, 1924.

Friedberg, Bernhard (Chaim). *Toldot ha-defus ha-'ivri be-Polaniyah*. Tel Aviv, 1950.
Friedman, Jerome. *The Most Ancient Testimony: Sixteenth-Century Christian-Hebraica in the Age of Renaissance Nostalgia*. Athens: Ohio University Press, 1983.
Fudeman, Kirsten A. "Glosses of Hebrew: Medieval French." In *Encyclopedia of Hebrew Language and Linguistics*. Edited by Geoffrey Khan, 1–5. Leiden: Brill, 2016.
Fuenn, Joseph. *Keneset Yisrael*. Warsaw, 1887.
Gager, John. "Simon Peter, the Founder of Christianity or the Savior of Israel?" In *Toledot Yeshu: The Life Story of Jesus*. Edited by Peter Schäfer, Michael Meerson, and Yaacov Deutsch, 221–45. Tübingen: Mohr Siebeck, 2014.
Galinsky, Judah. "The Impact of Ḥasidei Ashkenaz in Northern France: The Evidence of Sefer Ḥasidut and Ḥayyei Olam." *Jewish History* 34, no. 1–3 (2021).
Gaziel, Ahuva. "Spontaneous Generation in Medieval Jewish Philosophy and Theology." *History and Philosophy of the Life Sciences* 34, no. 3 (2012): 461–79.
Genette, Gérard. *Paratexts: Thresholds of Interpretation*. Cambridge: Cambridge University Press, 1997.
Gillespie, Alexandra. *Print Culture and the Medieval Author: Chaucer, Lydgate, and Their Books, 1473–1557*. Oxford: Oxford University Press, 2006.
Ginzburg, Carlo. *The Cheese and the Worms: The Cosmos of a Sixteenth-Century Miller*. Translated by John and Anne Tedeschi. Baltimore: Johns Hopkins University Press, 1980.
Ginzburg, Carlo. "Microhistory: Two or Three Things That I Know About It." *Critical Inquiry* 20, no. 1 (Autumn 1993): 10–35.
Giusberti, Fabio, and Francesca Roversi Monaco. "Economy and Demography." In *A Companion to Medieval and Renaissance Bologna*. Edited by Sarah Rubin Blanshei, 155–84. Leiden: Brill, 2018.
Glaisyer, Natasha. "Calculating Credibility: Print Culture, Trust and Economic Figures in Early Eighteenth-Century England." *Economic History Review* 60, no. 4 (2007): 685–711.
Glasberg Gail, Debra. "*Scientific Authority and Jewish Law in Early Modern Italy*." PhD diss., Columbia University, 2016.
Gondos, Andrea. *Kabbalah in Print: The Study and Popularization of Jewish Mysticism in Early Modernity*. Albany: SUNY Press, 2020.
Grafton, Anthony, and Joanna Weinberg. *The Culture of Correction in Renaissance Europe*. London: British Library, 2011.
Grafton, Anthony, and Joanna Weinberg. *Forgers and Critics: Creativity and Duplicity in Western Scholarship*. Princeton, NJ: Princeton University Press, 1990.
Grafton, Anthony, and Joanna Weinberg. *"I Have Always Loved the Holy Tongue": Isaac Casaubon, the Jews, and a Forgotten Chapter in Renaissance Scholarship*. Cambridge, MA: Belknap Press of Harvard University Press, 2011.
Grafton, Anthony, and Joanna Weinberg. *Inky Fingers: The Making of Books in Early Modern Europe*. Cambridge, MA: Harvard University Press, 2020.
Grafton, Anthony, and Joanna Weinberg. "'Pandects of the Jews': A French, Swiss

and Italian Prelude to John Selden." In *Jewish Books and Their Readers Aspects of the Intellectual Life of Christians and Jews in Early Modern Europe*. Edited by Scott Mandelbrote and Joanna Weinberg, 169–88. Leiden: Brill, 2016.

Grendi, Edoardo. "Micro-analisi e storia sociale." *Quaderni storici* 12, no. 35 (2) (1977): 506–520.

Grendi, Edoardo. "Micro-analyse et histoire sociale." Translated by Pierre Savy. *Écrire l'histoire* 3 (2009): 67–80.

Grendi, Edoardo. "Ripensare la microstoria?" *Quaderni Storici* 29, no. 86 (2) (1994): 539–49.

Grendler, Paul F. "The Destruction of Hebrew Books in Venice, 1568." *Proceedings of the American Academy for Jewish Research* 45 (1978): 1–29.

Grendler, Paul F. *The Roman Inquisition and the Venetian Press*. Princeton, NJ: Princeton University Press, 1977.

Grossman, Avraham. *Hakhmei Tzarfat ha-rishonim: Koroteihem, darkham be-hanhagat ha-tzibur, ve-yetziratam ha-ruḥanit*. Jerusalem: Magnes Press, 2001.

Grünbaum, Max. *Jüdischdeutsche Chrestomathie: Zugleich ein Beitrag zur Kunde der Hebräischen Literatur*. Leipzig: F. A. Brockhaus, 1882.

Güdemann, Moritz. *Geschichte des Erziehungswesens und der Cultur der Abendländischen Juden während des Mittelalters und der neueren Zeit*. Vol. 1. Vienna: A. Hölder, 1880.

Gueta, Alessandro. "Religious Life and Jewish Erudition in Pisa: Yehiel Nissim Da Pisa and the Crisis of Aristotelianism." In *Cultural Intermediaries: Jewish Intellectuals in Early Modern Italy*. Edited by David Ruderman, 86–108. Philadelphia: University of Pennsylvania Press, 2004.

Gueta, Anat. "Ha-sefarim ha-mudpasim shel shenot ha-shin ke-makor le-ḥeker ḥaye ha-ru'ah shel ha-ḥevrah ha-yehudi." PhD diss., Bar Ilan University, 2002.

Guiley, Rosemary. *Encyclopedia of Angels*. New York: Facts on File, 1996.

Habermann, A. M. *Ha-madpis Cornelio Adelkind u-beno Daniel u-reshimat ha-sefarim she-nidpesu al yedeihem*. Jerusalem: Rubin Mass, 1980.

Habermann, A. M. *Ha-madpis Daniel Bombergi ve-reshimat sifrei beit defuso*. Safed: Museum of Printing Art, 1978.

Habermann, A. M. "Ha-madpis Yisrael ha-Zifroni u-beno Elishama." In *Perakim b'toldot ha-madpisim ha-ivri'im v'inyanei sefarim*. Edited by A. M. Haberman, 216–91. Jerusalem: Rubin Mass, 1978.

Habermann, A. M. *Ha-sefer ha-ivri be-hitpatḥuto: Me-simanim le-otiyot u-me-megillah le-sefer*. Jerusalem: Rubin Mass, 1968.

Hacker, Joseph. "Al gezerat tat'nu (1096)." *Zion* 31, no. 1 (1966): 225–31.

Hacker, Joseph. "Ha-derashot ha-sephradit be-me'ah ha-16 bein sifrut le-makor histori." *Pe'amim* 26 (1986): 108–27.

Hacker, Joseph R. "Sixteenth-Century Jewish Internal Censorship of Hebrew Books." In *The Hebrew Book in Early Modern Italy*. Edited by Joseph R. Hacker and Adam Shear, 109–20. Philadelphia: University of Pennsylvania Press, 2011.

Hacker, Joseph R., and Adam Shear. *The Hebrew Book in Early Modern Italy*. Philadelphia: University of Pennsylvania Press, 2011.

ha-Cohen, Meir. *Hagahot Maimoniyot, Hilkhot avodah zarah*. Bar Ilan Responsa Database.

Halbertal, Moshe. *Concealment and Revelation: Esotericism in Jewish Thought and Its Philosophical Implications*. Translated by Jackie Feldman. Princeton, NJ: Princeton University Press, 2007.

Halbertal, Moshe. *People of the Book: Canon, Meaning, and Authority*. Cambridge, MA: Harvard University Press, 1997.

Halbertal, Moshe, and Avishai Margalit. *Idolatry*. Translated by Naomi Goldblum. Cambridge, MA: Harvard University Press, 1992.

Hallamish, Moshe. "Te'udah le-toldot ha-pulmus al ha-kabbalah b'Italia bereishit ha-me'ah ha-17." *Bar Ilan Annual* 22 (1988): 179–204.

Harris, Neil. "The History of the Book in Italy." In *The Oxford Companion to the Book*. Vol. 1. Edited by Michael F. Suarez, S. J. Woudhuysen, and H. R. Woudhuysen, 257–65. Oxford: Oxford University Press, 2010.

Harvey, Warren Zev. "Hasdai Crescas's Critique of the Theory of the Acquired Intellect." PhD diss., Columbia University, 1973.

Hayles, N. Katherine. *How We Became Posthuman*. Chicago: University of Chicago Press, 1999.

Heckethorn, Charles William. *The Printers of Basle in the XV. & XVI. Centuries: Their Biographies, Printed Books and Devices*. London: T. Fisher Unwin, 1897.

Heller, Marvin J. "Behold, You Are Beautiful, My Love: The Use of Ornamental Frames in Hebrew Incunabula." In *Further Studies in the Making of the Early Hebrew Book*, 3–35. Leiden: Brill, 2013.

Heller, Marvin J. *Further Studies in the Making of the Early Hebrew Book*. Leiden: Brill, 2013.

Heller, Marvin J. Introduction to *The Sixteenth Century Hebrew Book: An Abridged Thesaurus*. Vol. 1, xiii–xvi. Leiden: Brill, 2004.

Heller, Marvin J. *Printing the Talmud: A History of the Earliest Printed Editions of the Talmud*. New York: I. M. HaSefer, 1993.

Heller, Marvin J. *The Sixteenth Century Hebrew Book: An Abridged Thesaurus*. 2 vols. Leiden: Brill, 2004.

Heller, Marvin J. *Studies in the Making of the Early Hebrew Book*. Leiden: Brill, 2008.

Hendel, Ronald. "What Is a Biblical Book?" In *From Author to Copyist: Essays on the Composition, Redaction, and Transmission of the Hebrew Bible in Honor of Zipi Talshir*. Edited by Cana Werman, 283–302. University Park: Penn State University Press, 2015.

Herodotus. *The History of Herodotus*. Vol. 1. Translated by G. C. Macaulay. London: Macmillan, 1904.

Hilgert, Earle. "Johann Froben and the Basel University Scholars, 1513–1523." *Library Quarterly* 41, no. 2 (1971): 141–69.

Horowitz, Elliot. "Processions, Piety and Jewish Confraternities." In *The Jews of Early Modern Venice*. Edited by Robert C. Davis and Benjamin Ravid, 231–48. Baltimore: Johns Hopkins University Press, 2001.

Horowitz, Elliot. "Yeshiva and Hevra: Educational Control and Confraternal Organization in Sixteenth-Century Italy." In *Shlomo Simonsohn Jubilee Volume* [Hebrew side]. Edited by Daniel Carpi, 123–47. Tel Aviv: Tel Aviv University, 1993.

Hsia, Ronnie Po-Chia. "Christian Ethnography of Jews in Early Modern Germany." In *The Expulsion of the Jews and After*. Edited by Raymond Waddington, 223–35. New York: Garland, 1994.

Hundert, Gershon David. *Jews in Poland-Lithuania in the Eighteenth Century*. Berkeley: University of California Press, 2004.

Huss, Boaz. *Ke-zohar ha-raki'a: Perakim be-hitkablut ha-Zohar u-ve-havnayat erko ha-simli*. Jerusalem: Ben-Zvi Institute, 2008.

Huss, Boaz. *The Zohar: Reception and Impact*. Translated by Yudith Nave. London: Littman Library of Jewish Civilization, 2016.

Idel, Moshe. *Kabbalah in Italy, 1280–1510*. New Haven, CT: Yale University Press, 2011.

Idel, Moshe. "Printing Kabbalah in the Sixteenth Century Jewish Culture." In *Early Modern Europe: Essays in Honor of David B. Ruderman*. Edited by Richard I. Cohen, Natalie B. Dohrmann, Adam Shear, and Elchanan Reiner, 85–97. Pittsburgh, PA: Hebrew Union College Press, 2014.

Idel, Moshe. *R. Menakhem Rekanati Ha-Mekubal*. Jerusalem: Schocken Books, 1998.

Idelson-Shein, Iris. "Shabbethei Bass and the Construction—and Deconstruction—of a Jewish Library." *Jewish Culture and History* 22, no. 1 (2021): 1–16.

Irosolomitano, Dominico. *Sefer ha-zikuk*. New York: The Jewish Theological Seminary of America, 1890.

Isaac b. Moses. *Sefer Or zaru'a, hilkhot shaliḥ ẓibbur*. Vol. 1. Bar Ilan Responsa Database.

Jacob b. Asher. *Arba'ah turim: Orah ḥayyim, hilkhot birkot ha-shakhar ve-sha'ar ha-berachot*. Vilna, 1923.

Jardine, Lisa. *Erasmus, Man of Letters: The Construction of Charisma in Print*. Princeton, NJ: Princeton University Press, 1993.

Johns, Adrian. "How to Acknowledge a Revolution." *American Historical Review* 107, no. 1 (2002): 106–25.

Johns, Adrian. *The Nature of the Book: Print and Knowledge in the Making*. Chicago: University of Chicago Press, 1998.

Johns, Adrian. *Piracy: The Intellectual Property Wars from Gutenberg to Gates*. Chicago: University of Chicago Press, 2010.

Jones, G. Lloyd. *The Discovery of Hebrew in Tudor England: A Third Language*. Manchester, UK: Manchester University Press, 1983.

Jones, Howard. *Printing the Classical Text*. Utrecht: Hes & De Graaf, 2004.

Joseph ha-Cohen. *Emek ha-bakhah*. Krakow: M. Letteris, 1895.

Kahana, Maoz. "Old Prophesies, Multiple Modernities: The Stormy Afterlife of a Medieval Pietist in Early Modern Ashkenaz." *Jewish History* 34, no. 1–3 (2021).

Kallendorf, Craig. *Printing Virgil: The Transformation of the Classics in the Renaissance.* Leiden: Brill, 2019.

Kanarfogel, Ephraim. *The Intellectual History and Rabbinic Culture of Medieval Ashkenaz.* Detroit, MI: Wayne State University Press, 2013.

Kanarfogel, Ephraim. *Jewish Education and Society in the High Middle Ages.* Detroit, MI: Wayne State University Press, 1992.

Kanarfogel, Ephraim. *Peering Through the Lattices: Mystical, Magical, and Pietistic Dimensions in the Tosafist Period.* Detroit, MI: Wayne State University Press, 2000.

Kanarfogel, Ephraim. "R. Judah 'he-Hasid' and the Rabbinic Scholars of Regensburg: Interactions, Influences, and Implications." *Jewish Quarterly Review* 96, no. 1 (2006): 17–37.

Kant, Immanuel. *The Metaphysics of Morals.* Translated by Mary Gregor. Cambridge: Cambridge University Press, 1991.

Kant, Immanuel. "Of the Injustice of Counterfeiting Books." In *Essays and Treatises on Moral, Political, and Various Philosophical Subjects.* Vol. 1, 222–36. London: William Richardson, 1799.

Karo, Joseph. "Hakdamah" [introduction] to *Shulhan arukh.* Jerusalem: Ketuvim, 1992. Bar Ilan Responsa Database.

Katz, Jacob. *Exclusiveness and Tolerance: Studies in Jewish-Gentile Relations in Medieval and Modern Times.* New York: Oxford University Press, 1961.

Katz, Jacob. *Tradition and Crisis: Jewish Society at the End of the Middle Ages.* Translated by Bernard Dov Cooperman. Syracuse, NY: Syracuse University Press, 2000.

Kirschenbaum, Matthew G. *Mechanisms: New Media and the Forensic Imagination.* Cambridge, MA: MIT Press, 2012.

Kogot, Simha. "The Language of Sefer Hasidim." In *Studies in Medieval Jewish History and Literature.* Vol. 2. Edited by Isadore Twersky, 95–109. Cambridge, MA: Harvard University Center for Jewish Studies, 1984.

Labarthe, Olivier, and Bernard Lescaze. *Registres de la Compagnie des pasteurs de Genève: 1575–1582.* Vol. 4. Geneva: Librairie Droz, 1974.

Landshuth, Eliezer. *Sefer amudei ha-avodah.* Berlin, 1884.

Lange, Isaak S., ed. *Peirushei al ha-Torah.* Jerusalem: Lange, 1974.

Langer, Ruth. *Cursing the Christians? A History of the Birkat Haminim.* Oxford: Oxford University Press, 2011.

Laras, Joseph. "Igrot m'Rabbi Ovadiah Sforno." *Sinai* 62 (1968): 262–67.

Lasker, Daniel J. "Chasdai Crescas." In *History of Jewish Philosophy.* Edited by Daniel H. Frank and Oliver Leaman, 399–414. London: Routledge, 1997.

Lehman, Marjorie. *The En Yaaqov: Jacob ibn Habib's Search for Faith in the Talmud Corpus.* Detroit, MI: Wayne State University Press, 2012.

Lehnardt, Andreas, and Judith Olszowy-Schlanger, eds. *Books within Books: New Discoveries in Old Book Bindings.* Leiden: Brill, 2014.

Levene, Dan. "May These Curses Go Out and Flee." In *Magical and Religious Literature of Late Antiquity*. Vol. 2. Edited by Shaul Shaked and Siam Bhayro. Leiden: Brill, 2013.

Lieberman, Saul. *Tosefta kifshuta*. Vol. 3. New York: Jewish Theological Seminary of America, 1962.

Loew, Judah b. Bezallel. *Be'er ha-golah*. Jerusalem: Maḥon Yerushalayim, 2000. Bar Ilan Responsa Project.

Lowry, Martin. *The World of Aldus Manutius: Business and Scholarship in Renaissance Venice*. Ithaca, NY: Cornell University Press, 1979.

Luzzatto, Jacob b. Isaac. *Sefer kavvanot ha-Agadot*. Basel, 1580.

Luzzatto, Samuel David. *Autobiografia di S. D. Luzzatto preceduta da alcune notizie storico-letterarie sulla famiglia Luzzatto*. Padua: Crescini, 1882.

Luzzatto, Samuel David. *Mavo le-maḥzor b'nai Roma*. Tel Aviv: D'vir, 1966.

Magnússon, Sigurður Gylfi, and István M. Szijártó. *What Is Microhistory?: Theory and Practice*. New York: Taylor & Francis, 2013.

Maier, Johann. "I 'Sefer Hasidim': Il manoscrito Parmenese 3280 e l'Edizione di Bologna, 1538. Observazioni critiche." In *Manoscritti, frammenti e libri ebraici nell'Italia dei Secoli XV–XVI: Atti del VII Congresso Internazionale dell'AISG, S. Miniato, 7–8–9 Novembre 1988*. Edited by Giuliano Tamani and Angelo Vivian, 129–36. Rome: Carucci, 1991.

Maimonides, Moses. *The Guide of the Perplexed*. Translated by Shlomo Pines. Chicago: University of Chicago Press, 1963.

Malkiel, David. *Reconstructing Ashkenaz: The Human Face of Franco-German Jewry, 1000–1250*. Stanford, CA: Stanford University Press, 2008.

Manetsch, Scott M. *Calvin's Company of Pastors: Pastoral Care and the Emerging Reformed Church, 1536–1609*. Oxford: Oxford University Press, 2013.

Marcus, Hannah. *Forbidden Knowledge: Medicine, Science, and Censorship in Early Modern Italy*. Chicago: University of Chicago Press, 2020.

Marcus, Ivan G. "From Politics to Martyrdom: Shifting Paradigms in the Hebrew Narratives of the 1096 Crusade Riots." *Prooftexts* 2, no. 1 (1982): 40–52.

Marcus, Ivan G. "History, Story and Collective Memory: Narrativity in Early Ashkenazic Culture." *Prooftexts* 10, no. 3 (September 1990): 365–88.

Marcus, Ivan G. "A Jewish-Christian Symbiosis: The Culture of Early Ashkenaz." In *Cultures of the Jews*. Edited by David Biale, 449–516. New York: Schocken, 2002.

Marcus, Ivan G. "The Organization of the 'ḥaqdamah' and 'hilekhoth Ḥasiduth' in Eleazar of Worms' 'Sefer Ha-Roqeaḥ.'" *Proceedings of the American Academy for Jewish Research* 36 (1968): 85–94.

Marcus, Ivan G. *Piety and Society: The Jewish Pietists of Medieval Germany*. Leiden: Brill, 1981.

Marcus, Ivan G. "The Recensions and Structure of 'Sefer Ḥasidim.'" *Proceedings of the American Academy for Jewish Research* 45 (1978): 131–53.

Marcus, Ivan G. *Rituals of Childhood*. New Haven, CT: Yale University Press, 2015.

Marcus, Ivan G. *Sefer Hasidim and the Ashkenazic Book in Medieval Europe*. Philadelphia: University of Pennsylvania Press, 2018.

Marcus, Ivan. [Yisrael.] *Sefer Ḥasidim: K'tav-yad Parmah H-3280*. Jerusalem: Dinur Center, 1985.

Margoliot, Reuven, ed. *Sefer Ḥasidim*. Jerusalem: Mossad ha-Rav Kook, 1961. Bar Ilan Responsa Project.

Margoliot, Reuven. *Sefer Ha-Zohar al Hamishah Humshe Torah*. Jerusalem: Mosad HaRav Kook, 1964.

Marino, Marco. *Sefer Gan Eden*. Basel, 1580.

Martini, Annett. "Ritual Consecration in the Context of Writing the Holy Scrolls: Jews in Medieval Europe Between Demarcation and Acculturation." *European Journal of Jewish Studies* 11, no. 2 (2017): 174–202.

Marx, Alexander. "Aldus and the First Use of Hebrew Type in Venice." *Papers of Bibliographical Society of America* 13 (1919): 64–67.

Marx, Alexander. "Glimpses of the Life of an Italian Rabbi of the First Half of the Sixteenth Century (David ibn Yahya)." *Hebrew Union College Annual* 1 (1924): 605–24.

Marx, Alexander. "A Jewish Cause Celebre in Sixteenth Century Italy (the Pesakim of 1519)." In *Abhandlungen zur Erinnerung an Hirsch Perez Chajes*. Vol. 2. Edited by Victor Aptowitzer et al., 149–93. Vienna: Alexander Kohut Memorial Foundation, 1933.

Marx, Alexander. "R. Joseph of Arles and Rabbi Yochanan Treves." In *Studies in Memory of Moses Schorr*. Edited by Louis Ginzburg and Abraham Weiss, 189–210. New York: Professor Moses Schorr Memorial Committee, 1944.

Marx, Alexander. "R. Yosef ish Arli be-tor moreh ve-rosh yeshivah be-Siena." In *Sefer yovel: Likhvod Levi Gintzburg, ḥelek ivri*. Vol. 2, 271–304. New York: American Academy for Jewish Research, 1946.

Mayer, Yakov Z. "Metarbut k'tav ha-yad le-tarbut ha-defus." PhD diss., Tel Aviv University, 2018.

McKittrick, David. *Print, Manuscript and the Search for Order, 1450–1830*. Cambridge: Cambridge University Press, 2003.

Mentz, Steven. "The Nature of the Book: Print and Knowledge in the Making, by Adrian Johns." Review. *Journal of Interdisciplinary History* 30, no. 4 (Spring 2000): 636–37.

Meroz, Ronit. *Ha-biyografyah ha-ruḥanit shel Rabi Shim'on Bar Yoḥai: Diyun bi-yesodotaṿ ha-teḳsṭu'aliyim shel ha-Zohar*. Jerusalem: Mosad Bialik, 2018.

Milano, Attilio. *Storia degli Ebrei in Italia*. Torino: Einaudi, 1992.

Milikowsky, Chaim. "Gehenom u-poshei yisrael al pi 'Seder Olam.'" *Tarbiz* 55, no. 3 (1986): 311–44.

Minnis, A. J. *Medieval Theory of Authorship: Scholastic Literary Attitudes in the Later Middle Ages*. Philadelphia: University of Pennsylvania Press, 1988.

Molà, Luca. *The Silk Industry of Renaissance Venice*. Baltimore: Johns Hopkins University Press, 2000.

Moyn, Samuel. *Origins of the Other: Emmanuel Levinas between Revelation and Ethics*. Ithaca, NY: Cornell University Press, 2005.

Muzzarelli, Maria Giuseppina. "Ebrei a Bologna nel XVI Secolo." In *Bologna nell'Età Moderna (Secoli XVI–XVIII)*. Edited by Adriano Prosperi, 857–91. Bologna: Bononia University Press, 2008.

Muzzarelli, Maria Giuseppina. "Ebrei, Famiglie e Citta: Gli Sforno Di Bologna." *Zakhor* 3 (1999): 59–77.

Muzzarelli, Maria Giuseppina. "Ferrara, ovvero un porto placido e sicuro tra XV è XVI secolo." In *Vita e cultura Ebraica nello stato Estense*. Edited by Euride Fregni and Mauro Perani, 235–57. Bologna: Edizioni Fattoadarte, 2012.

Naquin, Nicholas. "On the Shoulders of Hercules: Erasmus, the Froben Press and the 1516 Jerome Edition in Context." PhD diss., Princeton University, 2013.

Neubauer, Adolf, and Moritz Stern. *Hebräische Berichte über die Judenverfolgungen während der Kreuzzüge*. Berlin: Simion, 1892.

Neubauer, Adolph, ed. *Catalogue of the Hebrew Manuscripts in the Bodleian Library and in the College Libraries of Oxford*. Oxford: Clarendon Press, 1886.

Nielsen, Bruce. "Daniel van Bombergen, a Bookman of Two Worlds." In *The Hebrew Book in Early Modern Italy*. Edited by Joseph R. Hacker and Adam Shear, 56–75. Philadelphia: University of Pennsylvania Press, 2011.

Nordmann, Achilles. "Geschichte der Juden in Basel seit dem Ende der Zweiten Gemeinde bis zur Einführung der Glaubens- und Gewissensfreiheit: 1397–1875." *Basler Zeitschrift für Geschichte und Altertumskunde* 13 (1914): 1–190.

Offenberg, Adri K. *A Choice of Corals: Facets of Fifteenth-Century Hebrew Printing*. Nieuwkoop, Netherlands: De Graaf, 1992.

Pallmann, Heinrich. "Ambrosius Froben von Basel als Drucker des Talmud." *Archiv für Geschichte des deutschen Buchhandels* 7 (1882): 44–61.

Parente, Fausto. "The Index, the Holy Office and the Condemnation of the Talmud and Publication of Clement VIII's Index Church." In *Church, Censorship and Culture in Early Modern Italy*. Edited by Gigliola Fragnito, 163–94. Cambridge: Cambridge University Press, 2001.

Parkes, Malcom B. *Pause and Effect: An Introduction to the History of Punctuation in the West*. Berkeley: University of California Press, 1993.

Parks, George B. "The Pier Luigi Farnese Scandal: An English Report." *Renaissance News* 15, no. 3 (1962): 193–200.

Pasternak, Nurit. "Marchion in Hebrew Manuscripts: State Censorship in Florence, 1472." In *The Hebrew Book in Early Modern Italy*. Edited by Joseph R. Hacker and Adam Shear, 27–55. Philadelphia: University of Pennsylvania Press, 2011.

Patterson, Annabel M. *Censorship and Interpretation: The Conditions of Writing and Reading in Early Modern England*. Madison: University of Wisconsin Press, 1984.

Perani, Mauro, and Bracha Rivlin. *Vita religiosa Ebraica a Bologna nel Cinquecento: Gli statuti della Confraternita dei Solerti*. Florence: Giuntina, 2000.

Petrucci, Armando. *Public Lettering: Script, Power, and Culture.* Chicago: University of Chicago Press, 1993.

Pettegree, Andrew. *The Book in the Renaissance.* New Haven, CT: Yale University Press, 2010.

Piergiovanni, Paola Massa. "Technological Typologies and Economic Organisation of Silk Workers in Italy, from the XIVth to the XVIIIth Centuries." *Journal of European Economic History* 22, no. 3 (1993): 543–64.

Poni, Carlo. "The Circular Silk Mill: A Factory Before the Industrial Revolution in Early Modern Europe." *History of Technology* 21 (1999): 65–85.

Poni, Carlo. *La seta in Italia: Una grande industria prima della Rivoluzione Industriale.* Bologna: Il Mulino, 2009.

Poni, Carlo. "Per la storia del distretto industriale serico di Bologna (Secoli XVI–XIX)." *Quaderni Storici* 25, no. 1 (2014): 93–167.

Popper, William. *The Censorship of Hebrew Books.* New York: Knickerbocker, 1899.

Prebor, Gila. "'Sefer ha-Zikkuk' shel Dominico Yerushalmi." *Italia* 18 (2008): 7–302.

Prijs, Joseph. *Die Basler Hebräischen Drucke, 1492–1866: Im Auftrag der Öffentlichen Bibliothek der Universität Basel.* Olten: Urs Graf, 1965.

Pulega, Dinora. "La tipographia bolognese dei Giaccarelli." *L'Archiginnasio* 35 (1940): 87–107.

Rabbinovicz, Raphael Nathan Nata. *Ma'amar al hadpasat ha-Talmud.* Munich: A. Huber, 1877.

Rabin, Chaim. "Zemanim u-derachim be-po'al she-be-lashon 'Sefer Ḥasidim." *Papers of the Fourth World Congress of Jewish Studies* 2 (1968): 113–16.

Raspe, Lucia. *Jüdische Hagiographie im Mittelalterlichen Aschkenas.* Tübingen: Mohr Siebeck, 2006.

Ravid, Benjamin. "The Venetian Government and the Jews." In *The Jews of Early Modern Venice.* Edited by Robert C. Davis and Benjamin Ravid, 3–30. Baltimore: Johns Hopkins University Press, 2001.

Raz-Krakotzkin, Amnon. *The Censor, the Editor, and the Text: The Catholic Church and the Shaping of the Jewish Canon in the Sixteenth Century.* Philadelphia: University of Pennsylvania Press, 2007.

Recanati, Menaḥem b. Benjamin. *Piske halakhot.* Bologna, 1538.

Recanati, Menaḥem b. Benjamin. *Sefer ta'amei ha-miẓvot.* Basel, 1581.

Reif, Stefan C. *Hebrew Manuscripts at Cambridge University Library.* Cambridge: Cambridge University Press, 1997.

Reif, Stefan C. *Judaism and Hebrew Prayer: New Perspectives on Jewish Liturgical History.* Cambridge: Cambridge University Press, 1993.

Reif, Stefan C. *Shabbethai Sofer and His Prayer-Book.* Cambridge: Cambridge University Press, 1979.

Reiner, Elchanan. "The Ashkenazi Elite at the Beginning of the Modern Era: Manuscript Versus Printed Book." In *Polin: Studies in Polish Jewish History.* Vol. 10, *Jews in*

Early Modern Poland. Edited by Gershon David Hundert, 85–98. London: Littman Library of Jewish Civilization, 1997.

Reiner, Elchanan. "A Biography of an Agent of Culture: Eliezer Altschul of Prague and His Literary Activity." In *Schöpferische momente des Europäischen Judentums in der Frühen Neuzeit*. Edited by Michael Graetz, 229–47. Heidelberg: Universitätsverlag C. Winter, 2000.

Reiner, Elchanan. "Temurot be-yeshivot polin ve-ashkenaz be-me'ot ha-16–17 ve-ha-viku'aḥ al ha-pilpul." In *Studies in Jewish Culture in Honor of Chone Shmeruk*. Edited by Israel Bartal, Ezra Mendelssohn, and Chava Turniansky, 9–80. Jerusalem: Zalman Shazar Center, 1993.

Richardson, Brian. *Manuscript Culture in Renaissance Italy*. Cambridge: Cambridge University Press, 2009.

Richardson, Brian. *Print Culture in Renaissance Italy: The Editor and the Vernacular Text, 1470–1600*. Cambridge: Cambridge University Press, 1994.

Richardson, Brian. *Printing, Writers and Readers in Renaissance Italy*. Cambridge: Cambridge University Press, 1999.

Rosen-Zvi, Ishay, and Adi Ophir. "Goy: Toward a Genealogy." *Diné Israel* 28 (2011): 69–122.

Rosenthal, Avraham. "Daniel Bomberg and His Talmud Editions." In *Gli Ebrei e Venezia: Secoli XIV–XVIII*. Edited by Gaetano Cozzi, 375–416. Milan: Edizioni Communità, 1987.

Rosenzweig, Claudia. "A Note on an Old Jewish Bibliotaphos." *Zutot* 17, no. 1 (2020): 49–57.

Roth, Cecil. *Jewish Life in Renaissance Italy*. Philadelphia: Jewish Publication Society, 1959.

Rouse, Mary A., and Richard H. Rouse. "La Naissance des Index." *Histoire de l'édition française* 1 (1982): 77–85.

Rubinstein, Jeffrey L. *Talmudic Stories*. Baltimore: Johns Hopkins University Press, 2003.

Ruderman, David B. *Early Modern Jewry: A New Cultural History*. Princeton, NJ: Princeton University Press, 2010.

Ruderman, David B, ed. *Preachers of the Italian Ghetto*. Berkeley: University of California Press, 1992.

Saperstein, Marc. "Italian Jewish Preaching: An Overview." In *Preachers of the Italian Ghetto*. Edited by David Ruderman, 22–40. Berkeley: University of California Press, 1992.

Schäfer, Peter. "The Ideal of Piety of the Ashkenazi Hasidim and Its Roots in Jewish Tradition." *Jewish History* 4, no. 2 (1990): 9–23.

Schäfer, Peter. "Jews and Christians in the High Middle Ages: The Book of the Pious." In *The Jews of Europe in the Middle Ages Tenth to Fifteenth Centuries: Proceedings of the International Symposium Held at Speyer*. Edited by Christoph Cluse, 29–42. Turnhout: Brepols, 2004.

Schäfer, Peter. "Research into Rabbinic Literature: An Attempt to Define the Status Quaestionis." *Journal of Jewish Studies* 37, no. 2 (1986), 139–52.

Schäfer, Peter, Michael Meerson, and Yaacov Deutsch, eds. *Toledot Yeshu: The Life Story of Jesus*. Tübingen: Mohr Siebeck, 2014.

Schaffer, Simon, and Steven Shapin. *The Leviathan and the Air Pump: Hobbes, Boyle, and the Experimental Life*. Princeton, NJ: Princeton University Press, 2011.

Scholem, Gershom. *Major Trends in Jewish Mysticism*. New York: Schocken, 2011.

Sebastiani, Valentina. *Johann Froben, Printer of Basel: A Biographical Profile and Catalogue of His Editions*. Leiden: Brill, 2018.

Sforno, Ovadiah. *Or ammim*. Bologna, 1537.

Shapin, Steven. *The Scientific Revolution*. Chicago: University of Chicago Press, 2018.

Shapiro, Marc. "Torah Study on Christmas Eve." *Journal of Jewish Thought and Philosophy* 8, no. 2 (1999): 319–53.

Shear, Adam. *The Kuzari and the Shaping of Jewish Identity, 1167–1900*. Cambridge: Cambridge University Press, 2008.

Sheehan, Jonathan. *The Enlightenment Bible*. Princeton, NJ: Princeton University Press, 2005.

Shemesh, Rikva. "On the Narrative Discourse in Tannaitic Language: An Exploration of the Ma'aseh and Pa'am Ahat Discourse Units." *Hebrew Studies* 49 (2008): 99–123.

Sherira Gaon. *Letter of Rav Sherira Gaon*. Translated by D. Metzger. Jerusalem: Neve Asher Institute, 1998. Bar Ilan Responsa Database.

Shoham-Steiner, Ephraim. "Mi-Shpeyer le-Regensburg: N'dodei mishpaḥat he-ḥasid mi-ḥevel ha-Rhine le-ḥevel Danube." *Zion* 81, no. 2 (2016): 149–76.

Shuger, Debora. *Censorship and Cultural Sensibility: The Regulation of Language in Tudor-Stuart England*. Philadelphia: University of Pennsylvania Press, 2013.

Shulvass, Moses A. *The Jews in the World of the Renaissance*. Translated by Elvin I. Kose. Leiden: Brill, 1973.

Shyovitz, David I. "Beauty and the Bestiary: Animals, Wonder, and Polemic in Medieval Ashkenaz the Jewish-Christian Encounter in Medieval Preaching." In *The Jewish-Christian Encounter in Medieval Preaching*. Edited by Jonathan Adams and Jussi Hanska, 215–39. New York: Routledge, 2014.

Shyovitz, David I. *A Remembrance of His Wonders: Nature and the Supernatural in Medieval Ashkenaz*. Philadelphia: University of Pennsylvania Press, 2017.

Shyovitz, David I. "Was Judah He-Ḥasid the 'Author' of Sefer Ḥasidim?" *Jewish History* 34, no. 1–3 (2021).

Shyovitz, David I. "'You Have Saved Me from the Judgment of Gehenna': The Origins of the Mourner's Kaddish in Medieval Ashkenaz." *AJS Review* 39, no. 1 (2015): 49–73.

Siegmund, Stefanie B. *The Medici State and the Ghetto of Florence: The Construction of an Early Modern Jewish Community*. Stanford, CA: Stanford University Press, 2006.

Simhoni, Yaakov N. "Ha-ḥasidut ha-ashkenazit be-yemei ha-beinayim." *Hatsefirah* (1917): 12–32.

Simonsohn, Shlomo, ed. *The Apostolic See and the Jews: Documents: 1522–1538*. Toronto: Pontifical Institute of Mediaeval Studies, 1990.

Simonsohn, Shlomo. *The Apostolic See and the Jews: History*. Toronto: Pontifical Institute of Mediaeval Studies, 1991.

Skloot, Joseph A. "Blood and Guts in Jewish Law: The Laws of the Forbidden and the Permitted and Religious Norms in Rabbi Moses Isserles' Glosses on the Shulḥan Arukh." Paper presented at the Norms and Normativity in History conference, Paris-Sorbonne University, March 2010.

Sládek, Pavel. "A Sixteenth-Century Rabbi as a Published Author: The Early Editions of Rabbi Mordecai Jaffe's *Levushim*." In *Connecting Histories: Jews and Their Others in Early Modern Europe*. Edited by Francesca Bregoli and David B. Ruderman, 49–66. Philadelphia: University of Pennsylvania Press, 2019.

Smail, Daniel Lord. *Legal Plunder: Households and Debt Collection in Late Medieval Europe*. Cambridge, MA: Harvard University Press, 2016.

Smith, Helen. "Acknowledgements and Dedications." In *Book Parts*. Edited by Dennis Duncan and Adam Smyth, 95–107. Oxford: Oxford University Press, 2019.

Smith, Helen. "'Imprinted by Simeon Such a Signe': Reading Early Modern Imprints Renaissance Paratexts." In *Renaissance Paratexts*. Edited by Helen Smith and Louise Wilson, 17–33. Cambridge: Cambridge University Press, 2011.

Smith, Pamela H. "Why Write a Book? From Lived Experience to the Written Word in Early Modern Europe." *Bulletin of the German Historical Institute* 47 (2010): 25–50.

Soloveitchik, Haym. "Le-ta'arikh ḥibburo shel Sefer Ḥasidim." In *Culture and Society in Medieval Jewish History: A Collection of Essays in Memory of Hayim Hillel Ben-Sasson*. Edited by Robert Bonfil, Menachem Ben-Sasson, and Joseph Hacker, 383–88. Jerusalem: Zalman Shazar Center for Jewish History, 1989.

Soloveitchik, Haym. "Olam Ke-Minhago Noheg." Review. *AJS Review* 23, no. 2 (1998): 223–34.

Soloveitchik, Haym. "Piety, Pietism and German Pietism: Sefer Ḥasidim and the Influence of Ḥasidei Ashkenaz." *Jewish Quarterly Review* 92, no. 3–4 (2002): 455–93.

Soloveitchik, Haym. "Three Themes in the 'Sefer Ḥasidim.'" *AJS Review* 1 (1976): 311–57.

Sonne, Isaiah. *Expurgation of Hebrew Books--the Work of Jewish Scholars: A Contribution to the History of the Censorship of Hebrew Books in Italy in the Sixteenth Century*. New York: The New York Public Library, 1943.

Sonne, Isaiah. "L'toldot kehilat Bologna b'tehilat ha'meah ha'16." *Hebrew Union College Annual* 16 (1941): 35–98.

Staehelin, Ernst. "Des Basler Buchdruckers Ambrosius Froben Talmudausgabe und Handel mit Rom." *Basler Zeitschrift für Geschichte und Altertumskunde* 30 (1930): 7–37.

Stallybrass, Peter. "Books and Scrolls: Navigating the Bible." In *Books and Readers in Early Modern England*. Edited by Jennifer Anderson and Elizabeth Sauer, 42–79. Philadelphia: University of Pennsylvania Press, 2002.

Starn, Randolph. "The Early Modern Muddle." *Journal of Early Modern History* 6, no. 3 (2002): 296–307.

Steinschneider, Moritz. *Catalogus librorum Hebraeorum in Bibliotheca Bodleiana*. Vol. 1. Berlin: A. Friedlaender, 1852–1860.

Stern, David, ed. *The Anthology in Jewish Literature*. New York: Oxford University Press, 2004.

Stern, David. *The Jewish Bible: A Material History*. Seattle: University of Washington Press, 2018.

Stern, Josef. *Matter and Form of Maimonides' Guide*. Cambridge, MA: Harvard University Press, 2013.

Stern, David. "The Rabbinic Bible in Its Sixteenth-Century Context." In *The Hebrew Book in Early Modern Italy*. Edited by Joseph R. Hacker and Adam Shear, 77–108. Philadelphia: University of Pennsylvania Press, 2011.

Stow, Kenneth R. *Alienated Minority: The Jews of Medieval Latin Europe*. Cambridge, MA: Harvard University Press, 1992.

Stow, Kenneth R. "The Burning of the Talmud in 1553, in Light of Sixteenth-Century Catholic Attitudes toward the Talmud." *Bibliothèque d'Humanisme et Renaissance* 34, no. 3 (1972): 435–59.

Stow, Kenneth R. "Ethnic Rivalry or Melting Pot: The 'Edot' in the Roman Ghetto." *Judaism* 41, no. 3 (1992): 286–96.

Stow, Kenneth R. *The Jews in Rome*. Leiden: Brill, 1995.

Strauss, Leo. *Persecution and the Art of Writing*. Glencoe, IL: Free Press, 1952.

Suarez, Michael Felix. *The Oxford Companion to the Book*. Oxford: Oxford University Press, 2010.

Sutherland, Kathryn. "Anglo American Editorial Theory." In *The Cambridge Companion to Textual Scholarship*. Edited by Neil Freistat and Julia Flanders, 42–60. Cambridge: Cambridge University Press, 2013.

Talmage, Frank. "R. David Kimḥi as Polemicist." *Hebrew Union College Annual* 38 (1967): 213–35.

Tamburini, Filippo. *Ebrei Saraceni Cristiani: Vita sociale e vita religiosa dai registri della Penitenziera Apostolica (Secoli XIV–XVI)*. Milan: Instituto di Propaganda Libraria, 1996.

Tefilah: Mireshit ve-ad aḥarit ha-shanah. Bologna, 1537.

Teller, Adam. "Culture and Money: The Economic Dimension of Cultural History and What It Can Teach Us." *Jewish Quarterly Review* 104, no. 2 (2014): 278–87.

Teplitsky, Joshua. *Prince of the Press: How One Collector Built History's Most Enduring and Remarkable Jewish Library*. New Haven, CT: Yale University Press, 2019.

Teter, Magda. *Jews and Heretics in Catholic Poland: A Beleaguered Church in the Post-Reformation Era*. Cambridge: Cambridge University Press, 2006.

Teter, Magda, and Edward Fram. "Apostasy, Fraud, and the Beginnings of Hebrew Printing in Cracow." *AJS Review* 30, no. 1 (2006): 31–66.

Timm, Erika. "The Migration of German Jews into Italy and the Emergence of Local

Rites of Seliḥot Recitation." In *The Jews of Europe Around 1400: Disruption, Crisis, and Resilience*. Edited by Lukas Clemens and Christoph Cluse, 173–93. Weisbaden, Germany: Harrassowitz Verlag, 2018.

Timm, Erika. "Zur Frühgeschichte der Yiddischen Erzählprosa: Eine neuaufgefundene Maise-Handschrift." *Beiträge zur Geschichte der deutschen Sprache und Literatur* 117 (1995): 243–80.

Tirosh-Rothschild [Samuelson], Hava. "Jewish Philosophy on the Eve of Modernity." In *History of Jewish Philosophy*. Edited by Oliver Leaman and Daniel H. Frank, 499–574. London: Routledge, 1997.

Tirosh-Samuelson, Hava. "Jewish Culture in Renaissance Italy: A Methodological Survey." *Italia* 9, no. 1–2 (1990): 63–96.

Tishby, Isaiah. *Studies in Kabbalah and Its Branches: Research and Sources* [in Hebrew]. Vol. 1. Jerusalem: Magnes Press, 1982.

Tkacz, Dov Ber. *Kuntres ha-shemot ha-ḥadash*. Tel Aviv: Ahavat Zion, 1960.

Toaff, Ariel. "Bologna Ebraica negli studi recenti." In *La cultura Ebraica a Bologna tra Medioevo E Rinascimento*. Edited by Mauro Perani, 13–28. Florence: Giuntina, 2002.

Toniolo, Alberta. "Els mercats de les sedes: Paper I Herència dels Sefardites a Bolognya en L'Edat Moderna." *Revista d'Història Medieval* 4 (1993): 25–44.

Toniolo, Alberta. "Los Sefarditas Españoles Y La sedería Italiana En La Primera Edad Moderna." *Revista de historia industrial* 12 (1997): 42–73.

Trauring, Philip. "Male Jewish Names in Poland from 1866." Blood and Frogs: Navigating Jewish Geneology, March 4, 2020. https://bloodandfrogs.com/2020/03/male-jewish-names-in-poland-from-1866.html.

Treves, Yohanan. *Mahzor kamcha d'Avishuna*. [*Maḥzor ke-fi minhag kehillat kodesh Roma*]. Bologna, 1540.

Trivellato, Francesca. "Microstoria/Microhistoire/Microhistory." *French Politics, Culture & Society* 33, no. 1 (2015): 122–34.

Trustees of Princeton University. Princeton University *Sefer Ḥasidim* Project Database. https://etc.princeton.edu/sefer_hasidim/index.php.

Turan, Sinai (Tamas). "Pirkei mavo le-toldot ha-pisuk ha-ivri." *Tarbiz* 71, no. 3–4 (2002): 449–530.

van Bekkum, Wout. "The Poetical Qualities of the Apostle Peter in Jewish Folktale." *Zutot* 3, no. 1 (2003): 16–25.

van Boxel, Piet W. "Cardinal Santoro and the Expurgation of Hebrew Literature." In *The Roman Inquisition, the Index and the Jews*. Edited by Stephan Wendehorst, 19–34. Brill: Leiden, 2004.

van Boxel, Piet W. "Hebrew Books and Censorship in Sixteenth Century Italy." In *Jewish Books and Their Readers: Aspects of the Intellectual Life of Christians and Jews in Early Modern Europe*. Edited by Scott Mandelbrote and Joanna Weinberg, 75–99. Leiden: Brill, 2016.

van Boxel, Piet W. *Jewish Books in Christian Hands: Theology, Exegesis and Conversion Under Gregory XIII (1572–1585)*. Vatican: Biblioteca Apostolica Vaticana, 2016.

van Boxel, Piet W. "Robert Bellarmine Reads Rashi: Rabbinic Bible Commentaries and the Burning of the Talmud." In *The Hebrew Book in Early Modern Italy*. Edited by Joseph R. Hacker and Adam Shear, 121–32. Philadelphia: University of Pennsylvania Press, 2011.

Veltri, Guiseppe. "Maharal against Azariah De' Rossi: The Other Side of Scepticism." In *Rabbinic Theology and Jewish Intellectual History: The Great Rabbi Loew of Prague*. Edited by Meir Seidler, 65–76. London: Routledge, 2013.

Vinograd, Yeshayahu. *Oẓar ha-sefer ha-Ivri: Reshimat ha-sefarim she-nidpesu be-ot ivrit me-reshit ha-defus ha-ivri bi-shenat 229 (1469) ad shenat 623 (1863)*, 2 vols. Jerusalem: Ha-makhon le-bibliyografyah memuḥshevet, 2011.

Wacker, Gudrun. "The Internet and Censorship in China: Gudrun Wacker." In *China and the Internet*. Edited by Christopher R. Hughes and Gudrun Wacker, 58–82. London: Taylor & Francis, 2003.

Weinberg, Joanna. "Johann Buxtorf Makes a Notebook." In *Canonical Texts and Scholarly Practices: A Global Comparative Approach*. Edited by Anthony Grafton and Glenn W. Most, 275–98. Cambridge: Cambridge University Press, 2016.

Weinryb, Bernard D. *The Jews of Poland: A Social and Economic History of the Jewish Community in Poland from 1100 to 1800*. Philadelphia: Jewish Publication Society, 1972.

Weinstein, Roni. *Kabbalah and Jewish Modernity*. Oxford: Littman Library of Jewish Civilization, 2016.

Weinstein, Roni. "Ma karah ha-na'ar Shemuel be-pinkaso ishi? Ḥinukh na'arim yehudim be-Italia be-mahalakh ha-Reformaẓiah ha-katolit." *Italia* 13–15 (2001): 131–68.

Weissler, Chava. *Voices of the Matriarchs: Listening to the Prayers of Early Modern Jewish Women*. Boston: Beacon, 1998.

Wirszubski, Chaim. *Pico Della Mirandola's Encounter with Jewish Mysticism*. Cambridge, MA: Harvard University Press, 1989.

Wistinetski, Jehuda, ed. *Sefer Ḥasidim: Al pi nosaḥ ketav yad asher be-Parmah*. Frankfurt-am-Main: M. A. Wahrmann, 1924.

Witcomb, Christopher L. C. E. *Copyright in the Renaissance: Printers and the Privilegio in Sixteenth-Century Venice and Rome*. Leiden: Brill, 2004.

Wolfson, Elliot R. "Beyond the Spoken Word: Oral Tradition and Written Transmission in Medieval Jewish Mysticism." In *Transmitting Jewish Traditions: Orality, Textuality, and Cultural Diffusion*. Edited by Yaakov Elman and Israel Gershoni, 166–224. New Haven, CT: Yale University Press, 2000.

Yadin-Israel, Azzan. "A Note on a Middle High German Calque in Sefer Hasidim." *Jewish Studies Quarterly* 19, no. 4 (2012): 385–87.

Yahalom, Shalom. "Viku'aḥ Barcelona u-ma'amad ha-aggadah be-mishnat ha-Ramban." *Zion* 69, no. 1 (2004): 25–43.

Yaḥya, Gedaliah ibn. *Sefer shalshelet ha-kabbalah*. Venice, 1587.

Yaḥya, Joseph b. David ibn. *Perush al ḥamesh megilot*. Bologna, 1538.

Yaḥya, Joseph b. David ibn. *Sefer Torah or*. Bologna, 1538.

Yassif, Eli. *The Hebrew Folktale: History, Genre, Meaning*. Translated by Jacqueline S. Teitelbaum. Indianapolis: Indiana University Press, 2009.

Yehuda he-Ḥasid. *Ẓava'at Yehuda he-Ḥasid*. Venice, 1583.

Yerushalmi, Yosef H. "Clio and the Jews: Reflections on Jewish Historiography in the Sixteenth Century." In *Essential Papers on Jewish Culture in Renaissance and Baroque Italy*. Edited by David Ruderman, 191–218. New York: New York University Press, 1992.

Zafren, Herbert C. "Elias Hutter's Hebrew Bibles." In *Joshua Bloch Memorial Volume: Studies in Booklore and History*. Edited by Abraham Berger, Lawrence Marwick, and Isidore S. Meyer, 29–39. New York: New York Public Library, 1960.

Zafren, Herbert C. "Hebrew Printing by and for Frankfurt Jews—to 1800." In *Jüdische Kultur in Frankfurt am Main van den Anfängen bis zur Gegenwart*. Edited by Karl E. Grözinger, 231–71. Wiesbaden: Harrassowitz, 1997.

Zarah, Menaḥem ibn. *Ḥamishah ḥumshei Torah ve-ḥamesh megillot*. Sabbionetta, 1567.

Zarah, Menaḥem ibn. *Ẓeidah le-derekh*. Sabbionetta, 1567.

Zeitlin, Solomon. "Mumar and Meshumad." *Jewish Quarterly Review* 54, no. 1 (July 1963): 84–86.

Zimmer, Eric. *Gaḥaltan shel ḥakhamim: Perakim be-toldot ha-rabanut be-Germanyah ba-me'ah ha-shesh-esreh uva-me'ah ha-sheva-esreh*. Be'er Sheva, Israel: Ben Gurion University of the Negev, 1999.

Zimmer, Yitzhak [Eric]. *Olam ke'minhago noheg: Erakim be-toldot ha'minhagim, hilkhotehem ve'gilgulehem*. Jerusalem: Merkaz Zalman Shazar, 1996.

Zinberg, Israel. *A History of Jewish Literature*. Vol. 8, *Italian Jewry in the Renaissance Era*. Translated by Bernard Martin. New York: K'tav, 1974.

Zonta, Mauro. "The Autumn of Medieval Jewish Philosophy: Latin Scholasticism in Late 15th-Century Hebrew Philosophical Literature." In *"Herbst Des Mittelalters"? Fragen Zur Bewertung Des 14. Und 15. Jahrhunderts*. Edited by Jan A. Aertsen and Martin Pickavé, 474–92. Berlin: De Gruyter, 2004.

Index

Illustrations are indicated by figure number in italics (e.g., *fig. 11*). Individual manuscripts are collected under the entry "manuscripts."